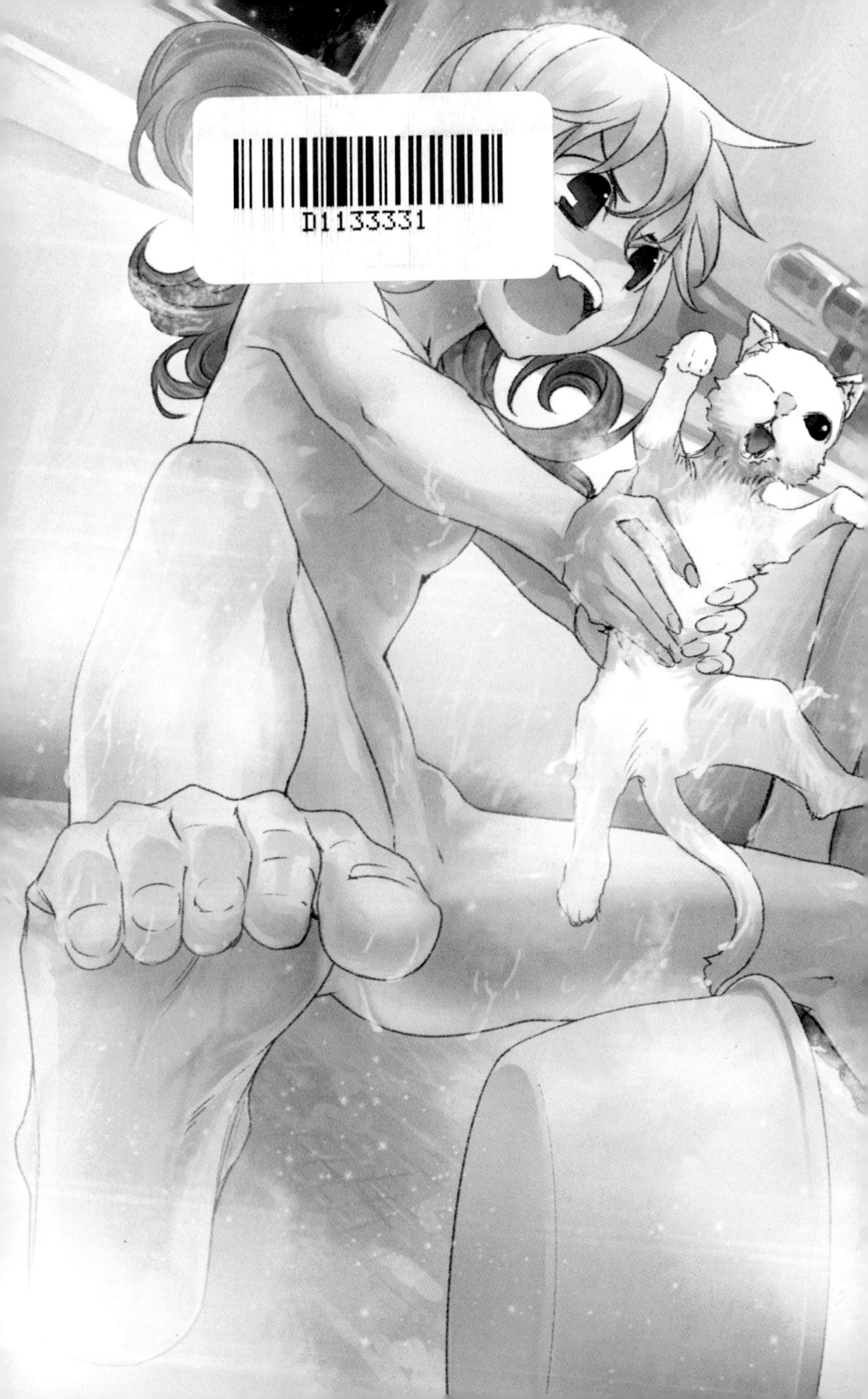

TABOO TATTOO 10

CONTENTS

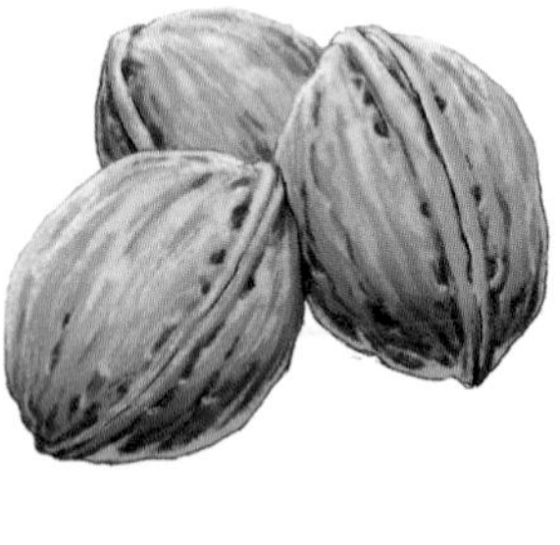

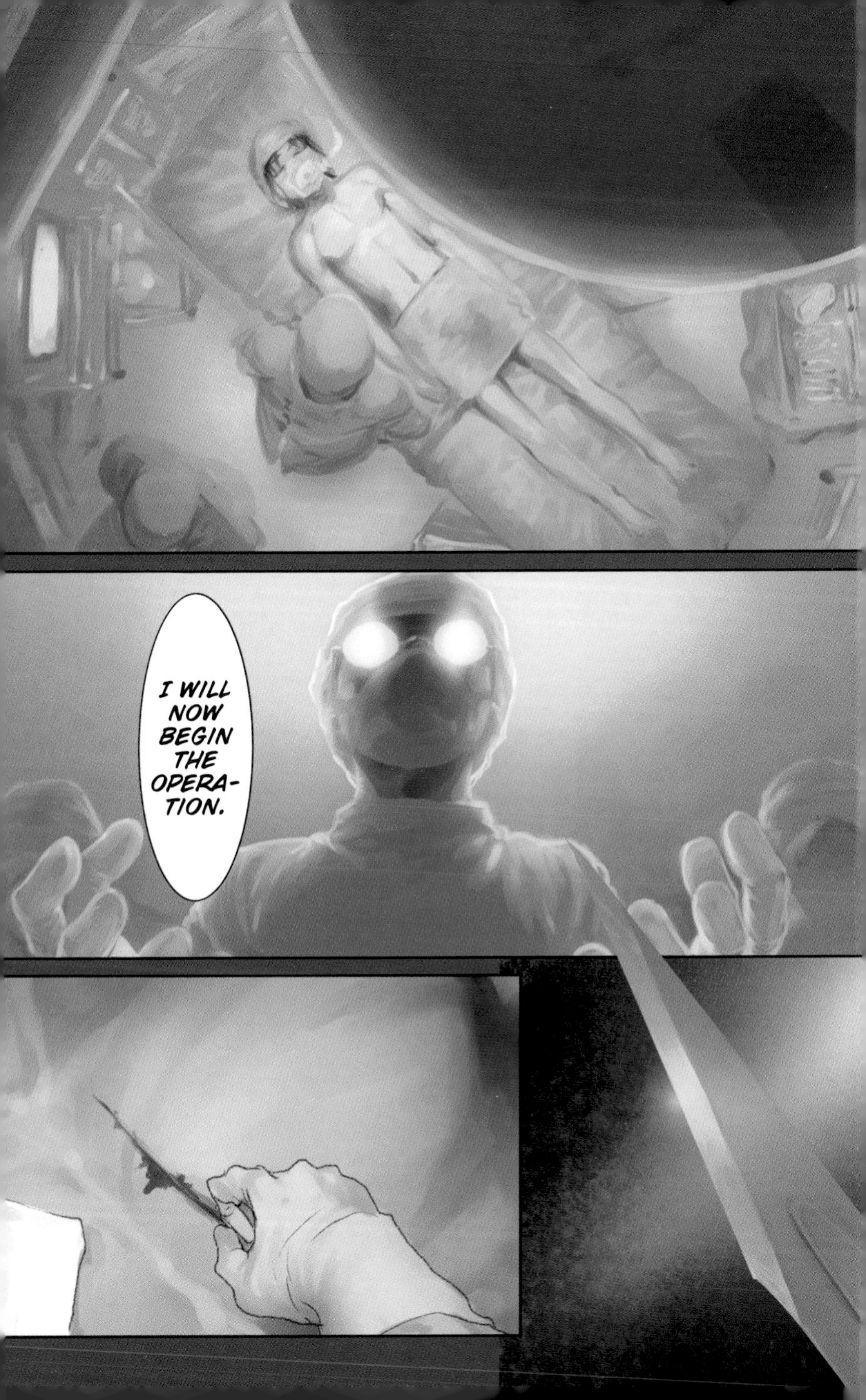
I WILL NOW BEGIN THE OPERA-TION.

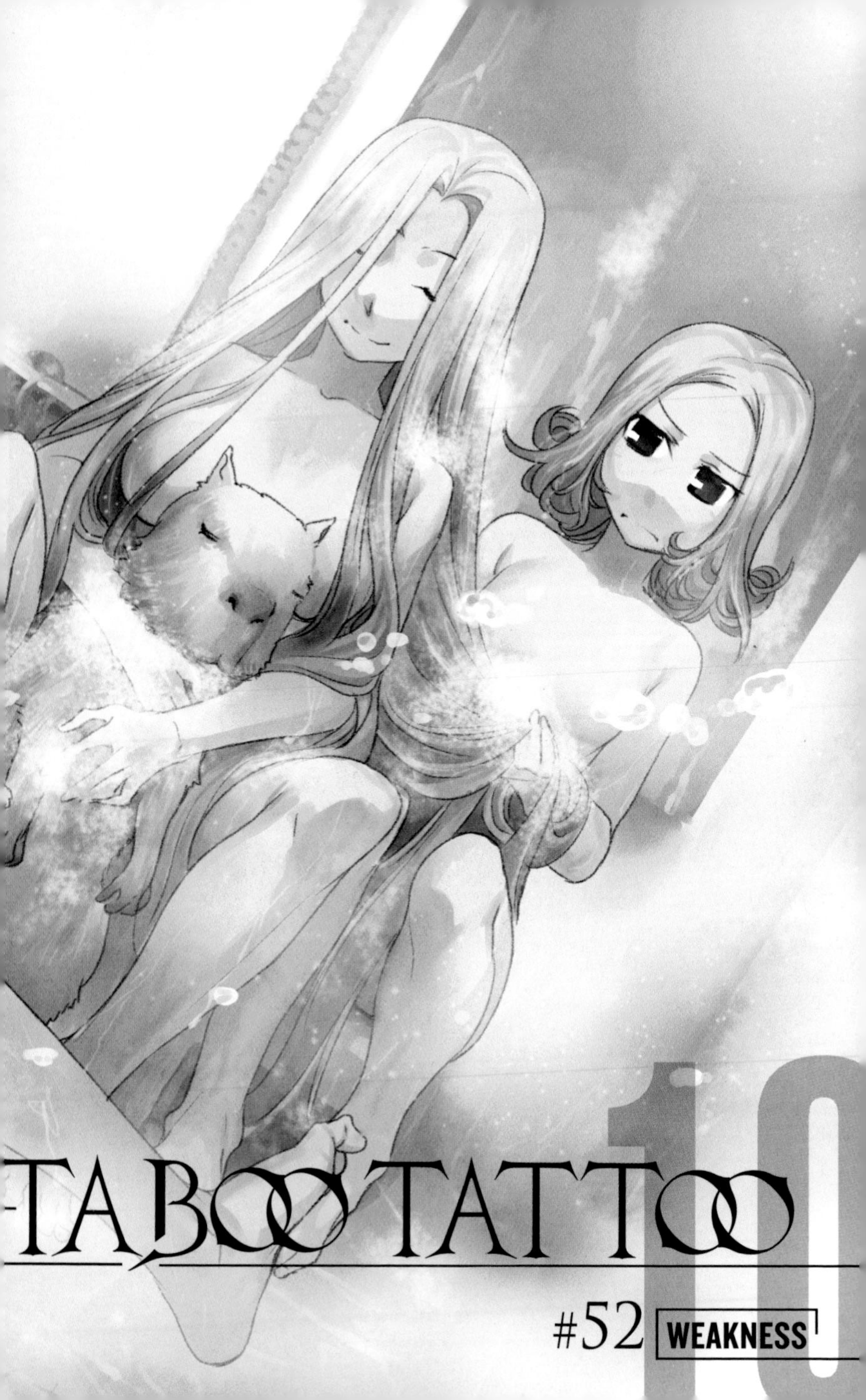
TABOO TATTOO
10
#52 WEAKNESS

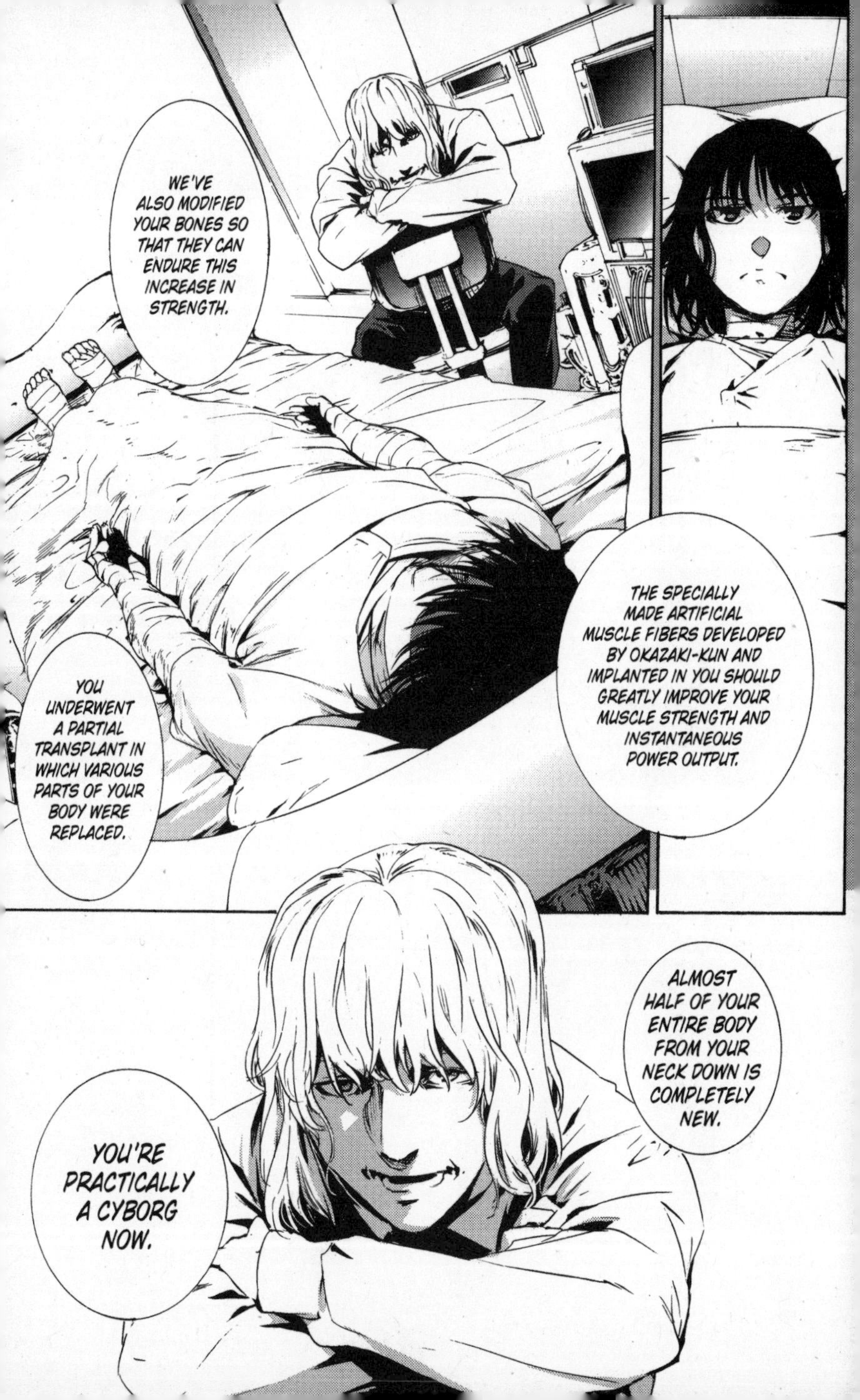
THE SPECIALLY MADE ARTIFICIAL MUSCLE FIBERS DEVELOPED BY OKAZAKI-KUN AND IMPLANTED IN YOU SHOULD GREATLY IMPROVE YOUR MUSCLE STRENGTH AND INSTANTANEOUS POWER OUTPUT.
WE'VE ALSO MODIFIED YOUR BONES SO THAT THEY CAN ENDURE THIS INCREASE IN STRENGTH.
YOU UNDERWENT A PARTIAL TRANSPLANT IN WHICH VARIOUS PARTS OF YOUR BODY WERE REPLACED.
ALMOST HALF OF YOUR ENTIRE BODY FROM YOUR NECK DOWN IS COMPLETELY NEW.
YOU'RE PRACTICALLY A CYBORG NOW.

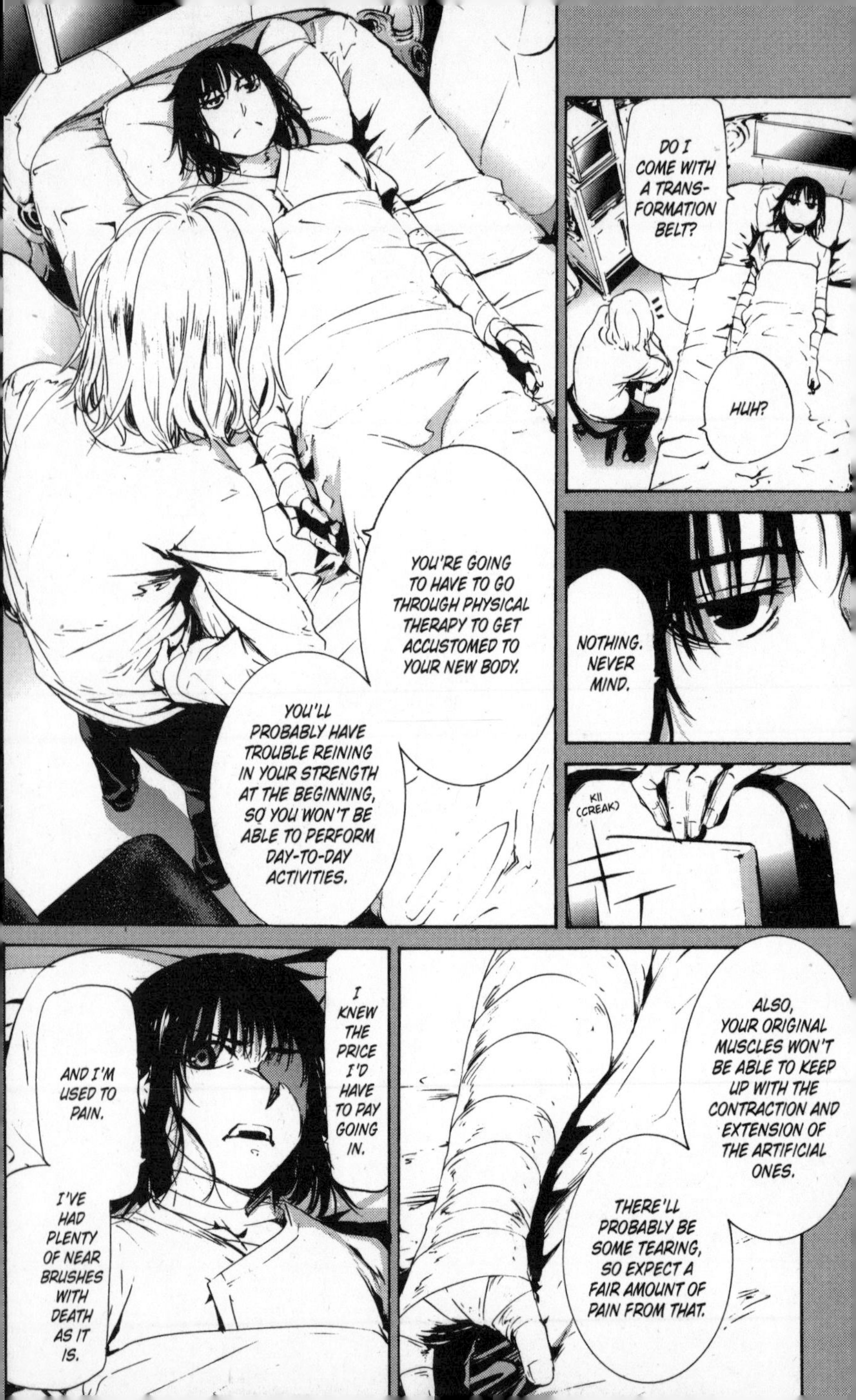
DO I COME WITH A TRANS-FORMATION BELT?
HUH?
NOTHING. NEVER MIND.
KII (CREAK)
YOU'RE GOING TO HAVE TO GO THROUGH PHYSICAL THERAPY TO GET ACCUSTOMED TO YOUR NEW BODY.
YOU'LL PROBABLY HAVE TROUBLE REINING IN YOUR STRENGTH AT THE BEGINNING, SO YOU WON'T BE ABLE TO PERFORM DAY-TO-DAY ACTIVITIES.
ALSO, YOUR ORIGINAL MUSCLES WON'T BE ABLE TO KEEP UP WITH THE CONTRACTION AND EXTENSION OF THE ARTIFICIAL ONES.
THERE'LL PROBABLY BE SOME TEARING, SO EXPECT A FAIR AMOUNT OF PAIN FROM THAT.
I KNEW THE PRICE I'D HAVE TO PAY GOING IN.
AND I'M USED TO PAIN.
I'VE HAD PLENTY OF NEAR BRUSHES WITH DEATH AS IT IS.

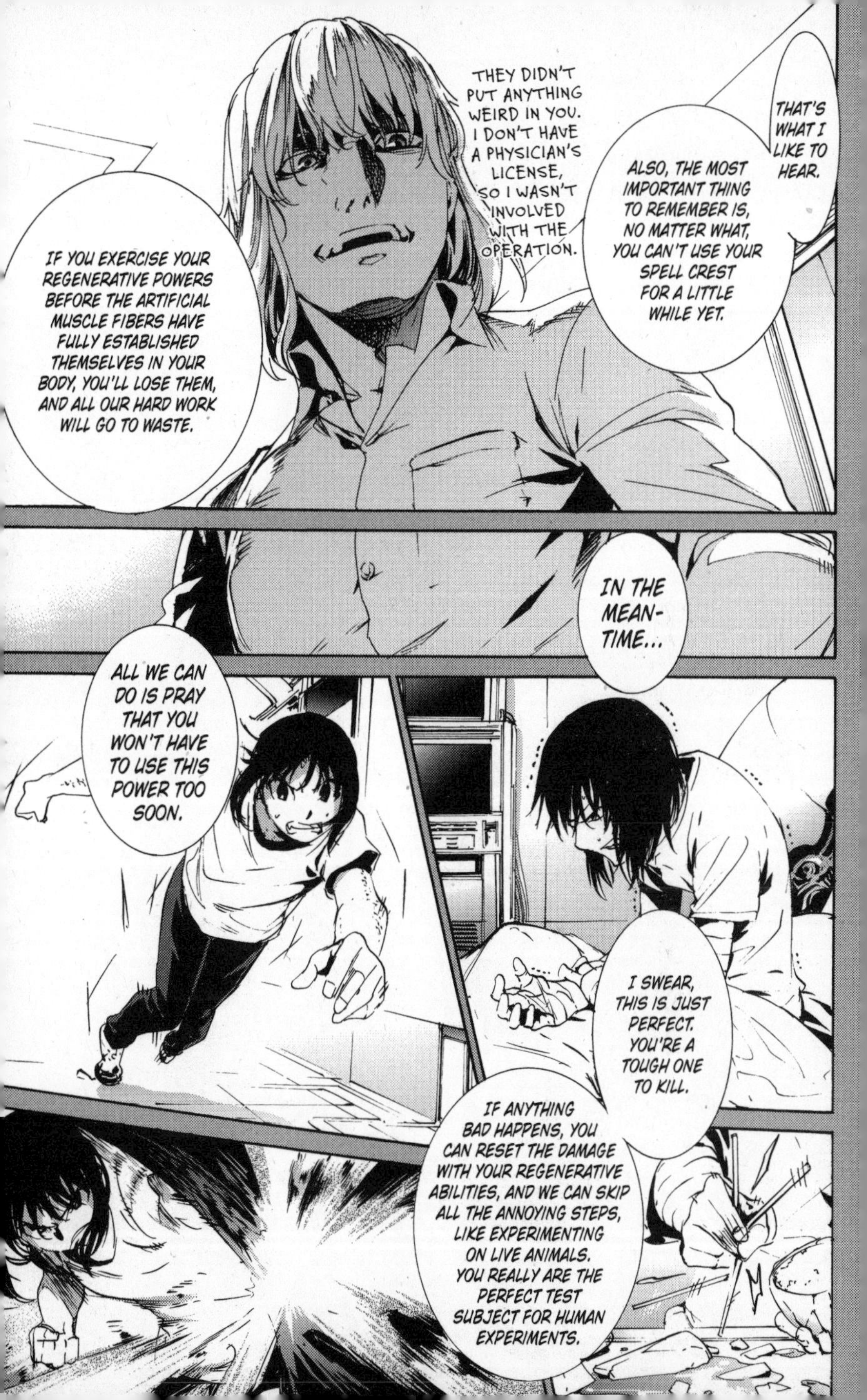
THAT'S WHAT I LIKE TO HEAR.
THEY DIDN'T PUT ANYTHING WEIRD IN YOU. I DON'T HAVE A PHYSICIAN'S LICENSE, SO I WASN'T INVOLVED WITH THE OPERATION.
ALSO, THE MOST IMPORTANT THING TO REMEMBER IS, NO MATTER WHAT, YOU CAN'T USE YOUR SPELL CREST FOR A LITTLE WHILE YET.
IF YOU EXERCISE YOUR REGENERATIVE POWERS BEFORE THE ARTIFICIAL MUSCLE FIBERS HAVE FULLY ESTABLISHED THEMSELVES IN YOUR BODY, YOU'LL LOSE THEM, AND ALL OUR HARD WORK WILL GO TO WASTE.
IN THE MEAN-TIME...
ALL WE CAN DO IS PRAY THAT YOU WON'T HAVE TO USE THIS POWER TOO SOON.
I SWEAR, THIS IS JUST PERFECT. YOU'RE A TOUGH ONE TO KILL.
IF ANYTHING BAD HAPPENS, YOU CAN RESET THE DAMAGE WITH YOUR REGENERATIVE ABILITIES, AND WE CAN SKIP ALL THE ANNOYING STEPS, LIKE EXPERIMENTING ON LIVE ANIMALS. YOU REALLY ARE THE PERFECT TEST SUBJECT FOR HUMAN EXPERIMENTS.

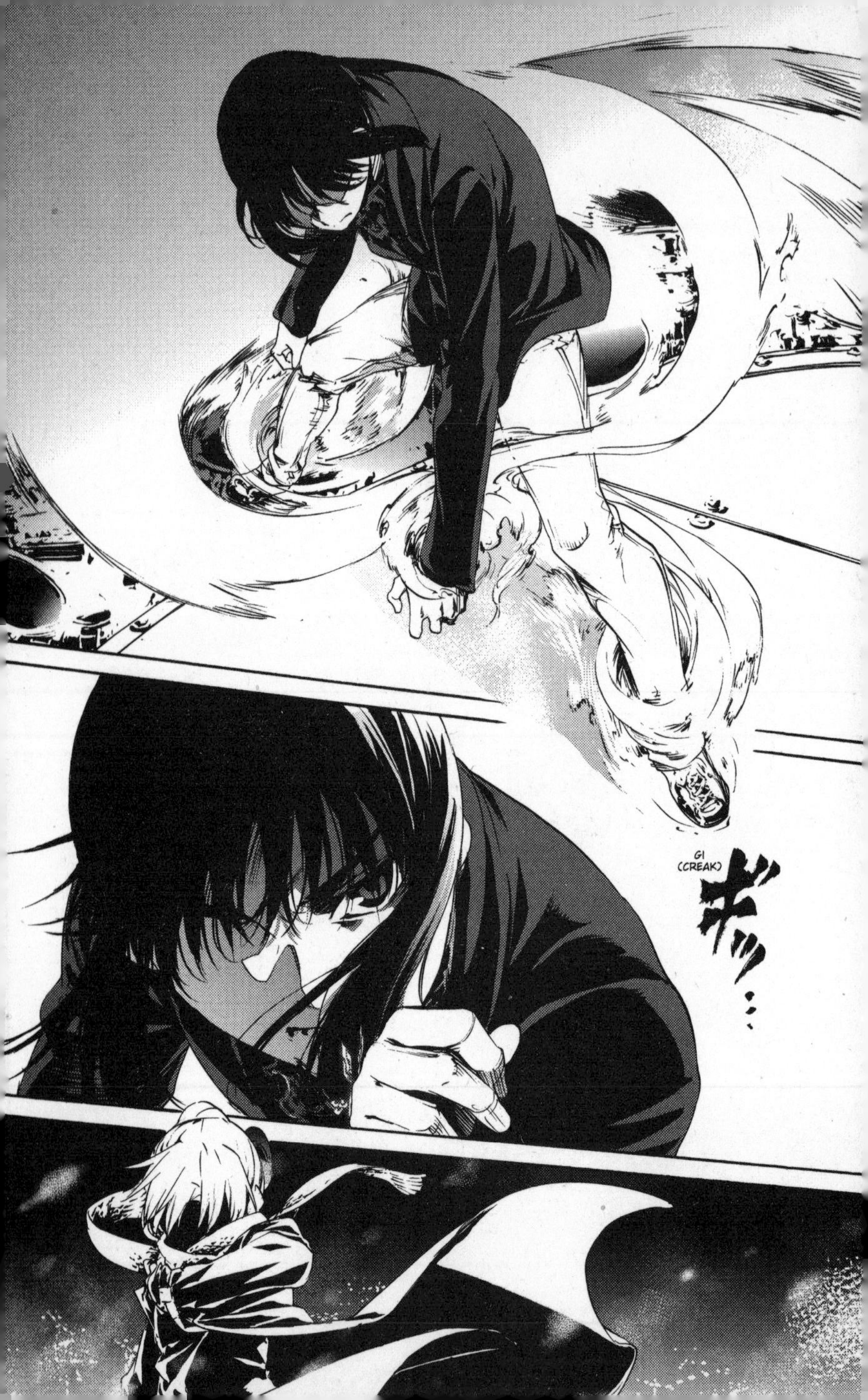
GI
(CREAK)
ギッ…

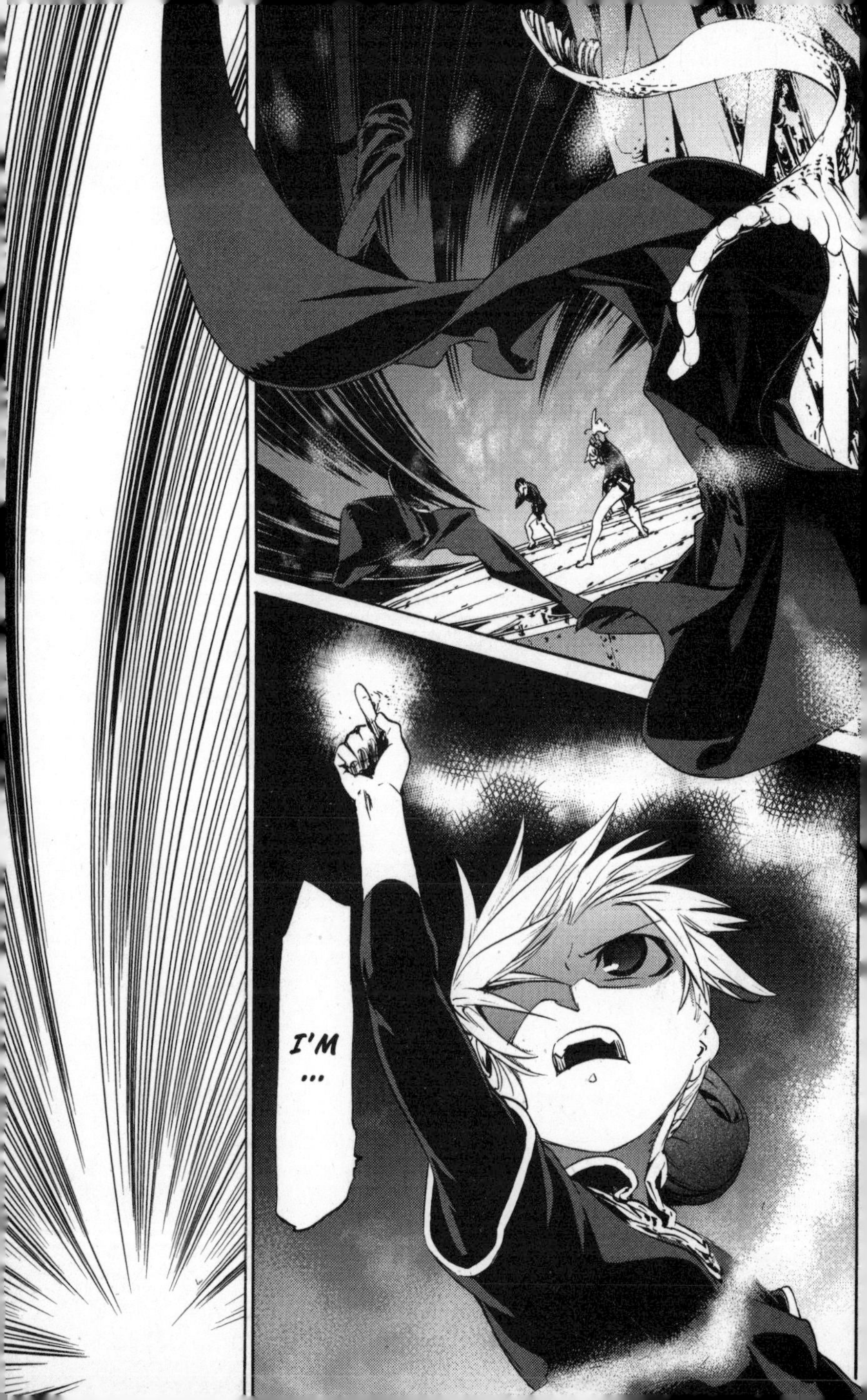
I'M ...

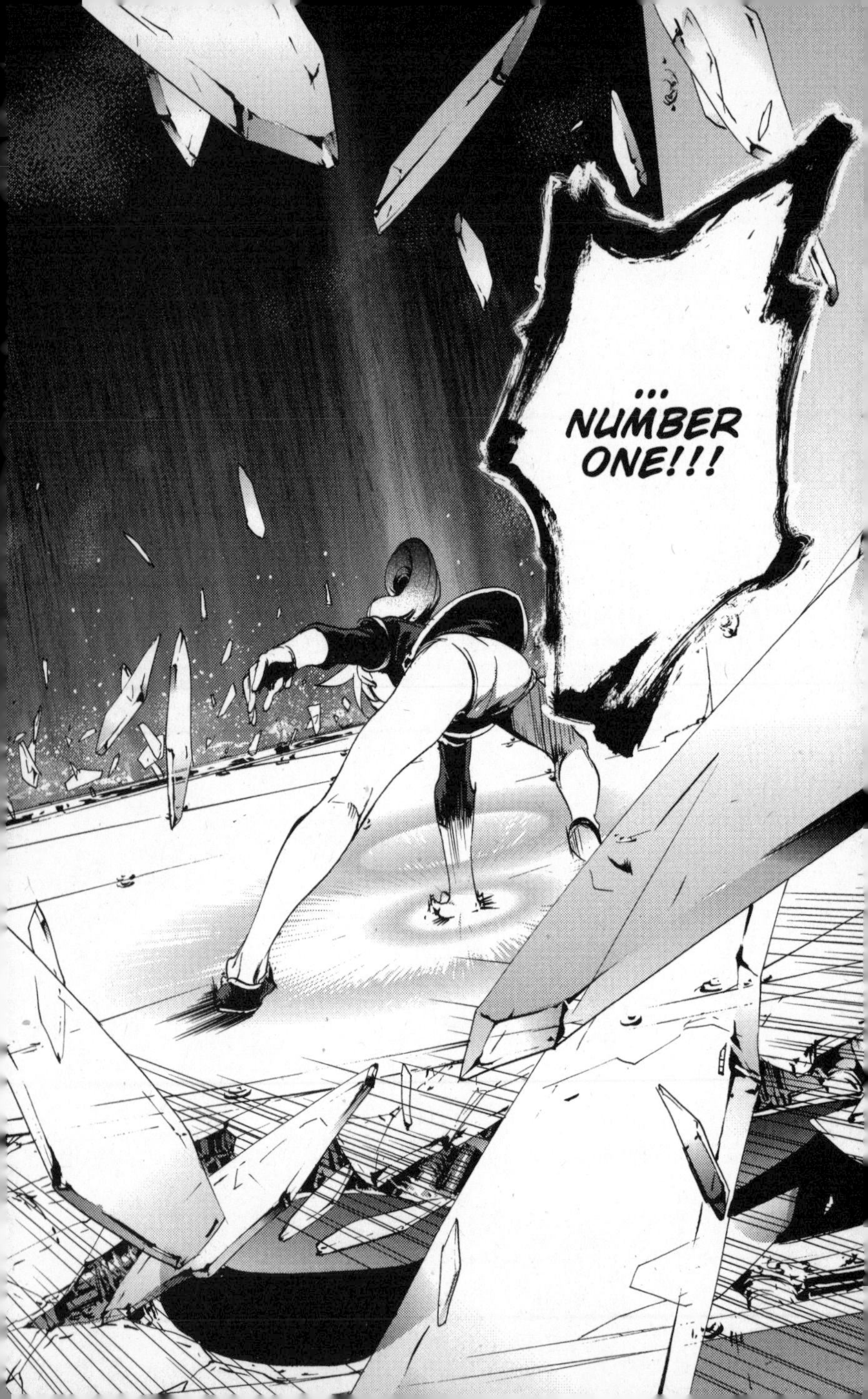
...NUMBER ONE!!!

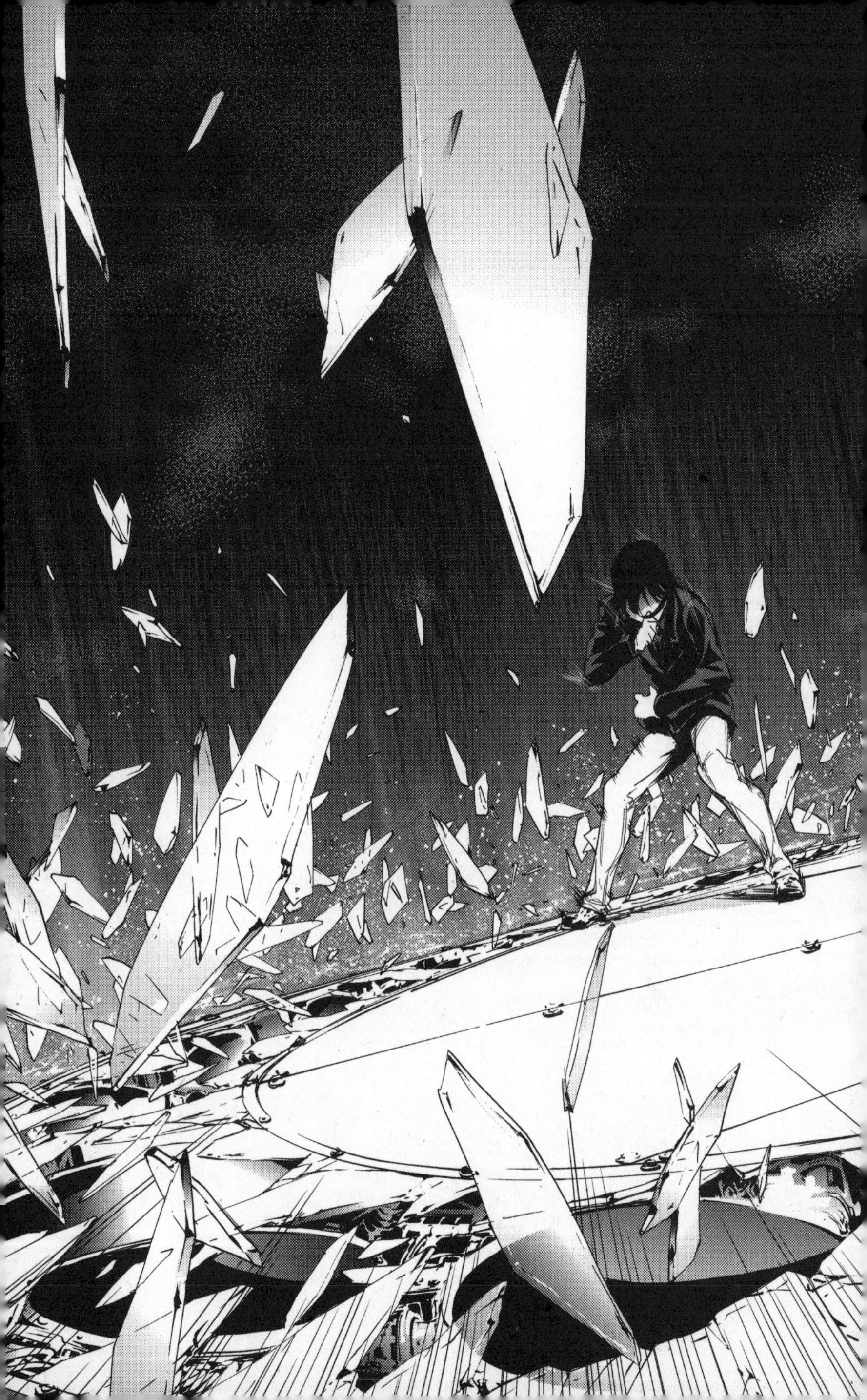

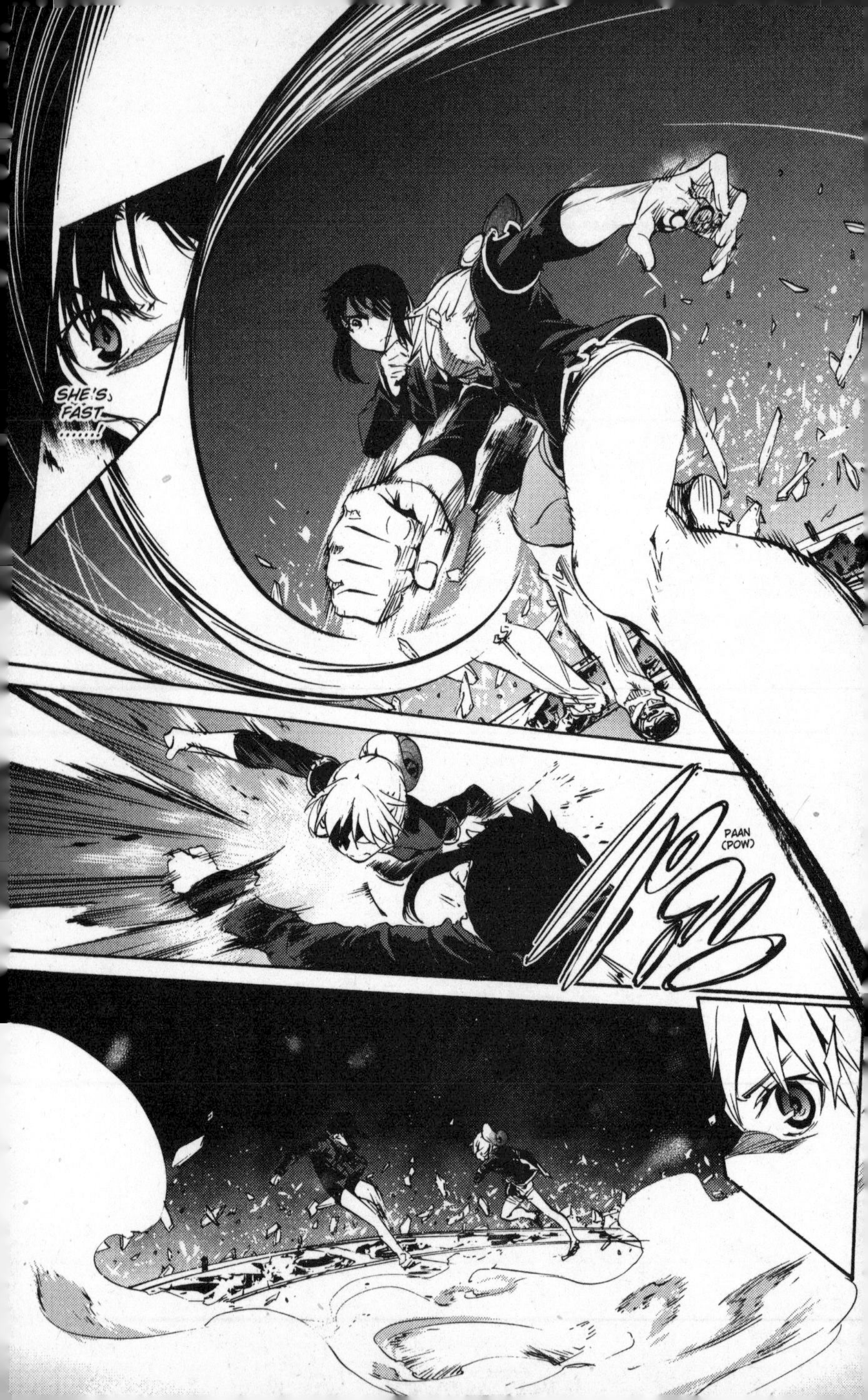
SHE'S FAST......!
PAAN (POW)

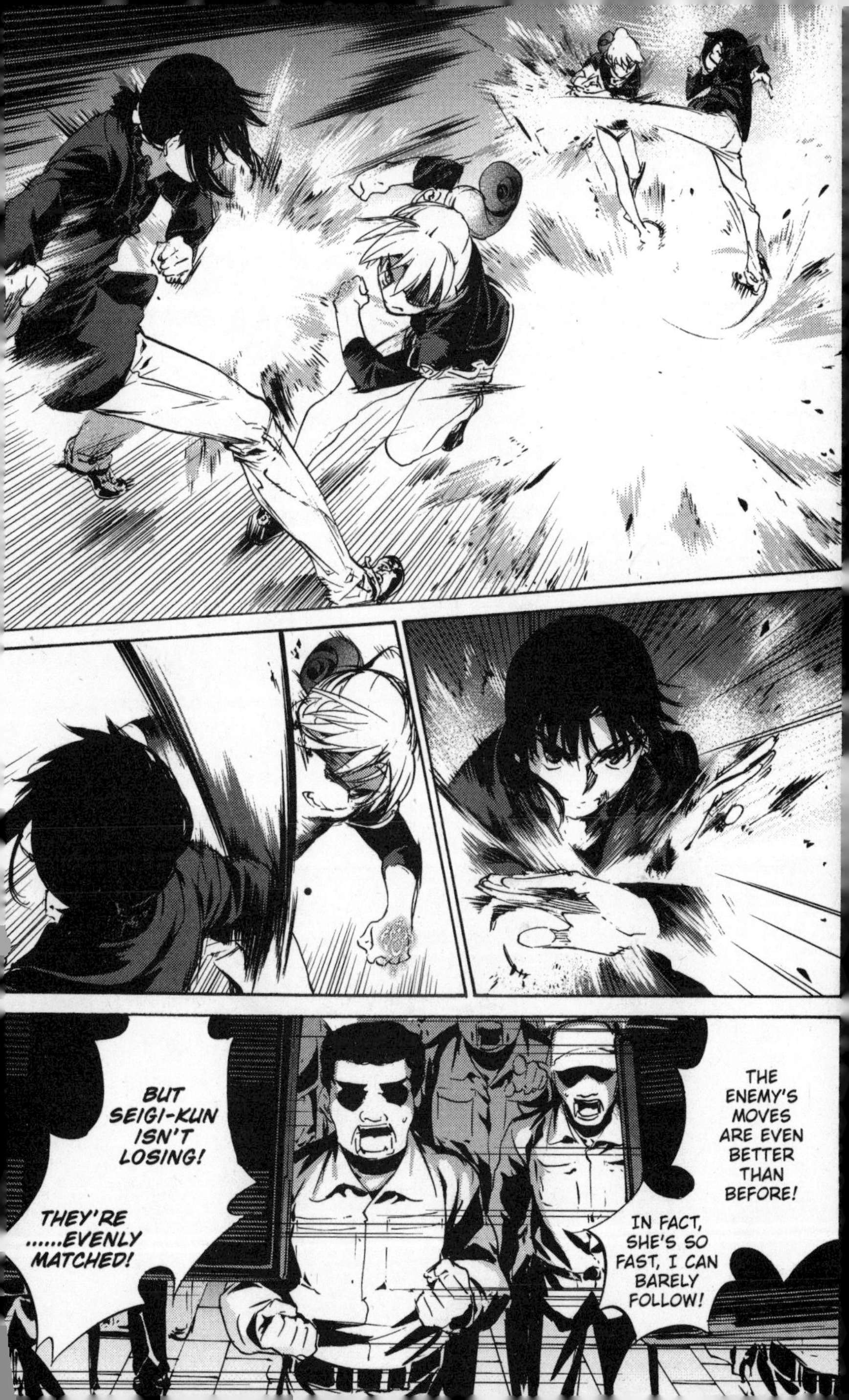
THE ENEMY'S MOVES ARE EVEN BETTER THAN BEFORE!
IN FACT, SHE'S SO FAST, I CAN BARELY FOLLOW!
BUT SEIGI-KUN ISN'T LOSING!
THEY'RE ......EVENLY MATCHED!

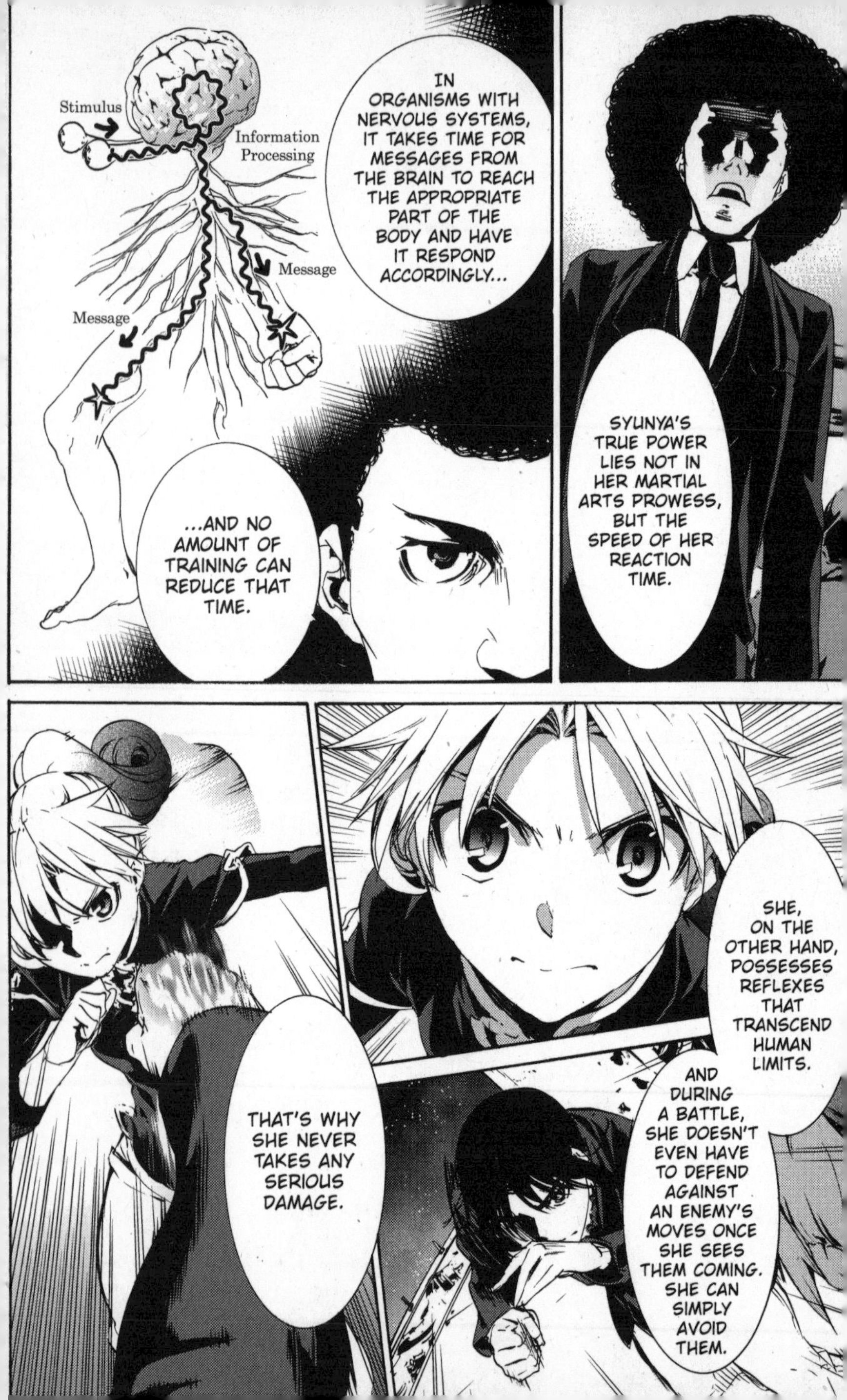
SYUNYA'S TRUE POWER LIES NOT IN HER MARTIAL ARTS PROWESS, BUT THE SPEED OF HER REACTION TIME.
IN ORGANISMS WITH NERVOUS SYSTEMS, IT TAKES TIME FOR MESSAGES FROM THE BRAIN TO REACH THE APPROPRIATE PART OF THE BODY AND HAVE IT RESPOND ACCORDINGLY...
Stimulus
Information Processing
Message
Message
...AND NO AMOUNT OF TRAINING CAN REDUCE THAT TIME.
SHE, ON THE OTHER HAND, POSSESSES REFLEXES THAT TRANSCEND HUMAN LIMITS.
AND DURING A BATTLE, SHE DOESN'T EVEN HAVE TO DEFEND AGAINST AN ENEMY'S MOVES ONCE SHE SEES THEM COMING. SHE CAN SIMPLY AVOID THEM.
THAT'S WHY SHE NEVER TAKES ANY SERIOUS DAMAGE.

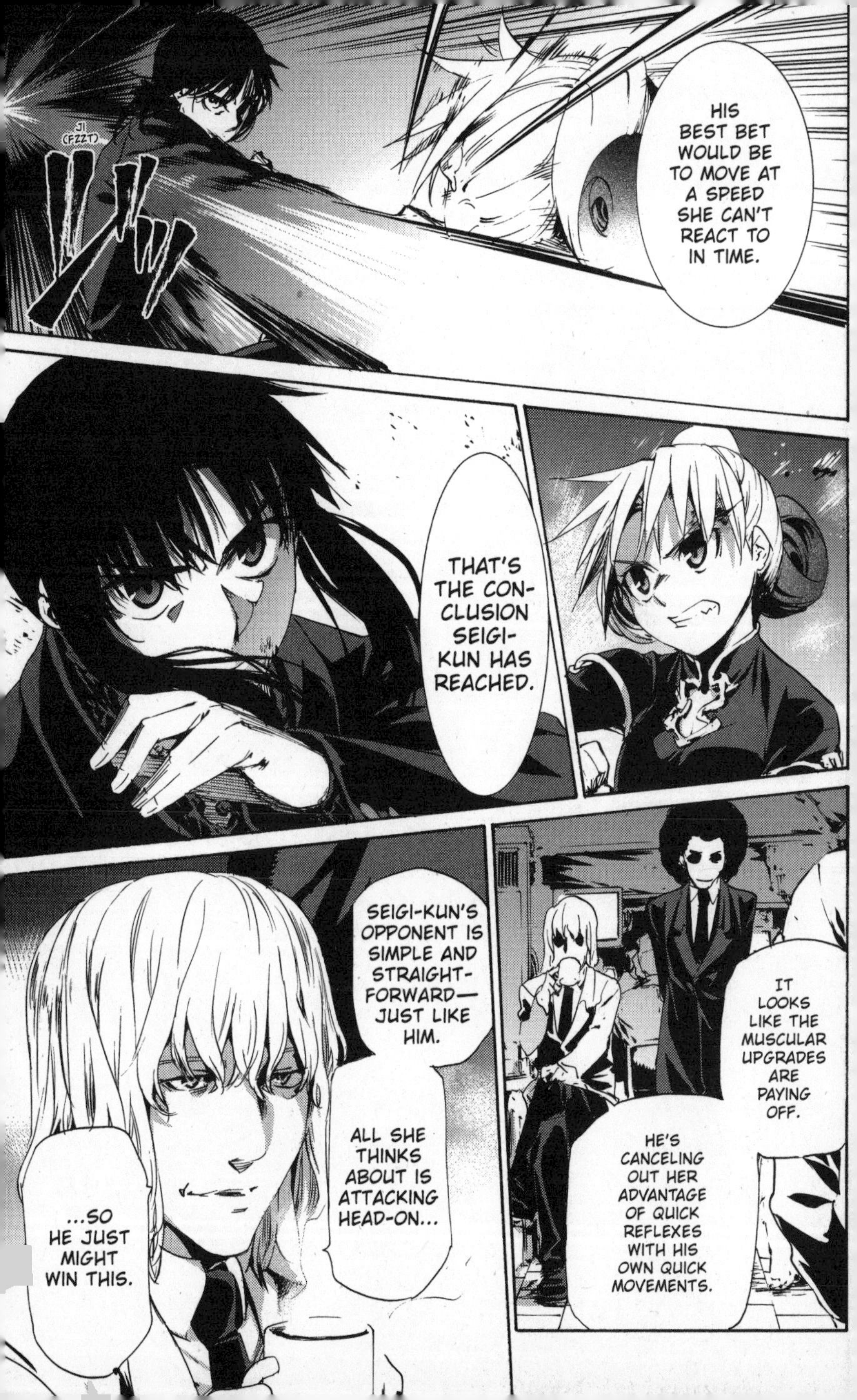
HIS BEST BET WOULD BE TO MOVE AT A SPEED SHE CAN'T REACT TO IN TIME.
JI (FZZT)
THAT'S THE CON-CLUSION SEIGI-KUN HAS REACHED.
IT LOOKS LIKE THE MUSCULAR UPGRADES ARE PAYING OFF.
HE'S CANCELING OUT HER ADVANTAGE OF QUICK REFLEXES WITH HIS OWN QUICK MOVEMENTS.
SEIGI-KUN'S OPPONENT IS SIMPLE AND STRAIGHT-FORWARD—JUST LIKE HIM.
ALL SHE THINKS ABOUT IS ATTACKING HEAD-ON...
...SO HE JUST MIGHT WIN THIS.

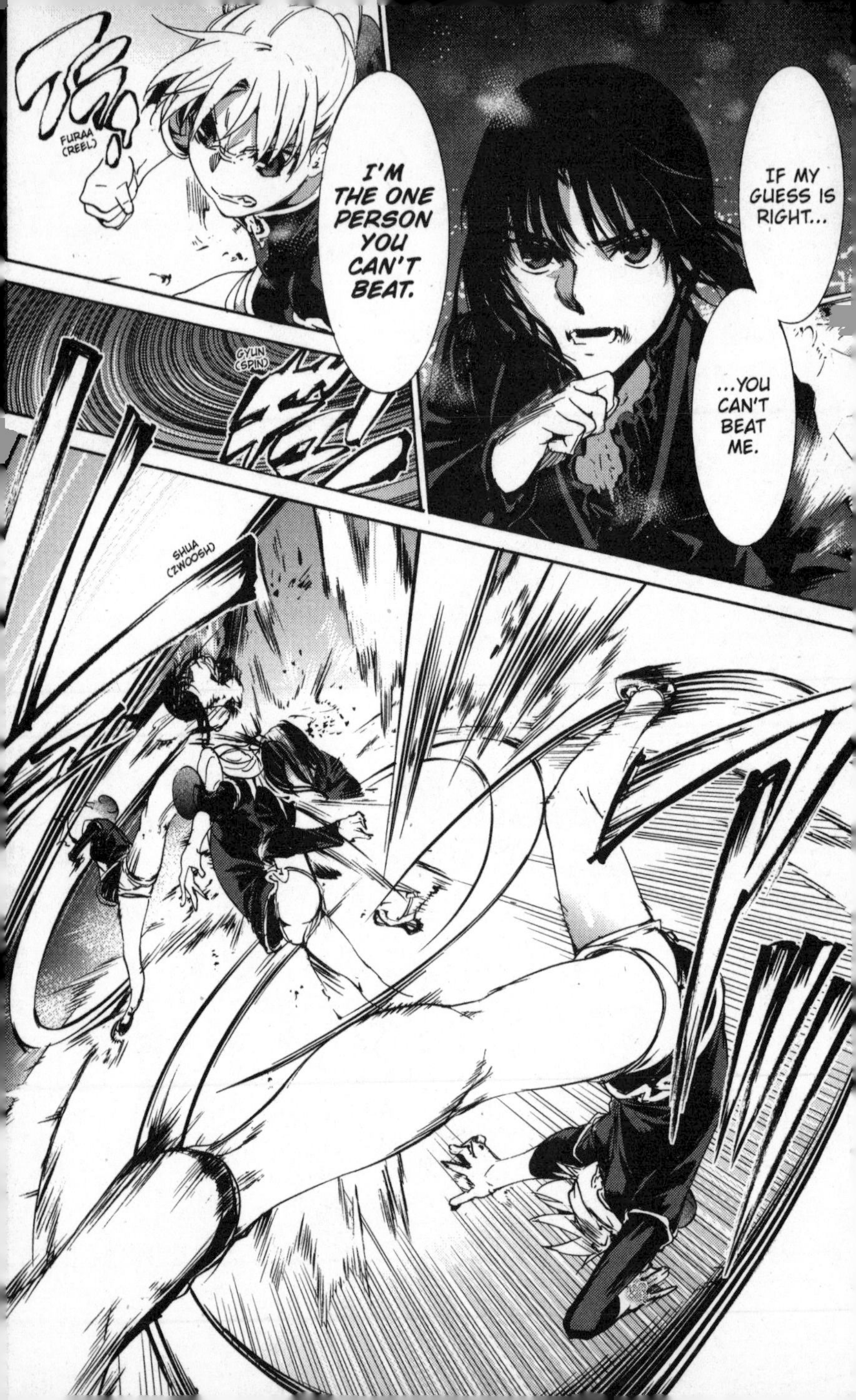

IF MY GUESS IS RIGHT...
...YOU CAN'T BEAT ME.
I'M THE ONE PERSON YOU CAN'T BEAT.
FURAA (REEL)
GYUN (SPIN)
SHUA (ZWOOSH)

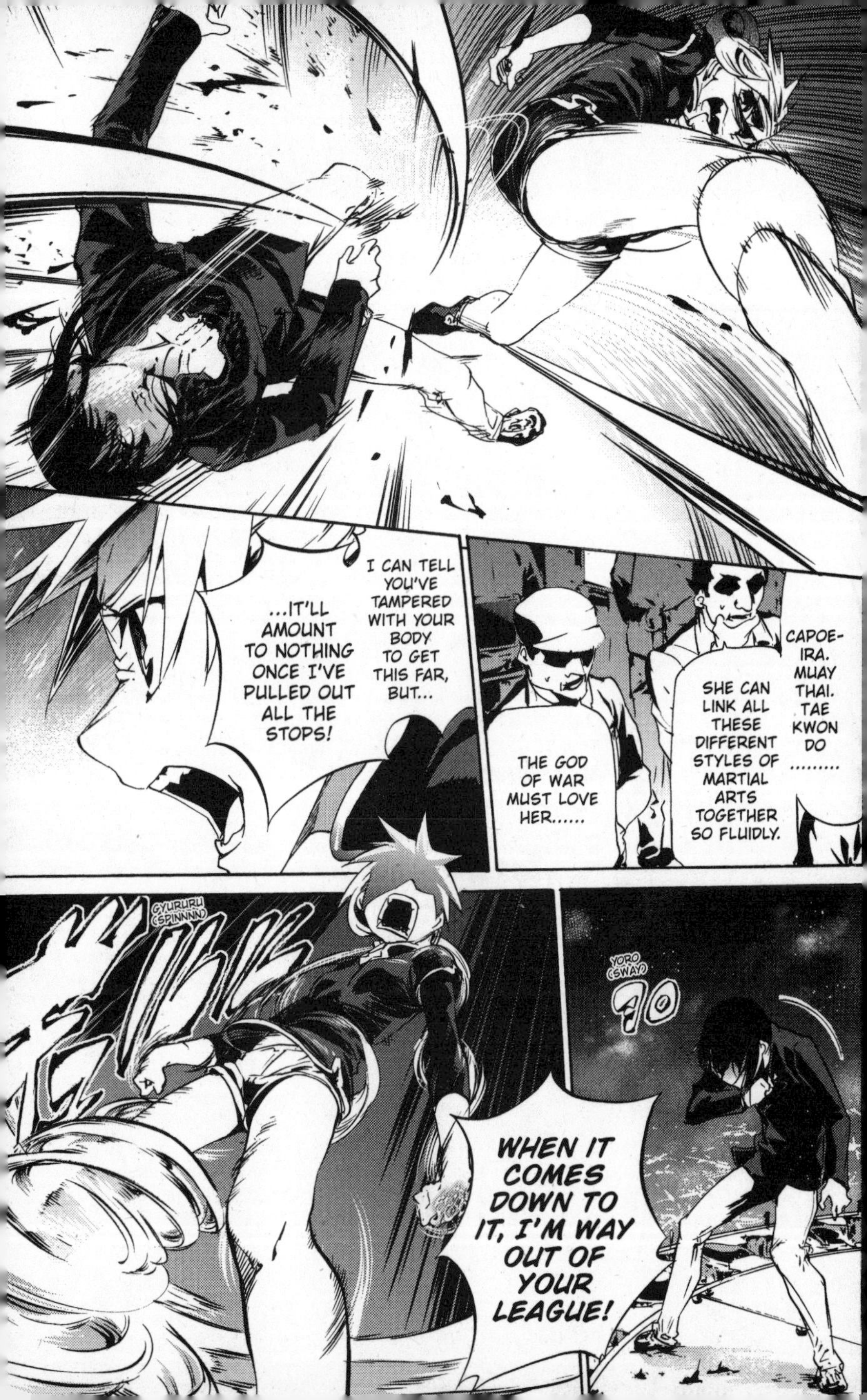
CAPOE-IRA. MUAY THAI. TAE KWON DO ....
SHE CAN LINK ALL THESE DIFFERENT STYLES OF MARTIAL ARTS TOGETHER SO FLUIDLY.
THE GOD OF WAR MUST LOVE HER......
I CAN TELL YOU'VE TAMPERED WITH YOUR BODY TO GET THIS FAR, BUT...
...IT'LL AMOUNT TO NOTHING ONCE I'VE PULLED OUT ALL THE STOPS!
YORO (SWAY)
GYURURU (SPINNNN)
WHEN IT COMES DOWN TO IT, I'M WAY OUT OF YOUR LEAGUE!

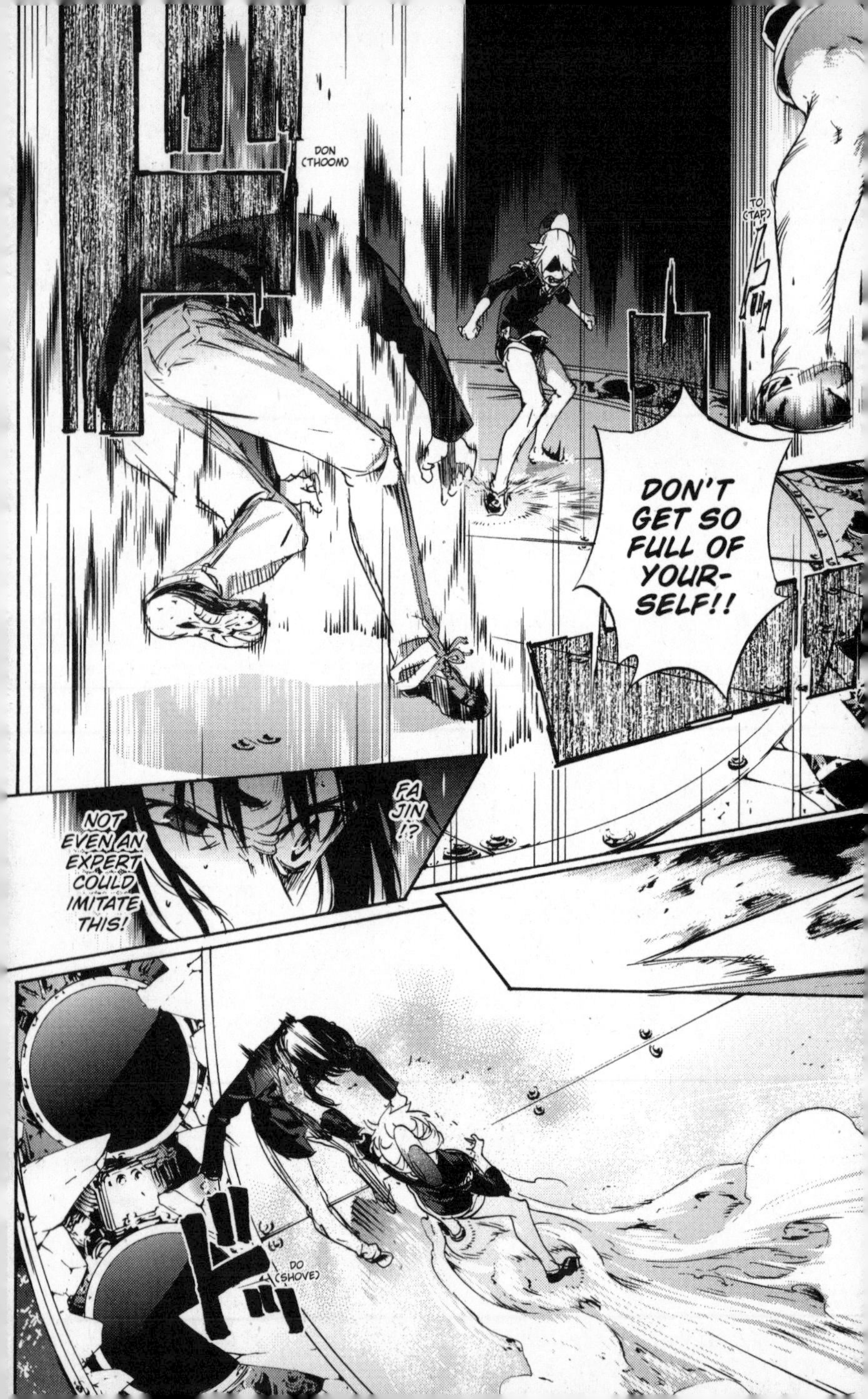
TO (TAP)
DON (THOOM)
DON'T GET SO FULL OF YOUR-SELF!!
FA JIN!?
NOT EVEN AN EXPERT COULD IMITATE THIS!
DO (SHOVE)

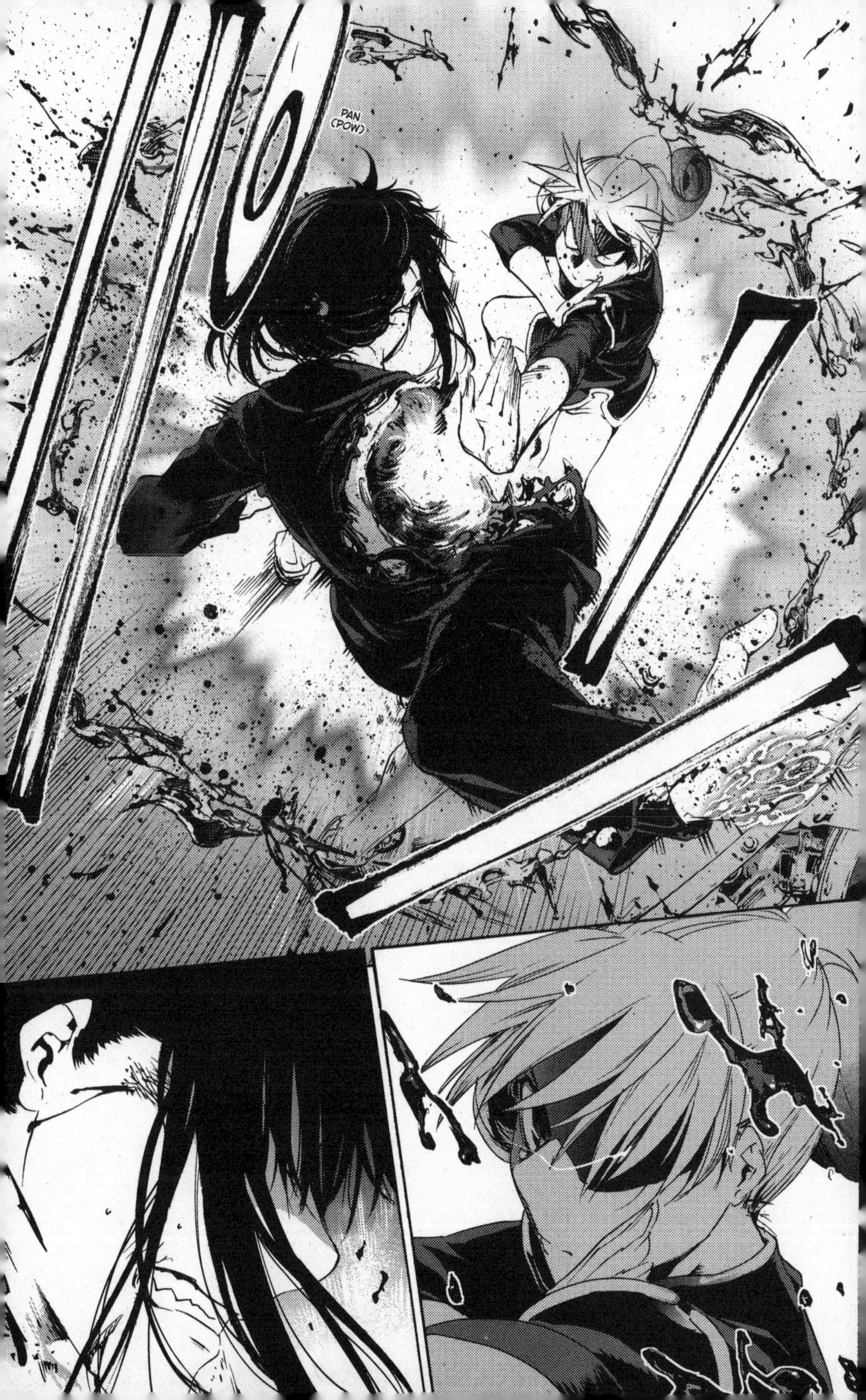
PAN
(POW)

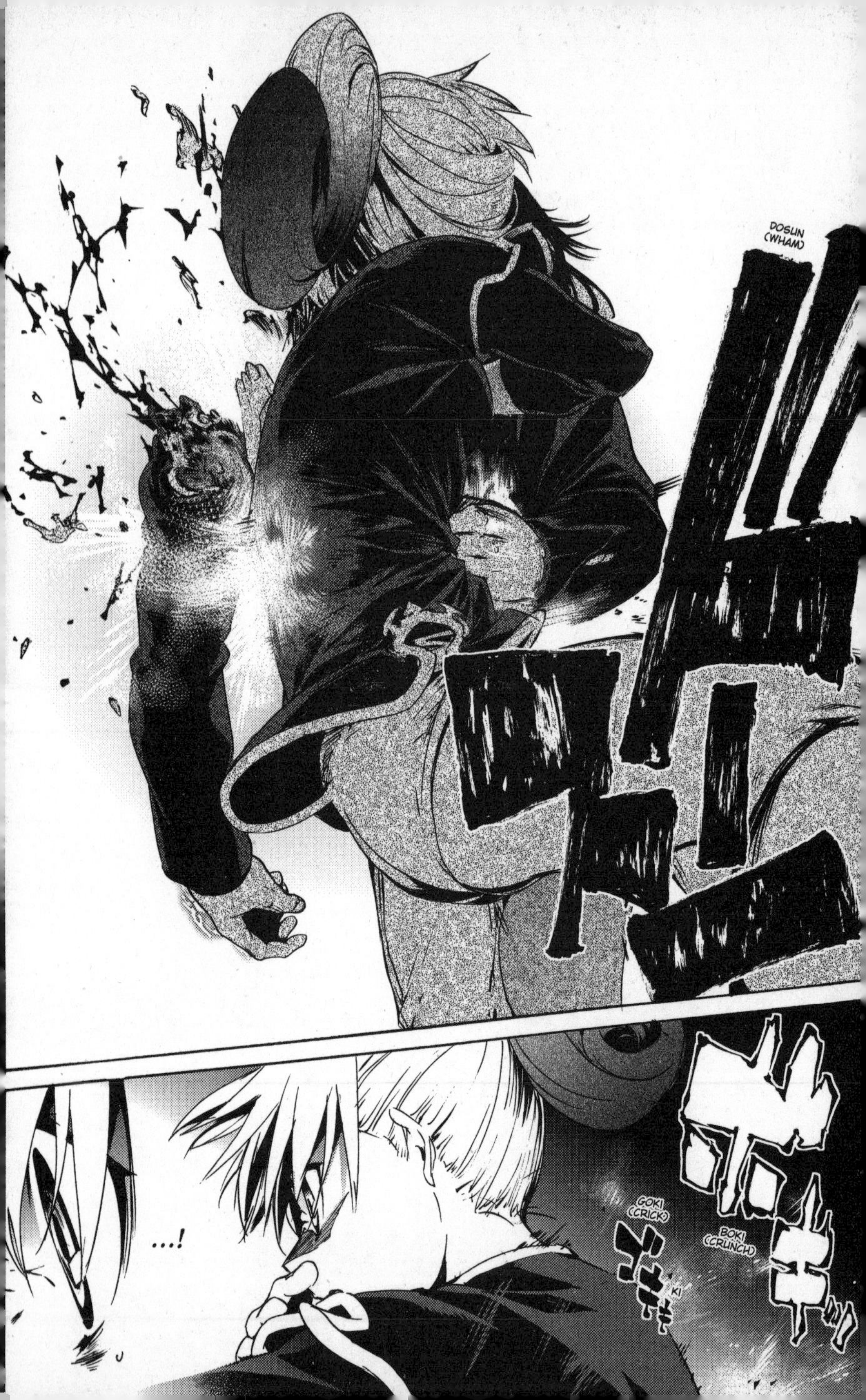
DOSUN (WHAM)
BOKI (CRUNCH)
GOKI (CRICK)
KI
...!

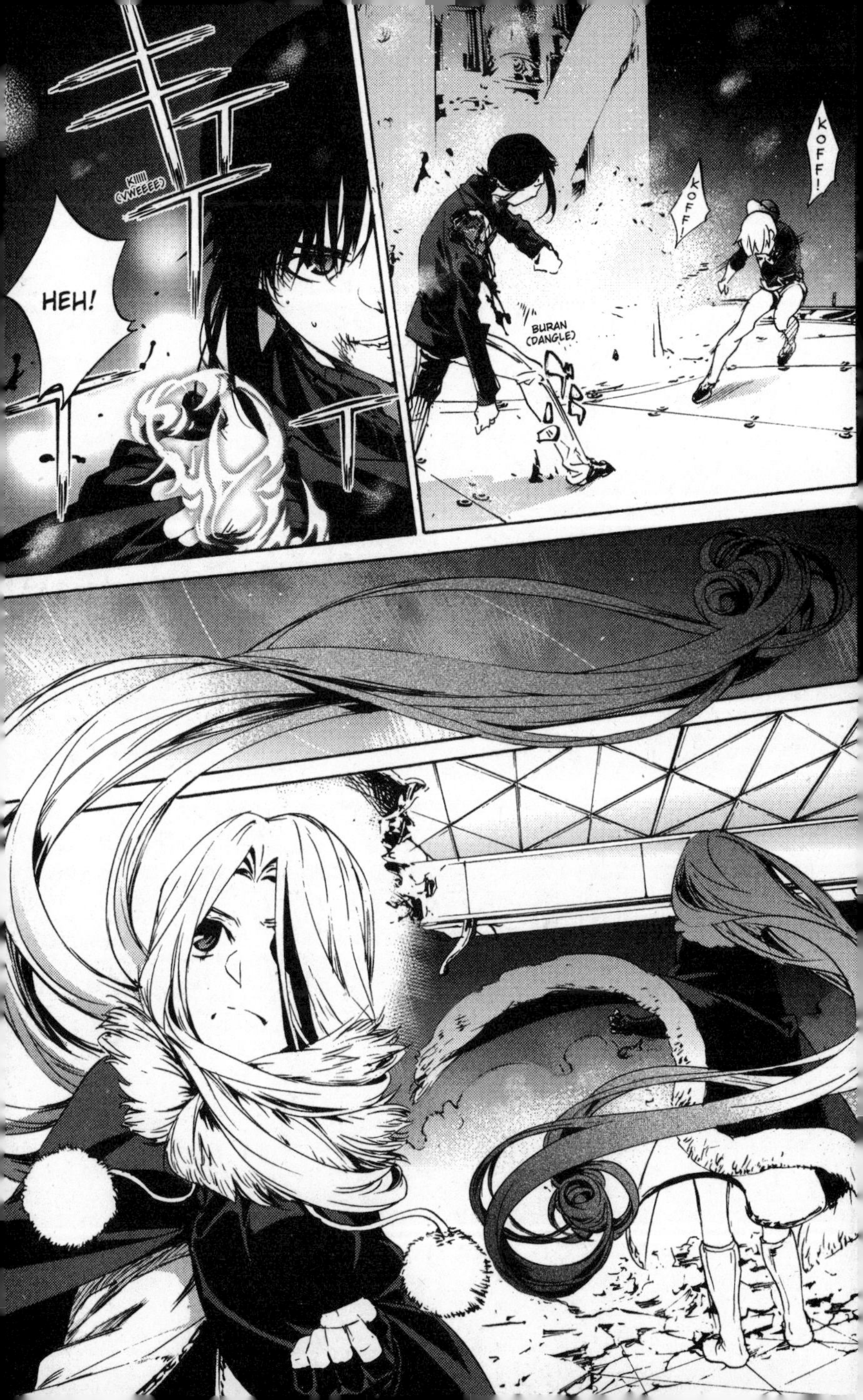
KOFF!
KOFF!
BURAN (DANGLE)
KIIIII (VWEEEE)
HEH!

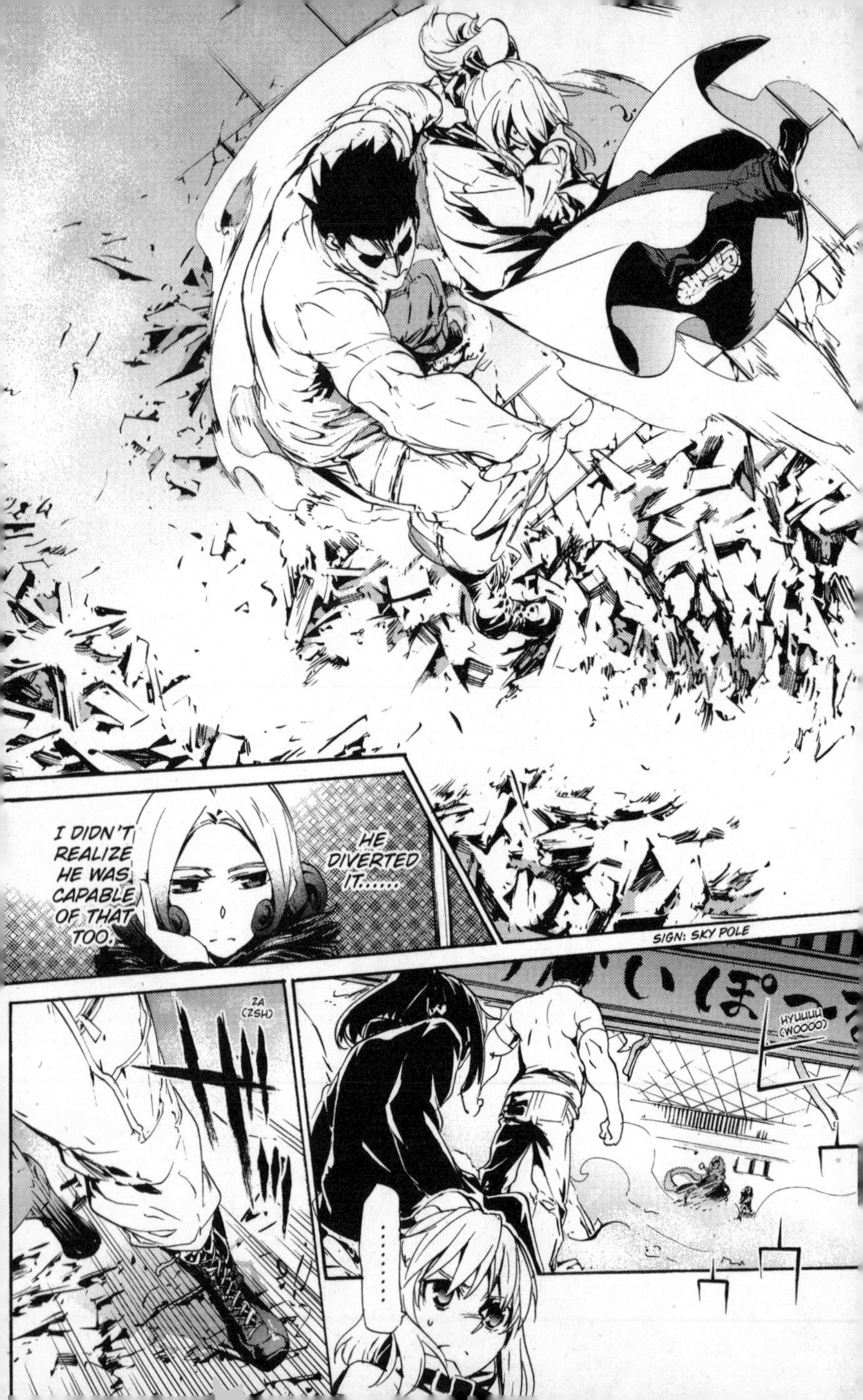
HE DIVERTED IT......
I DIDN'T REALIZE HE WAS CAPABLE OF THAT TOO.
SIGN: SKY POLE
HYUUUU (WOOOO)
ZA (ZSH)

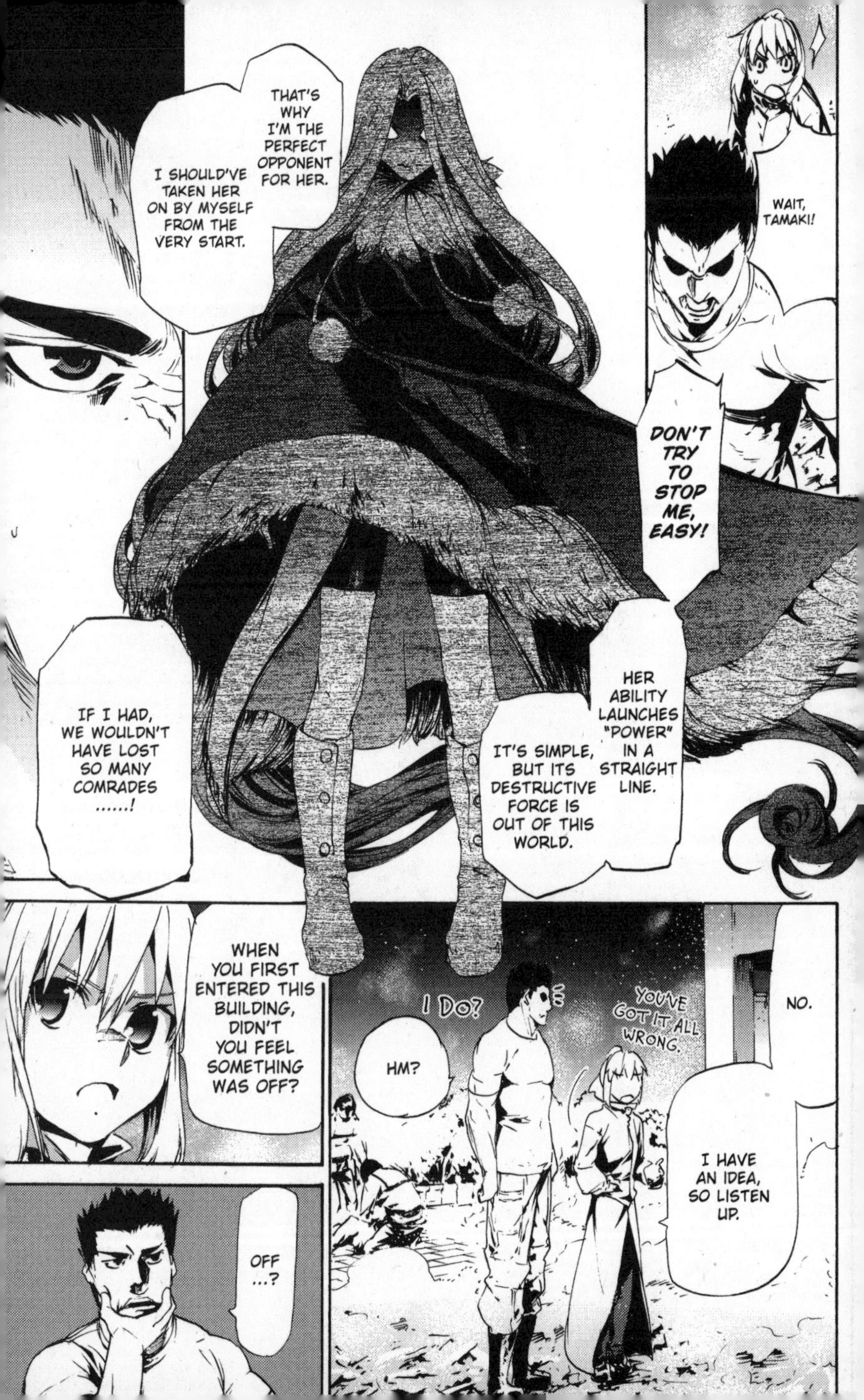
WAIT, TAMAKI!
DON'T TRY TO STOP ME, EASY!
HER ABILITY LAUNCHES "POWER" IN A STRAIGHT LINE.
IT'S SIMPLE, BUT ITS DESTRUCTIVE FORCE IS OUT OF THIS WORLD.
THAT'S WHY I'M THE PERFECT OPPONENT FOR HER.
I SHOULD'VE TAKEN HER ON BY MYSELF FROM THE VERY START.
IF I HAD, WE WOULDN'T HAVE LOST SO MANY COMRADES ......!
NO.
YOU'VE GOT IT ALL WRONG.
I DO?
HM?
I HAVE AN IDEA, SO LISTEN UP.
WHEN YOU FIRST ENTERED THIS BUILDING, DIDN'T YOU FEEL SOMETHING WAS OFF?
OFF ...?

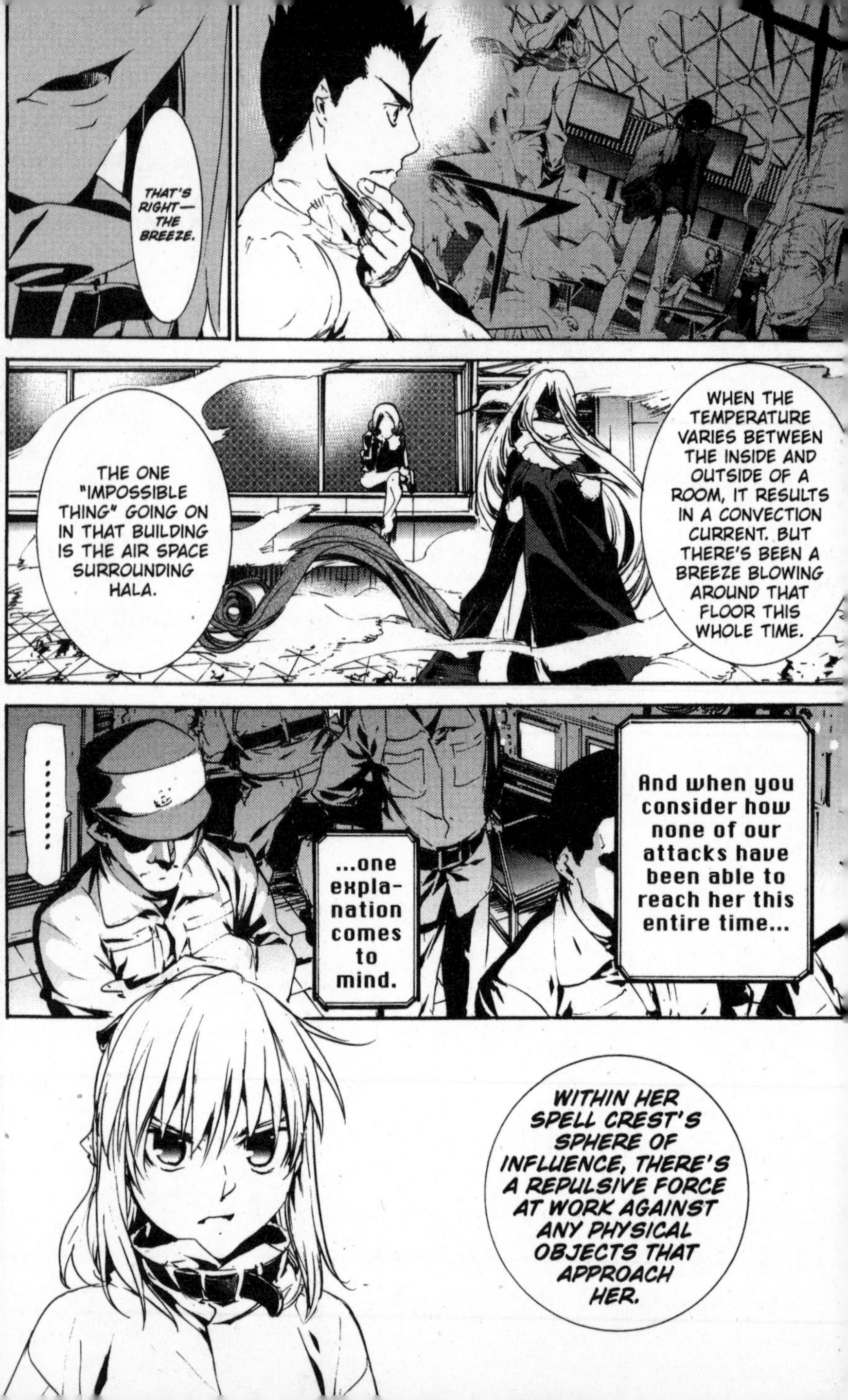
THAT'S RIGHT— THE BREEZE.
WHEN THE TEMPERATURE VARIES BETWEEN THE INSIDE AND OUTSIDE OF A ROOM, IT RESULTS IN A CONVECTION CURRENT. BUT THERE'S BEEN A BREEZE BLOWING AROUND THAT FLOOR THIS WHOLE TIME.
THE ONE "IMPOSSIBLE THING" GOING ON IN THAT BUILDING IS THE AIR SPACE SURROUNDING HALA.
And when you consider how none of our attacks have been able to reach her this entire time...
...one expla-nation comes to mind.
....
WITHIN HER SPELL CREST'S SPHERE OF INFLUENCE, THERE'S A REPULSIVE FORCE AT WORK AGAINST ANY PHYSICAL OBJECTS THAT APPROACH HER.

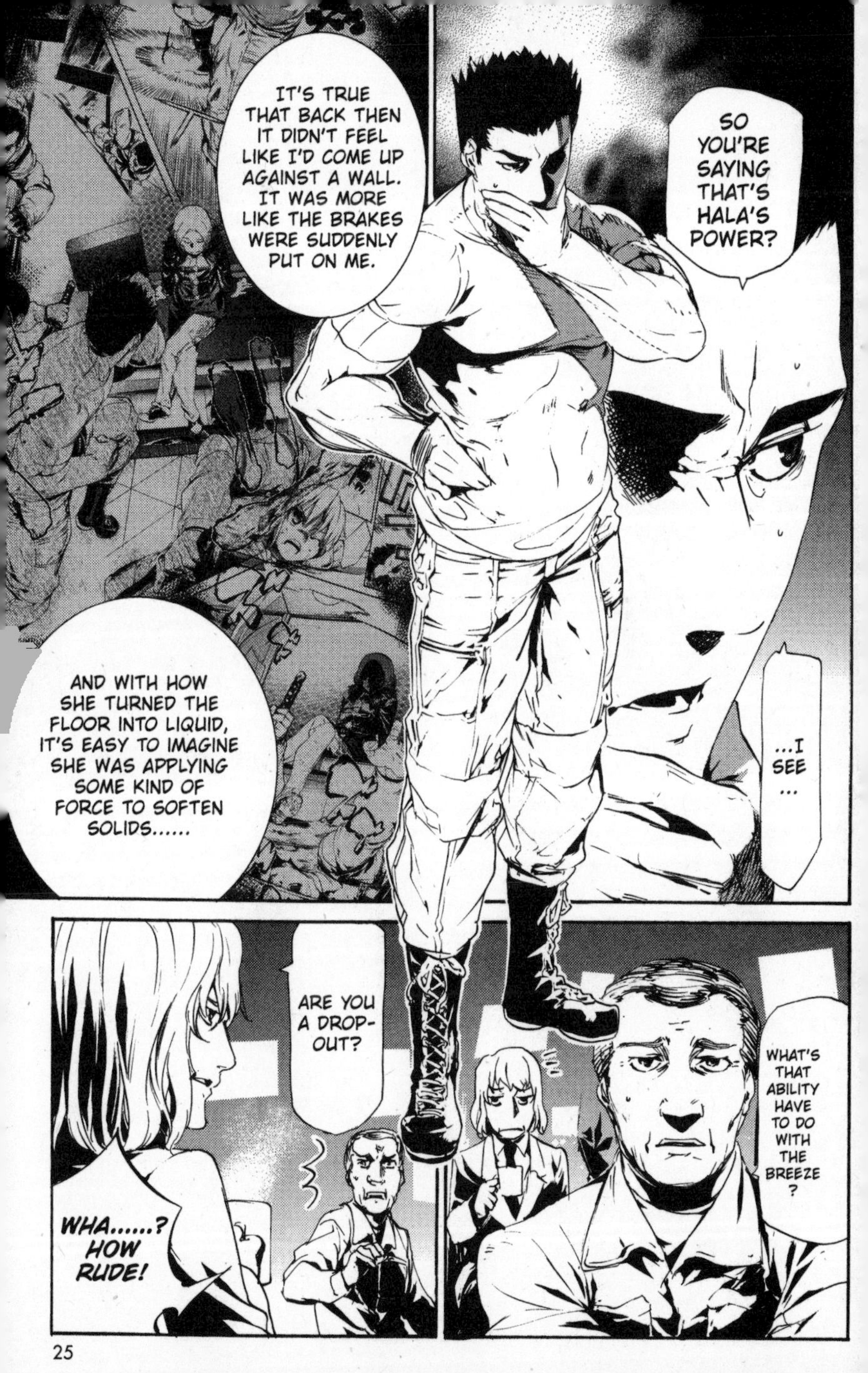
SO YOU'RE SAYING THAT'S HALA'S POWER?
...I SEE...
IT'S TRUE THAT BACK THEN IT DIDN'T FEEL LIKE I'D COME UP AGAINST A WALL. IT WAS MORE LIKE THE BRAKES WERE SUDDENLY PUT ON ME.
AND WITH HOW SHE TURNED THE FLOOR INTO LIQUID, IT'S EASY TO IMAGINE SHE WAS APPLYING SOME KIND OF FORCE TO SOFTEN SOLIDS......
WHAT'S THAT ABILITY HAVE TO DO WITH THE BREEZE?
ARE YOU A DROP-OUT?
WHA......? HOW RUDE!

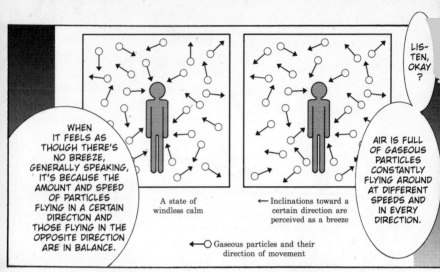

LIS-TEN, OKAY?
AIR IS FULL OF GASEOUS PARTICLES CONSTANTLY FLYING AROUND AT DIFFERENT SPEEDS AND IN EVERY DIRECTION.
← Inclinations toward a certain direction are perceived as a breeze
A state of windless calm
WHEN IT FEELS AS THOUGH THERE'S NO BREEZE, GENERALLY SPEAKING, IT'S BECAUSE THE AMOUNT AND SPEED OF PARTICLES FLYING IN A CERTAIN DIRECTION AND THOSE FLYING IN THE OPPOSITE DIRECTION ARE IN BALANCE.
Gaseous particles and their direction of movement
NOW, WHAT WOULD HAPPEN IF ONLY THE PARTICLES FLYING IN A CERTAIN DIRECTION SUDDENLY HAD THE BRAKES PUT ON THEM?
HMMMM.
THEY'D GO IN THE OP-POSITE DIREC-TION......
Windless calm
←Particles moving in the opposite direction have the brakes put on them
Overall, the air is moving in the direction of the arrows
I GET IT NOW! THERE'S A BREEZE!
PON (WHAP)

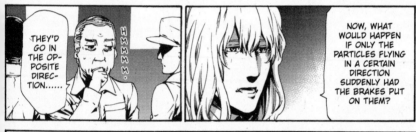

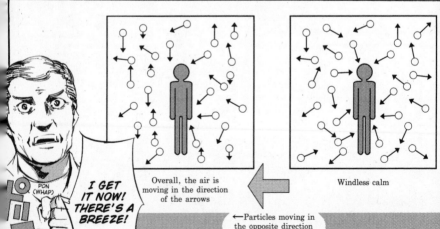

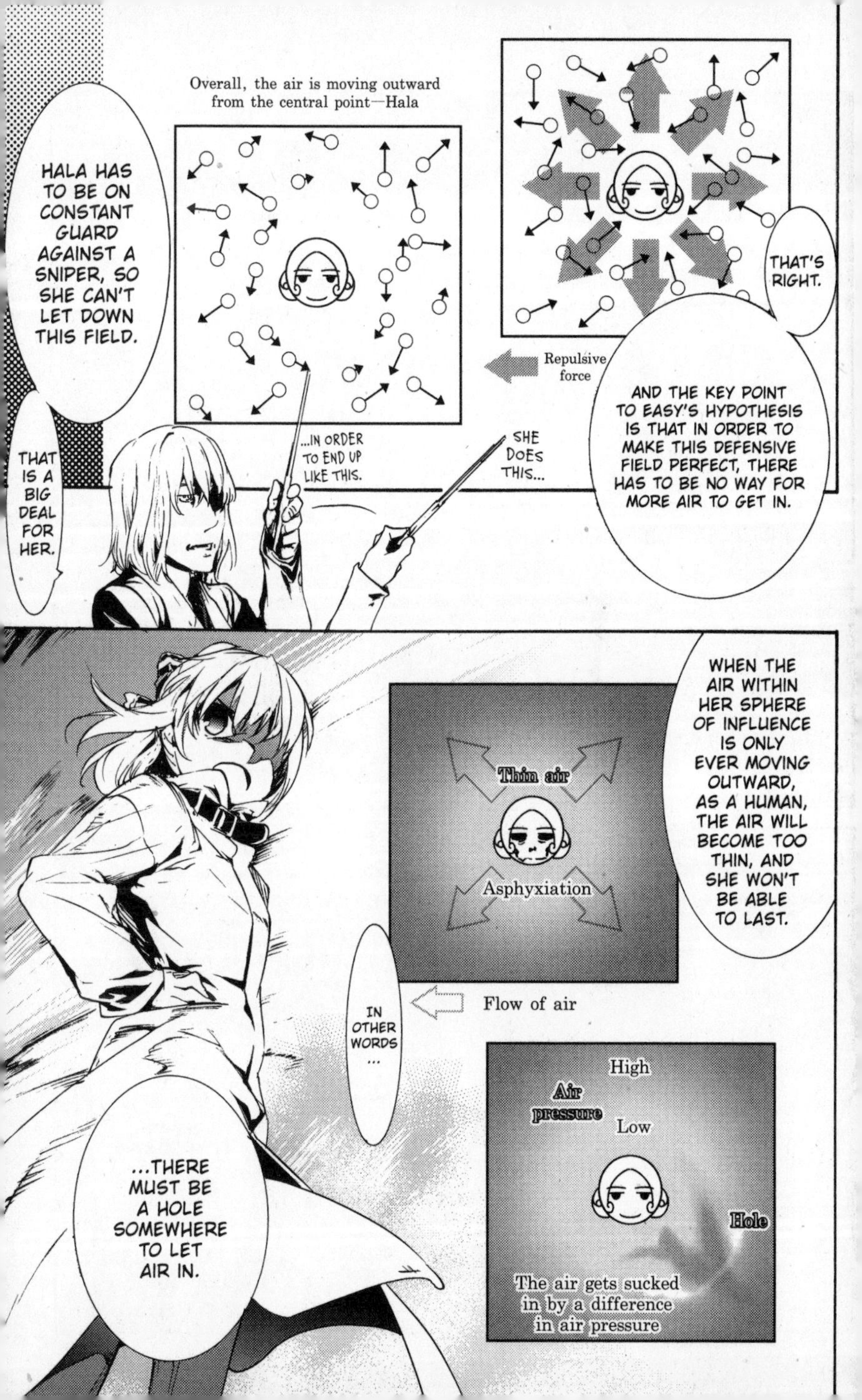

THAT'S RIGHT.
AND THE KEY POINT TO EASY'S HYPOTHESIS IS THAT IN ORDER TO MAKE THIS DEFENSIVE FIELD PERFECT, THERE HAS TO BE NO WAY FOR MORE AIR TO GET IN.
Repulsive force
Overall, the air is moving outward from the central point—Hala
SHE DOES THIS...
...IN ORDER TO END UP LIKE THIS.
HALA HAS TO BE ON CONSTANT GUARD AGAINST A SNIPER, SO SHE CAN'T LET DOWN THIS FIELD.
THAT IS A BIG DEAL FOR HER.
WHEN THE AIR WITHIN HER SPHERE OF INFLUENCE IS ONLY EVER MOVING OUTWARD, AS A HUMAN, THE AIR WILL BECOME TOO THIN, AND SHE WON'T BE ABLE TO LAST.
Thin air
Asphyxiation
Flow of air
IN OTHER WORDS...
High
Air pressure
Low
Hole
The air gets sucked in by a difference in air pressure
...THERE MUST BE A HOLE SOMEWHERE TO LET AIR IN.

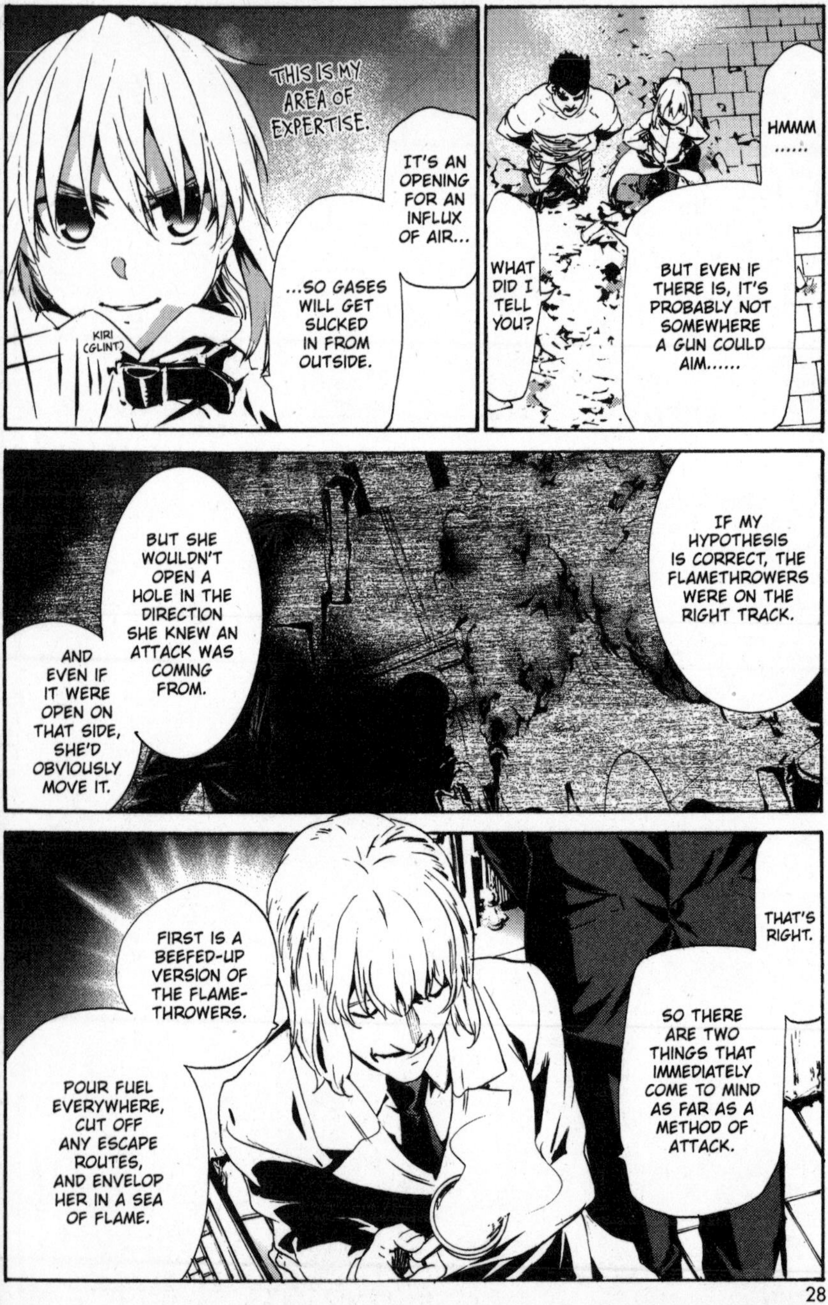
HMMM ......
BUT EVEN IF THERE IS, IT'S PROBABLY NOT SOMEWHERE A GUN COULD AIM......
WHAT DID I TELL YOU?
IT'S AN OPENING FOR AN INFLUX OF AIR...
...SO GASES WILL GET SUCKED IN FROM OUTSIDE.
THIS IS MY AREA OF EXPERTISE.
KIRI (GLINT)
IF MY HYPOTHESIS IS CORRECT, THE FLAMETHROWERS WERE ON THE RIGHT TRACK.
BUT SHE WOULDN'T OPEN A HOLE IN THE DIRECTION SHE KNEW AN ATTACK WAS COMING FROM.
AND EVEN IF IT WERE OPEN ON THAT SIDE, SHE'D OBVIOUSLY MOVE IT.
THAT'S RIGHT.
SO THERE ARE TWO THINGS THAT IMMEDIATELY COME TO MIND AS FAR AS A METHOD OF ATTACK.
FIRST IS A BEEFED-UP VERSION OF THE FLAME-THROWERS.
POUR FUEL EVERYWHERE, CUT OFF ANY ESCAPE ROUTES, AND ENVELOP HER IN A SEA OF FLAME.

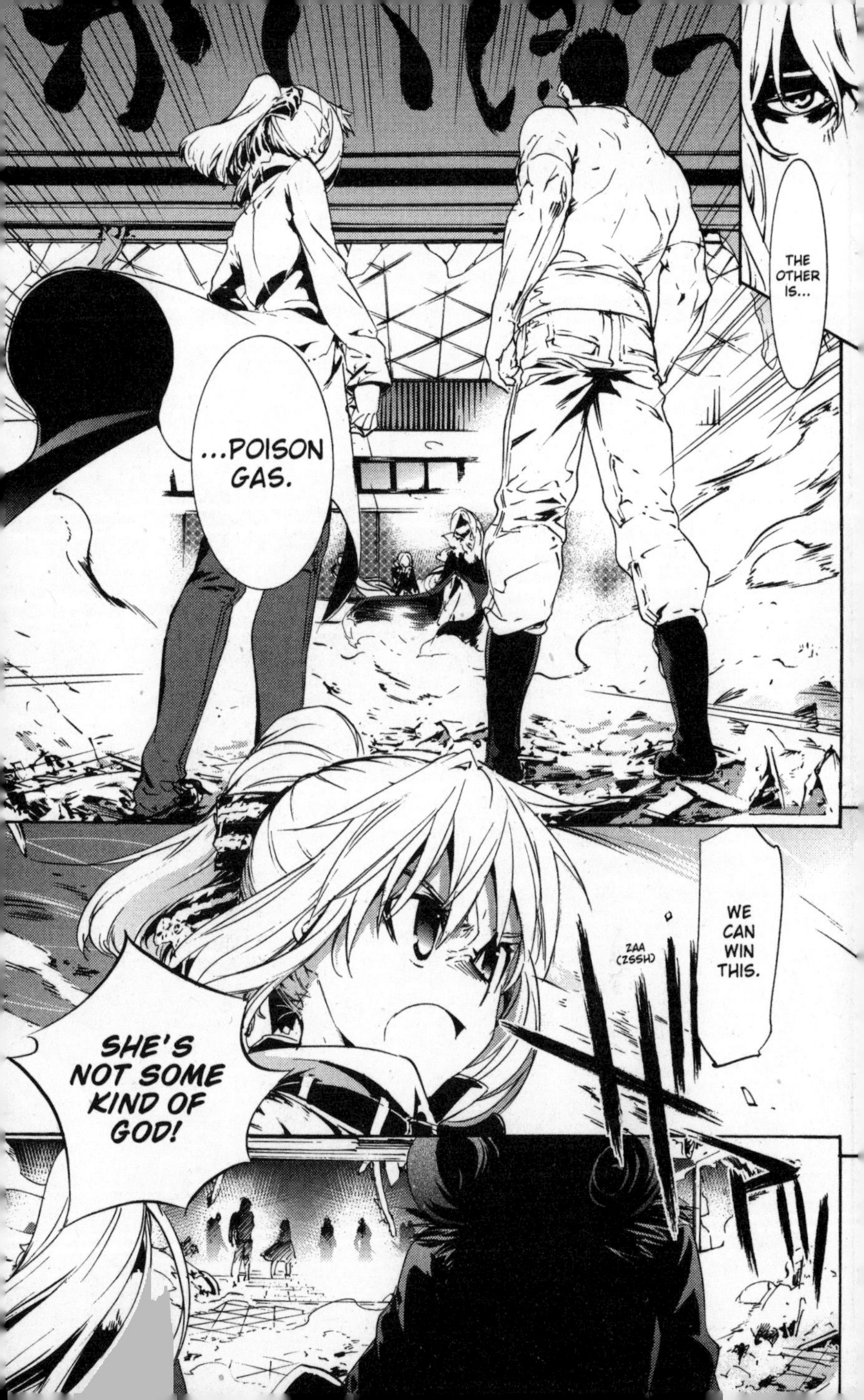
THE OTHER IS...
...POISON GAS.
WE CAN WIN THIS.
ZAA (ZSSH)
SHE'S NOT SOME KIND OF GOD!

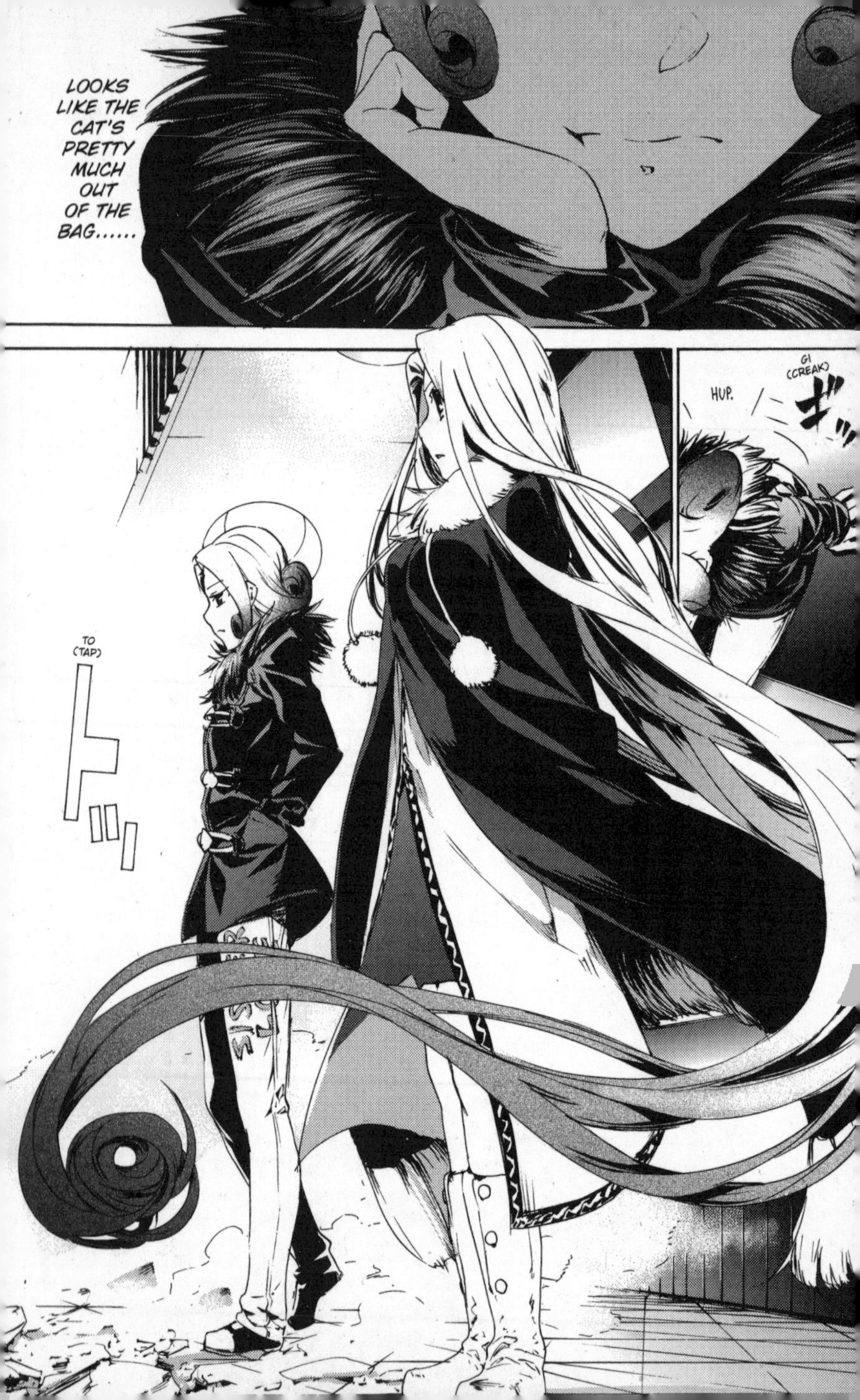
LOOKS LIKE THE CAT'S PRETTY MUCH OUT OF THE BAG......
HUP.
GI (CREAK)
ギッ
TO (TAP)
トッ

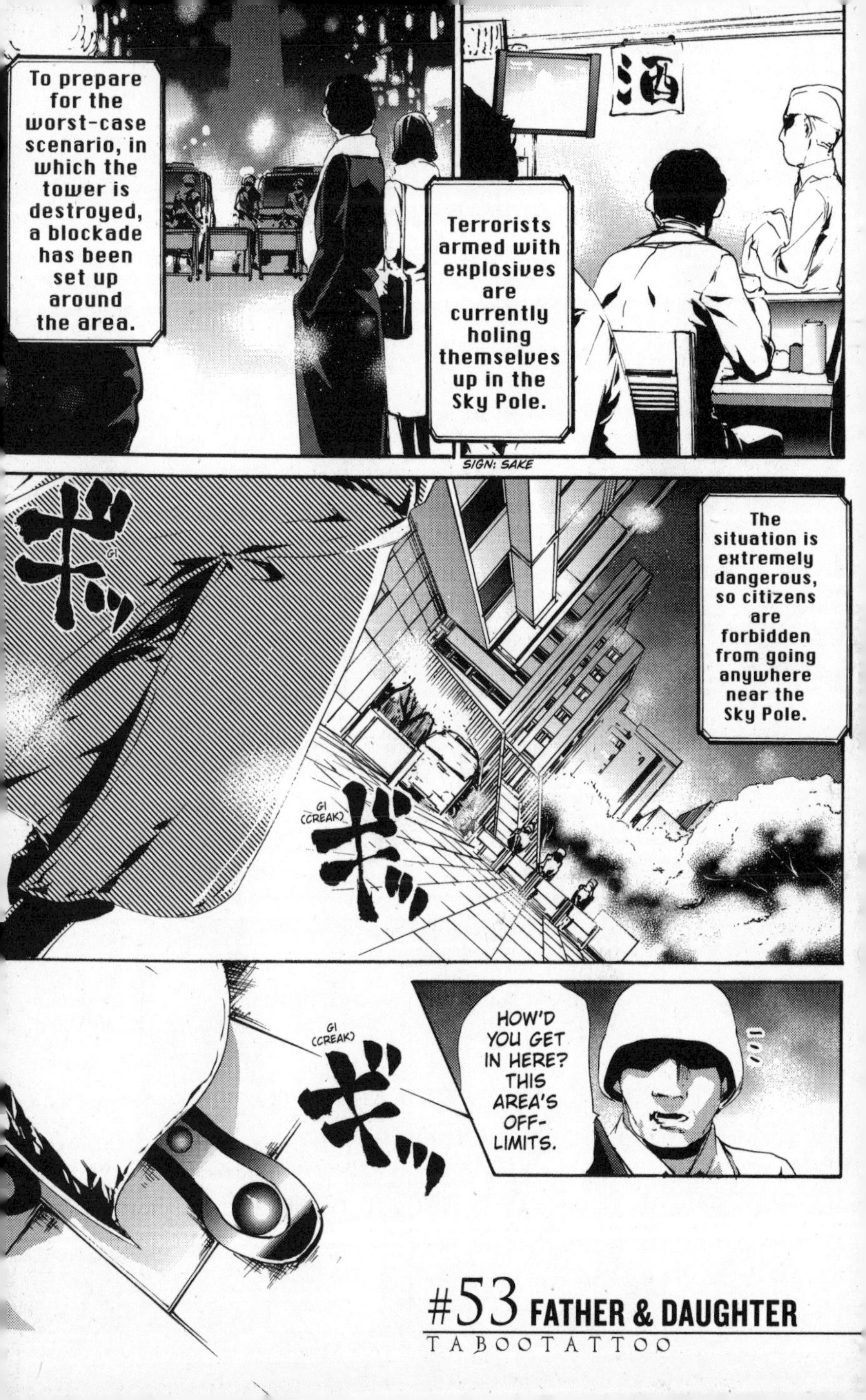
Terrorists armed with explosives are currently holing themselves up in the Sky Pole.
SIGN: SAKE
To prepare for the worst-case scenario, in which the tower is destroyed, a blockade has been set up around the area.
The situation is extremely dangerous, so citizens are forbidden from going anywhere near the Sky Pole.
GI
GI (CREAK)
...
HOW'D YOU GET IN HERE? THIS AREA'S OFF-LIMITS.
GI (CREAK)

#53 FATHER & DAUGHTER

TABOOTATTOO

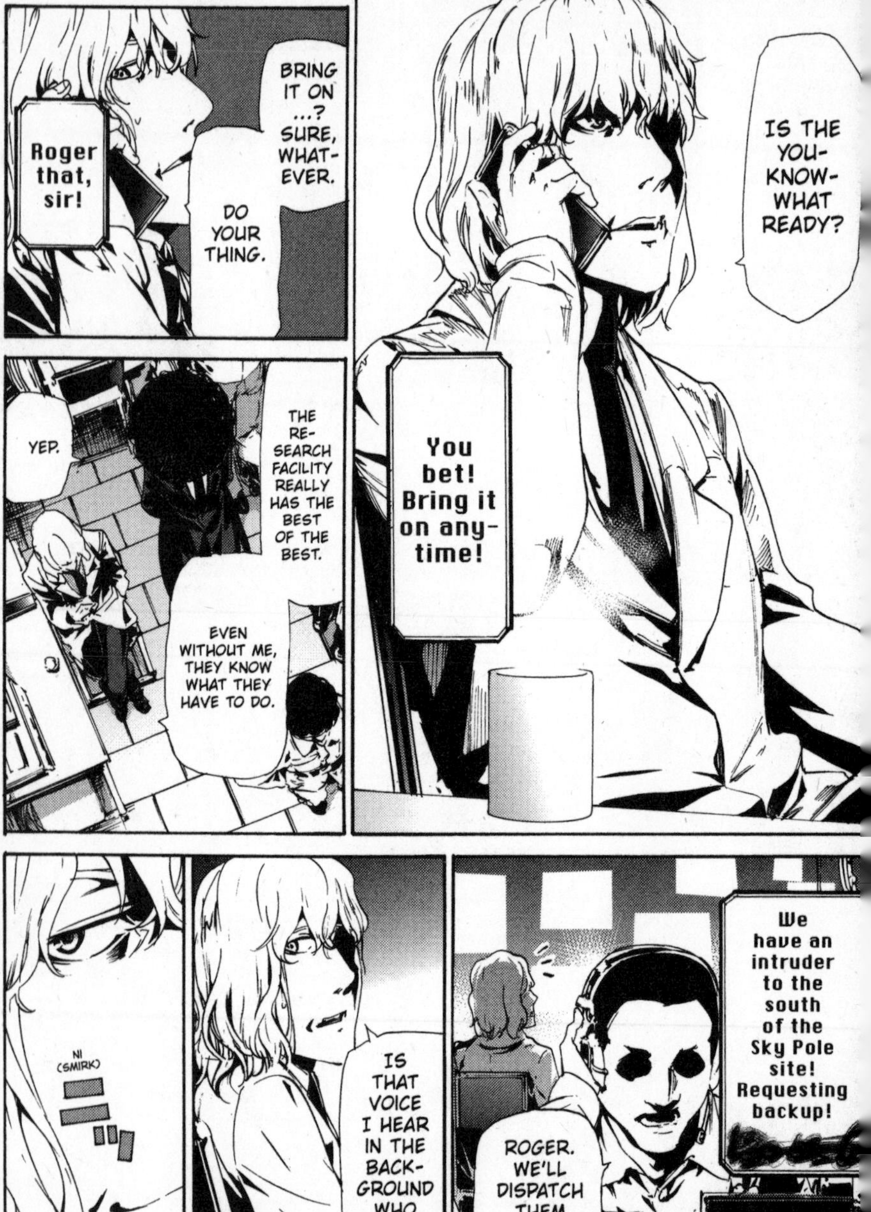
IS THE YOU-KNOW-WHAT READY?
You bet! Bring it on any-time!
BRING IT ON ...? SURE, WHAT-EVER.
Roger that, sir!
DO YOUR THING.
THE RE-SEARCH FACILITY REALLY HAS THE BEST OF THE BEST.
YEP.
EVEN WITHOUT ME, THEY KNOW WHAT THEY HAVE TO DO.
We have an intruder to the south of the Sky Pole site! Requesting backup!
ROGER. WE'LL DISPATCH THEM RIGHT AWAY.
IS THAT VOICE I HEAR IN THE BACK-GROUND WHO I THINK IT IS...?
NI (SMIRK)

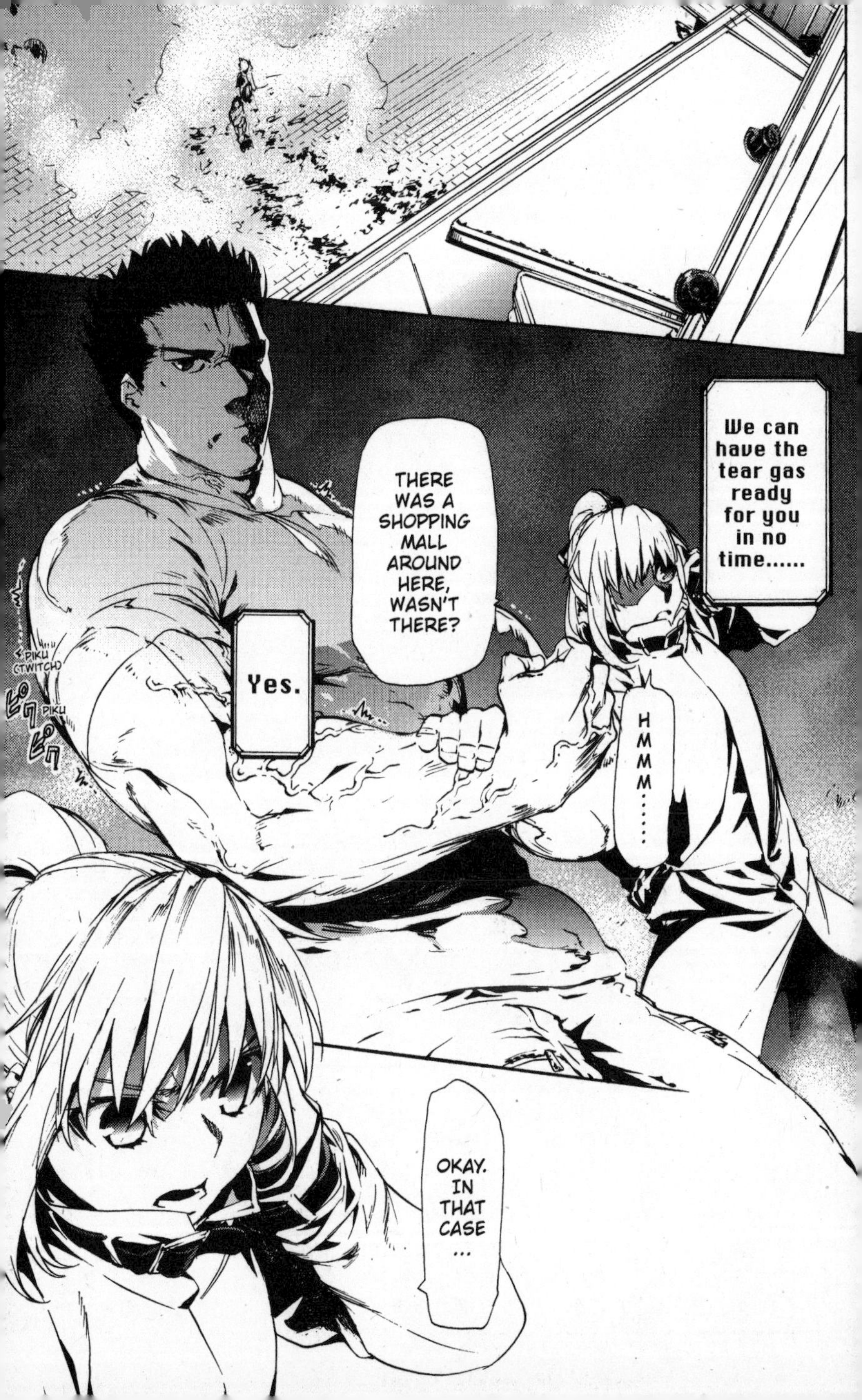
We can have the tear gas ready for you in no time......
THERE WAS A SHOPPING MALL AROUND HERE, WASN'T THERE?
Yes.
HMMM......
PIKU (TWITCH)
PIKU
OKAY. IN THAT CASE ...

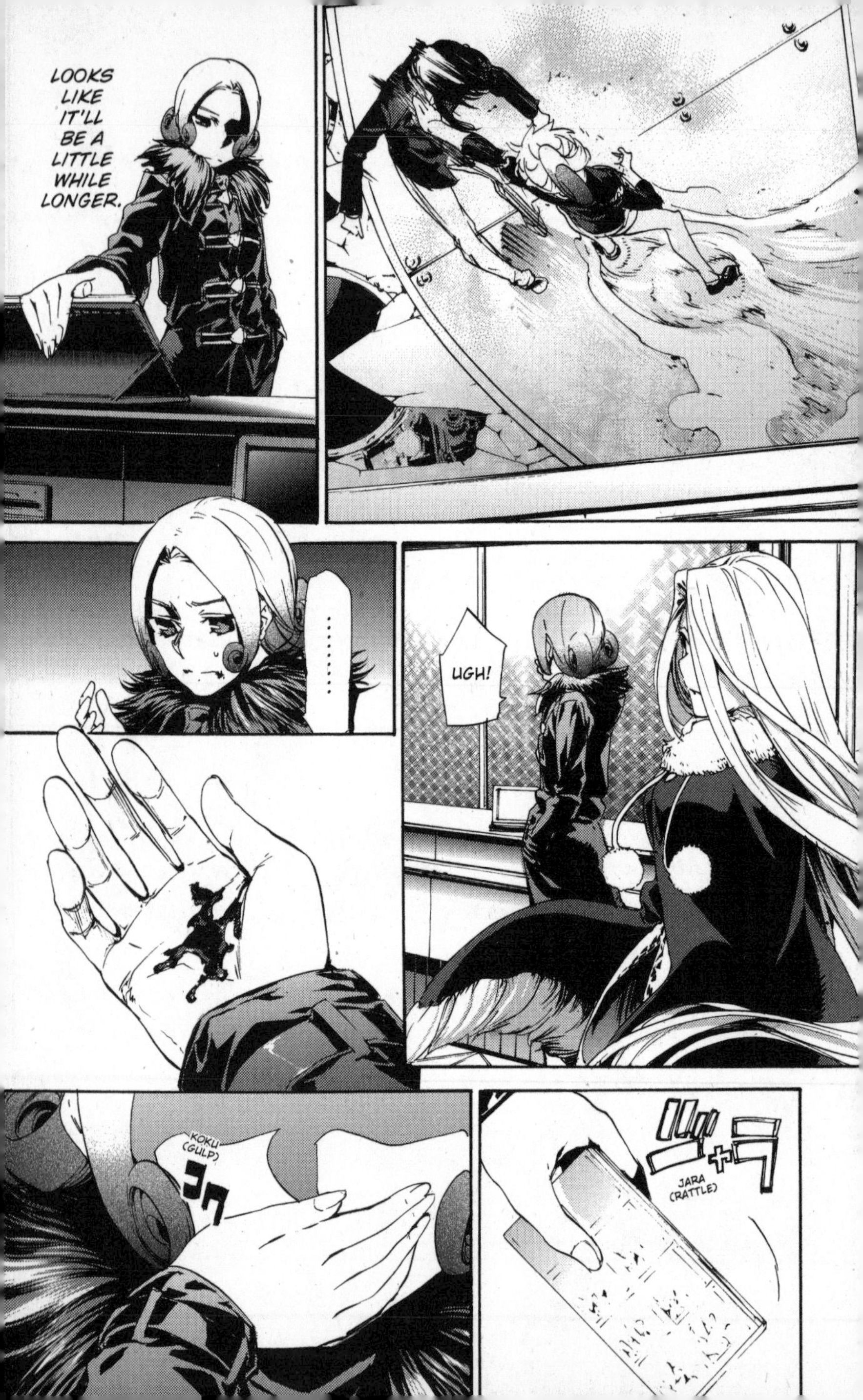
LOOKS LIKE IT'LL BE A LITTLE WHILE LONGER.
UGH!
....
JARA (RATTLE)
KOKU (GULP)

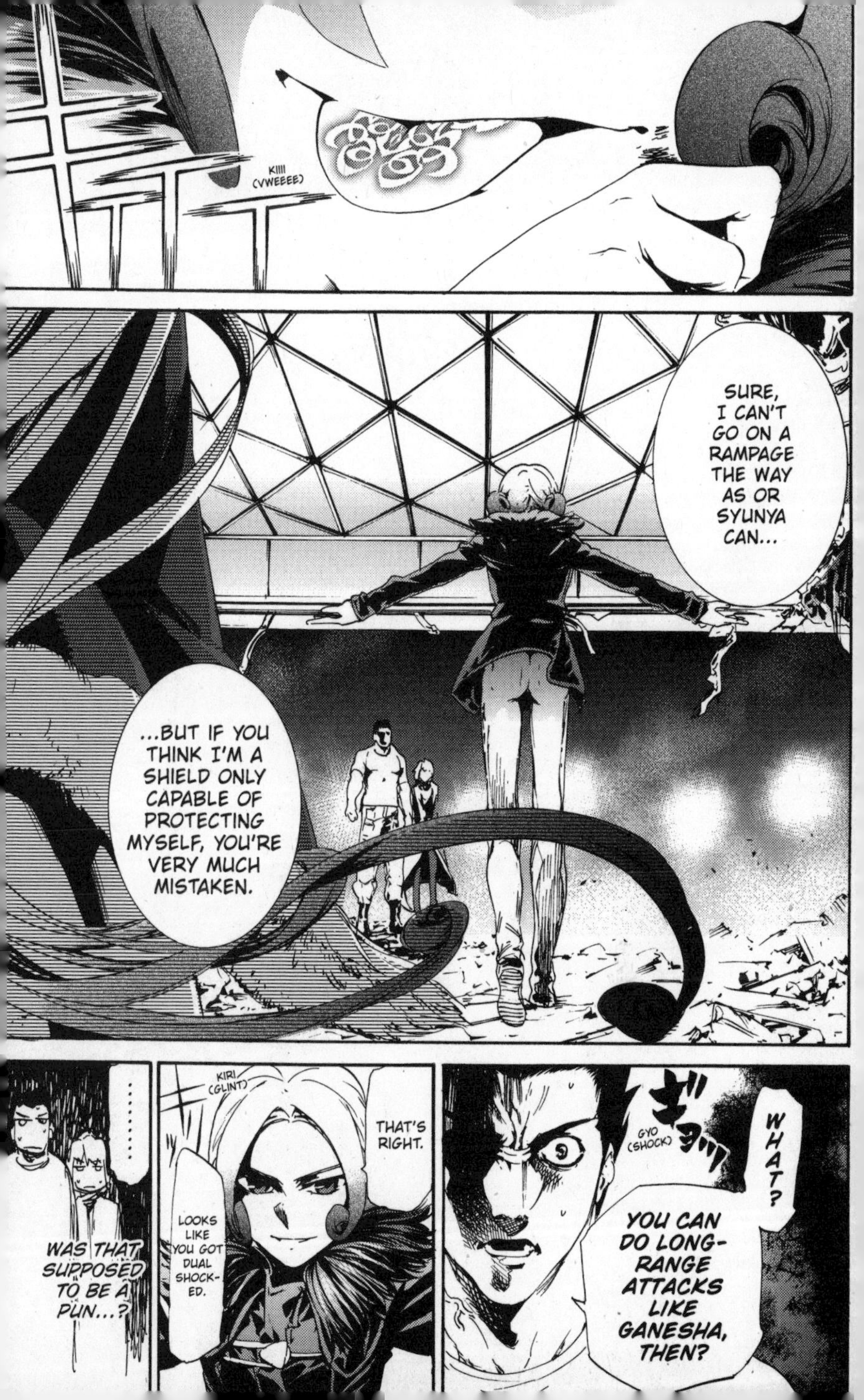
KIIII (VWEEEE)
SURE, I CAN'T GO ON A RAMPAGE THE WAY AS OR SYUNYA CAN...
...BUT IF YOU THINK I'M A SHIELD ONLY CAPABLE OF PROTECTING MYSELF, YOU'RE VERY MUCH MISTAKEN.
WHAT?
GYO (SHOCK)
YOU CAN DO LONG-RANGE ATTACKS LIKE GANESHA, THEN?
KIRI (GLINT)
THAT'S RIGHT.
LOOKS LIKE YOU GOT DUAL SHOCKED.
......
WAS THAT SUPPOSED TO BE A PUN...?

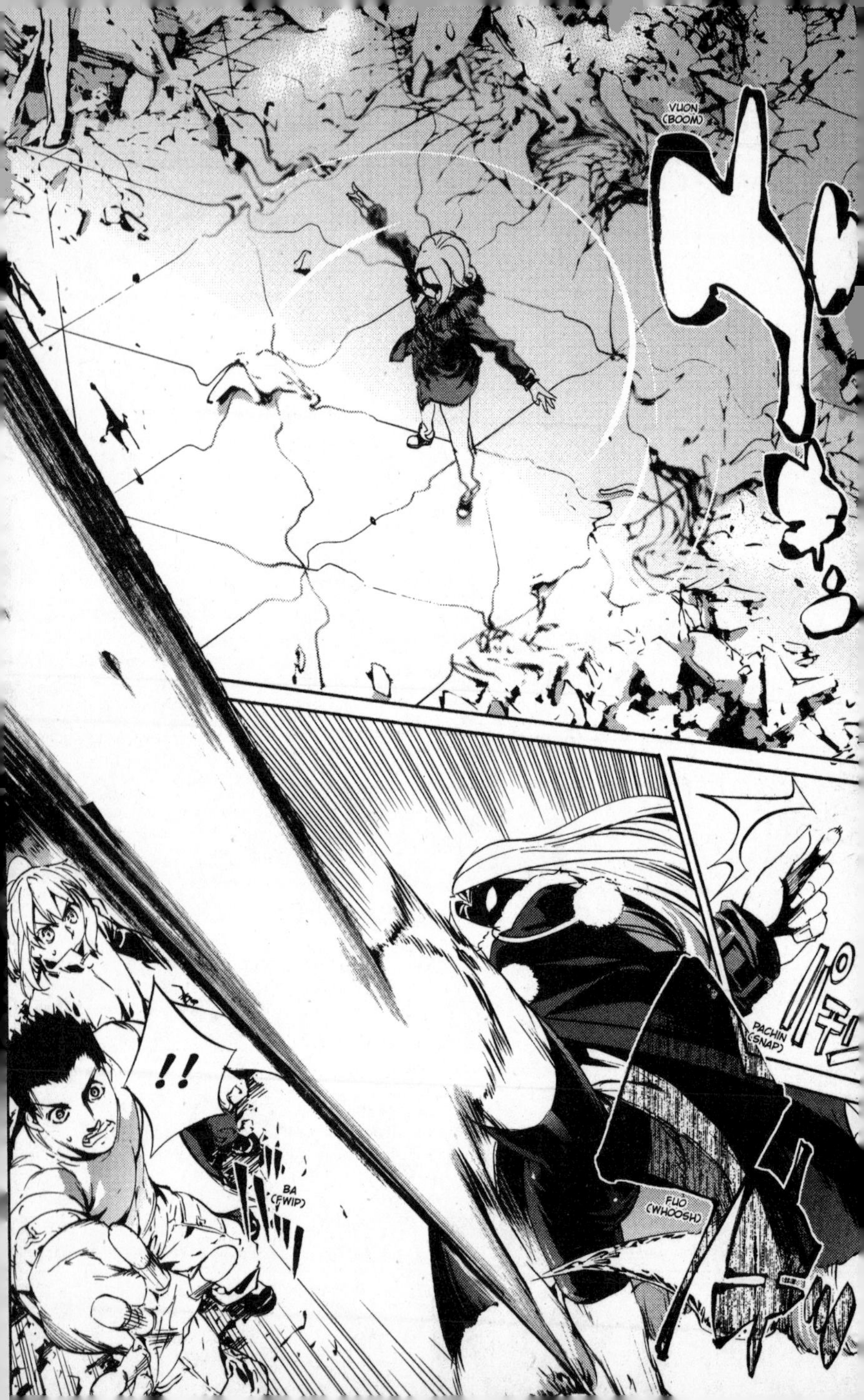
VUON
(BOOM)
PACHIN
(SNAP)
FUO
(WHOOSH)
!!
BA
(FWIP)

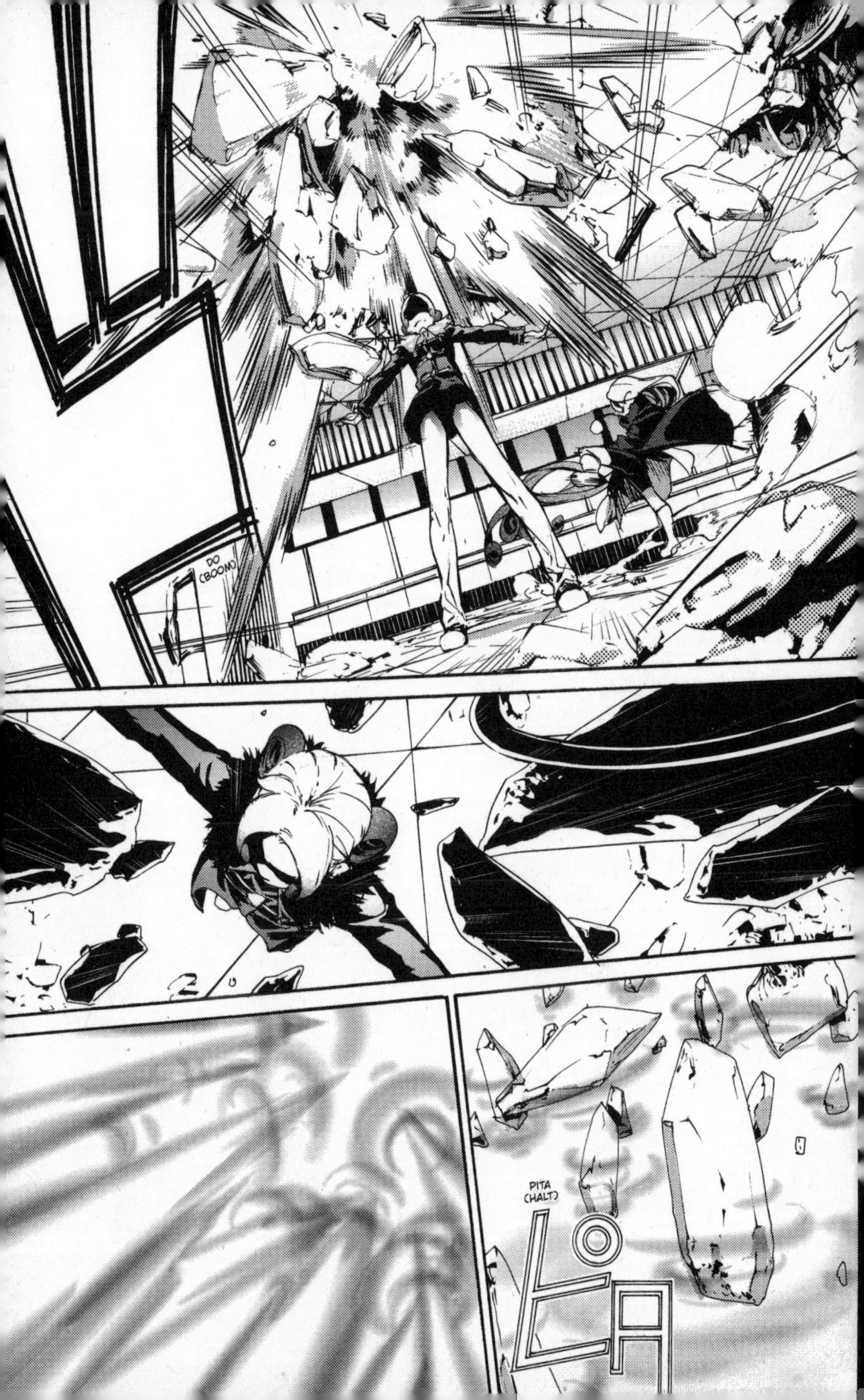
DO (BOOM)
PITA (HALT)
ピタ

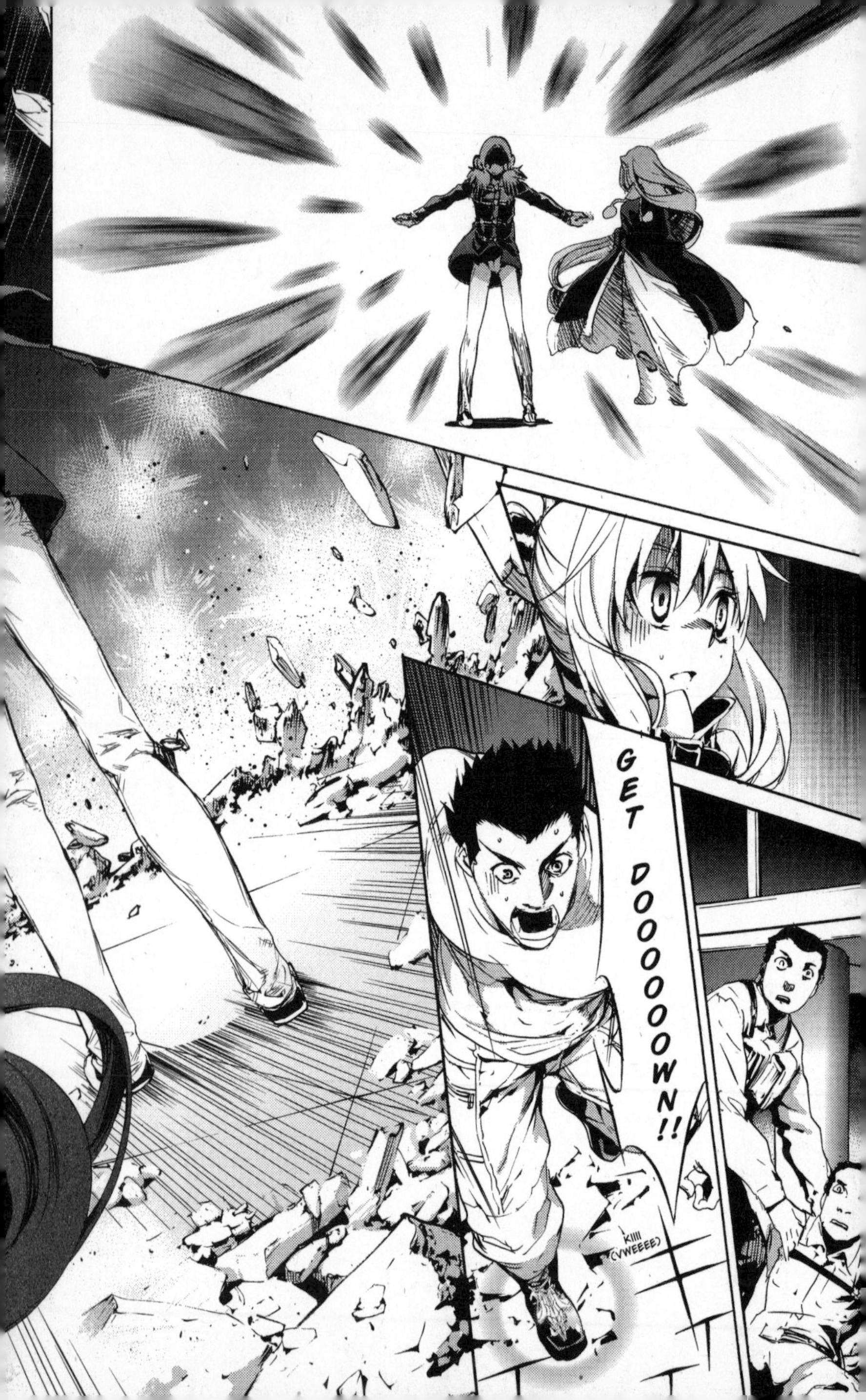
GET DOOOOOOOWN!!
KIIII
(VWEEEE)

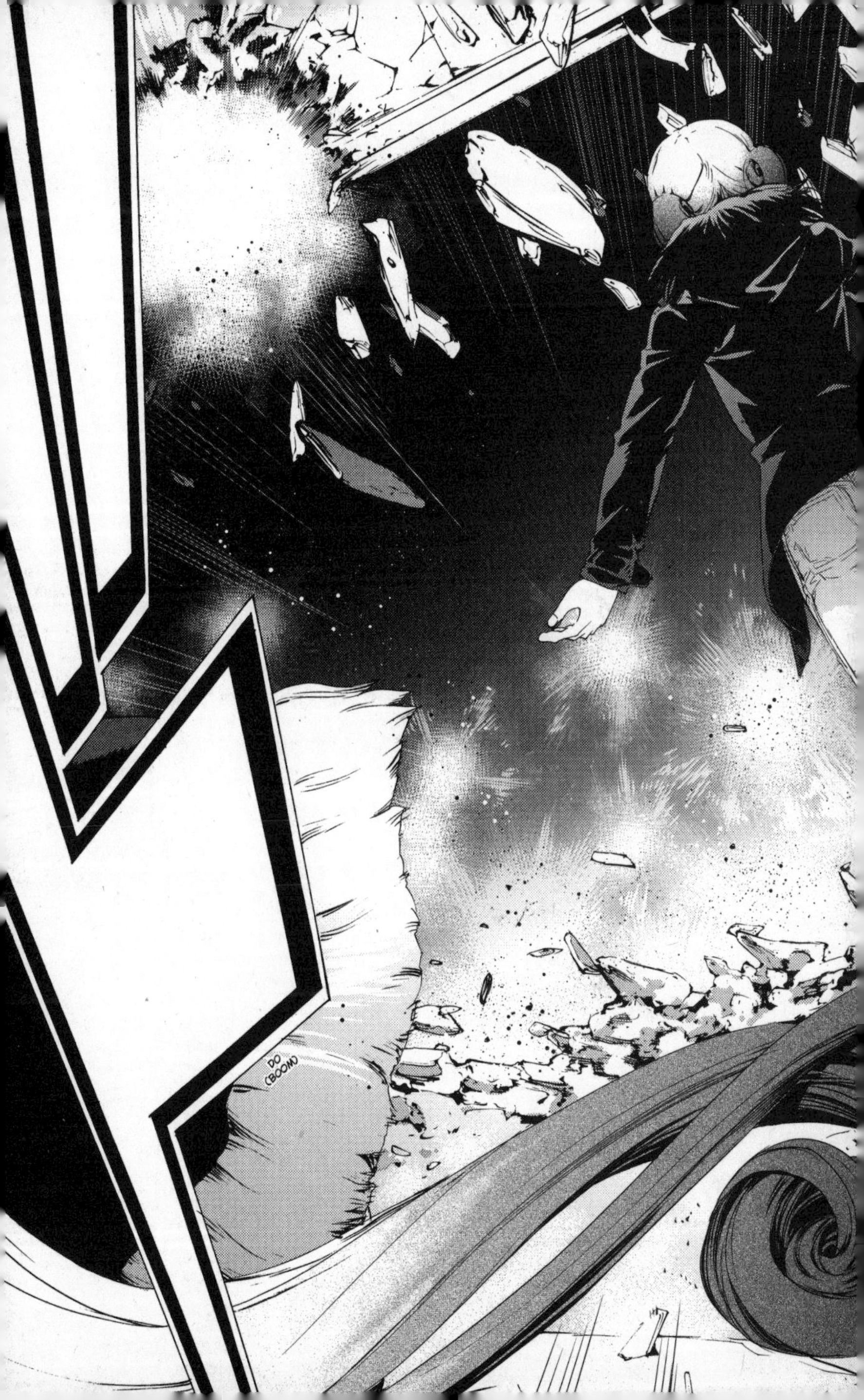
DO
(BOOM)

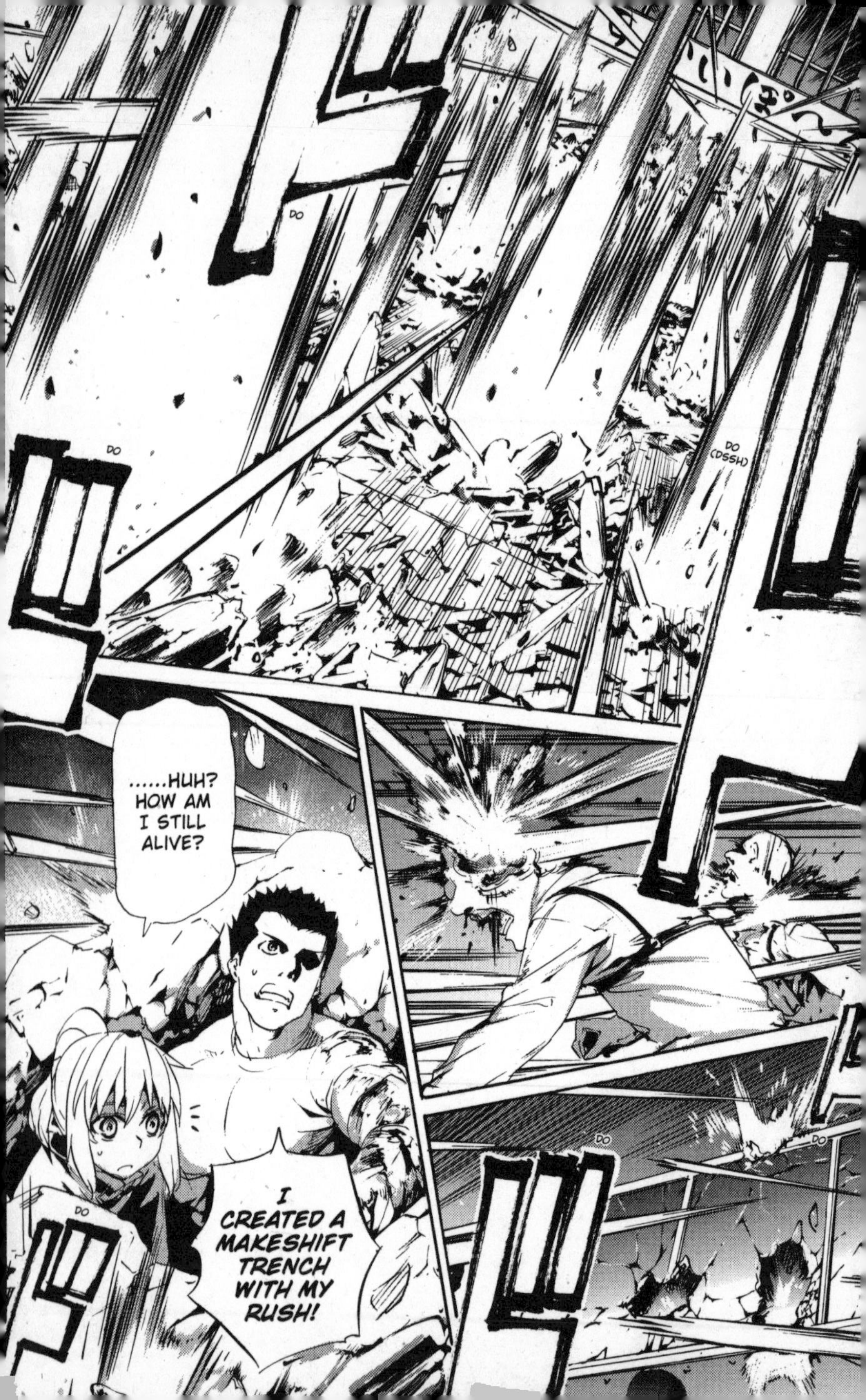
DO
DO
(DSSH)
DO
DO
DO
......HUH? HOW AM I STILL ALIVE?
I CREATED A MAKESHIFT TRENCH WITH MY RUSH!
DO

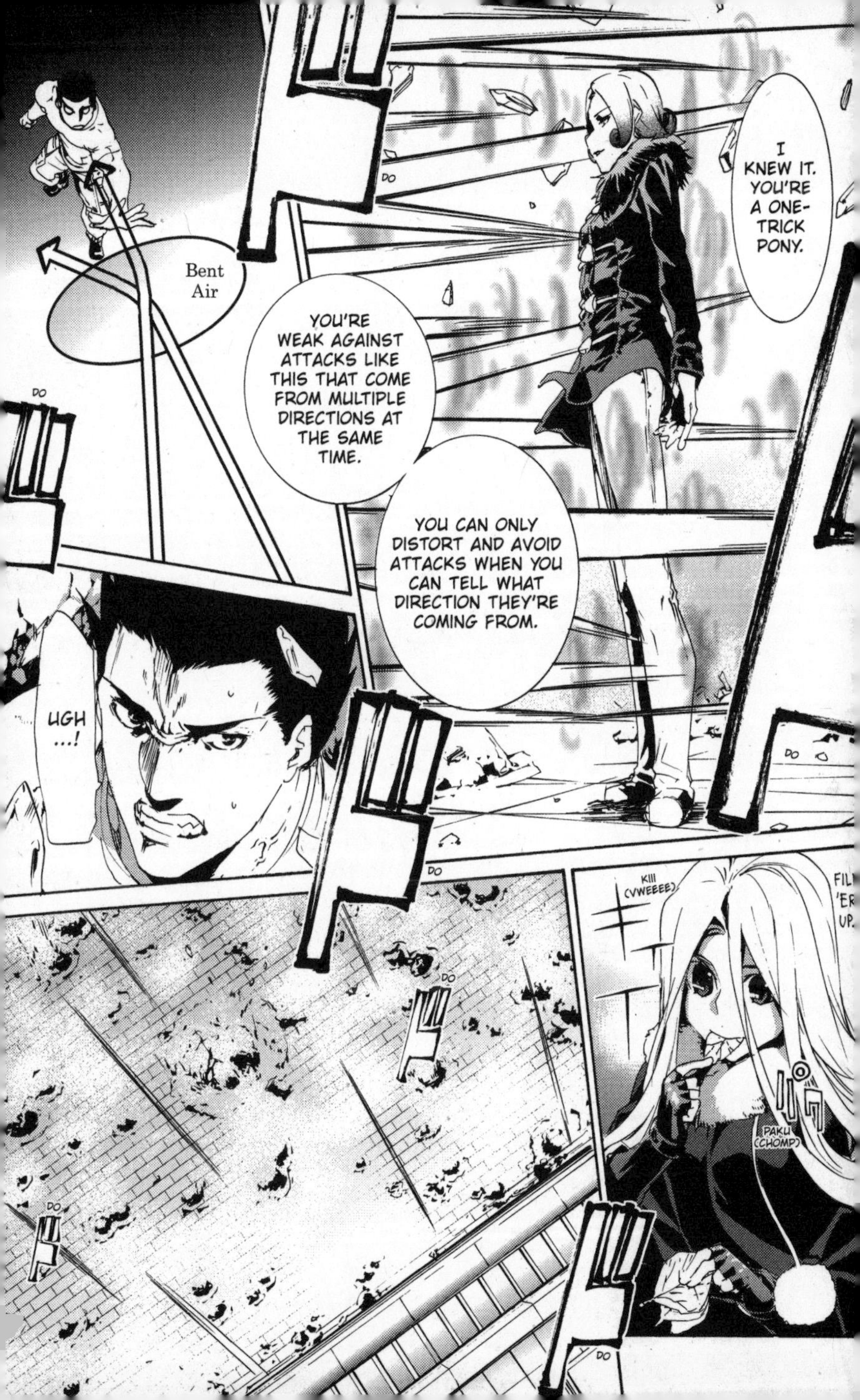

I KNEW IT. YOU'RE A ONE-TRICK PONY.
DO
YOU'RE WEAK AGAINST ATTACKS LIKE THIS THAT COME FROM MULTIPLE DIRECTIONS AT THE SAME TIME.
Bent Air
DO
YOU CAN ONLY DISTORT AND AVOID ATTACKS WHEN YOU CAN TELL WHAT DIRECTION THEY'RE COMING FROM.
DO
UGH ...!
FIL 'ER UP.
KIII (VWEEEE)
PAKU (CHOMP)
DO
DO
DO
DO

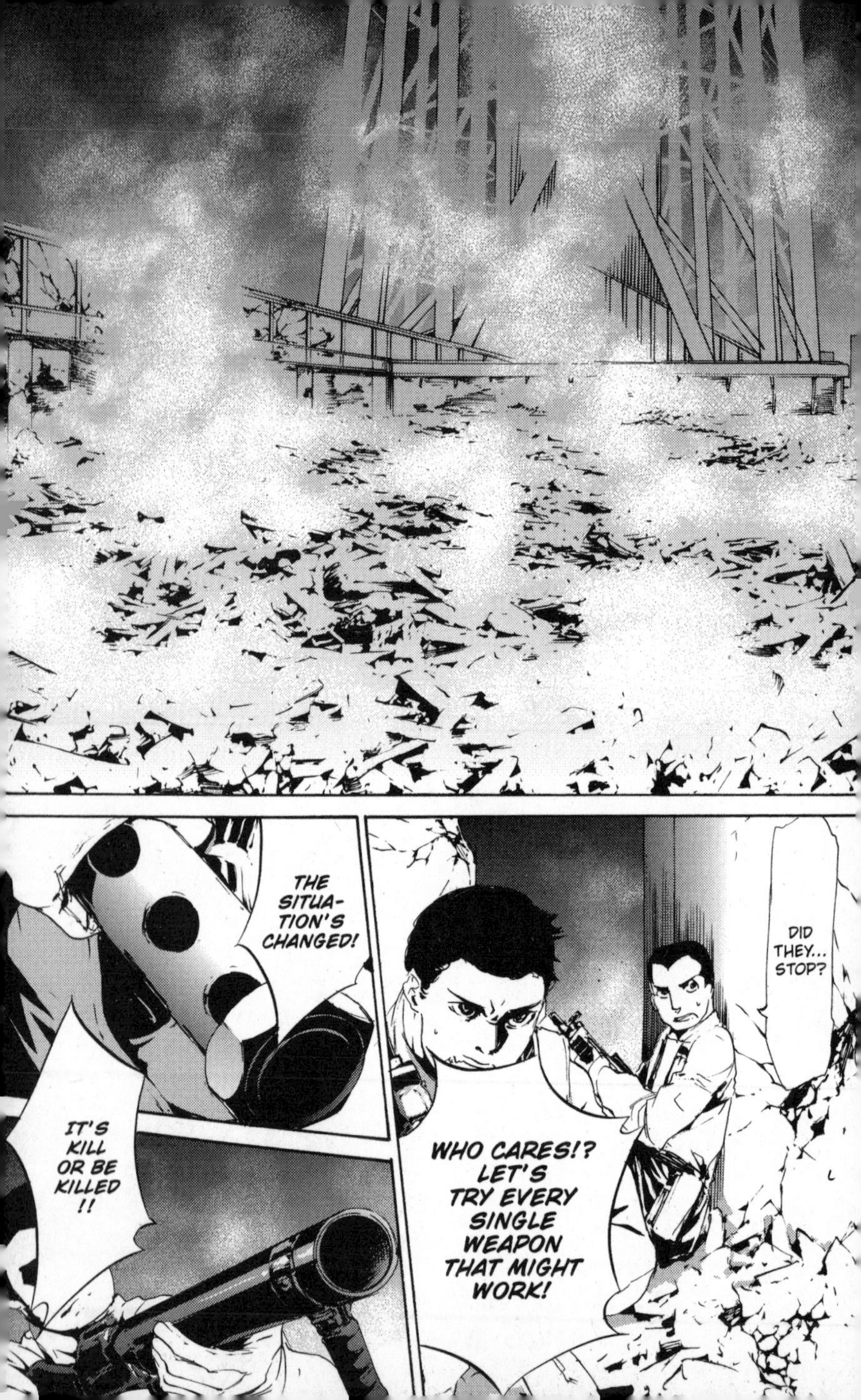
DID THEY... STOP?
WHO CARES!? LET'S TRY EVERY SINGLE WEAPON THAT MIGHT WORK!
THE SITUATION'S CHANGED!
IT'S KILL OR BE KILLED!!

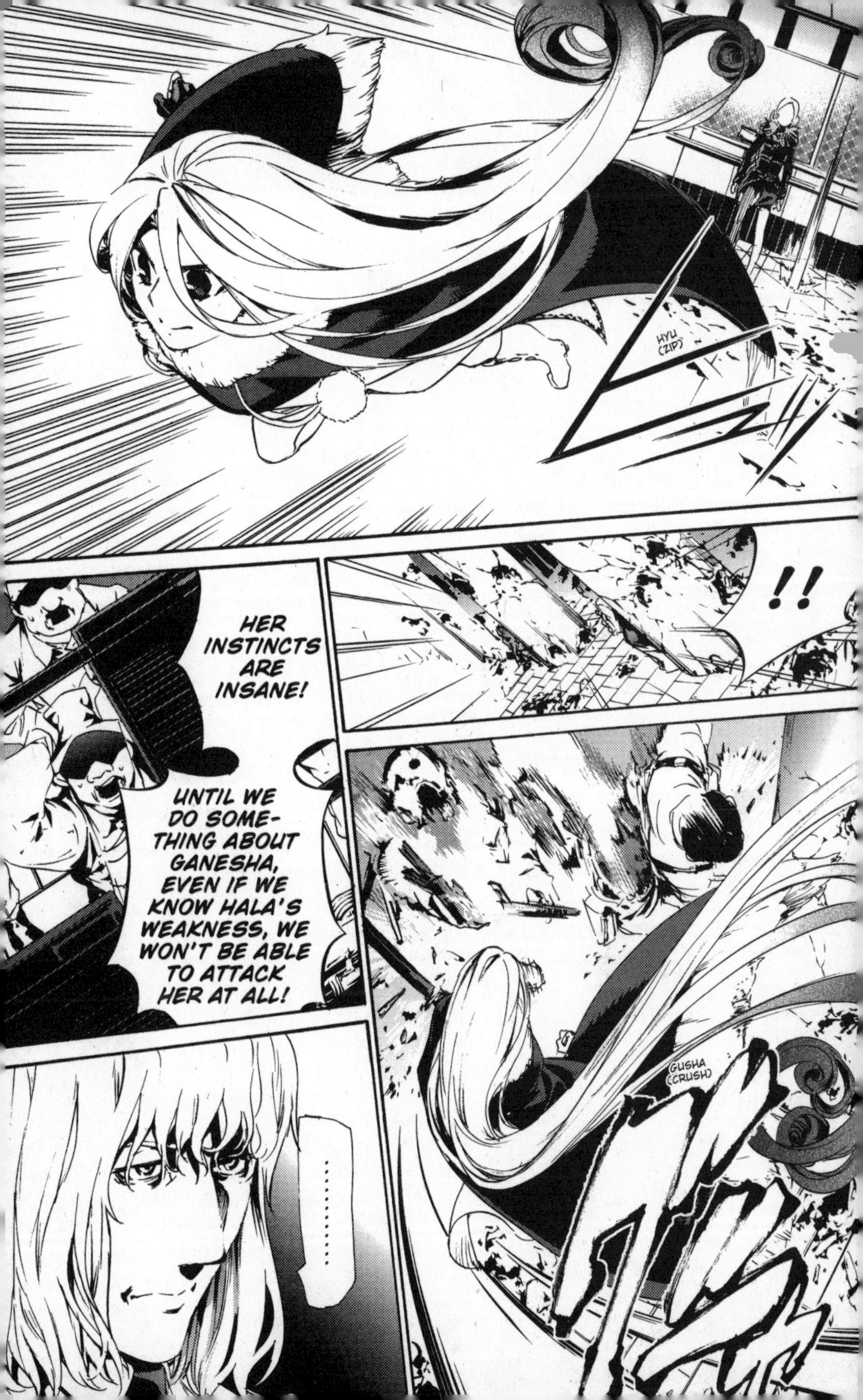
HYU (ZIP)
!!
HER INSTINCTS ARE INSANE!
UNTIL WE DO SOME-THING ABOUT GANESHA, EVEN IF WE KNOW HALA'S WEAKNESS, WE WON'T BE ABLE TO ATTACK HER AT ALL!
GUSHA (CRUSH)
......

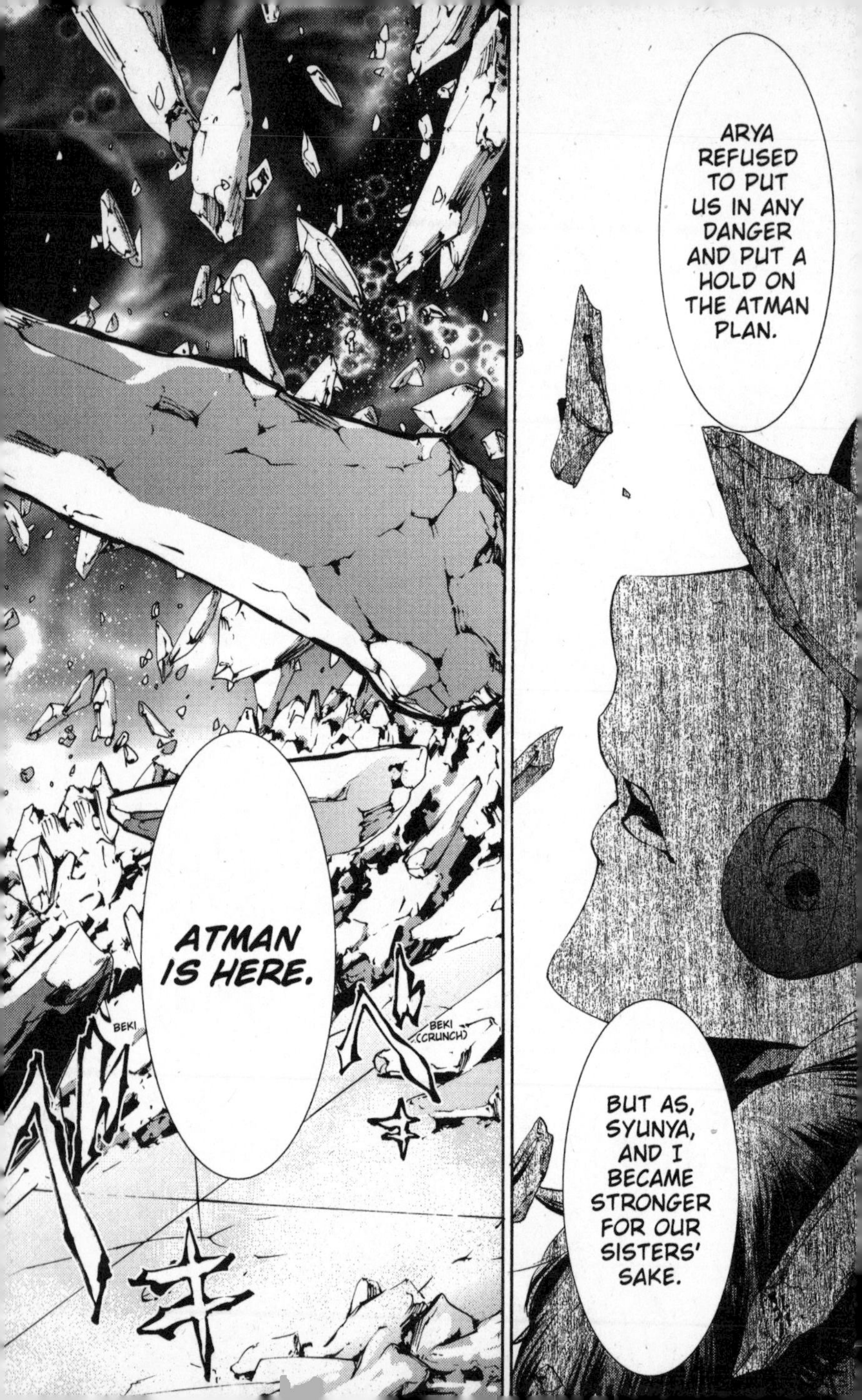
ARYA REFUSED TO PUT US IN ANY DANGER AND PUT A HOLD ON THE ATMAN PLAN.
BUT AS, SYUNYA, AND I BECAME STRONGER FOR OUR SISTERS' SAKE.
ATMAN IS HERE.
BEKI (CRUNCH)
BEKI

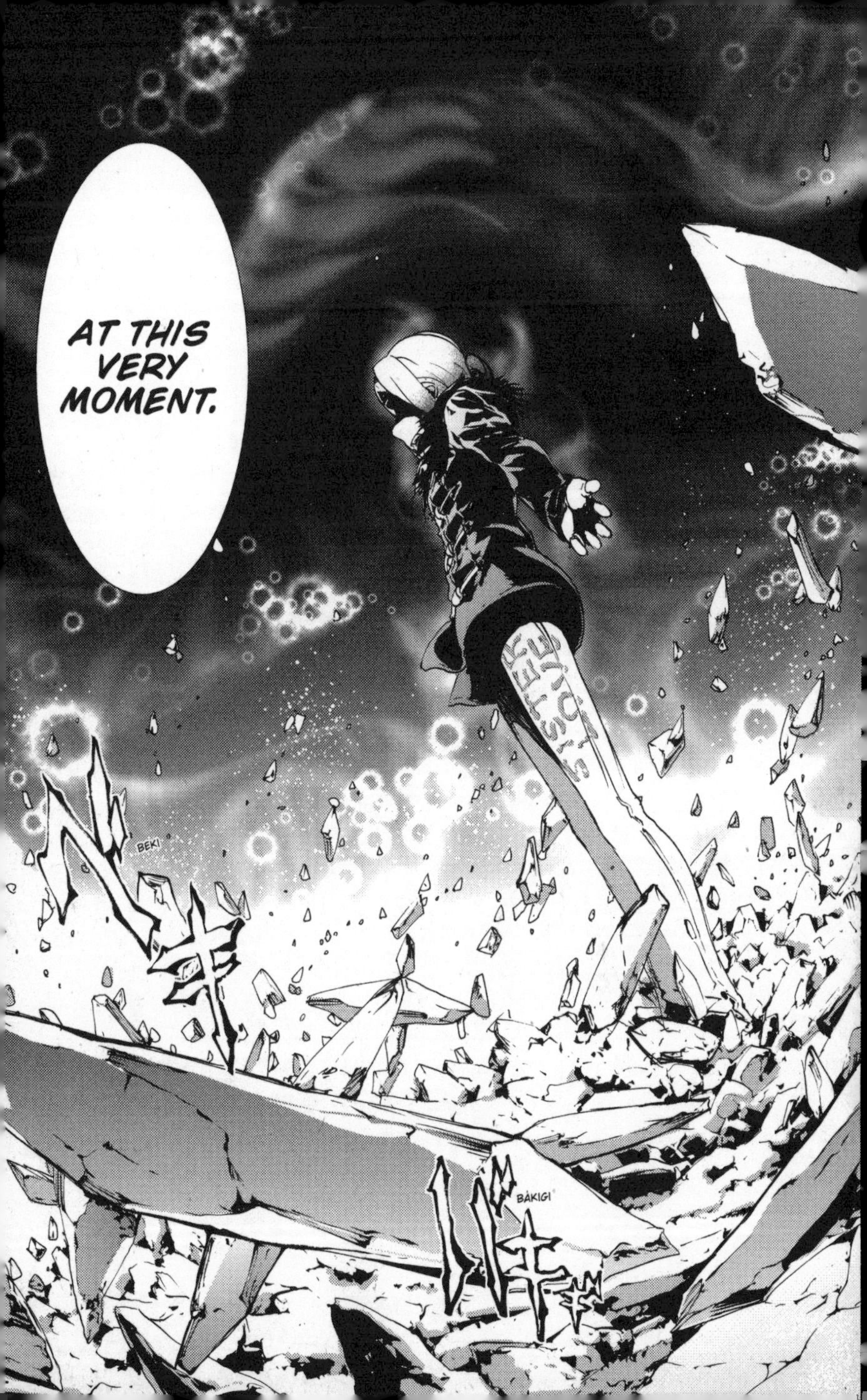
AT THIS VERY MOMENT.
BEKI
BAKIGI

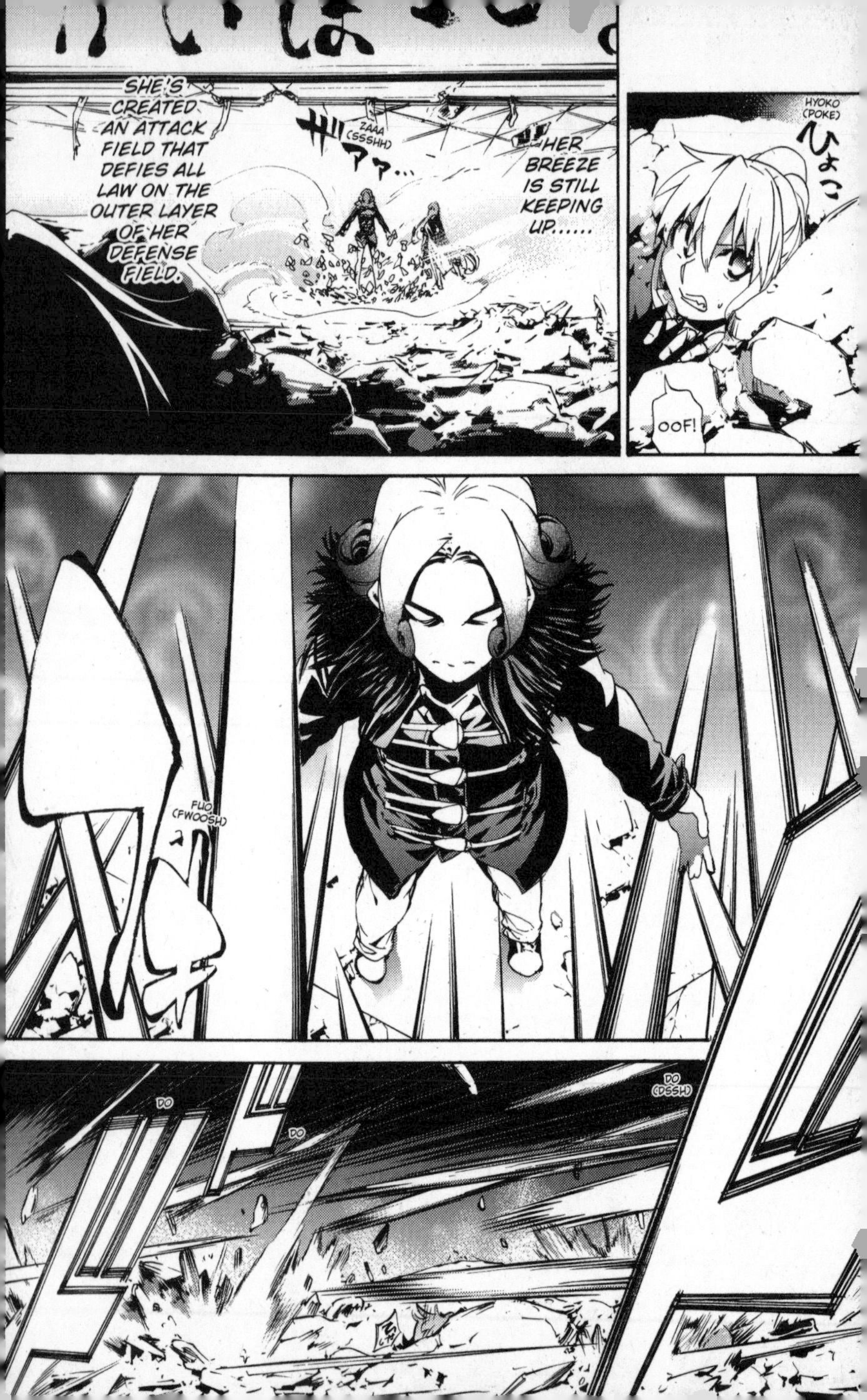
HYOKO (POKE)
ひょこ
OOF!
HER BREEZE IS STILL KEEPING UP......
ZAAA (SSSHH)
ザァ...
SHE'S CREATED AN ATTACK FIELD THAT DEFIES ALL LAW ON THE OUTER LAYER OF HER DEFENSE FIELD.
FUO (FWOOSH)
DO (DSSH)
DO
DO

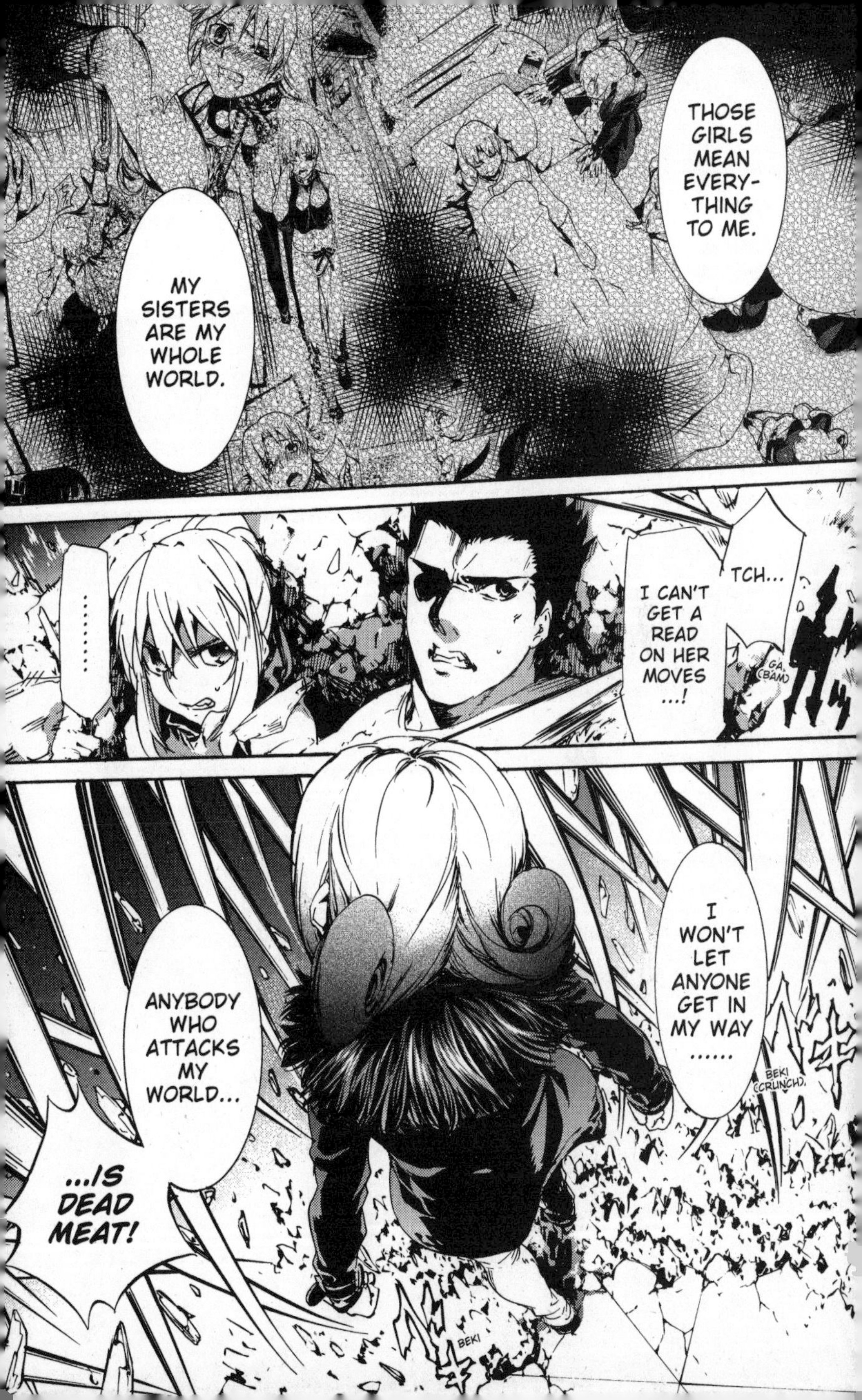
THOSE GIRLS MEAN EVERY-THING TO ME.
MY SISTERS ARE MY WHOLE WORLD.
GA (BAM)
TCH...
I CAN'T GET A READ ON HER MOVES ...!
......
I WON'T LET ANYONE GET IN MY WAY ......
BEKI (CRUNCH)
ANYBODY WHO ATTACKS MY WORLD...
...IS DEAD MEAT!
BEKI

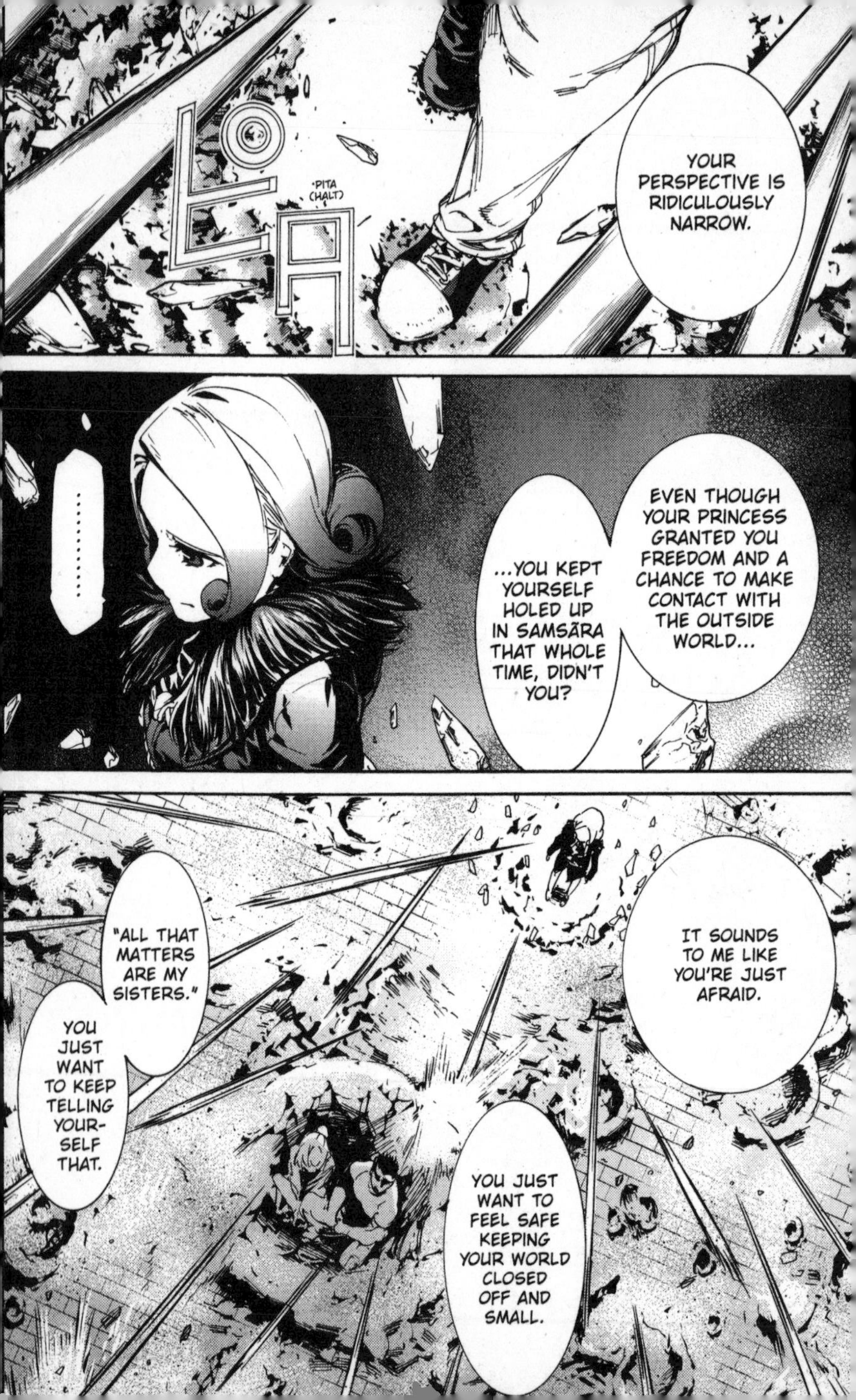
*PITA (HALT)
YOUR PERSPECTIVE IS RIDICULOUSLY NARROW.
EVEN THOUGH YOUR PRINCESS GRANTED YOU FREEDOM AND A CHANCE TO MAKE CONTACT WITH THE OUTSIDE WORLD...
...YOU KEPT YOURSELF HOLED UP IN SAMSĀRA THAT WHOLE TIME, DIDN'T YOU?
......
IT SOUNDS TO ME LIKE YOU'RE JUST AFRAID.
"ALL THAT MATTERS ARE MY SISTERS."
YOU JUST WANT TO KEEP TELLING YOUR-SELF THAT.
YOU JUST WANT TO FEEL SAFE KEEPING YOUR WORLD CLOSED OFF AND SMALL.

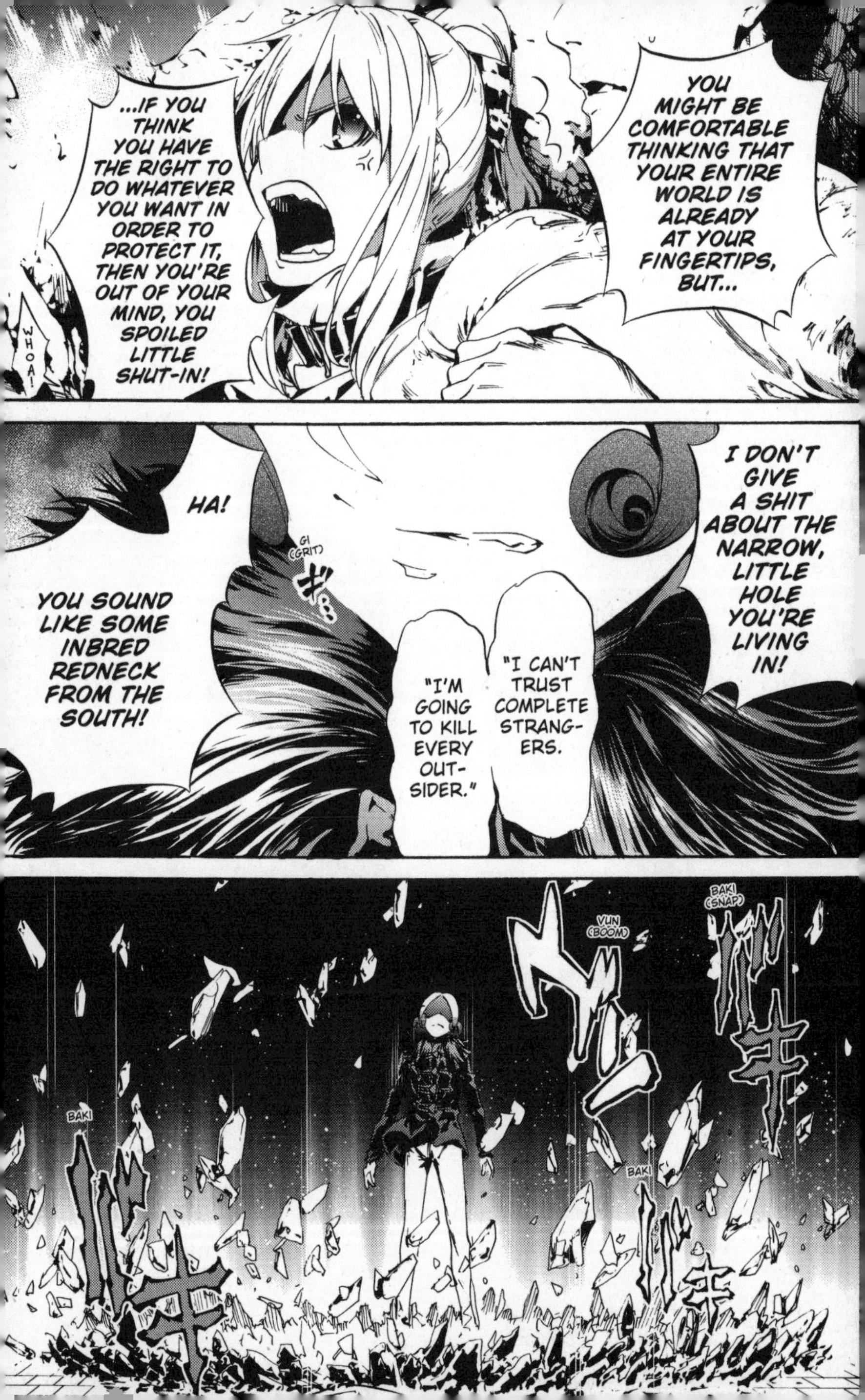
YOU MIGHT BE COMFORTABLE THINKING THAT YOUR ENTIRE WORLD IS ALREADY AT YOUR FINGERTIPS, BUT...
...IF YOU THINK YOU HAVE THE RIGHT TO DO WHATEVER YOU WANT IN ORDER TO PROTECT IT, THEN YOU'RE OUT OF YOUR MIND, YOU SPOILED LITTLE SHUT-IN!
WHOA!
I DON'T GIVE A SHIT ABOUT THE NARROW, LITTLE HOLE YOU'RE LIVING IN!
"I CAN'T TRUST COMPLETE STRANG-ERS.
"I'M GOING TO KILL EVERY OUT-SIDER."
GI (GRIT)
HA!
YOU SOUND LIKE SOME INBRED REDNECK FROM THE SOUTH!
BAKI (SNAP)
VUN (BOOM)
BAKI
BAKI

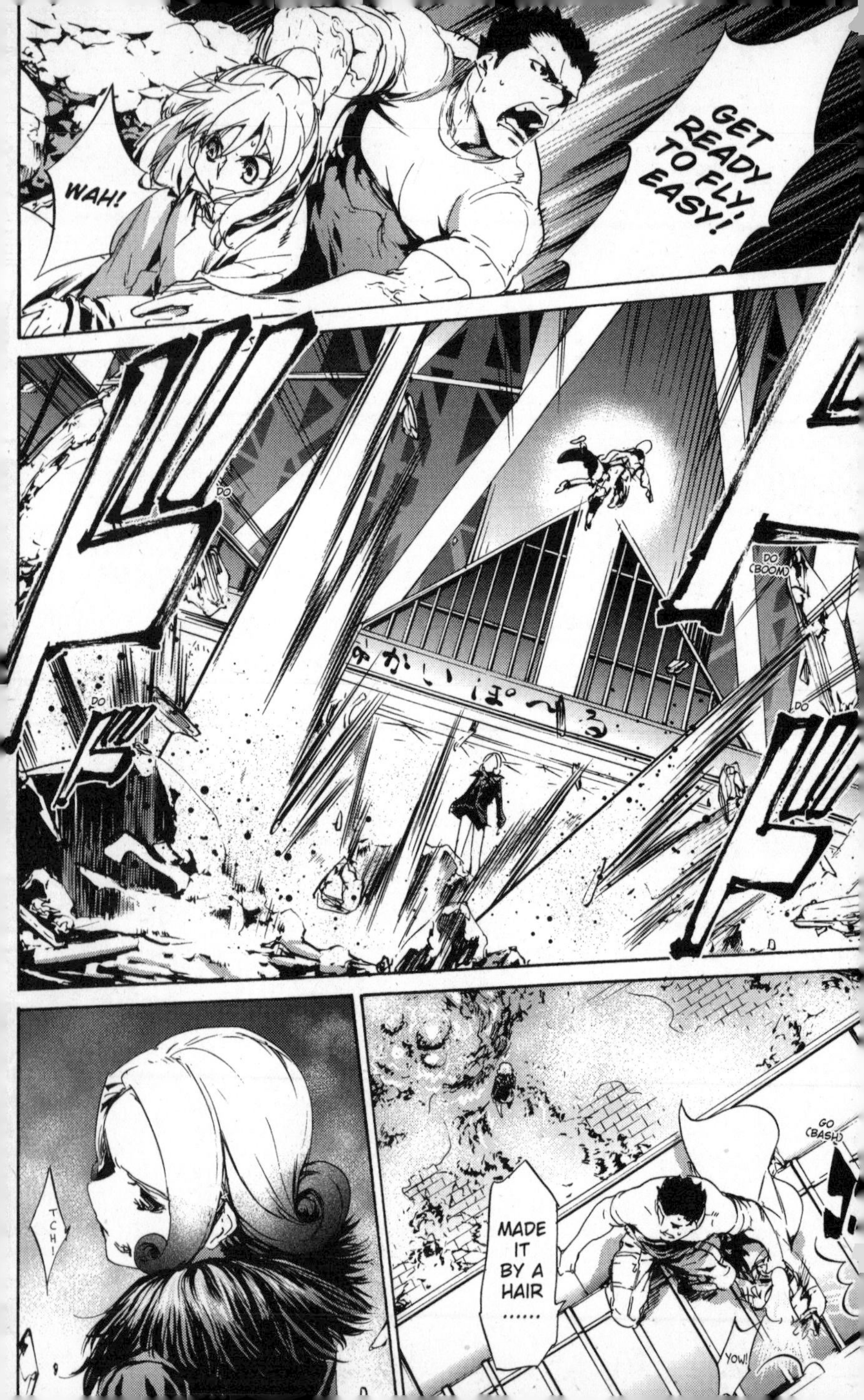
GET READY TO FLY, EASY!
WAH!
DO (BOOM)
DO
DO
DO
GO (BASH)
MADE IT BY A HAIR......
YOW!
TCH!

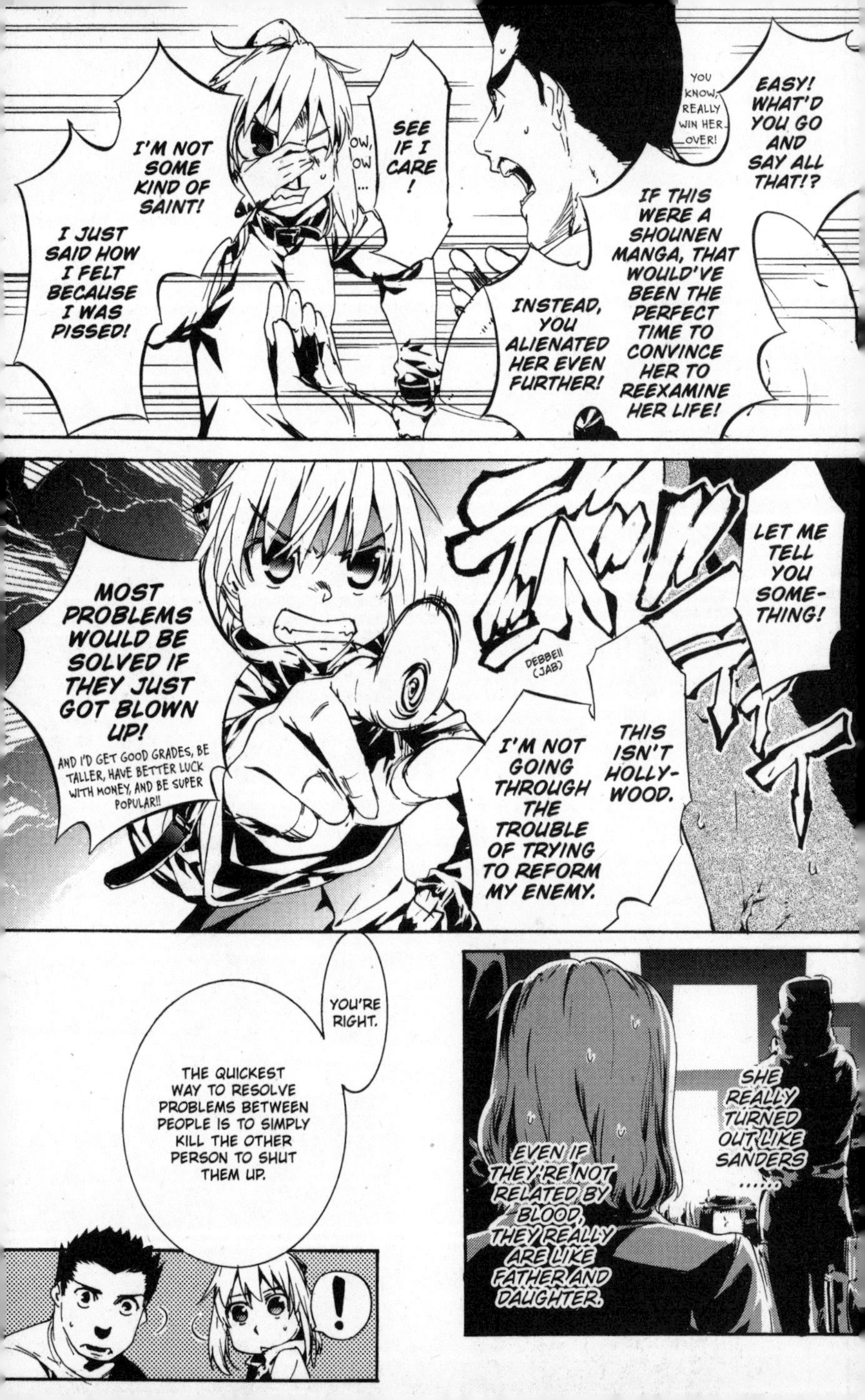
EASY! WHAT'D YOU GO AND SAY ALL THAT!?
IF THIS WERE A SHOUNEN MANGA, THAT WOULD'VE BEEN THE PERFECT TIME TO CONVINCE HER TO REEXAMINE HER LIFE!
YOU KNOW, REALLY WIN HER OVER!
INSTEAD, YOU ALIENATED HER EVEN FURTHER!
SEE IF I CARE!
OW, OW ...
I'M NOT SOME KIND OF SAINT!
I JUST SAID HOW I FELT BECAUSE I WAS PISSED!
LET ME TELL YOU SOMETHING!
DEBBEII (JAB)
THIS ISN'T HOLLYWOOD.
I'M NOT GOING THROUGH THE TROUBLE OF TRYING TO REFORM MY ENEMY.
MOST PROBLEMS WOULD BE SOLVED IF THEY JUST GOT BLOWN UP!
AND I'D GET GOOD GRADES, BE TALLER, HAVE BETTER LUCK WITH MONEY, AND BE SUPER POPULAR!!
SHE REALLY TURNED OUT LIKE SANDERS......
EVEN IF THEY'RE NOT RELATED BY BLOOD, THEY REALLY ARE LIKE FATHER AND DAUGHTER.
YOU'RE RIGHT.
THE QUICKEST WAY TO RESOLVE PROBLEMS BETWEEN PEOPLE IS TO SIMPLY KILL THE OTHER PERSON TO SHUT THEM UP.
!

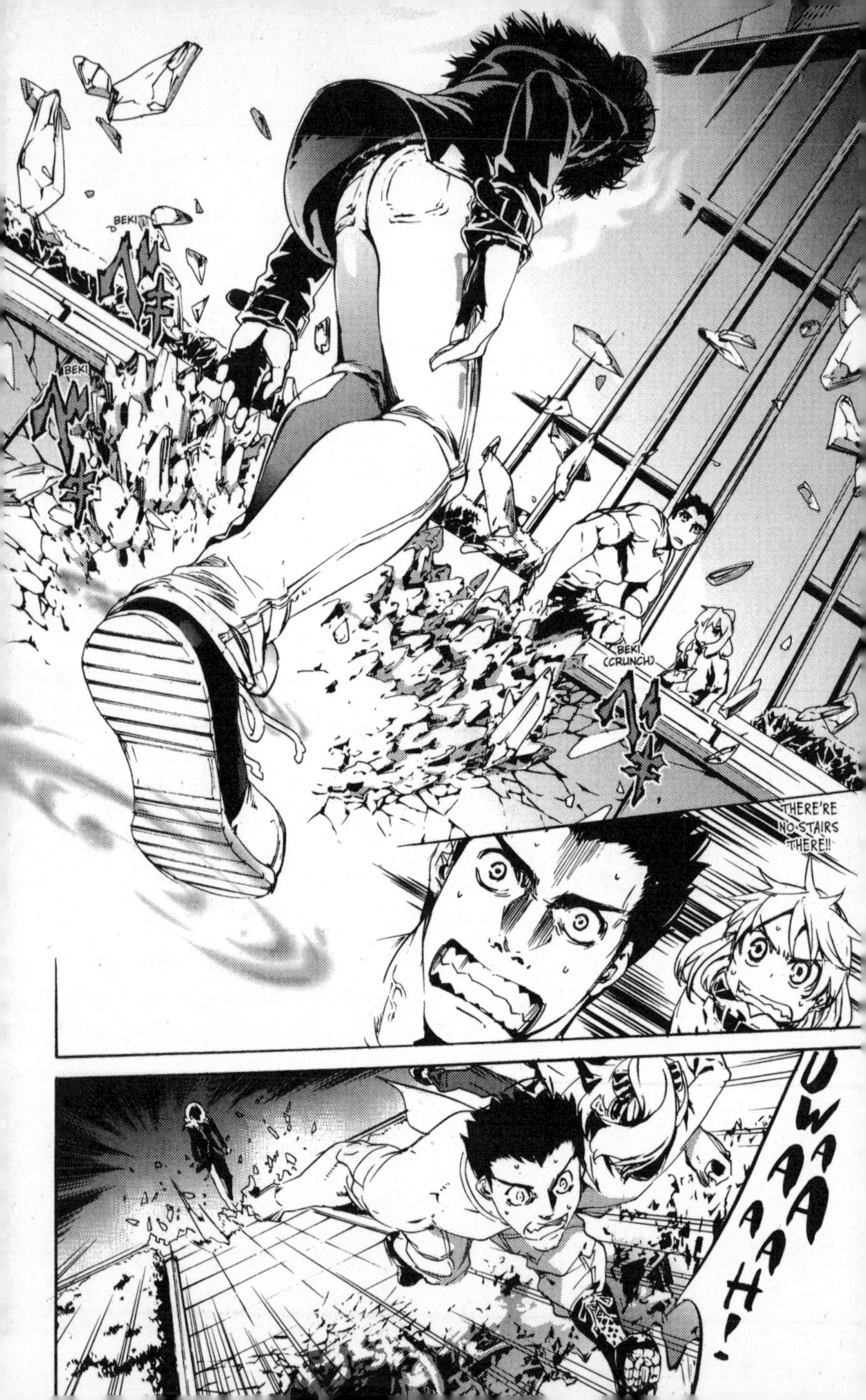
BEKI
BEKI
BEKI (CRUNCH)
THERE'RE NO STAIRS THERE!!
UWAAAAAH!

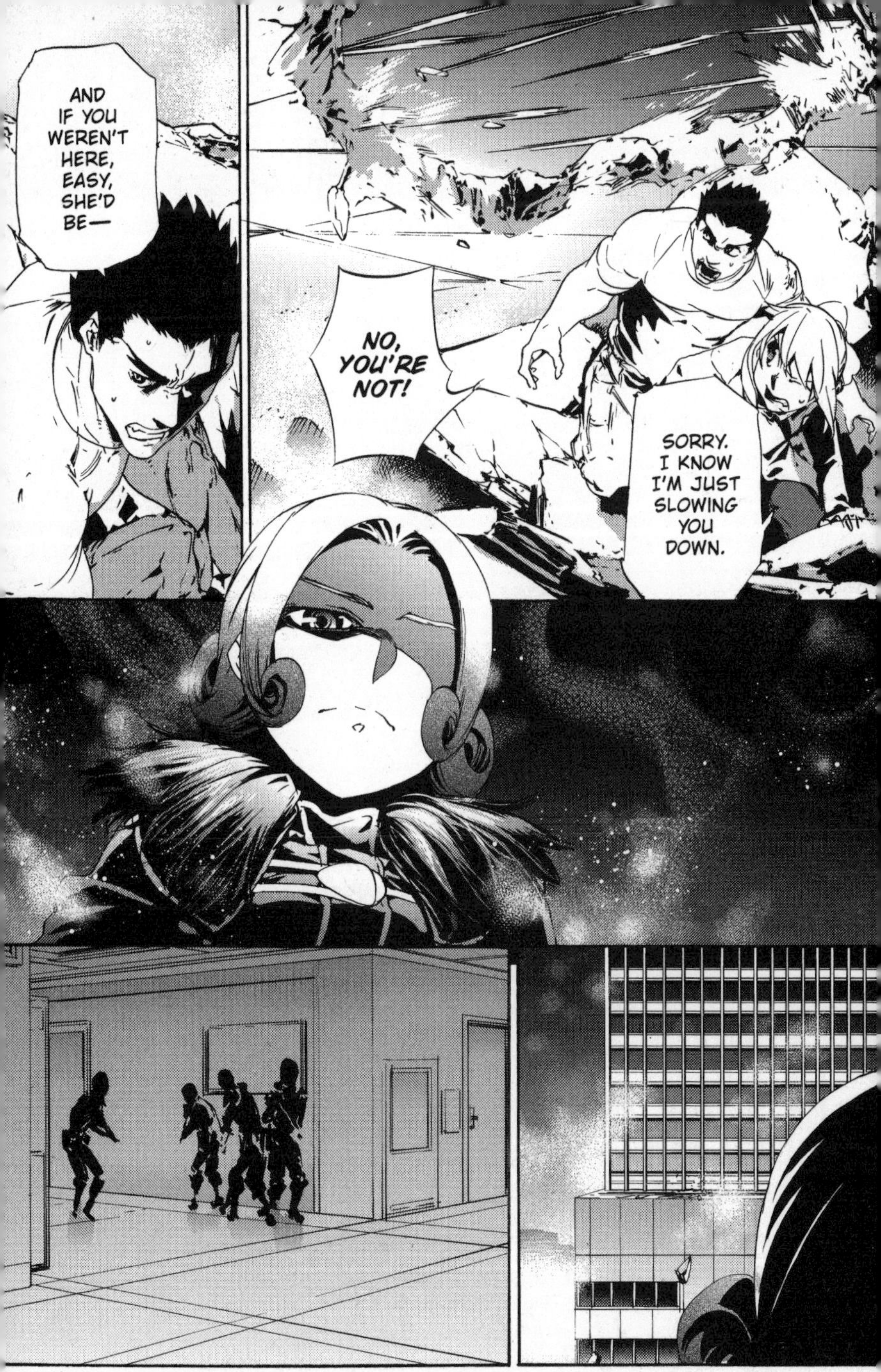
SORRY. I KNOW I'M JUST SLOWING YOU DOWN.
NO, YOU'RE NOT!
AND IF YOU WEREN'T HERE, EASY, SHE'D BE—

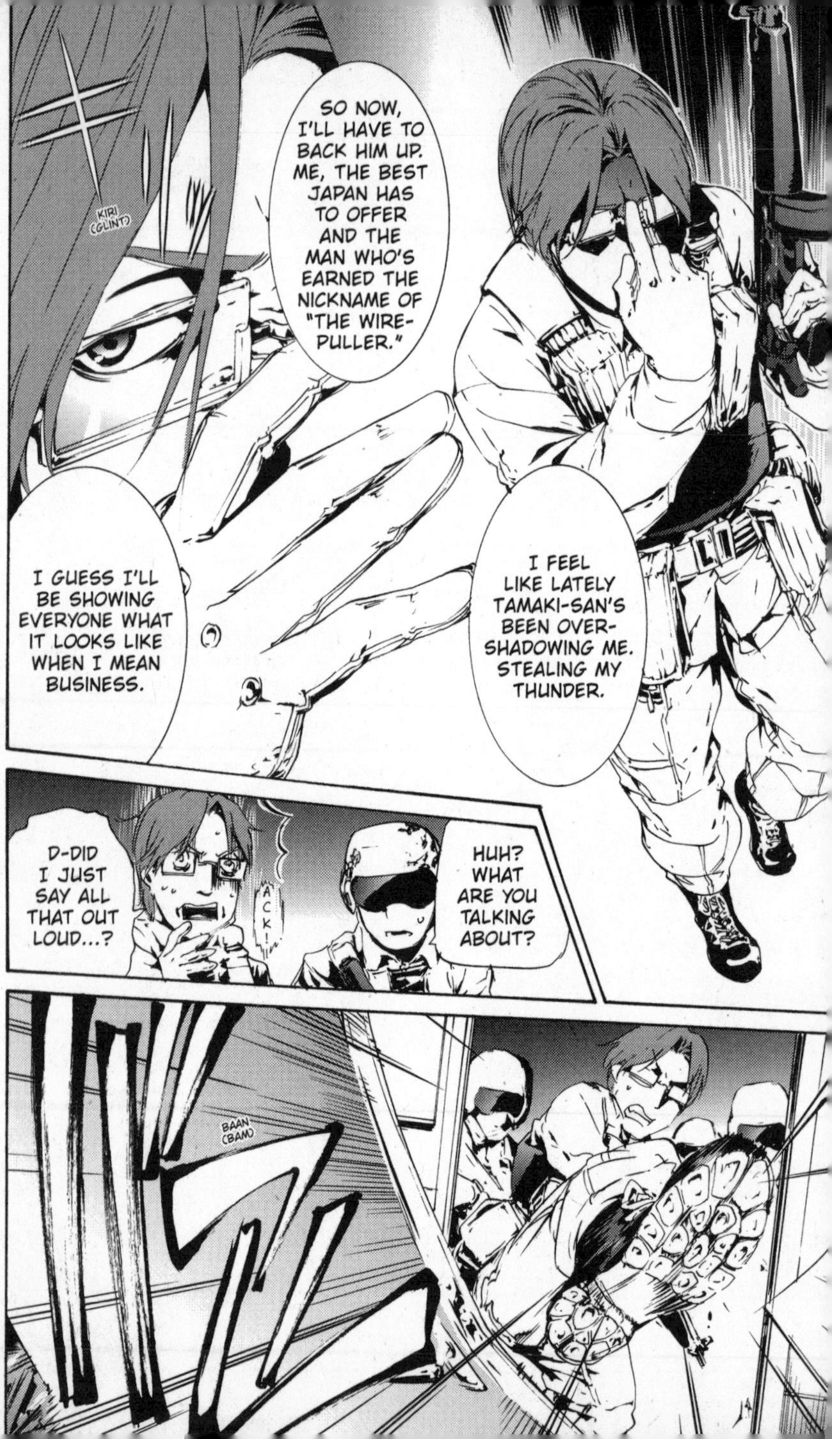
I FEEL LIKE LATELY TAMAKI-SAN'S BEEN OVER-SHADOWING ME. STEALING MY THUNDER.
SO NOW, I'LL HAVE TO BACK HIM UP. ME, THE BEST JAPAN HAS TO OFFER AND THE MAN WHO'S EARNED THE NICKNAME OF "THE WIRE-PULLER."
KIRI (GLINT)
I GUESS I'LL BE SHOWING EVERYONE WHAT IT LOOKS LIKE WHEN I MEAN BUSINESS.
HUH? WHAT ARE YOU TALKING ABOUT?
ACK!
D-DID I JUST SAY ALL THAT OUT LOUD...?
BAAN (BAM)

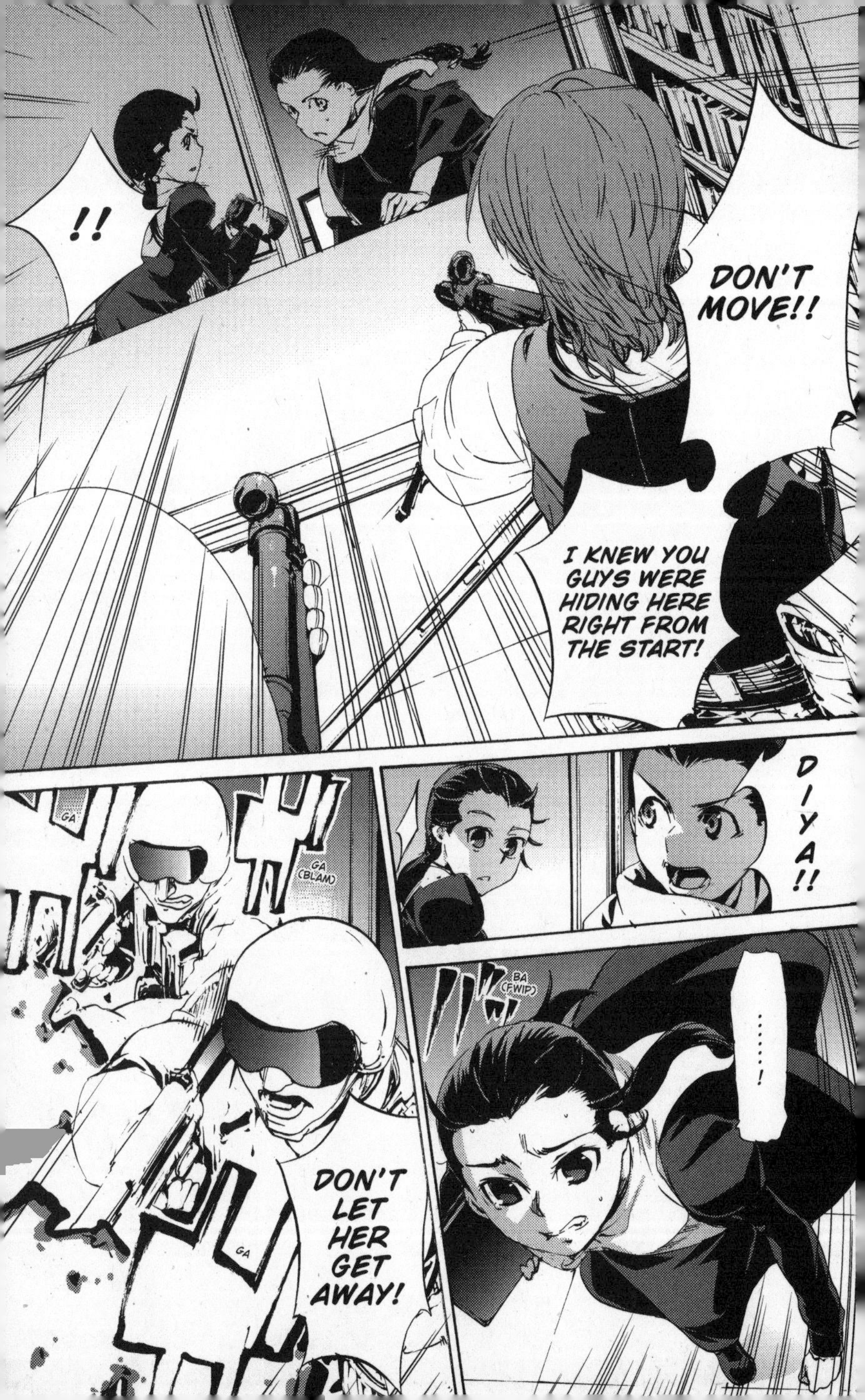
DON'T MOVE!!
!!
I KNEW YOU GUYS WERE HIDING HERE RIGHT FROM THE START!
DIYA!!
BA (FWIP)
......!
GA
GA (BLAM)
DON'T LET HER GET AWAY!
GA

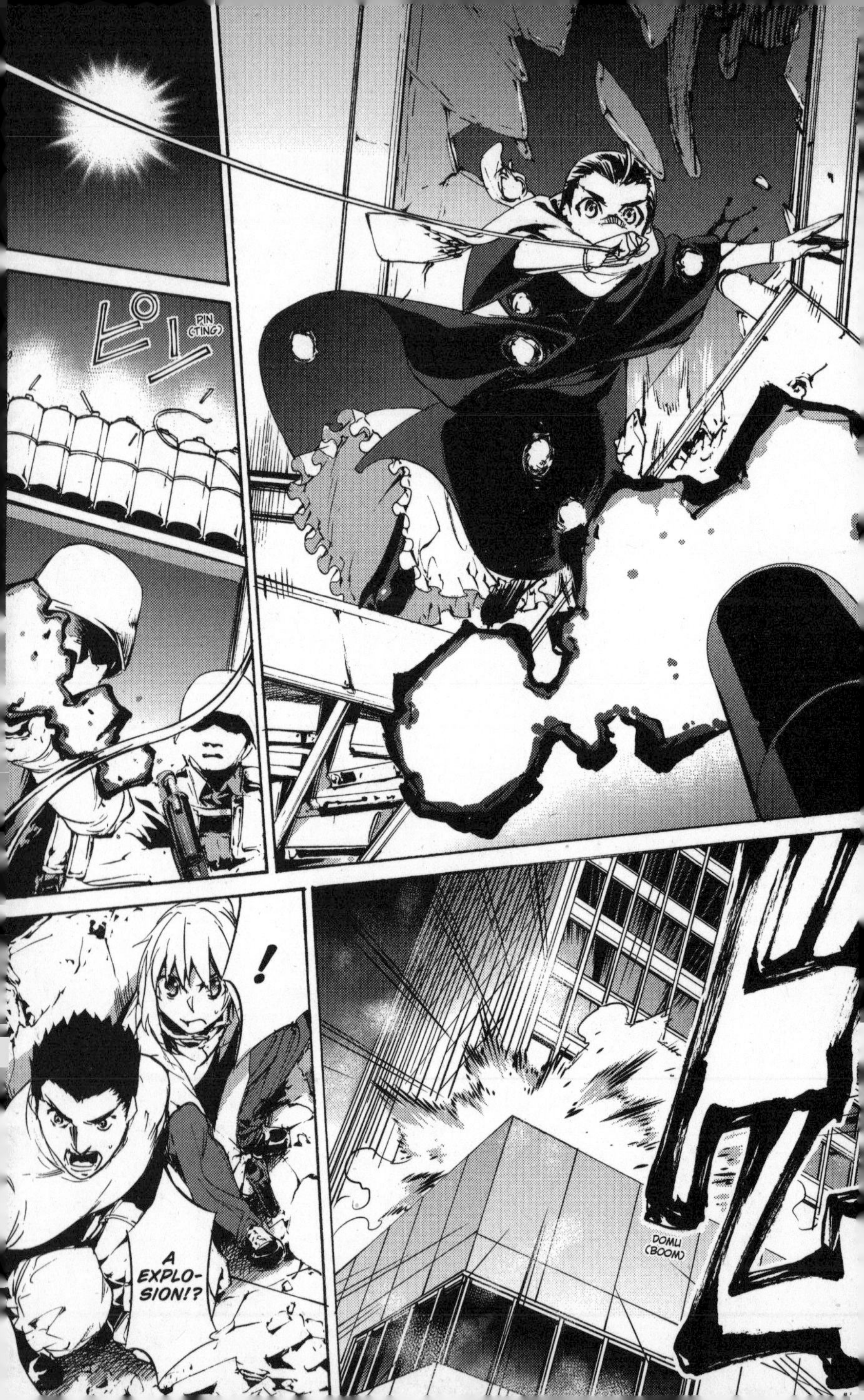
ピン
PIN (TING)
DOMU (BOOM)
!
A EXPLOSION!?

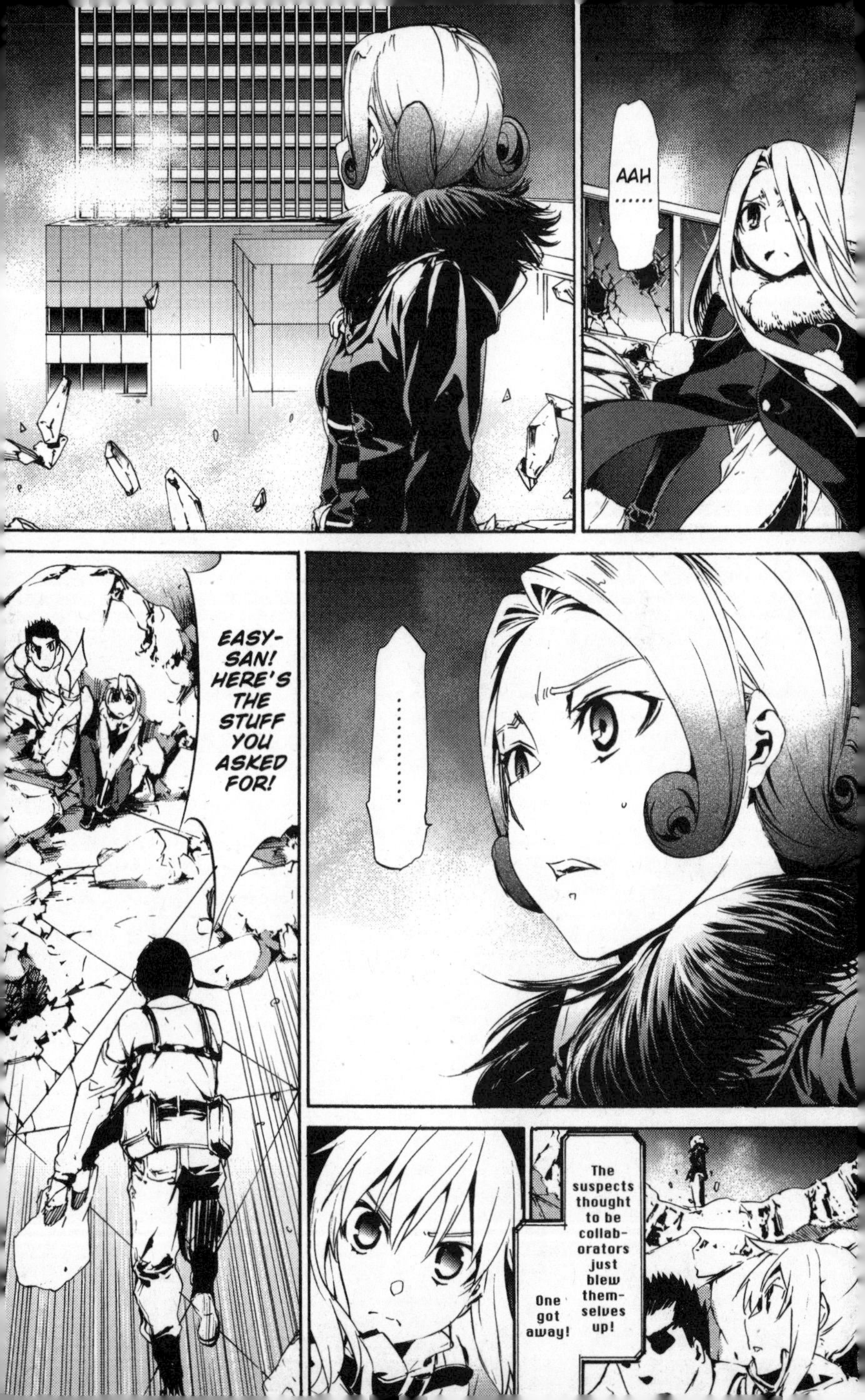
AAH ......
......
EASY-SAN! HERE'S THE STUFF YOU ASKED FOR!
The suspects thought to be collaborators just blew themselves up!
One got away!

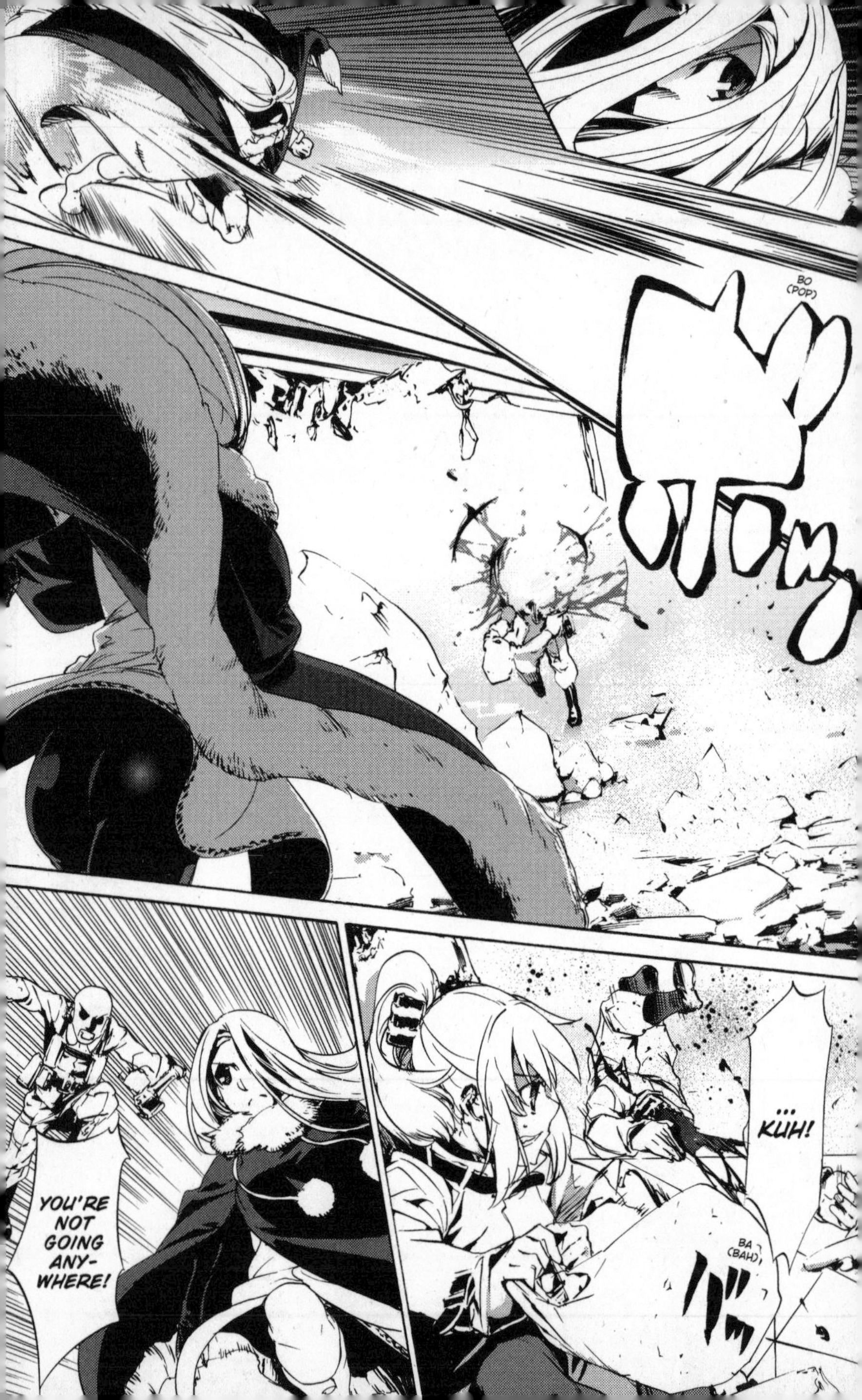
BO
(POP)
...KUH!
BA
(BAH)
YOU'RE NOT GOING ANY-WHERE!

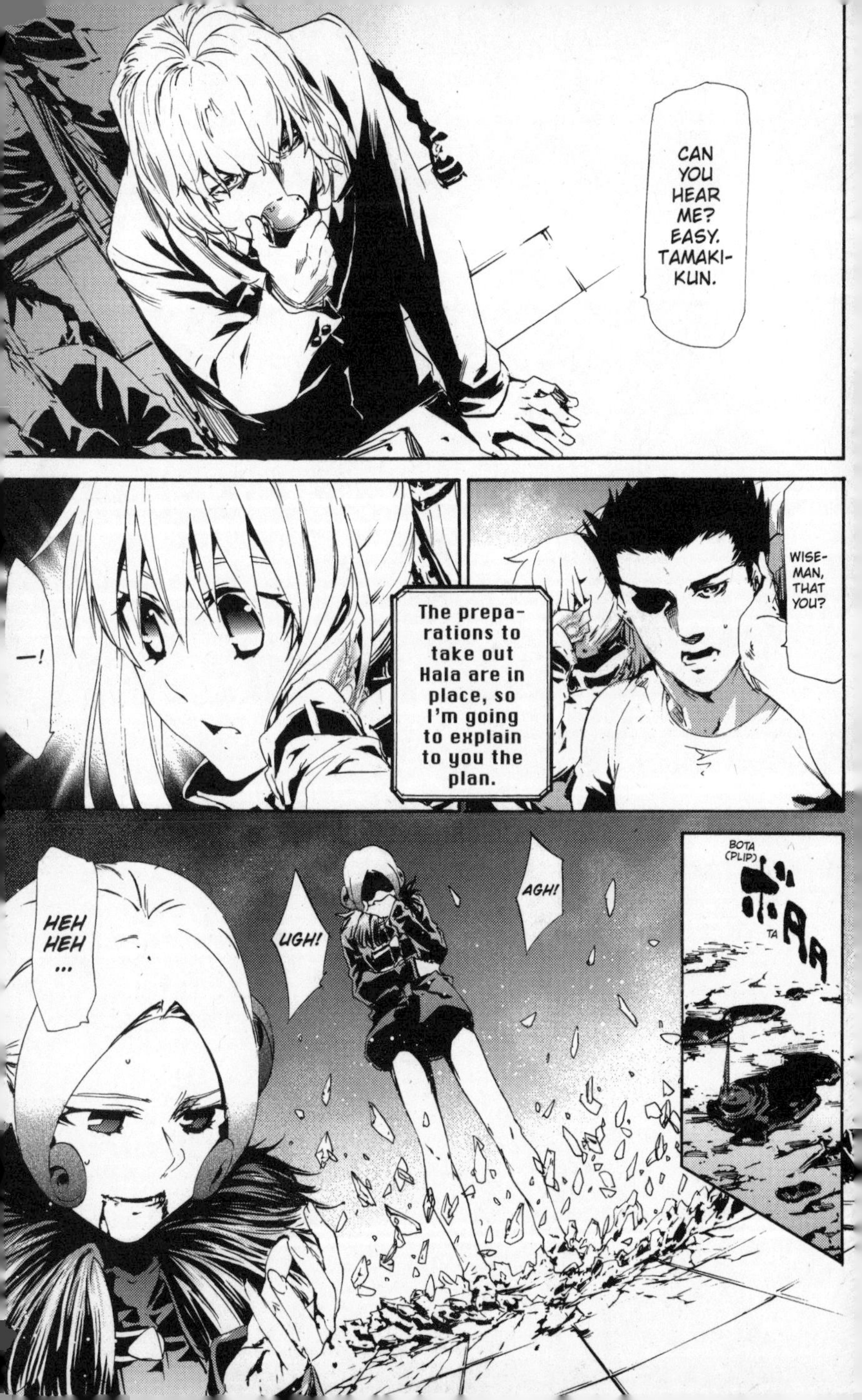
CAN YOU HEAR ME? EASY. TAMAKI-KUN.
WISE-MAN, THAT YOU?
The preparations to take out Hala are in place, so I'm going to explain to you the plan.
—!
BOTA (PLIP)
TA
AGH!
UGH!
HEH HEH ...

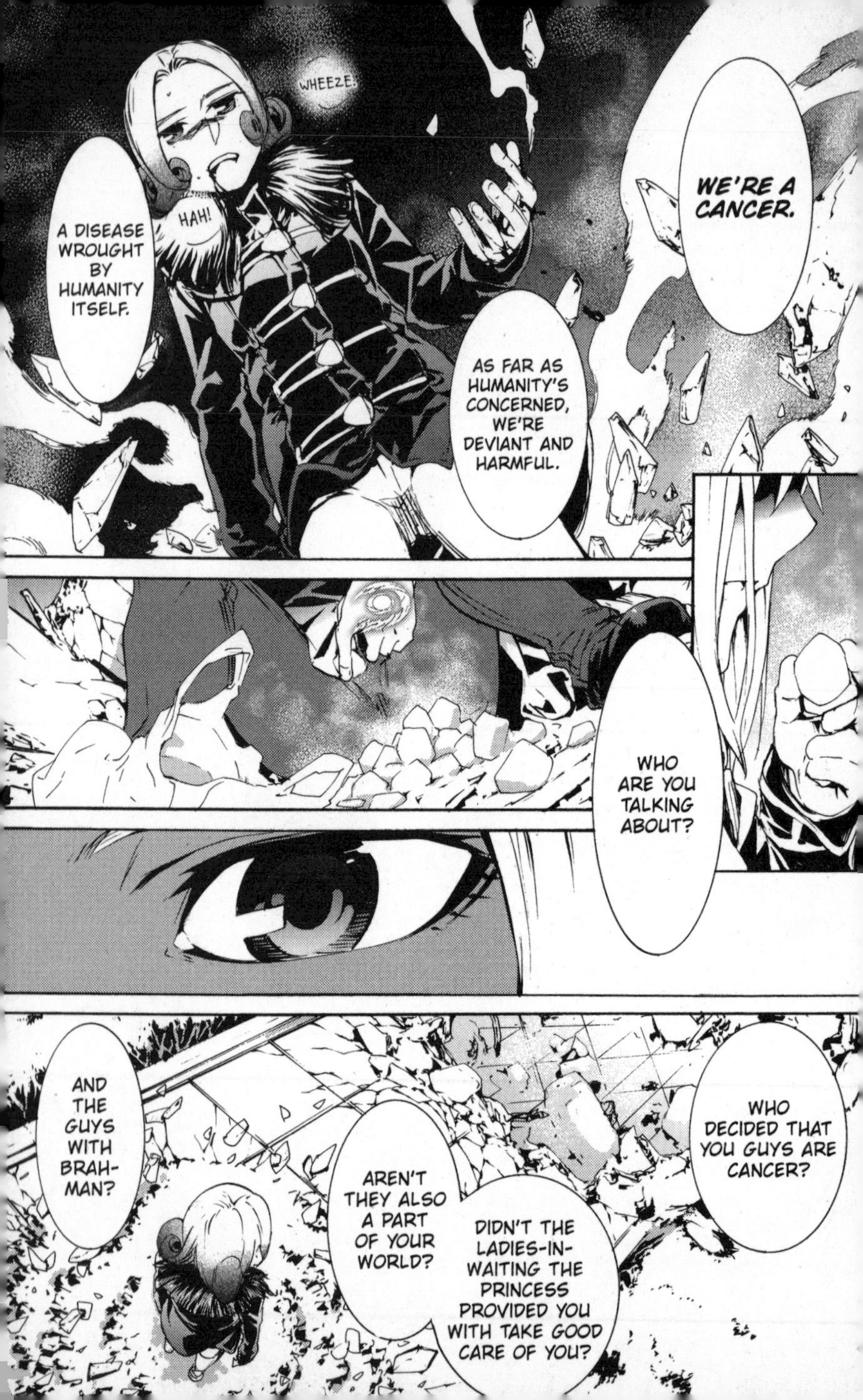
WE'RE A CANCER.
WHEEZE.
AS FAR AS HUMANITY'S CONCERNED, WE'RE DEVIANT AND HARMFUL.
HAH!
A DISEASE WROUGHT BY HUMANITY ITSELF.
WHO ARE YOU TALKING ABOUT?
WHO DECIDED THAT YOU GUYS ARE CANCER?
DIDN'T THE LADIES-IN-WAITING THE PRINCESS PROVIDED YOU WITH TAKE GOOD CARE OF YOU?
AREN'T THEY ALSO A PART OF YOUR WORLD?
AND THE GUYS WITH BRAH-MAN?

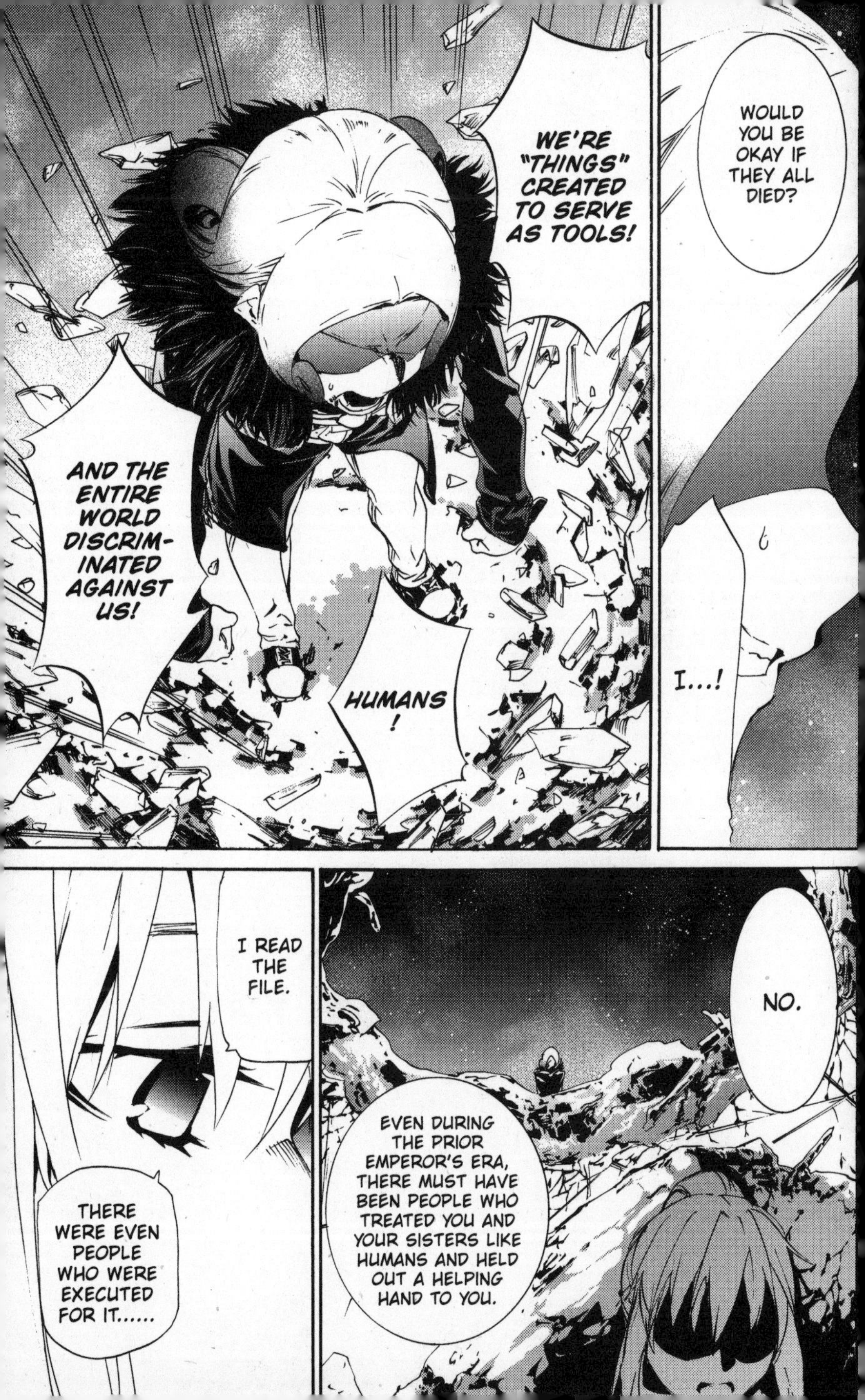
WOULD YOU BE OKAY IF THEY ALL DIED?
I...!
WE'RE "THINGS" CREATED TO SERVE AS TOOLS!
AND THE ENTIRE WORLD DISCRIMINATED AGAINST US!
HUMANS!
NO.
EVEN DURING THE PRIOR EMPEROR'S ERA, THERE MUST HAVE BEEN PEOPLE WHO TREATED YOU AND YOUR SISTERS LIKE HUMANS AND HELD OUT A HELPING HAND TO YOU.
I READ THE FILE.
THERE WERE EVEN PEOPLE WHO WERE EXECUTED FOR IT......

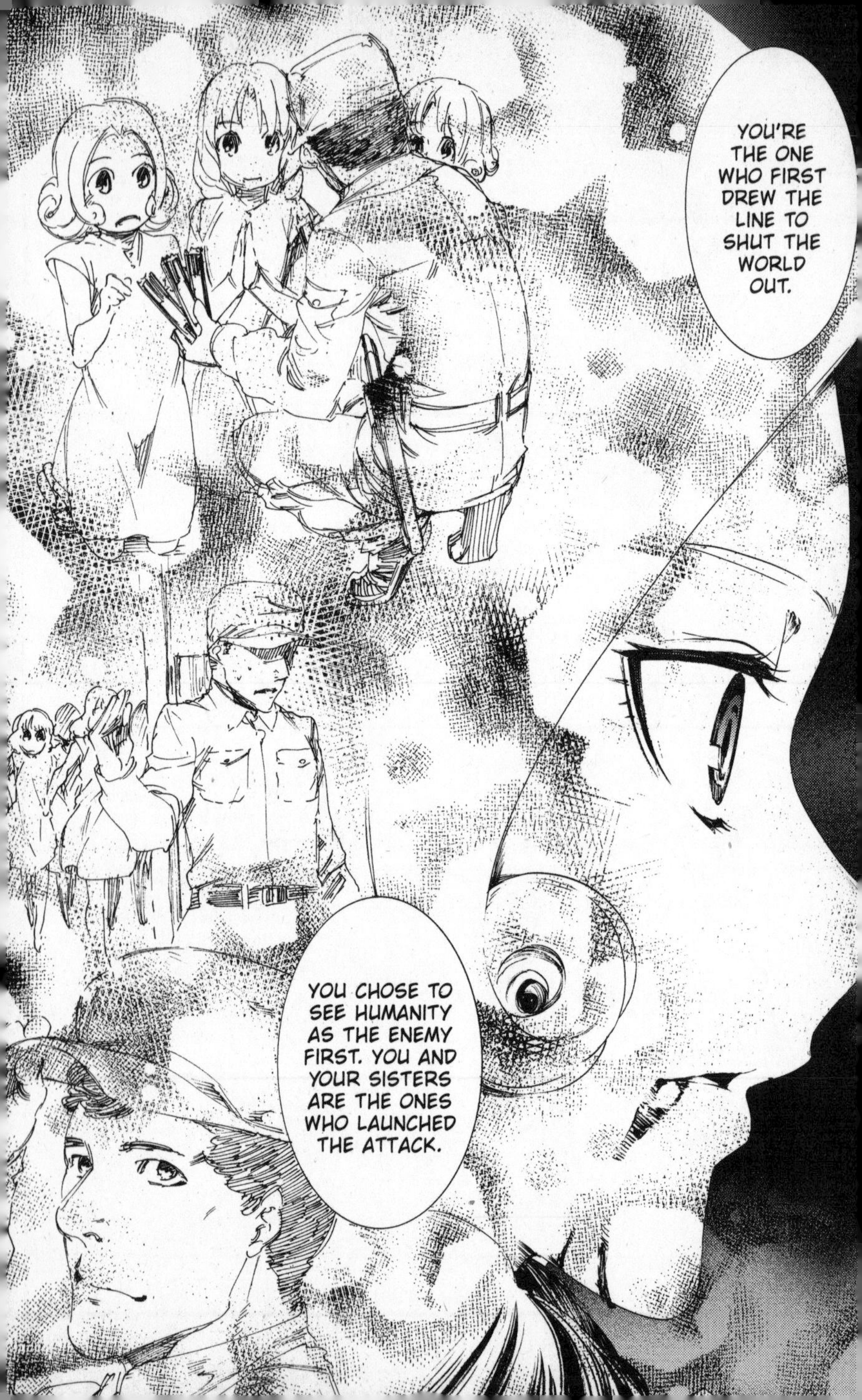
YOU'RE THE ONE WHO FIRST DREW THE LINE TO SHUT THE WORLD OUT.
YOU CHOSE TO SEE HUMANITY AS THE ENEMY FIRST. YOU AND YOUR SISTERS ARE THE ONES WHO LAUNCHED THE ATTACK.

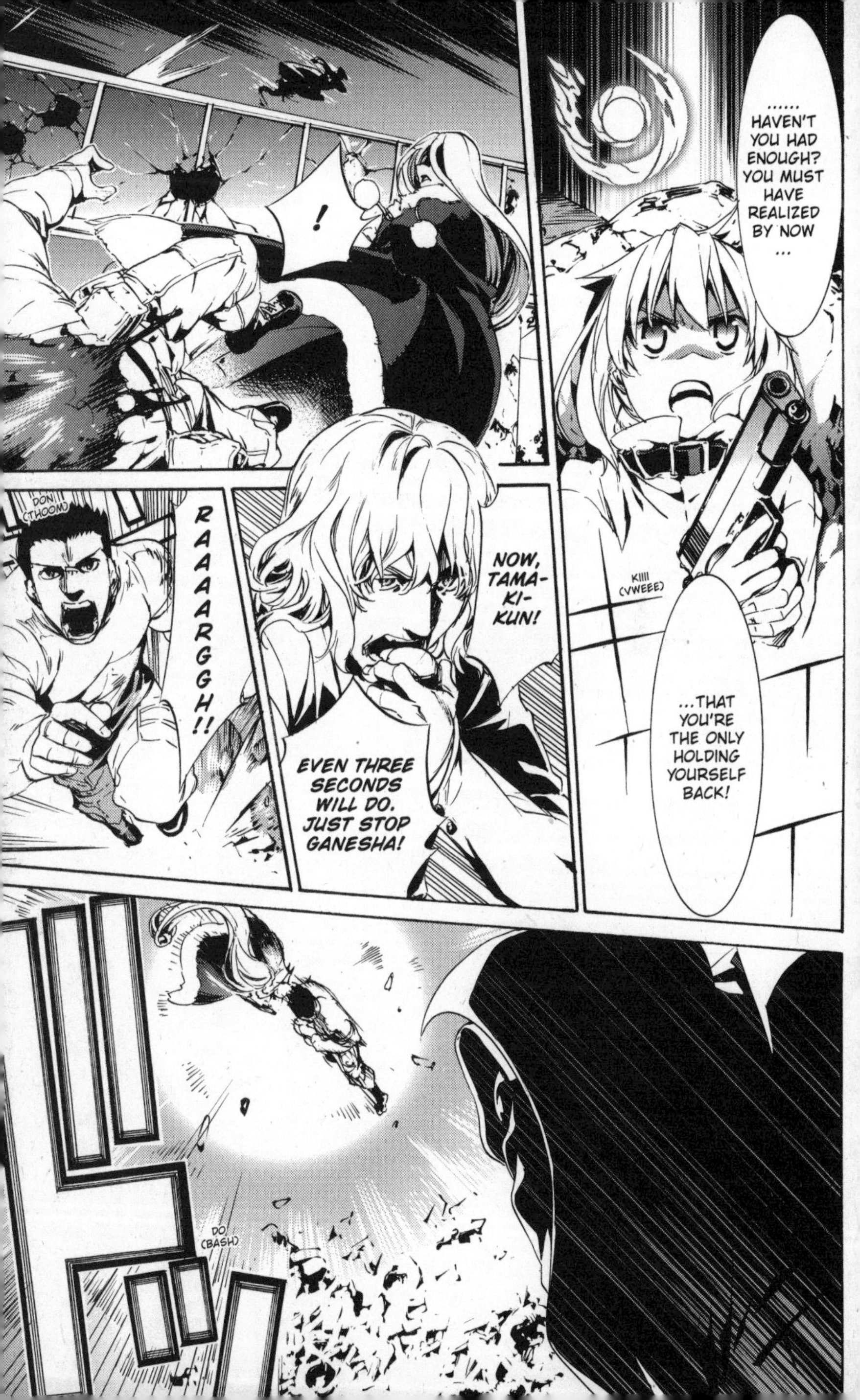

......HAVEN'T YOU HAD ENOUGH? YOU MUST HAVE REALIZED BY NOW ...
KIIII (VWEEE)
...THAT YOU'RE THE ONLY HOLDING YOURSELF BACK!
!
NOW, TAMA-KI-KUN!
EVEN THREE SECONDS WILL DO. JUST STOP GANESHA!
DON (THOOM)
RAAAAARGGH!!
DO (BASH)

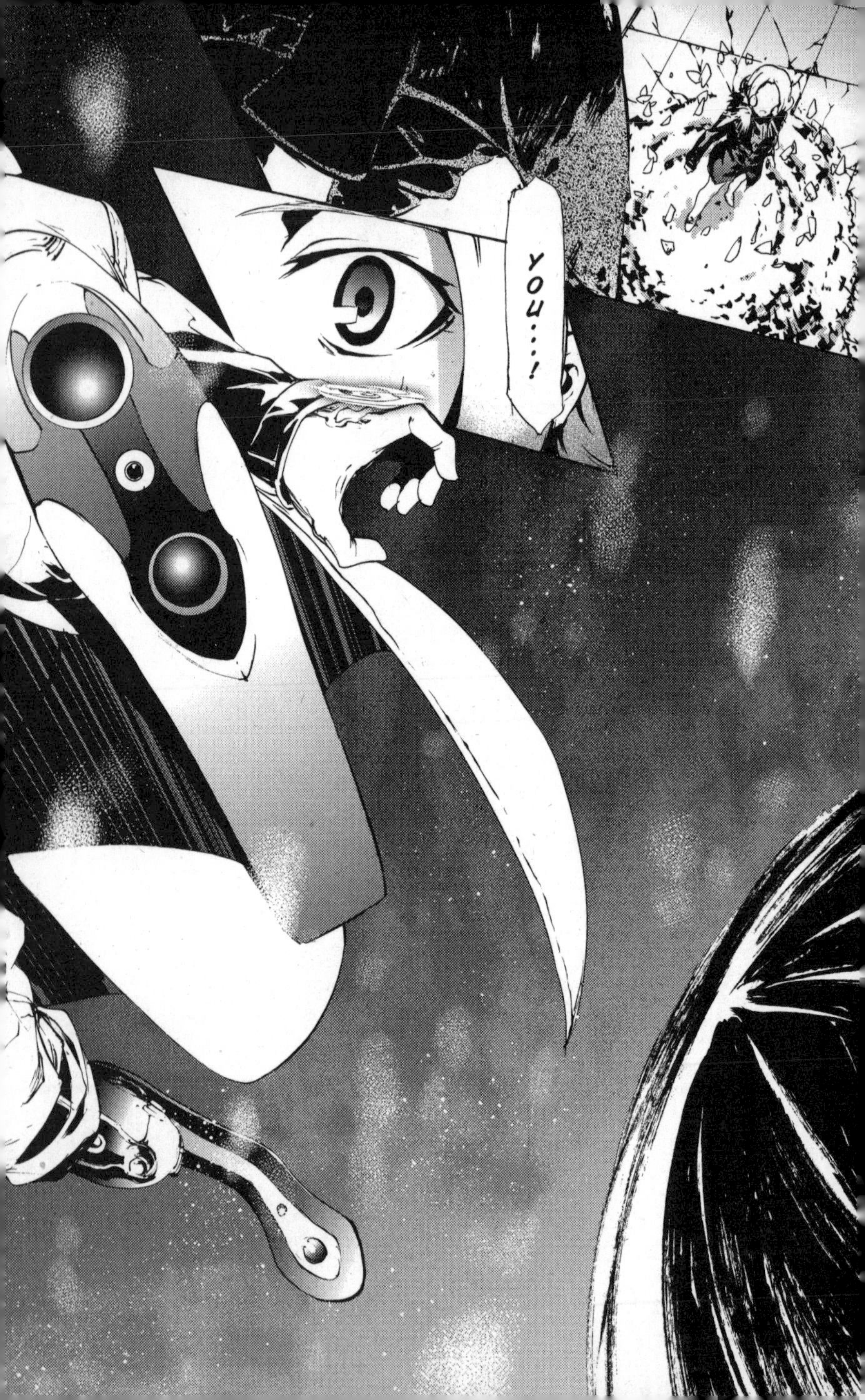
YOU...!

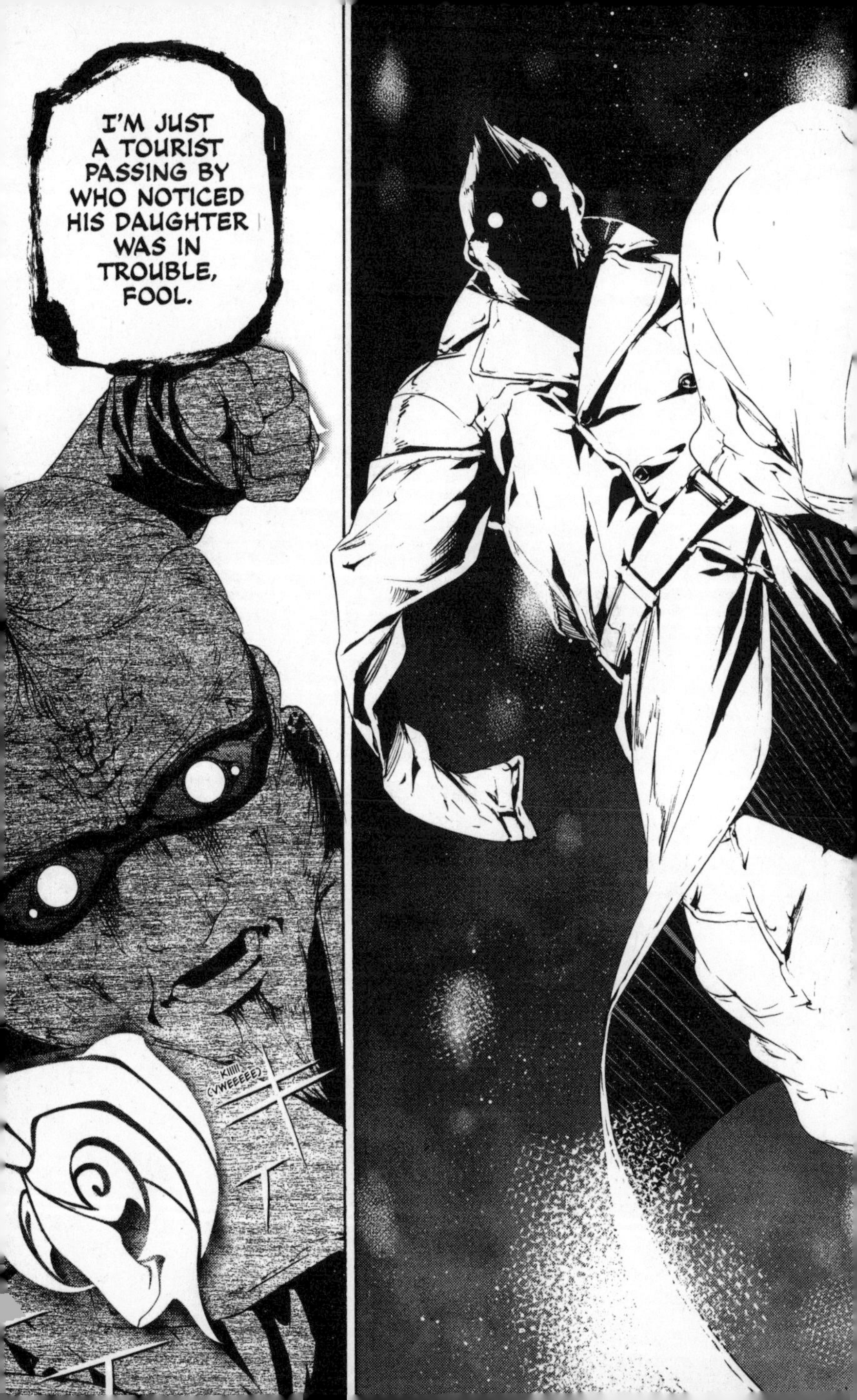
I'M JUST A TOURIST PASSING BY WHO NOTICED HIS DAUGHTER WAS IN TROUBLE, FOOL.
KIIIII (VWEEEEE)

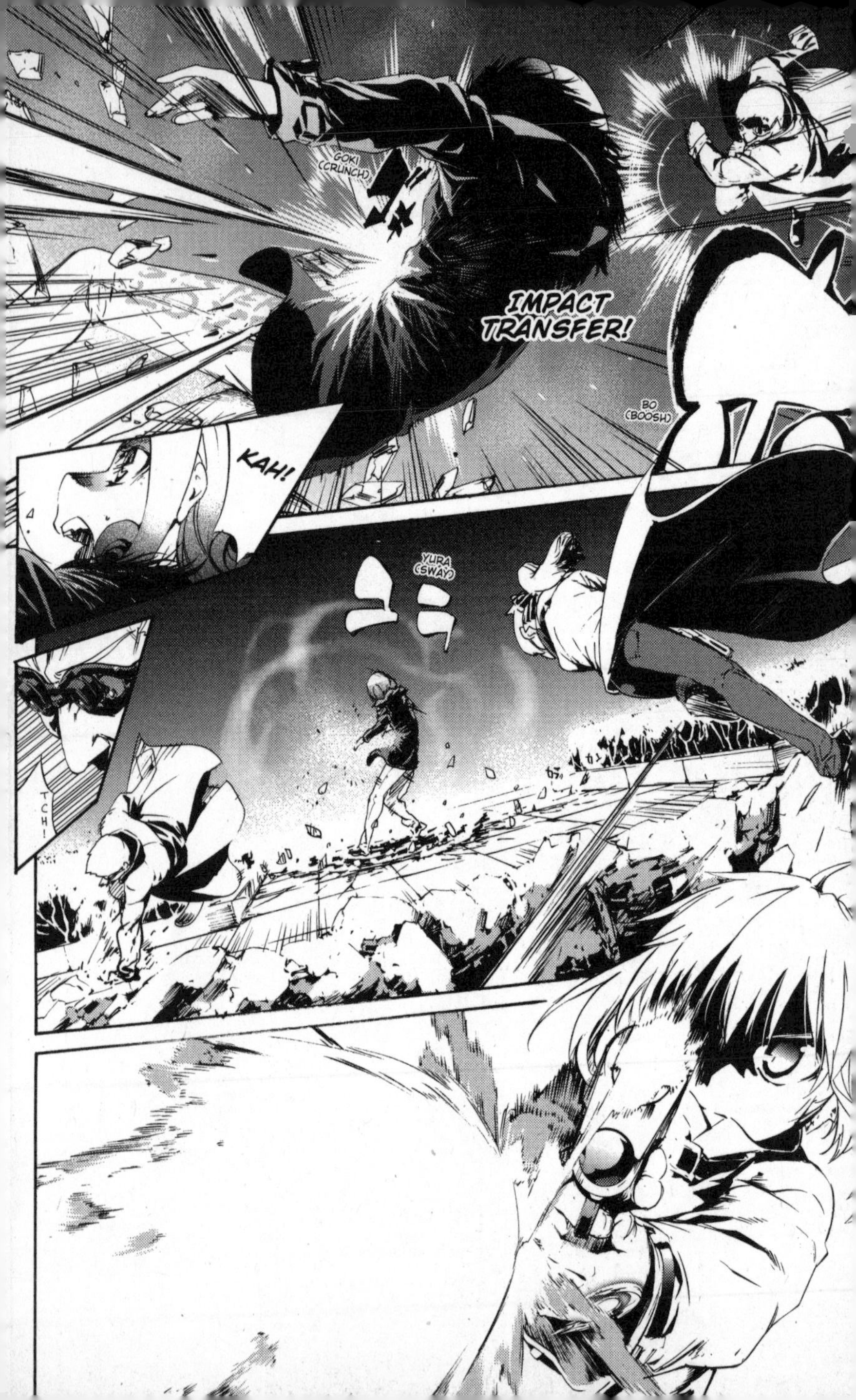
GOKI (CRUNCH)
IMPACT TRANSFER!
BO (BOOSH)
KAH!
YURA (SWAY)
ユラ
TCH!

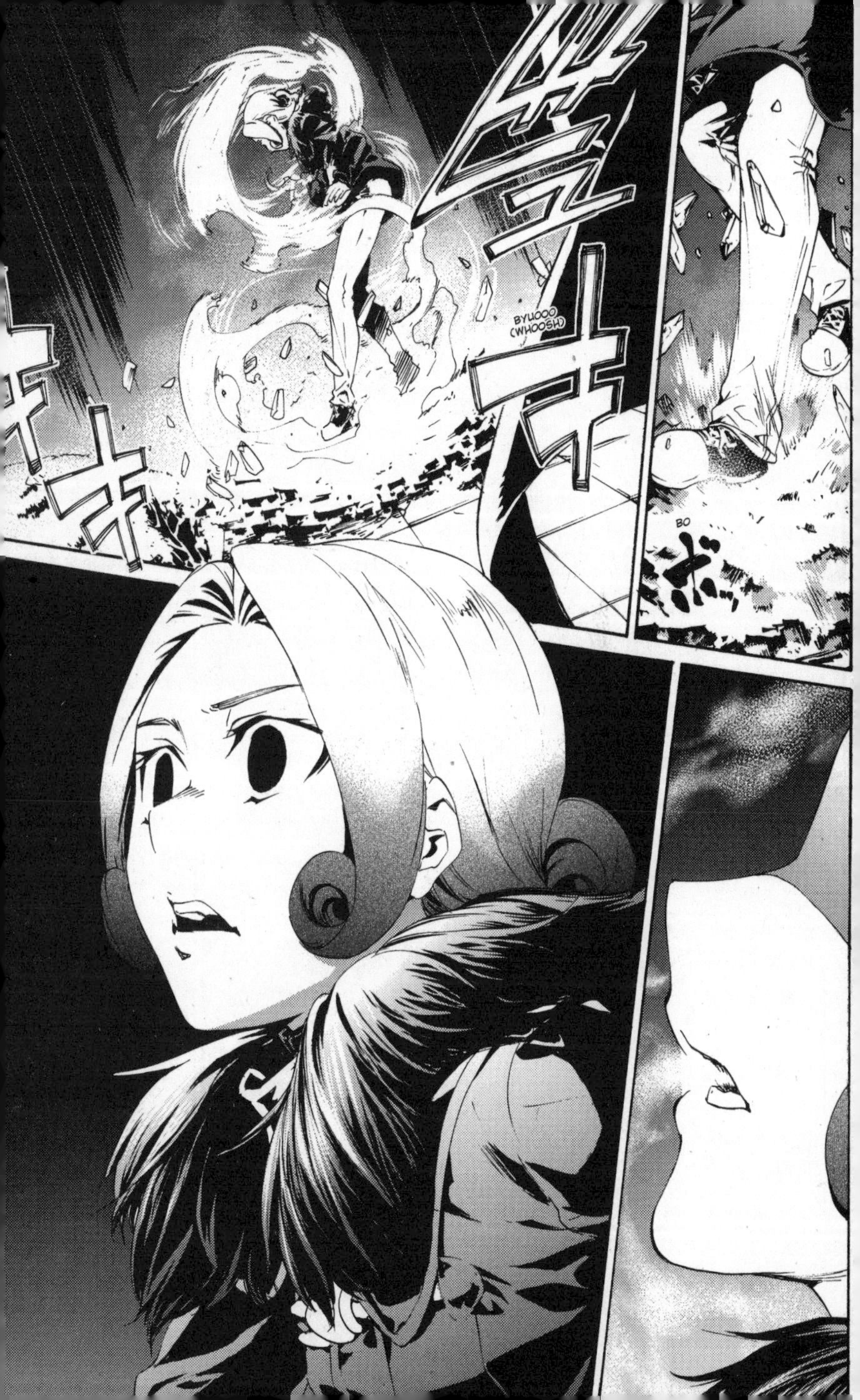
BO
BYUOOO
(WHOOSH)

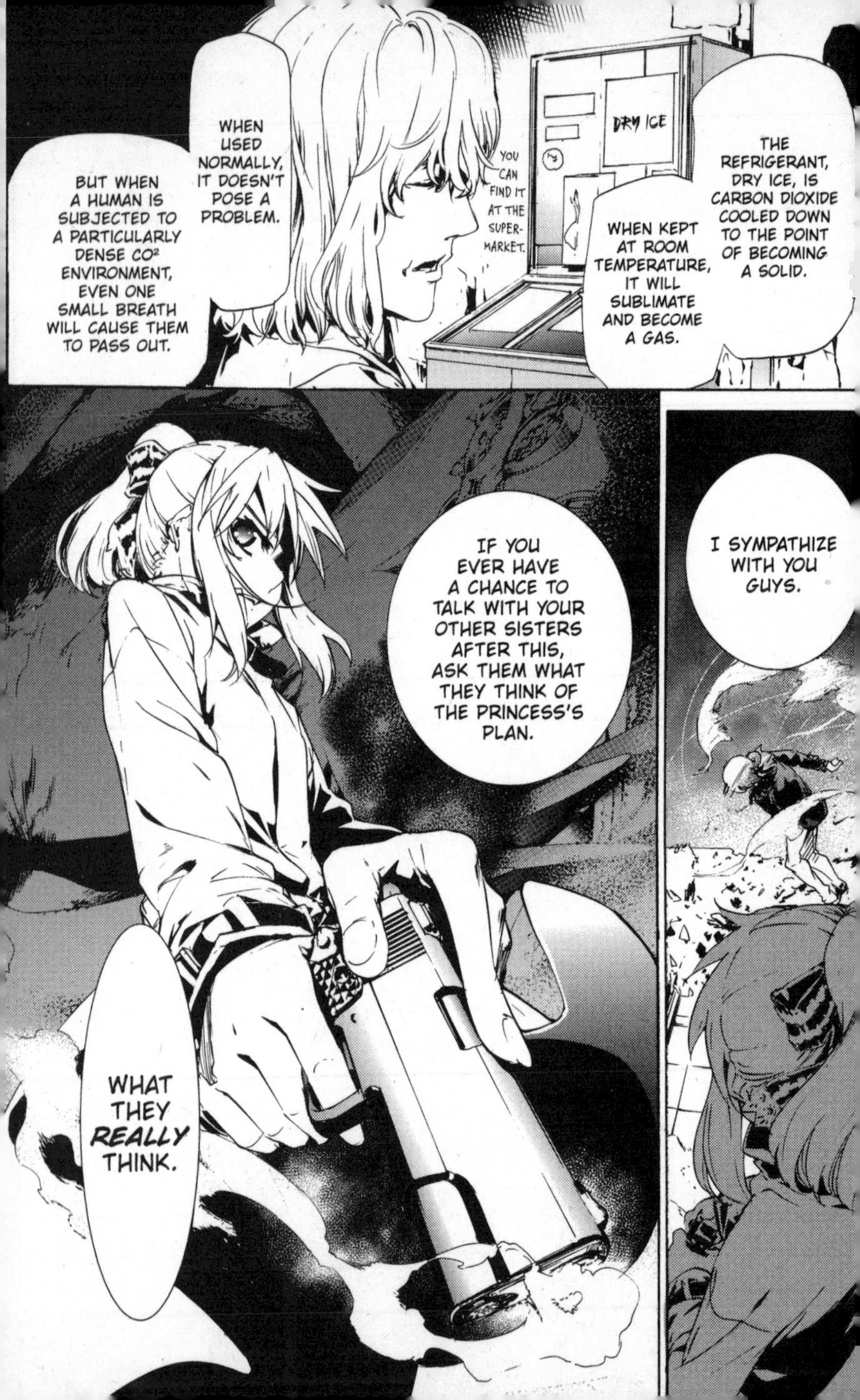
THE REFRIGERANT, DRY ICE, IS CARBON DIOXIDE COOLED DOWN TO THE POINT OF BECOMING A SOLID.
DRY ICE
WHEN KEPT AT ROOM TEMPERATURE, IT WILL SUBLIMATE AND BECOME A GAS.
YOU CAN FIND IT AT THE SUPER-MARKET.
WHEN USED NORMALLY, IT DOESN'T POSE A PROBLEM.
BUT WHEN A HUMAN IS SUBJECTED TO A PARTICULARLY DENSE CO_2 ENVIRONMENT, EVEN ONE SMALL BREATH WILL CAUSE THEM TO PASS OUT.
I SYMPATHIZE WITH YOU GUYS.
IF YOU EVER HAVE A CHANCE TO TALK WITH YOUR OTHER SISTERS AFTER THIS, ASK THEM WHAT THEY THINK OF THE PRINCESS'S PLAN.
WHAT THEY *REALLY* THINK.

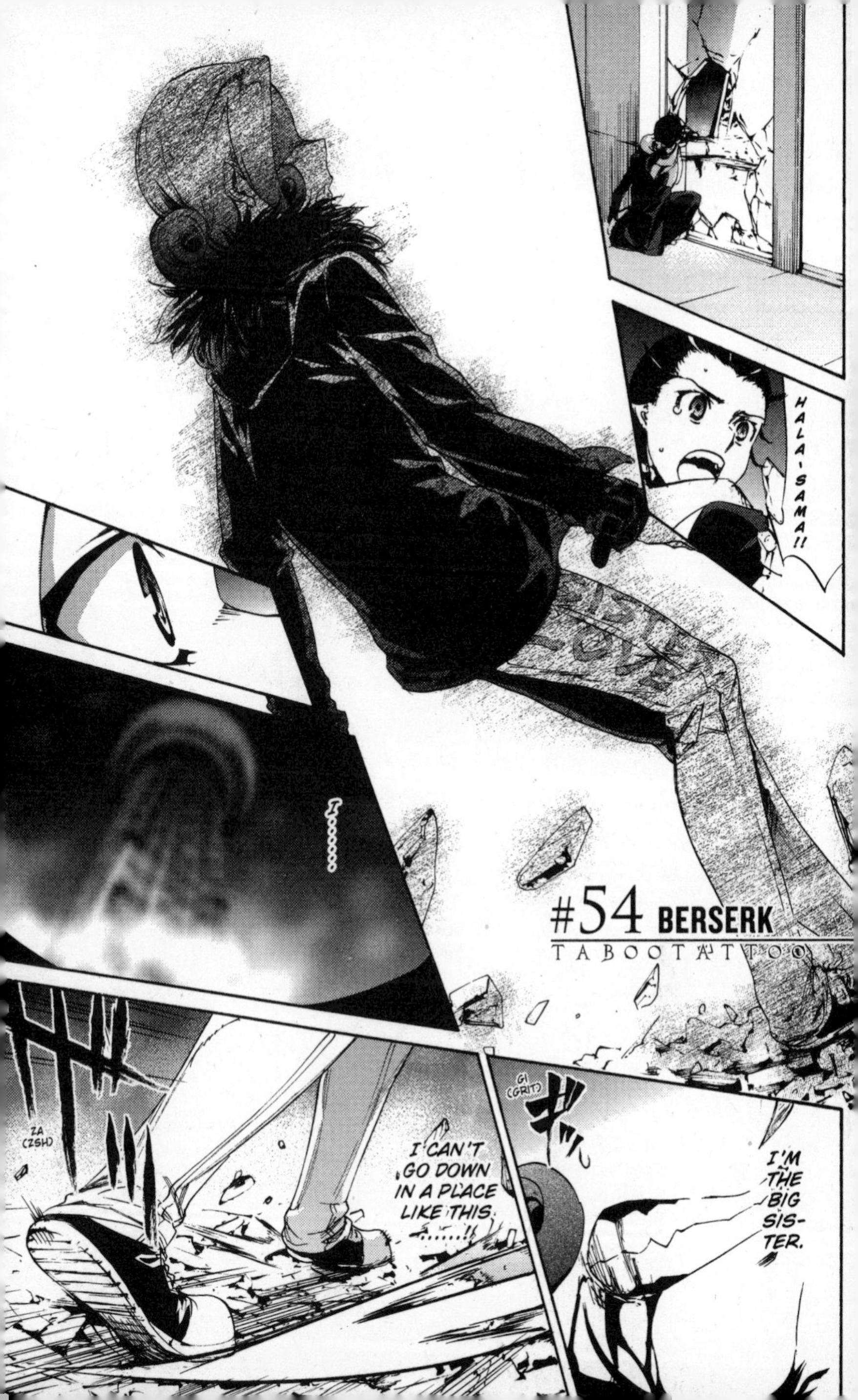

HALA-SAMA!!
#54 BERSERK
TABOO TATTOO
I......
GI (GRIT)
I'M THE BIG SISTER.
I CAN'T GO DOWN IN A PLACE LIKE THIS......!!
ZA (ZSH)

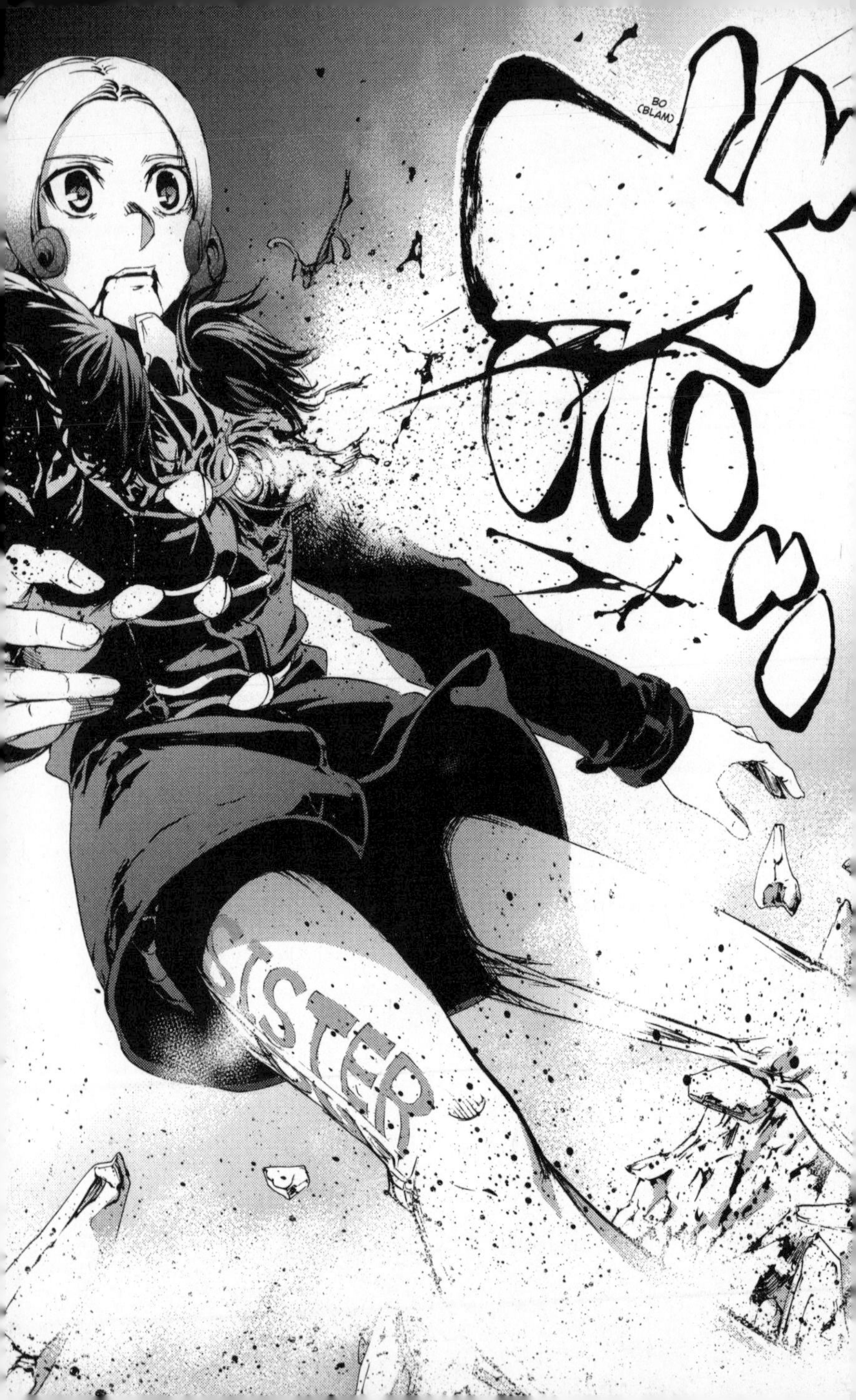
BO
(BLAM)
SISTER

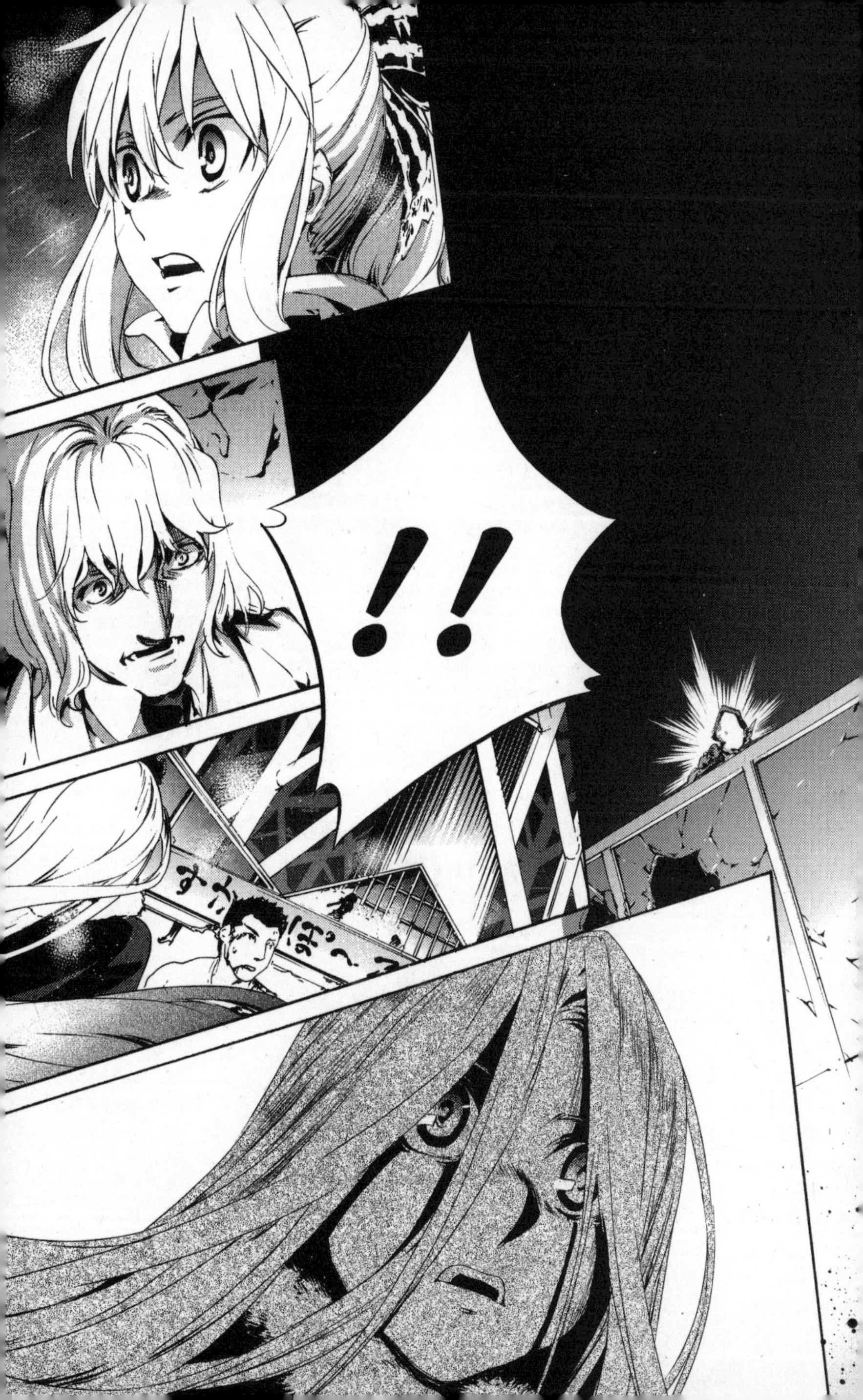
!!

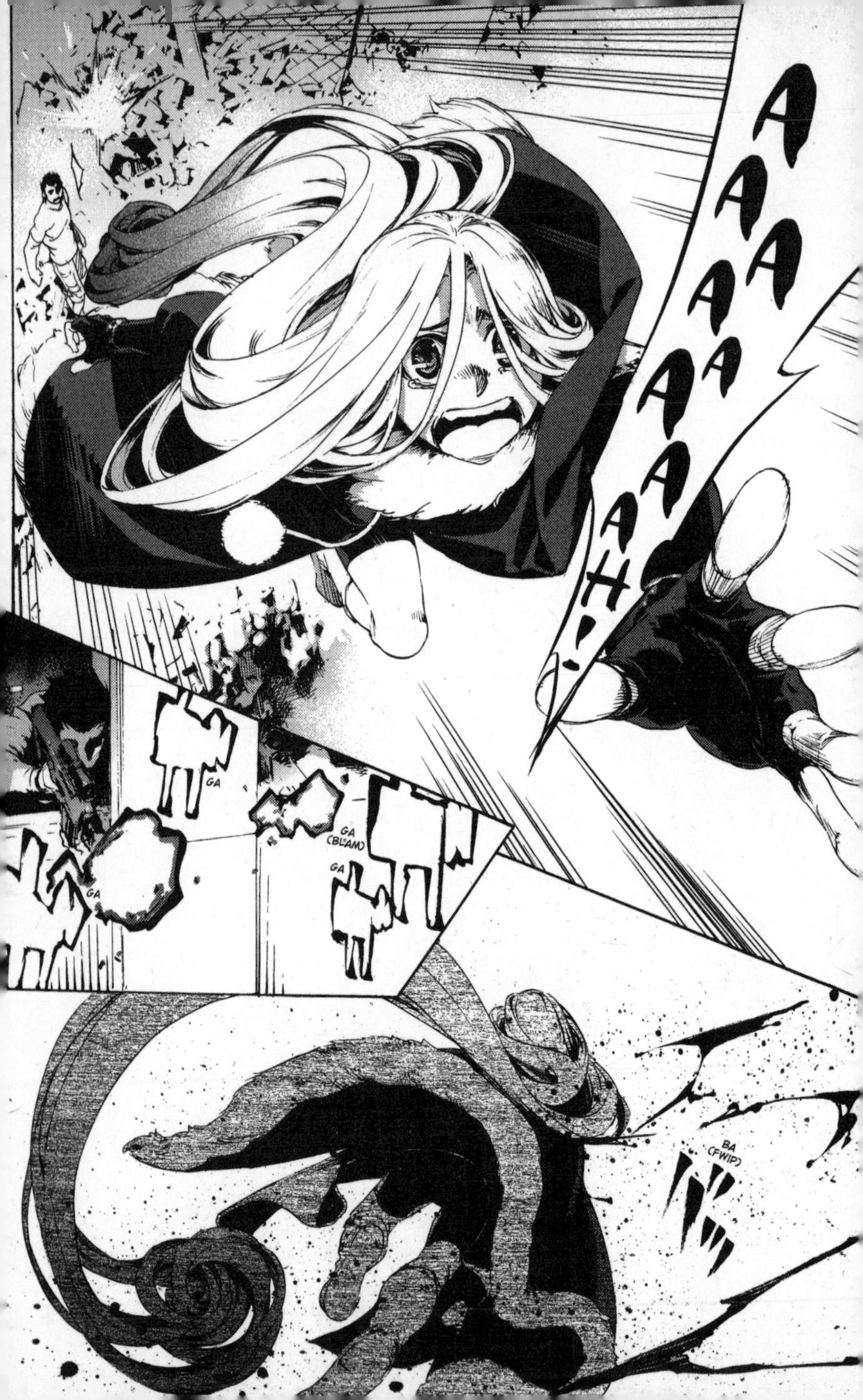
AAAAAAAAAAAH!!
GA
GA (BL'AM)
GA
GA
BA (FWIP)

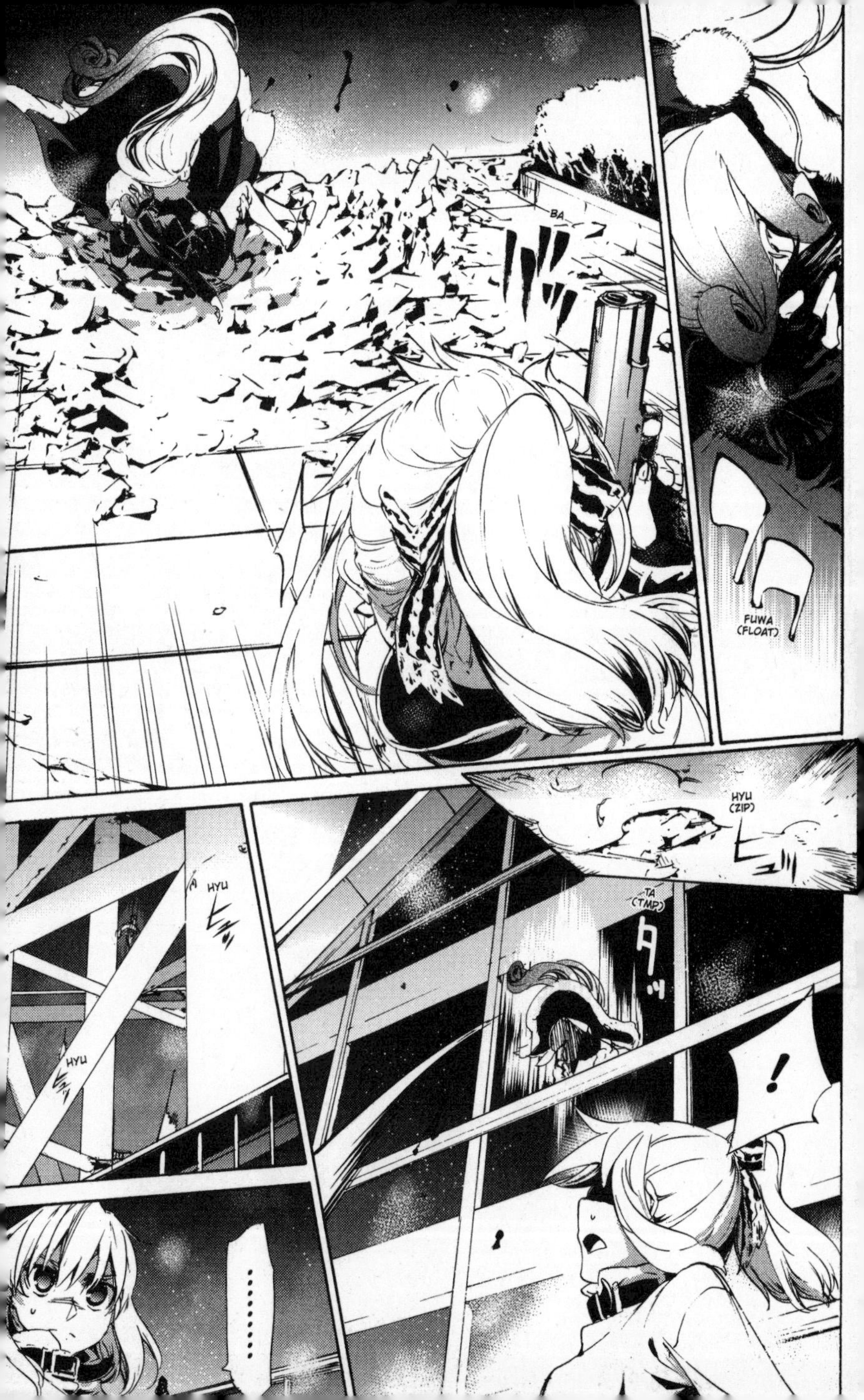
FUWA (FLOAT)
BA
HYU (ZIP)
TA (TMP)
!
HYU
HYU
......

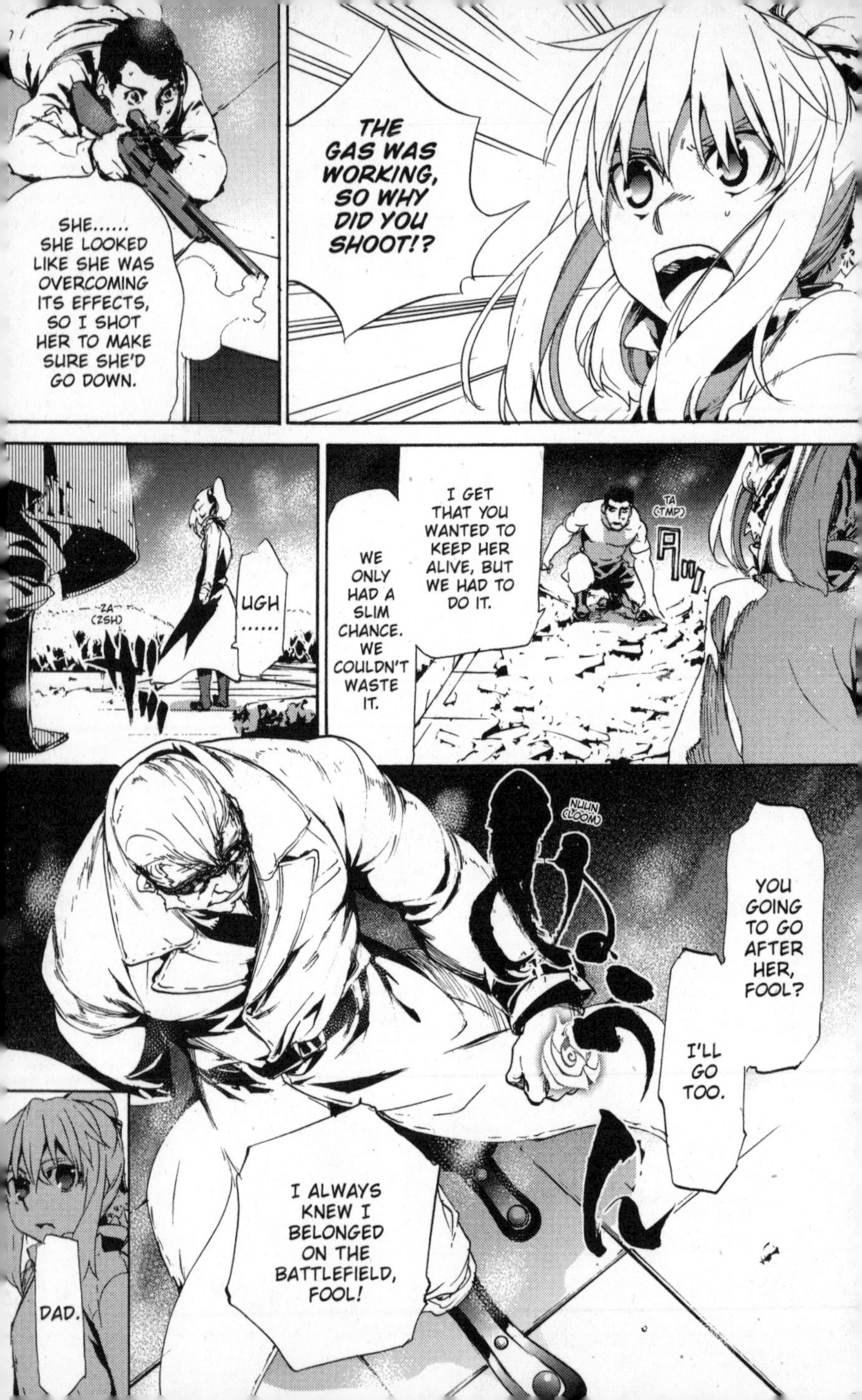
THE GAS WAS WORKING, SO WHY DID YOU SHOOT!?
SHE...... SHE LOOKED LIKE SHE WAS OVERCOMING ITS EFFECTS, SO I SHOT HER TO MAKE SURE SHE'D GO DOWN.
TA (TMP)
I GET THAT YOU WANTED TO KEEP HER ALIVE, BUT WE HAD TO DO IT.
WE ONLY HAD A SLIM CHANCE. WE COULDN'T WASTE IT.
UGH......
ZA (ZSH)
NUUN (LOOM)
YOU GOING TO GO AFTER HER, FOOL?
I'LL GO TOO.
I ALWAYS KNEW I BELONGED ON THE BATTLEFIELD, FOOL!
DAD.

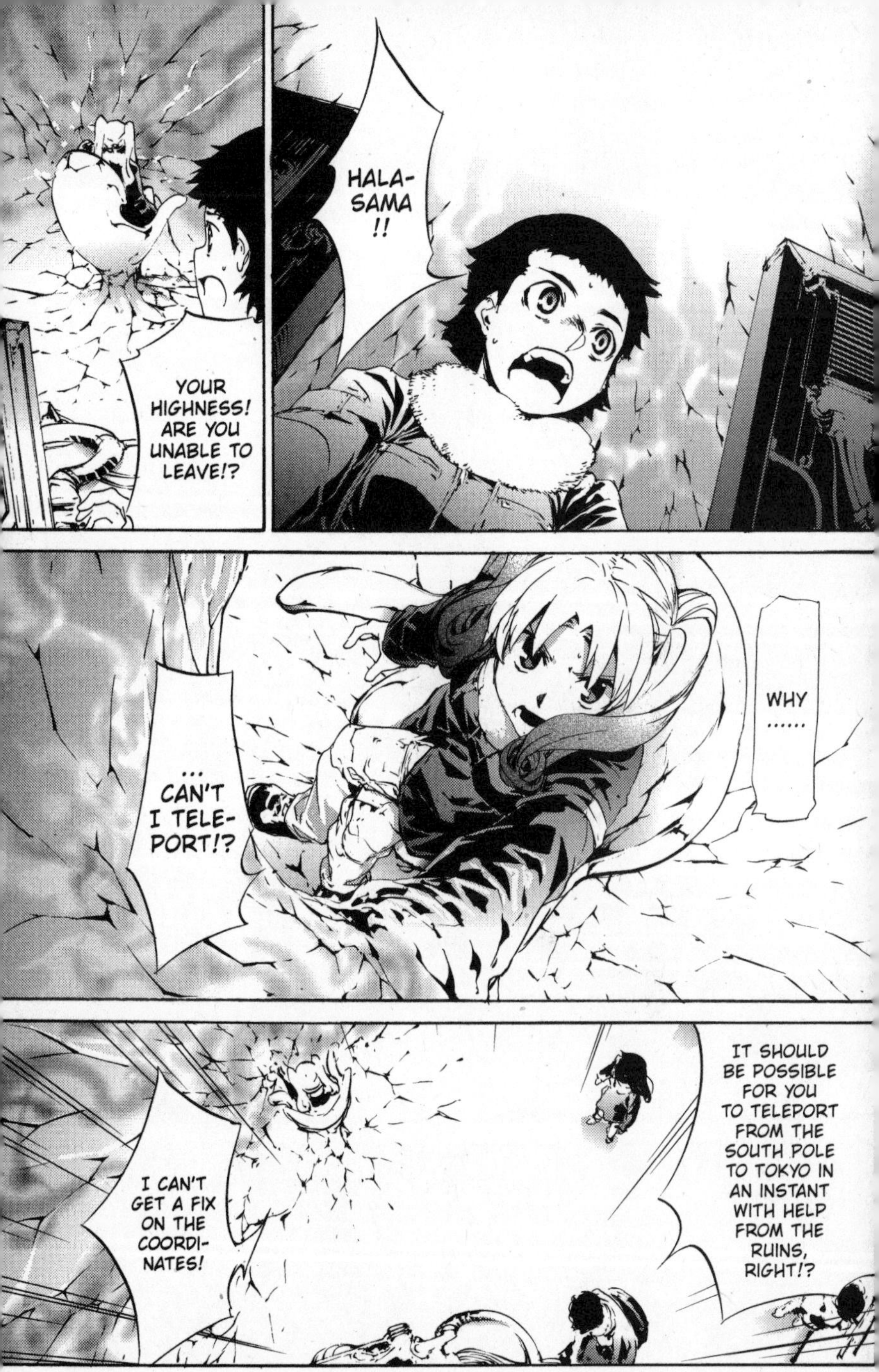
HALA-SAMA!!
YOUR HIGHNESS! ARE YOU UNABLE TO LEAVE!?
WHY......
...CAN'T I TELE-PORT!?
IT SHOULD BE POSSIBLE FOR YOU TO TELEPORT FROM THE SOUTH POLE TO TOKYO IN AN INSTANT WITH HELP FROM THE RUINS, RIGHT!?
I CAN'T GET A FIX ON THE COORDI-NATES!

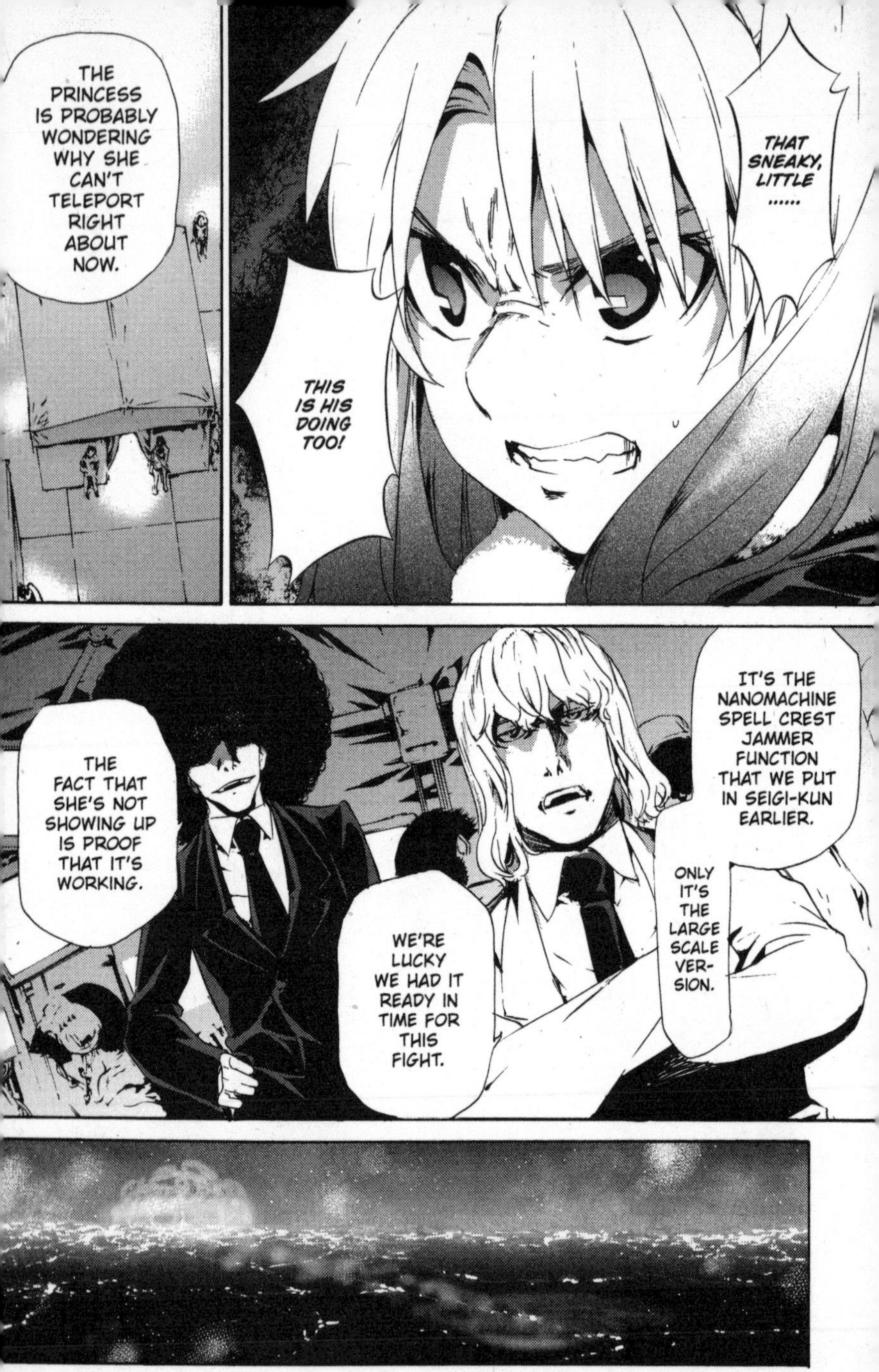
THAT SNEAKY, LITTLE ......
THIS IS HIS DOING TOO!
THE PRINCESS IS PROBABLY WONDERING WHY SHE CAN'T TELEPORT RIGHT ABOUT NOW.
IT'S THE NANOMACHINE SPELL CREST JAMMER FUNCTION THAT WE PUT IN SEIGI-KUN EARLIER.
ONLY IT'S THE LARGE SCALE VER-SION.
WE'RE LUCKY WE HAD IT READY IN TIME FOR THIS FIGHT.
THE FACT THAT SHE'S NOT SHOWING UP IS PROOF THAT IT'S WORKING.

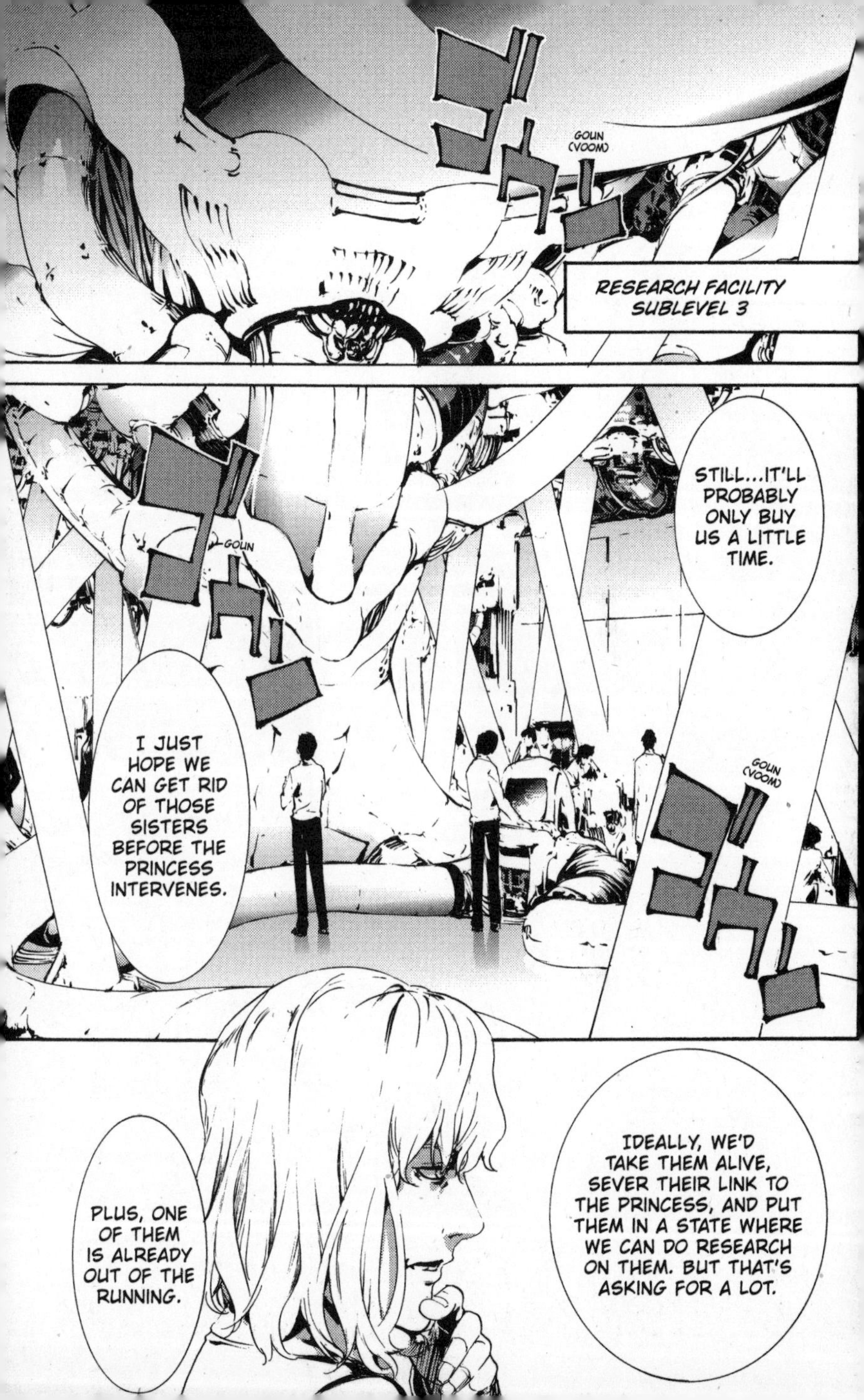
GOUN (VOOM)
RESEARCH FACILITY SUBLEVEL 3
STILL...IT'LL PROBABLY ONLY BUY US A LITTLE TIME.
GOUN (VOOM)
GOUN
I JUST HOPE WE CAN GET RID OF THOSE SISTERS BEFORE THE PRINCESS INTERVENES.
IDEALLY, WE'D TAKE THEM ALIVE, SEVER THEIR LINK TO THE PRINCESS, AND PUT THEM IN A STATE WHERE WE CAN DO RESEARCH ON THEM. BUT THAT'S ASKING FOR A LOT.
PLUS, ONE OF THEM IS ALREADY OUT OF THE RUNNING.

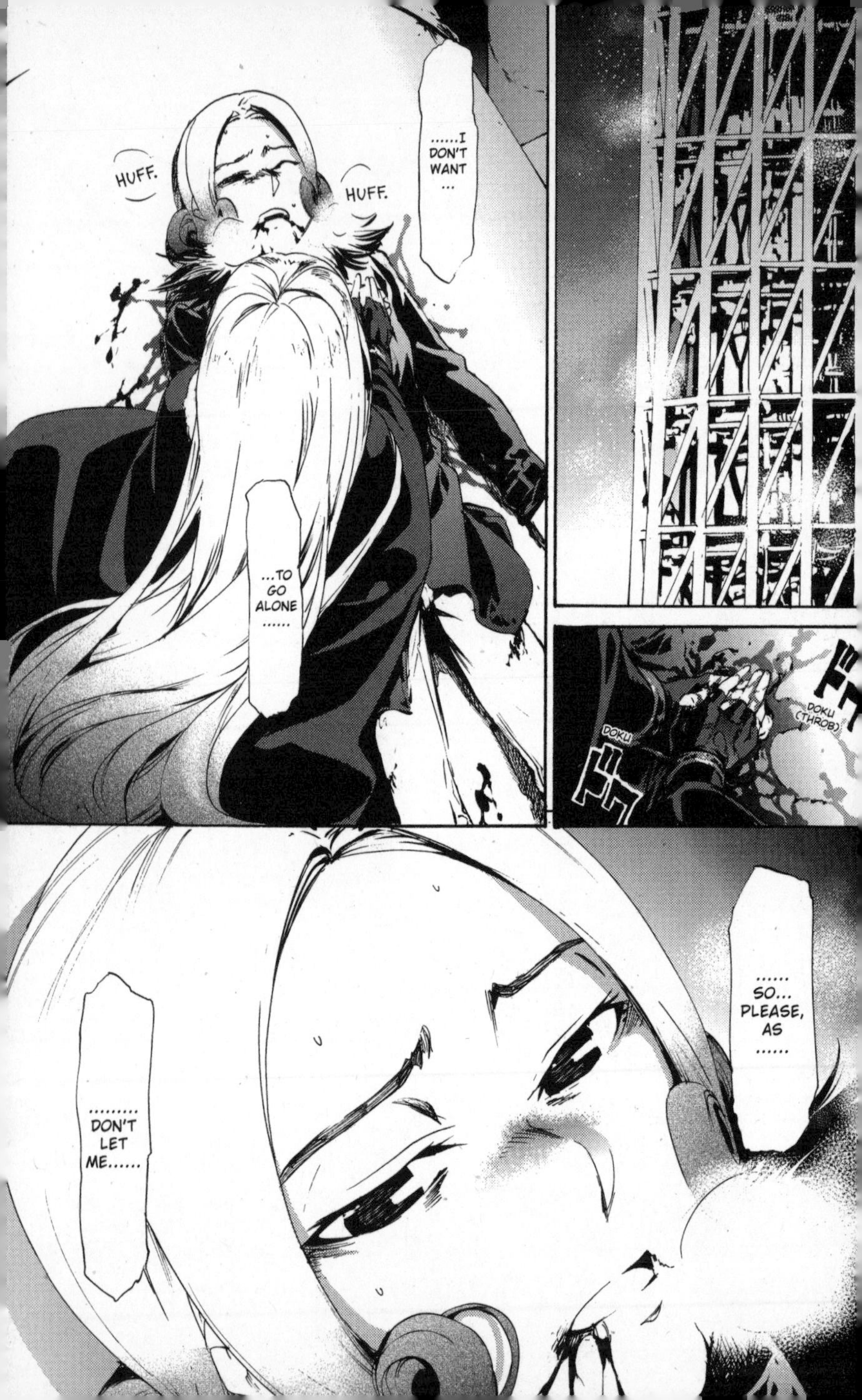
DOKU (THROB)
DOKU
......I DON'T WANT ...
HUFF.
HUFF.
...TO GO ALONE ......
......SO... PLEASE, AS ......
.........DON'T LET ME......

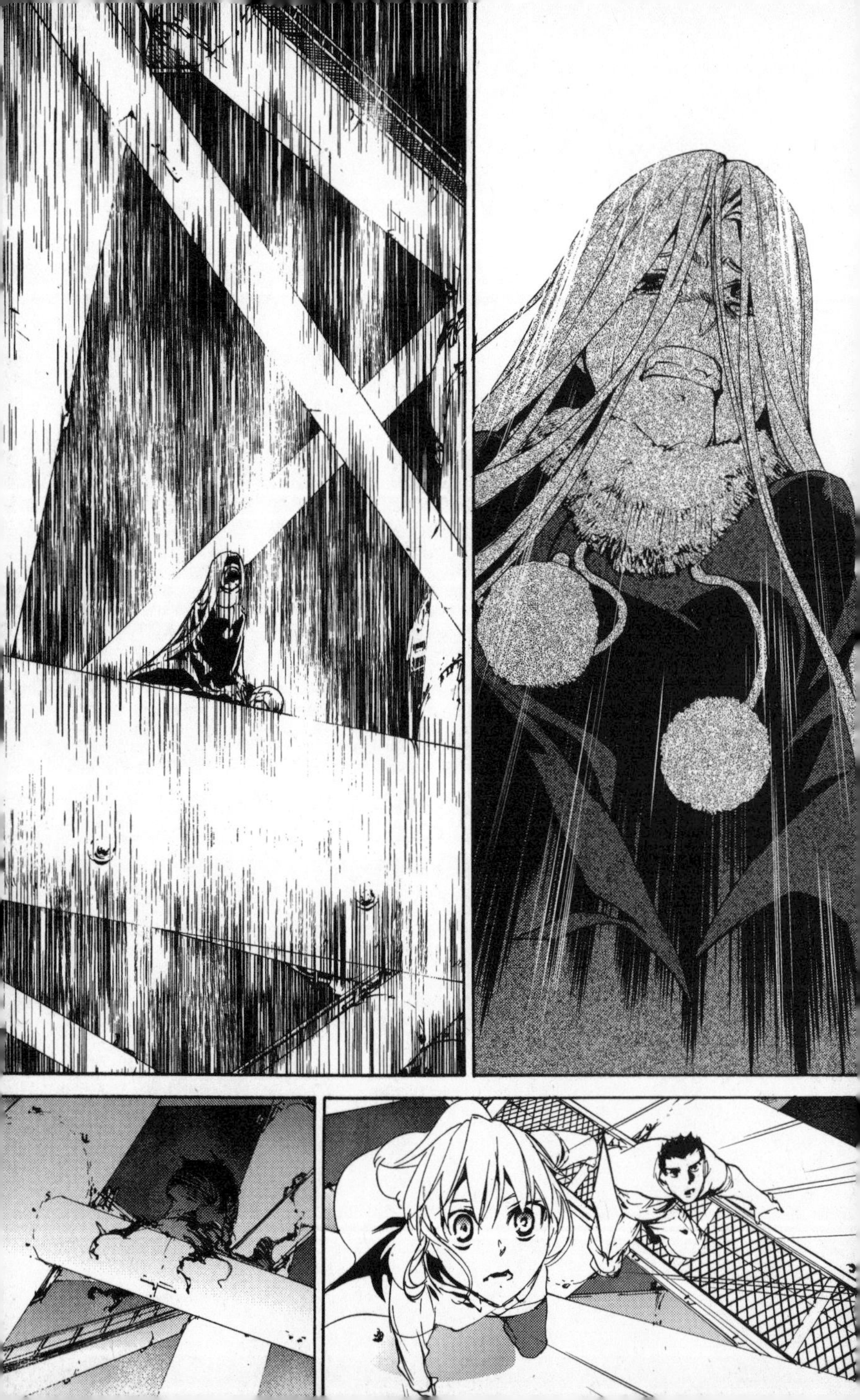

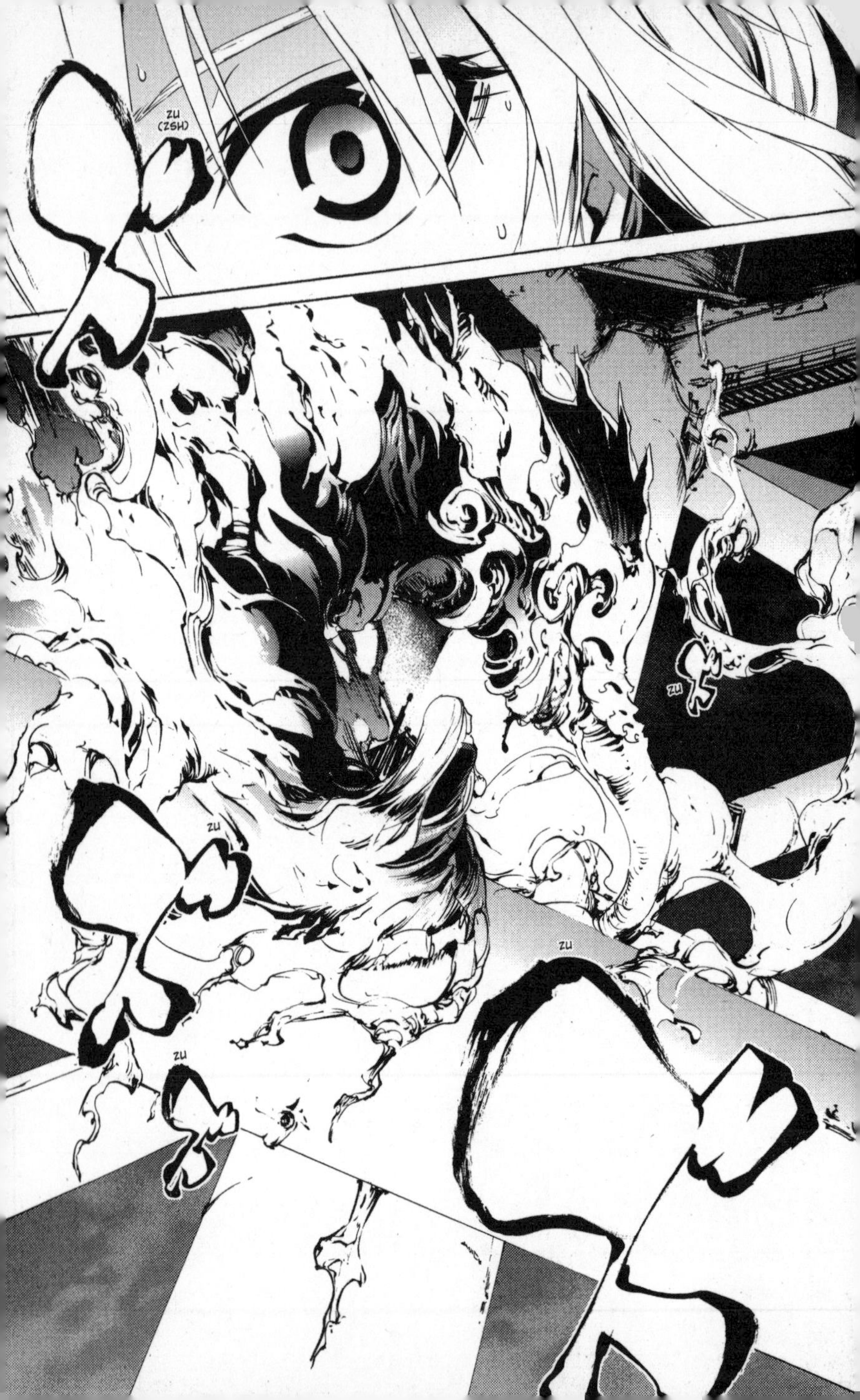
ZU
(ZSH)
ZU
ZU
ZU
ZU

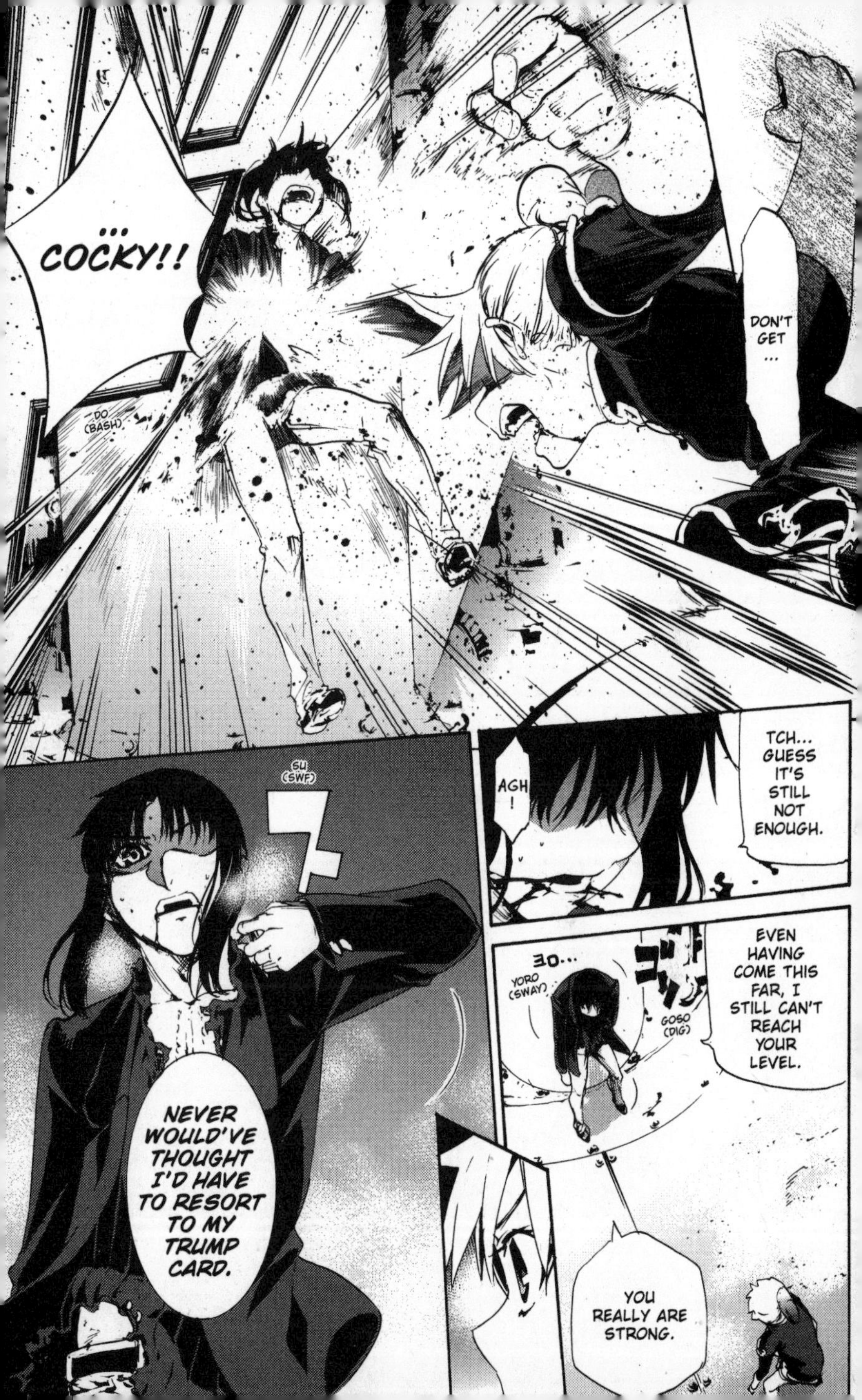
DON'T GET ...
... COCKY!!
DO (BASH)
TCH... GUESS IT'S STILL NOT ENOUGH.
AGH!
EVEN HAVING COME THIS FAR, I STILL CAN'T REACH YOUR LEVEL.
ヨロ...
YORO (SWAY)
GOSO (DIG)
YOU REALLY ARE STRONG.
SU (SWF)
NEVER WOULD'VE THOUGHT I'D HAVE TO RESORT TO MY TRUMP CARD.

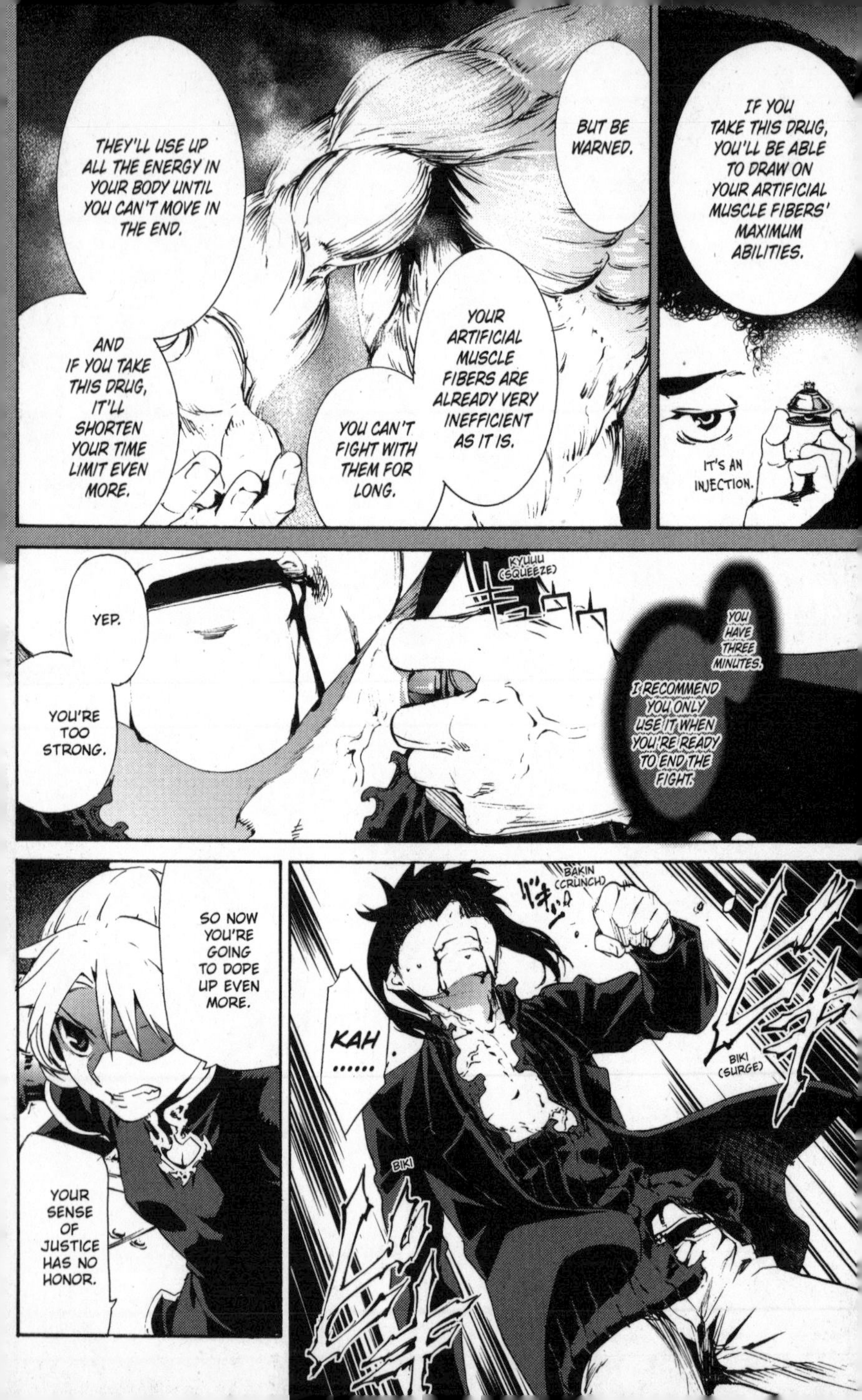
IF YOU TAKE THIS DRUG, YOU'LL BE ABLE TO DRAW ON YOUR ARTIFICIAL MUSCLE FIBERS' MAXIMUM ABILITIES.
IT'S AN INJECTION.
BUT BE WARNED.
YOUR ARTIFICIAL MUSCLE FIBERS ARE ALREADY VERY INEFFICIENT AS IT IS.
YOU CAN'T FIGHT WITH THEM FOR LONG.
THEY'LL USE UP ALL THE ENERGY IN YOUR BODY UNTIL YOU CAN'T MOVE IN THE END.
AND IF YOU TAKE THIS DRUG, IT'LL SHORTEN YOUR TIME LIMIT EVEN MORE.
YOU HAVE THREE MINUTES.
I RECOMMEND YOU ONLY USE IT WHEN YOU'RE READY TO END THE FIGHT.
KYUUU (SQUEEZE)
YEP.
YOU'RE TOO STRONG.
BAKIN (CRUNCH)
BIKI (SURGE)
KAH ......
BIKI
SO NOW YOU'RE GOING TO DOPE UP EVEN MORE.
YOUR SENSE OF JUSTICE HAS NO HONOR.

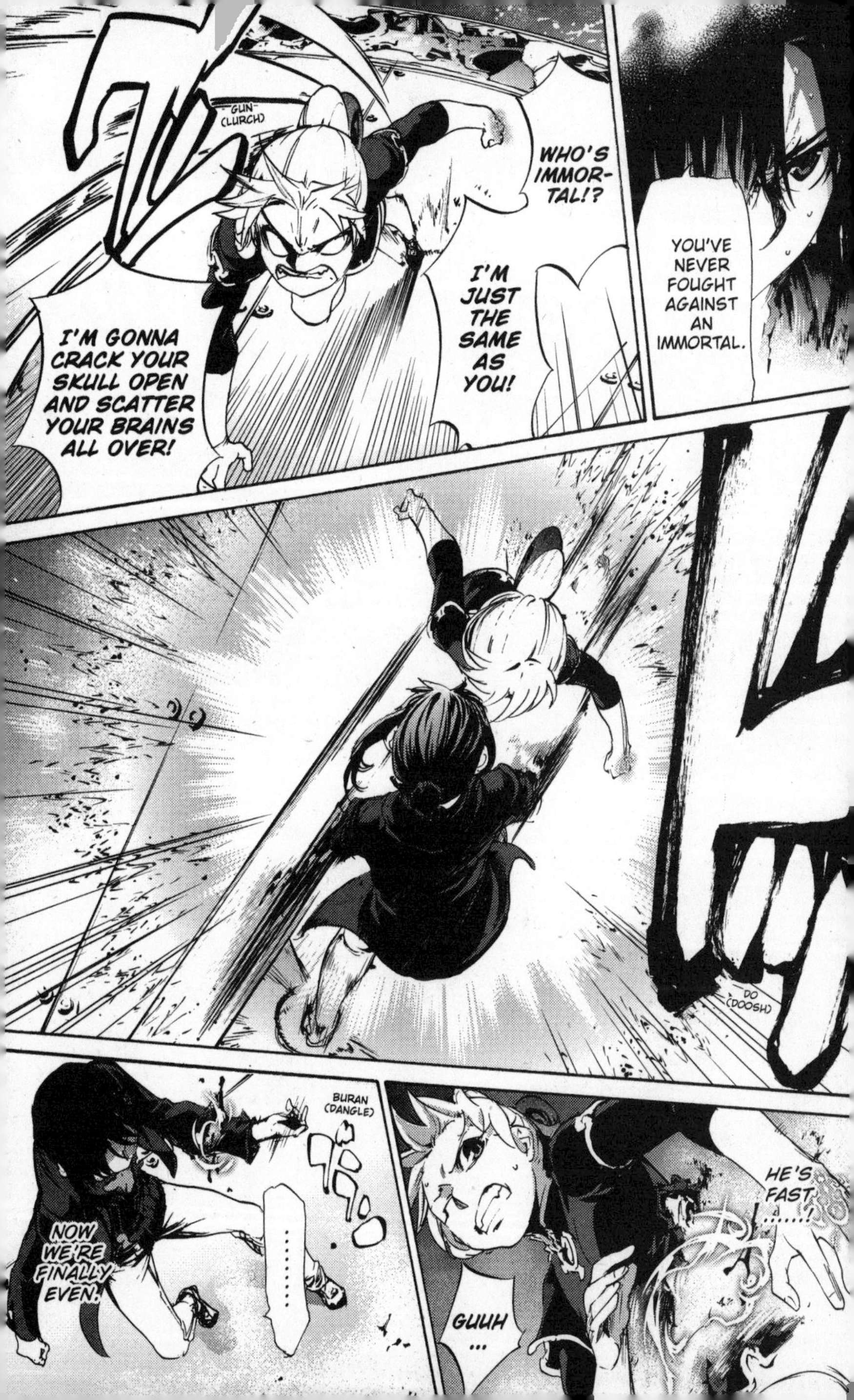
YOU'VE NEVER FOUGHT AGAINST AN IMMORTAL.
WHO'S IMMORTAL!?
I'M JUST THE SAME AS YOU!
GUN (LURCH)
I'M GONNA CRACK YOUR SKULL OPEN AND SCATTER YOUR BRAINS ALL OVER!
DO (DOOSH)
HE'S FAST......!
GUUH...
BURAN (DANGLE)
......
NOW WE'RE FINALLY EVEN.

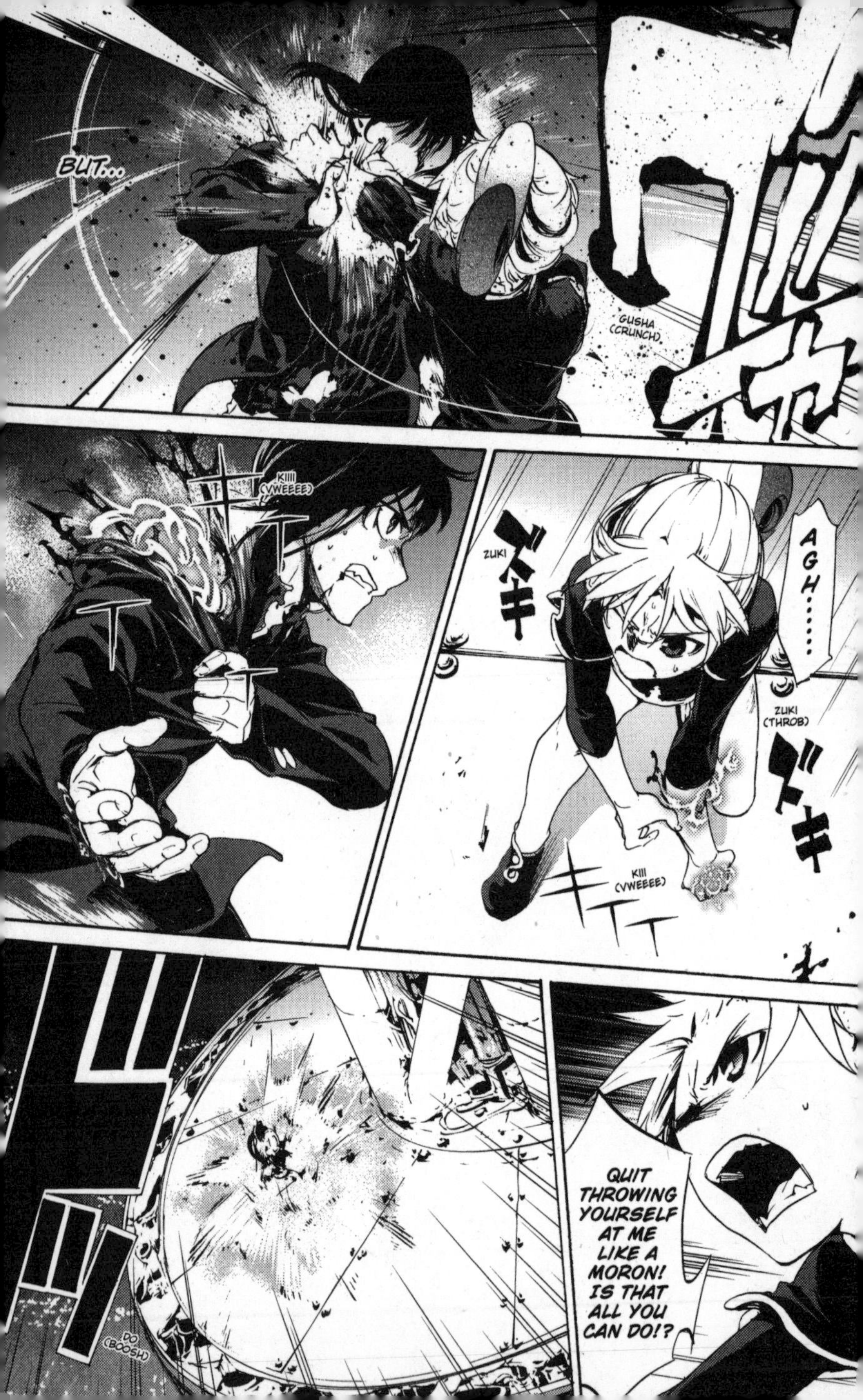
BUT...
GUSHA (CRUNCH)
ZUKI
AGH......
ZUKI (THROB)
KIII (VWEEEE)
KIIII (VWEEEE)
QUIT THROWING YOURSELF AT ME LIKE A MORON! IS THAT ALL YOU CAN DO!?
DO (BOOSH)

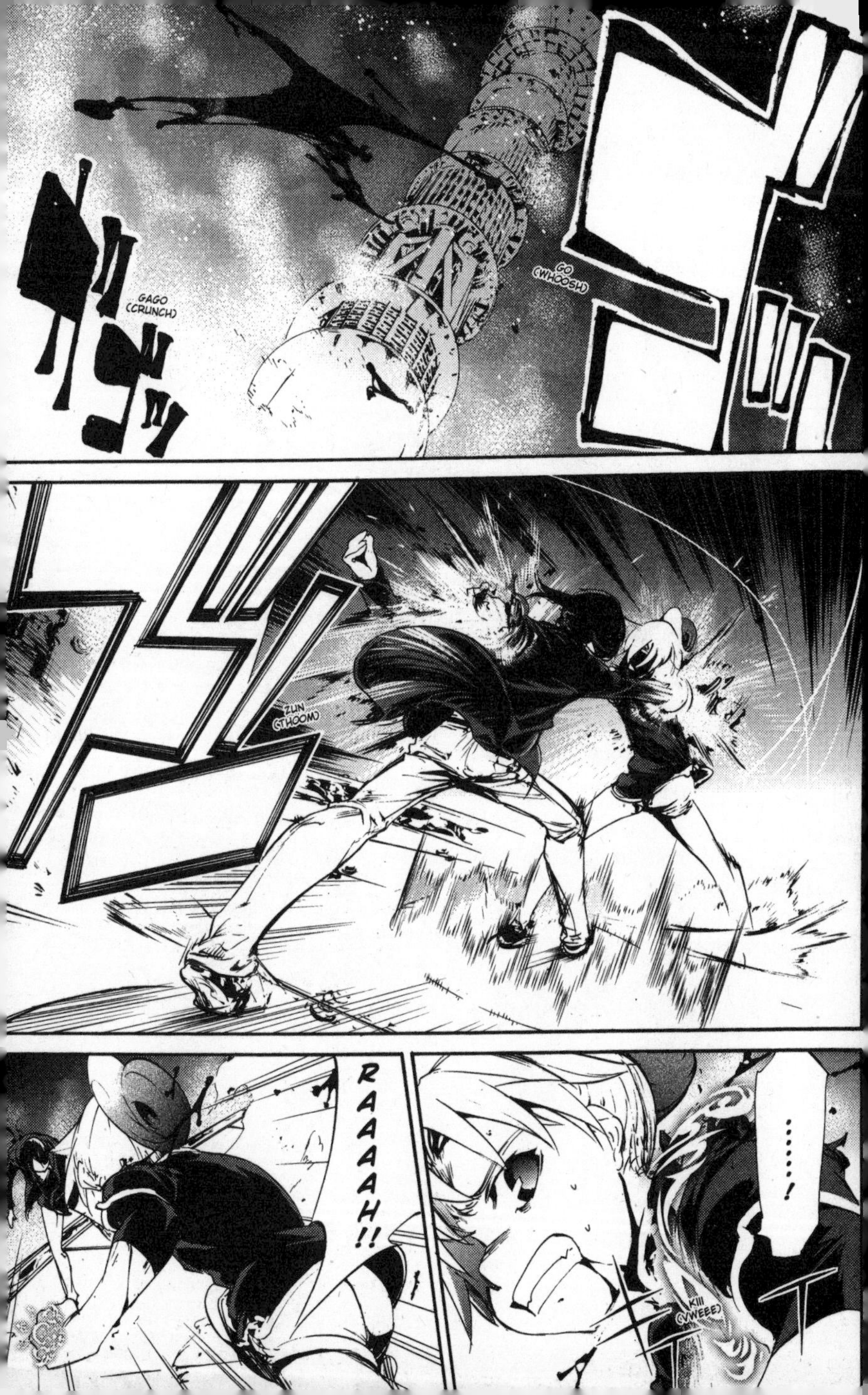
GO (WHOOSH)
GAGO (CRUNCH)
ZUN (THOOM)
......!
KIII (VWEEE)
RAAAAAH!!

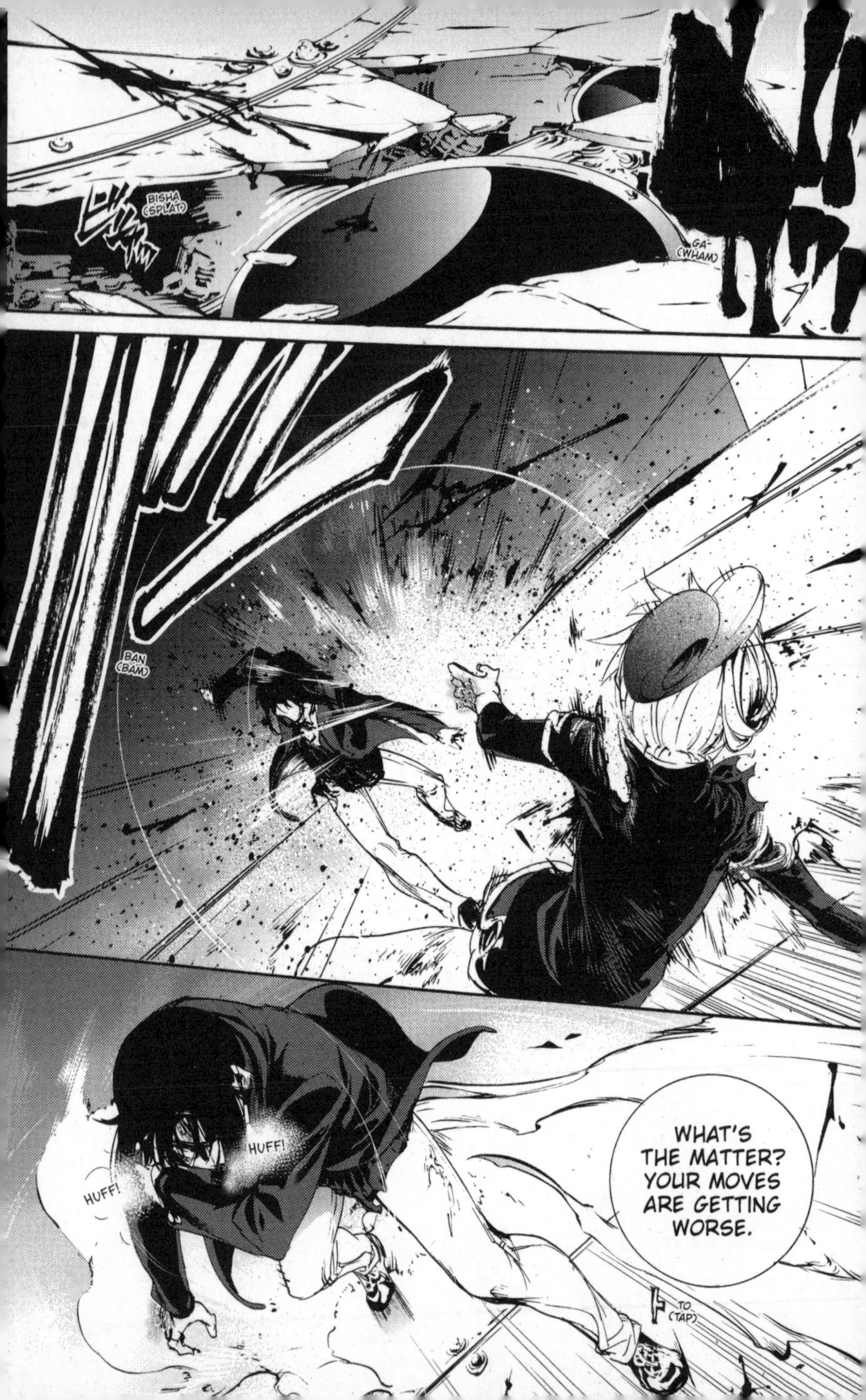
GA-
(WHAM)
BISHA
(SPLAT)
BAN
(BAM)
WHAT'S THE MATTER? YOUR MOVES ARE GETTING WORSE.
TO
(TAP)
HUFF!
HUFF!

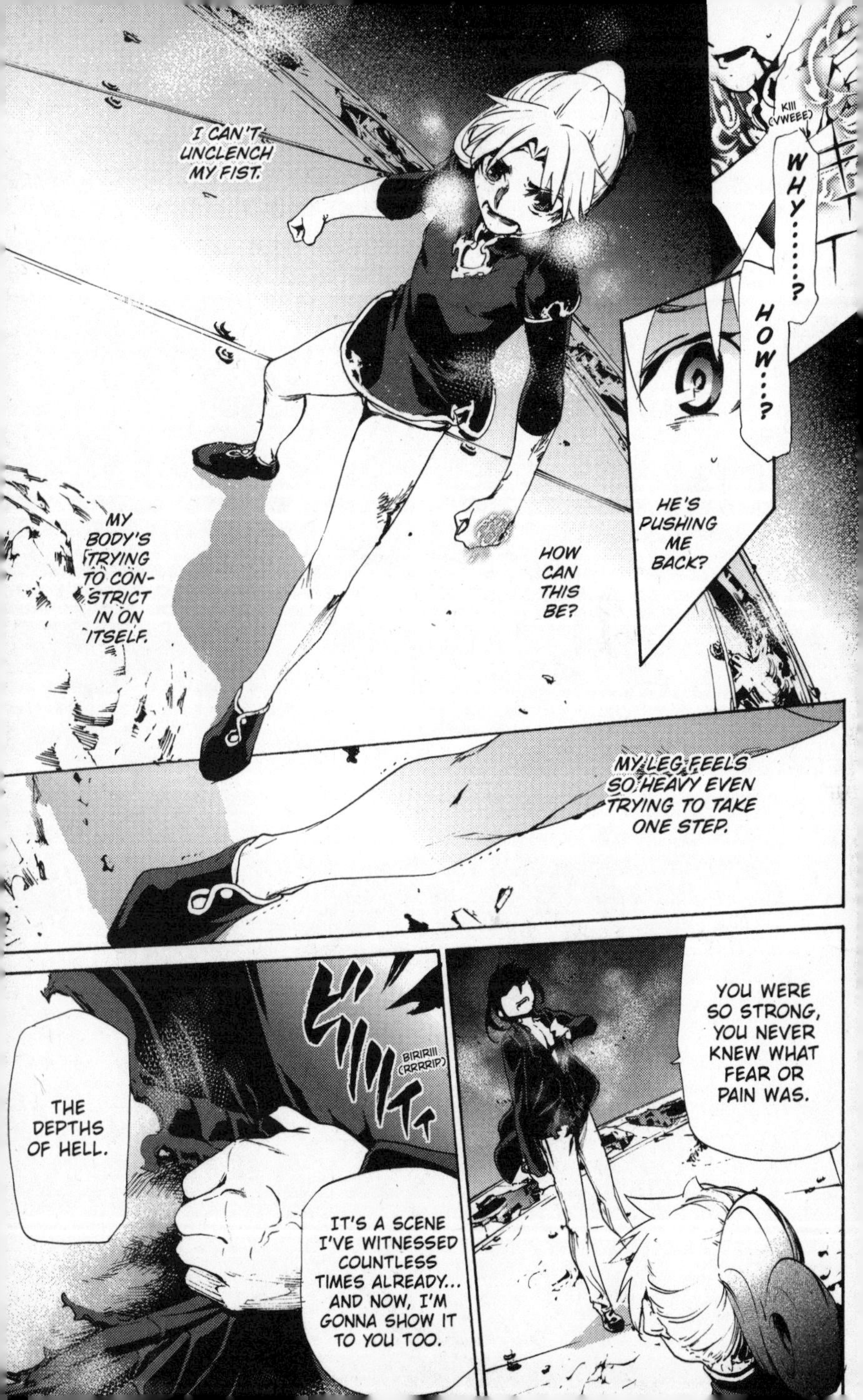
KIII (VWEEE)
WHY.....?
HOW...?
HE'S PUSHING ME BACK?
HOW CAN THIS BE?
I CAN'T UNCLENCH MY FIST.
MY BODY'S TRYING TO CON-STRICT IN ON ITSELF.
MY LEG FEELS SO HEAVY EVEN TRYING TO TAKE ONE STEP.
YOU WERE SO STRONG, YOU NEVER KNEW WHAT FEAR OR PAIN WAS.
BIRIRIII (RRRRIP)
IT'S A SCENE I'VE WITNESSED COUNTLESS TIMES ALREADY... AND NOW, I'M GONNA SHOW IT TO YOU TOO.
THE DEPTHS OF HELL.

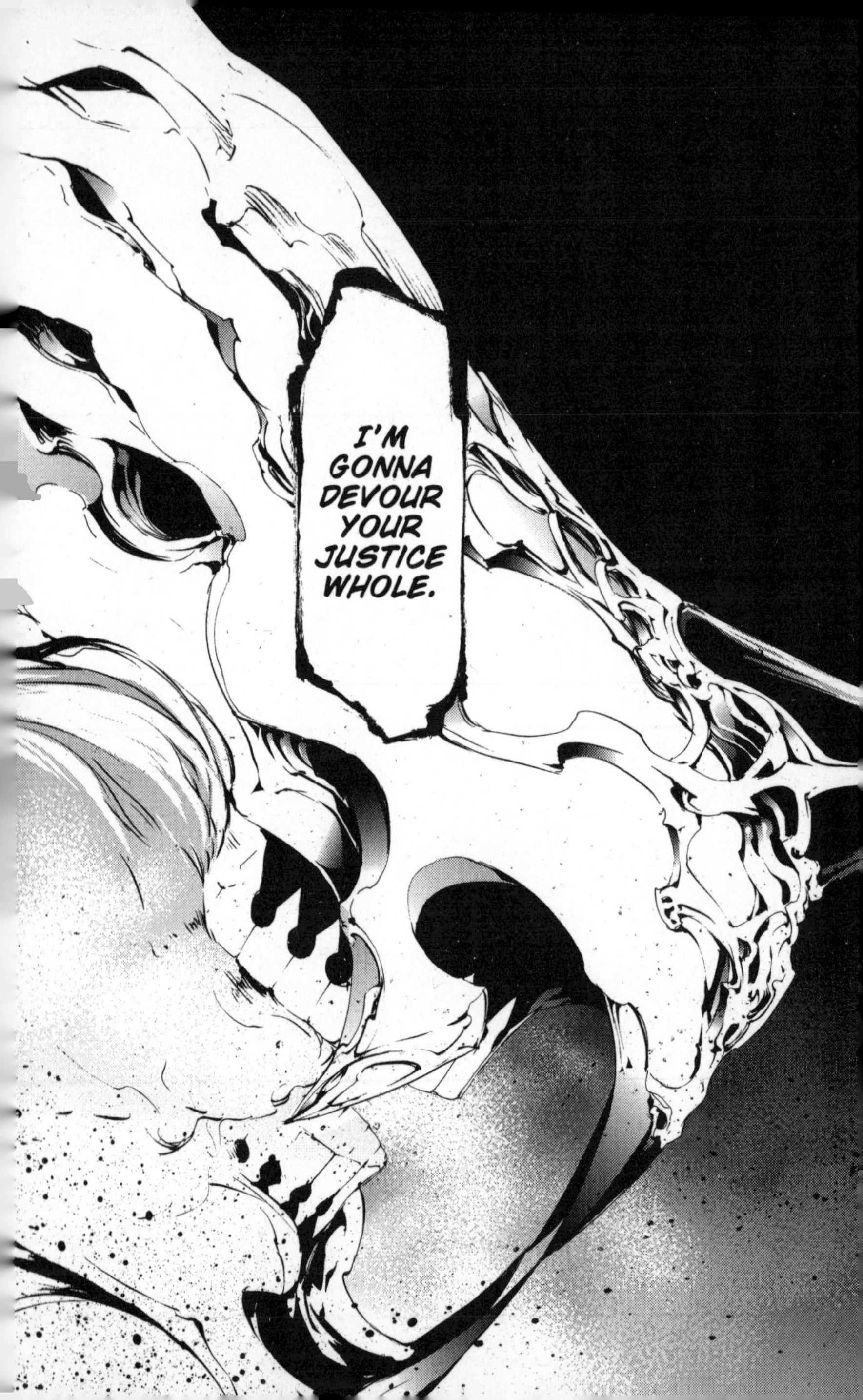
I'M GONNA DEVOUR YOUR JUSTICE WHOLE.

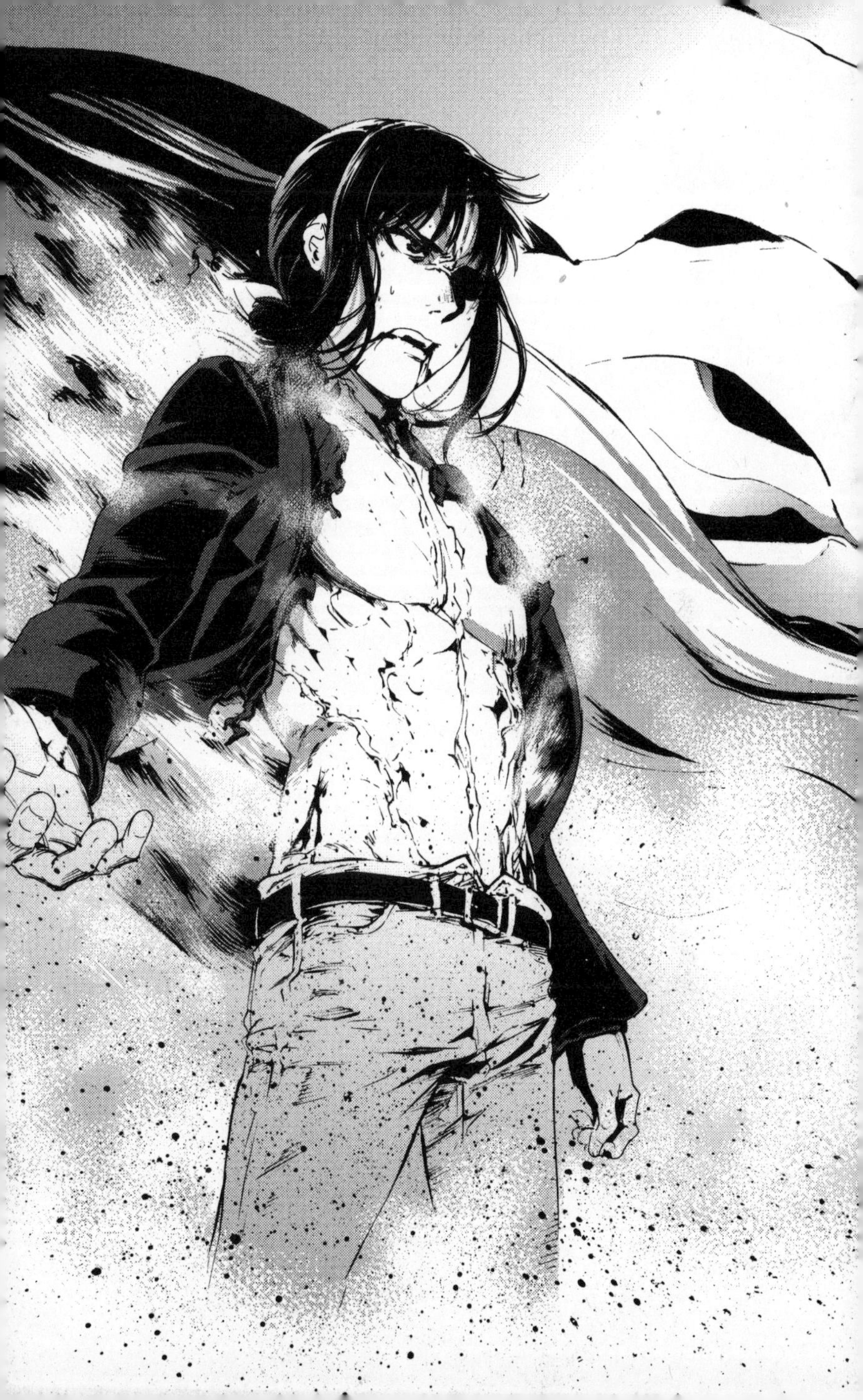

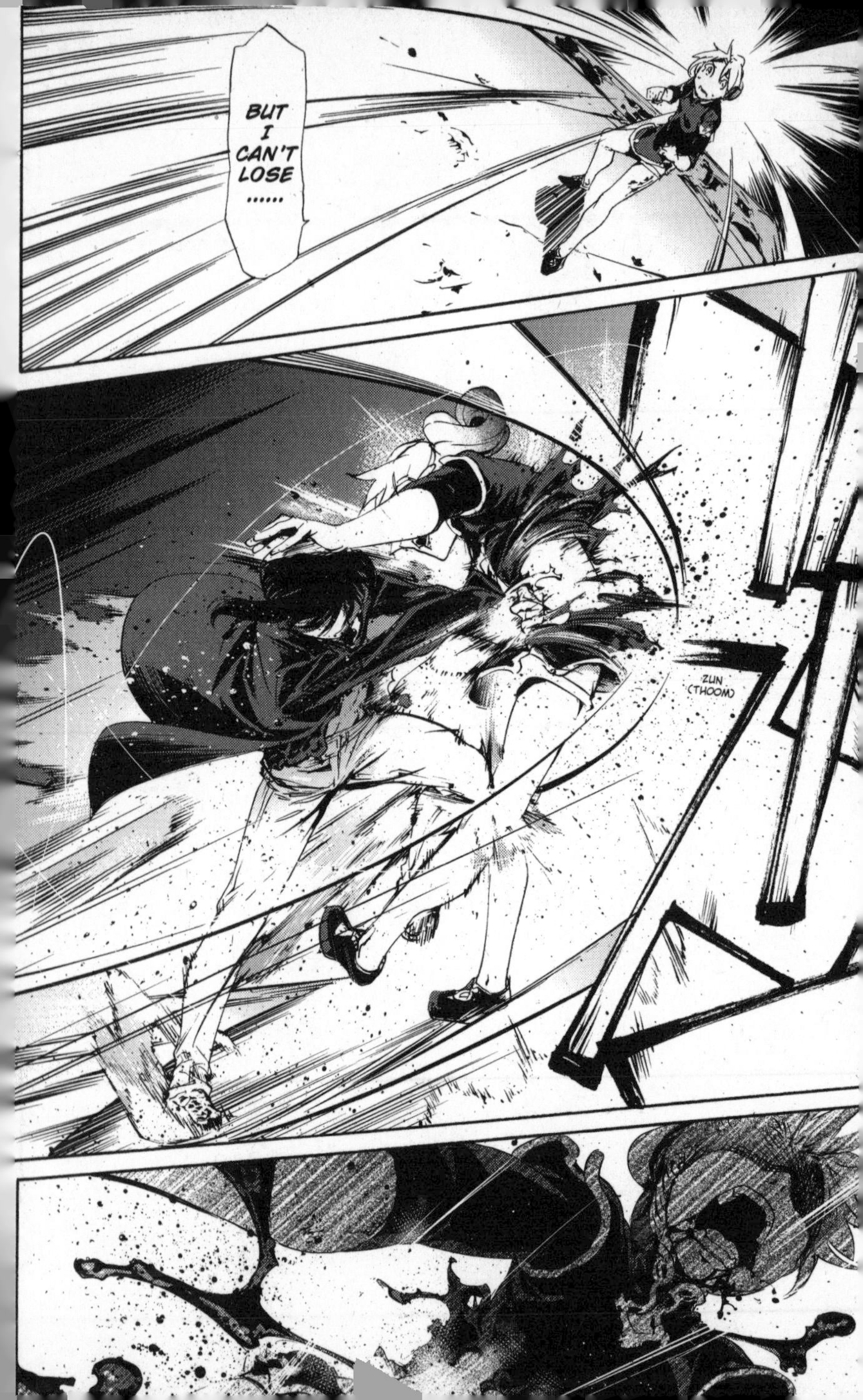
BUT I CAN'T LOSE ......
ZUN (THOOM)

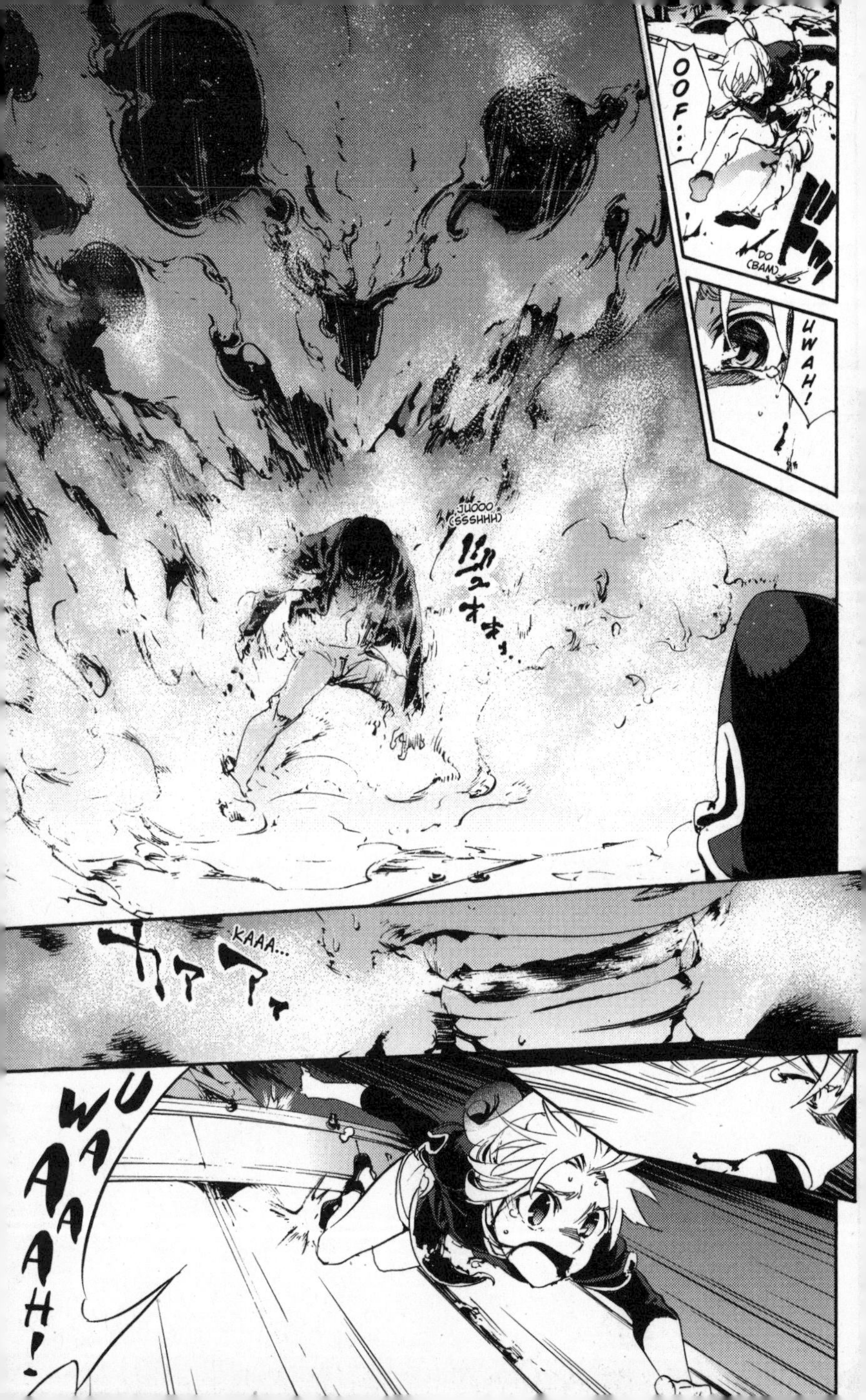
OOF...
DO (BAM)
UWAH!
JUOOO (SSSHHH)
KAAA...
UWAAAAAH!

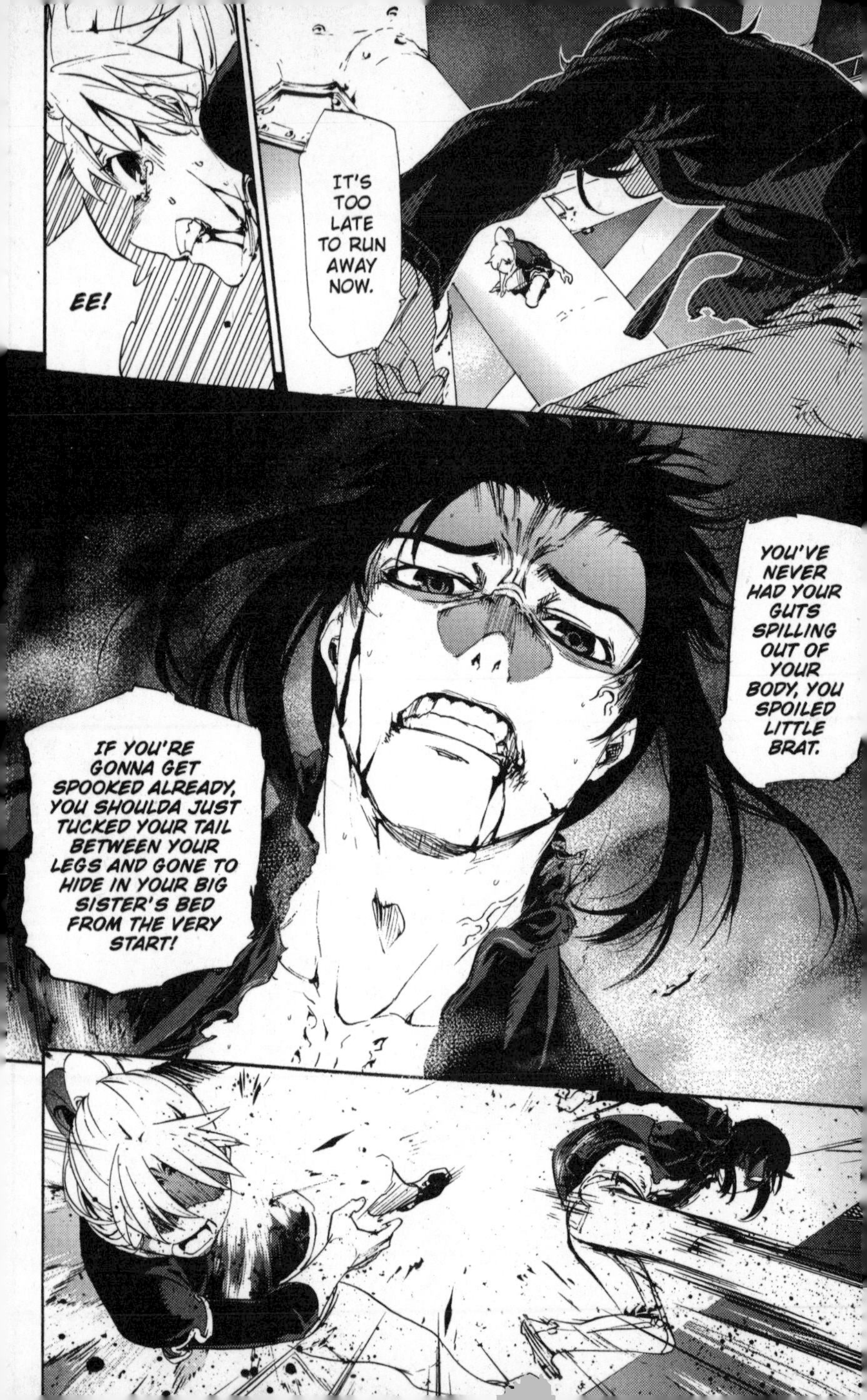
IT'S TOO LATE TO RUN AWAY NOW.
EE!
YOU'VE NEVER HAD YOUR GUTS SPILLING OUT OF YOUR BODY, YOU SPOILED LITTLE BRAT.
IF YOU'RE GONNA GET SPOOKED ALREADY, YOU SHOULDA JUST TUCKED YOUR TAIL BETWEEN YOUR LEGS AND GONE TO HIDE IN YOUR BIG SISTER'S BED FROM THE VERY START!

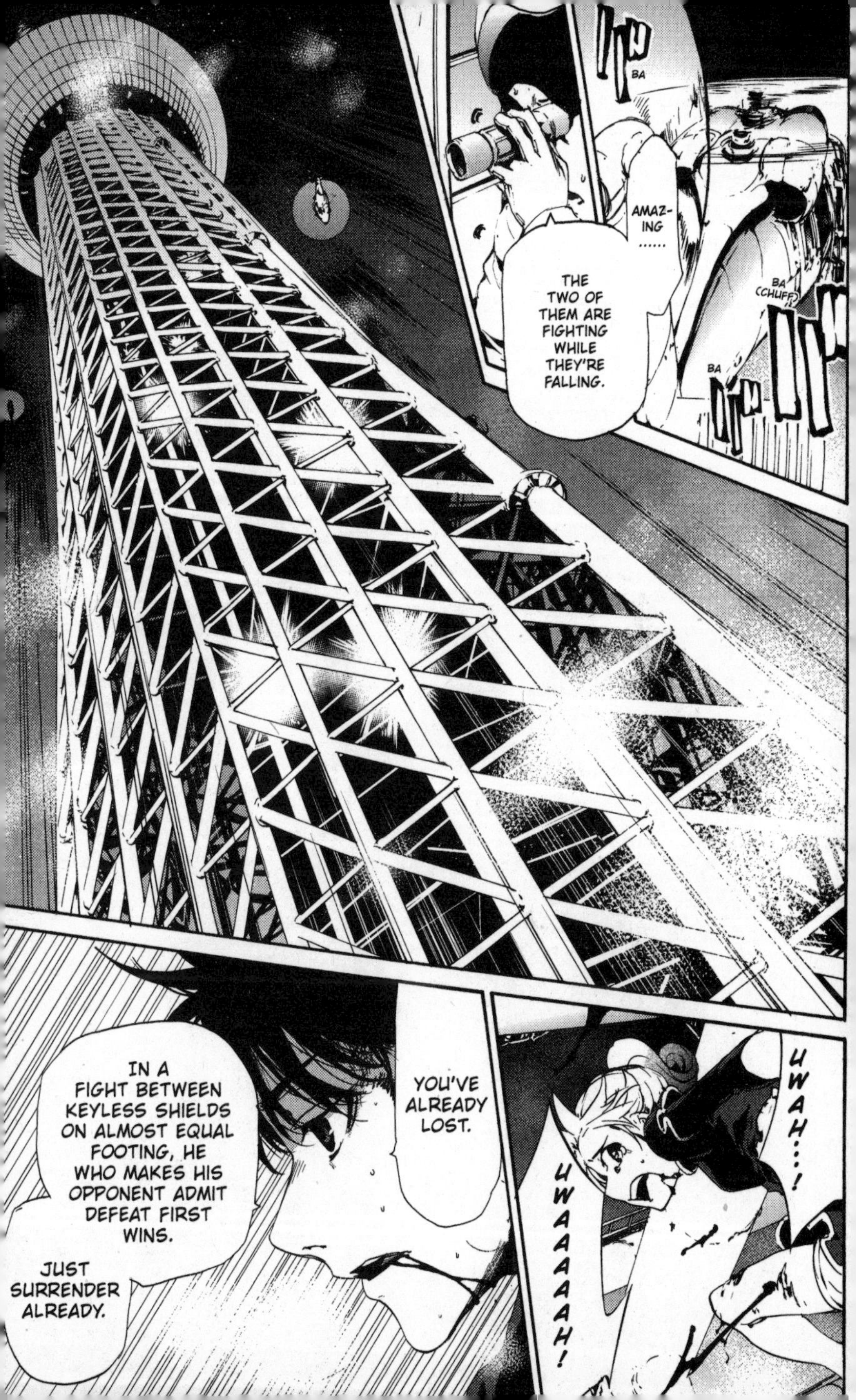
BA
AMAZ-ING ......
THE TWO OF THEM ARE FIGHTING WHILE THEY'RE FALLING.
BA (CHUFF)
BA
UWAH...!
UWAAAAAAH!
YOU'VE ALREADY LOST.
IN A FIGHT BETWEEN KEYLESS SHIELDS ON ALMOST EQUAL FOOTING, HE WHO MAKES HIS OPPONENT ADMIT DEFEAT FIRST WINS.
JUST SURRENDER ALREADY.

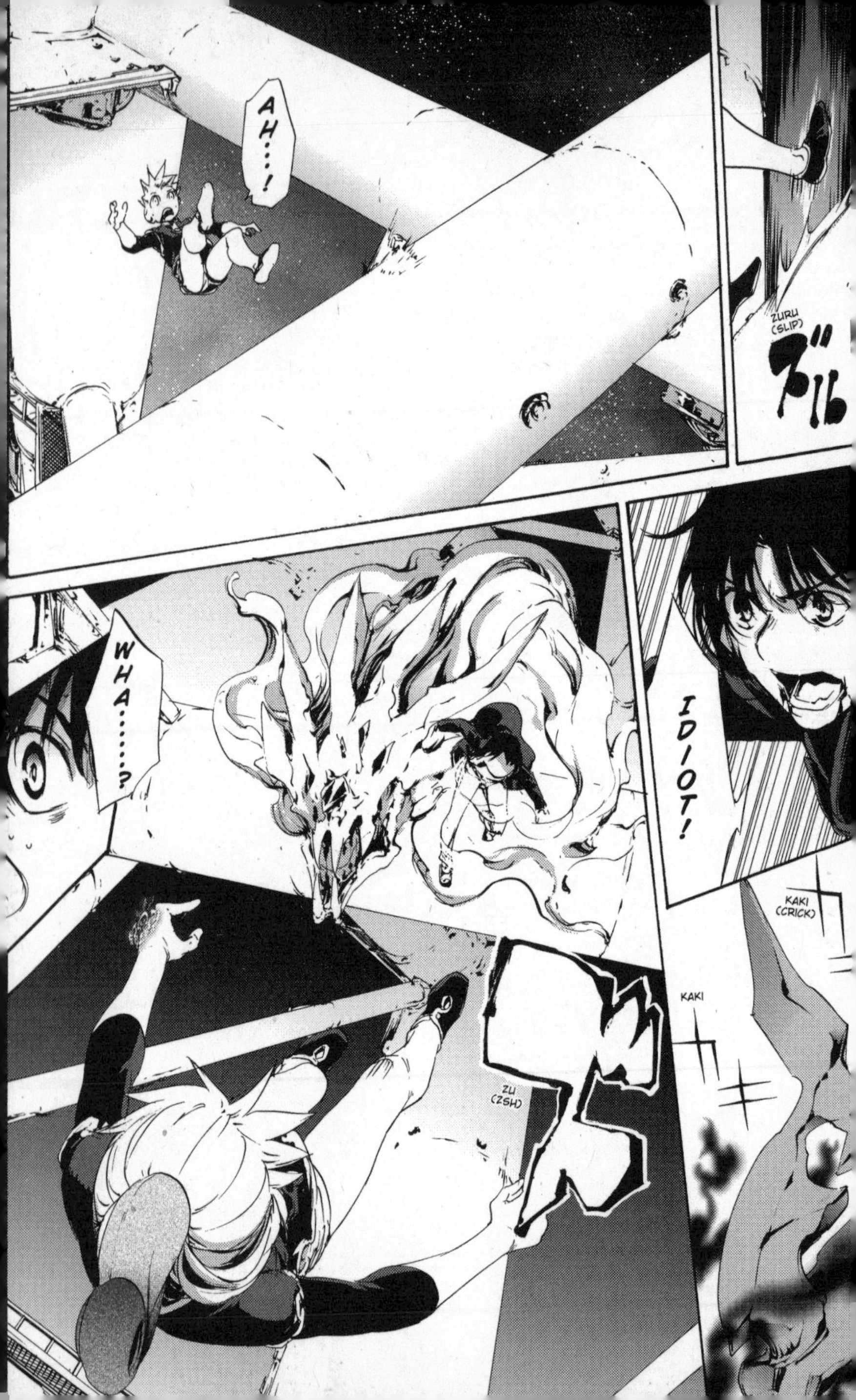

ZURU (SLIP)
ズル
AH...!
IDIOT!
WHA.....?
KAKI (CRICK)
KAKI
ZU (ZSH)

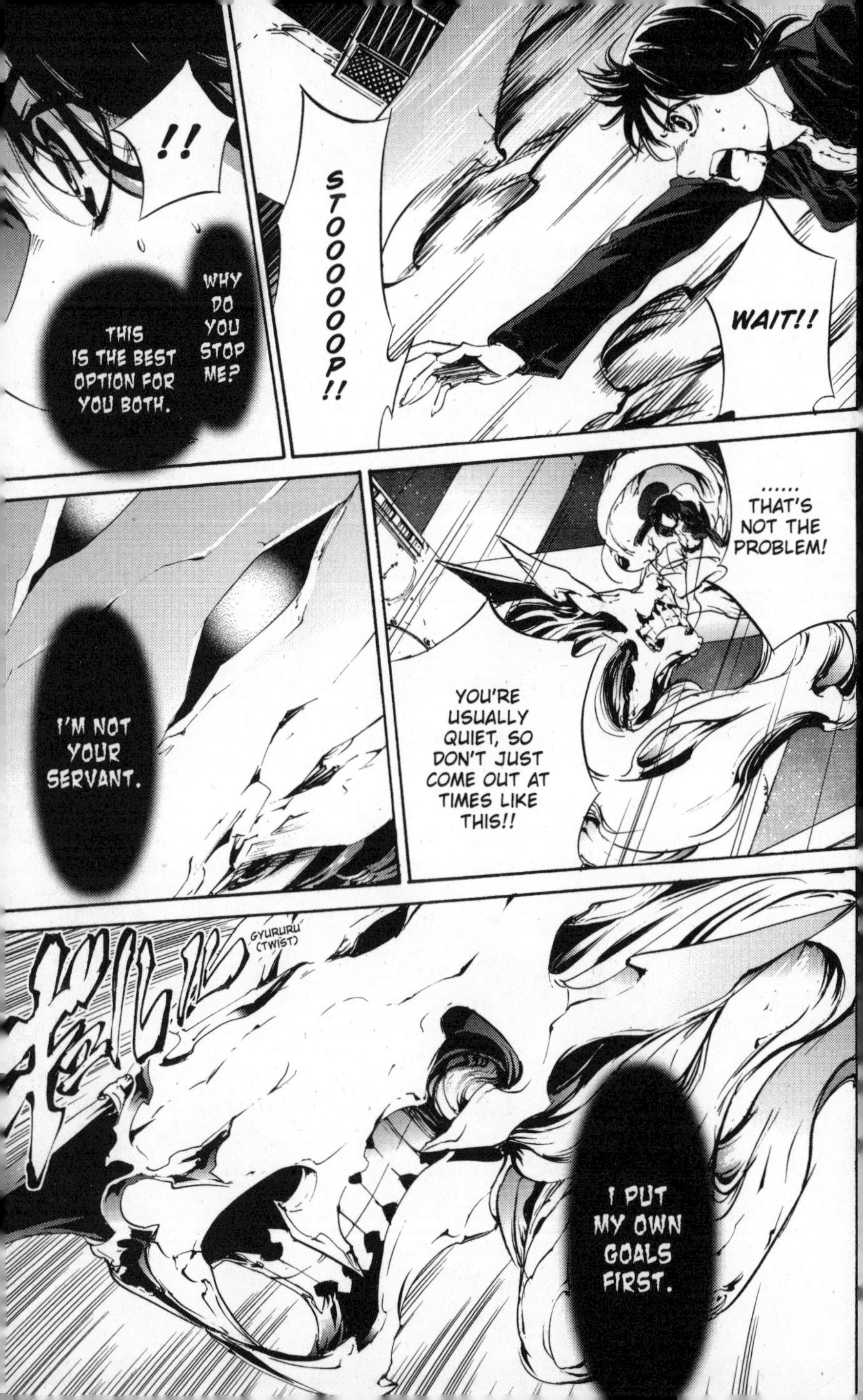
WAIT!!
STOOOOOOOP!!
!!
WHY DO YOU STOP ME?
THIS IS THE BEST OPTION FOR YOU BOTH.
......THAT'S NOT THE PROBLEM!
YOU'RE USUALLY QUIET, SO DON'T JUST COME OUT AT TIMES LIKE THIS!!
I'M NOT YOUR SERVANT.
GYURURU (TWIST)
I PUT MY OWN GOALS FIRST.

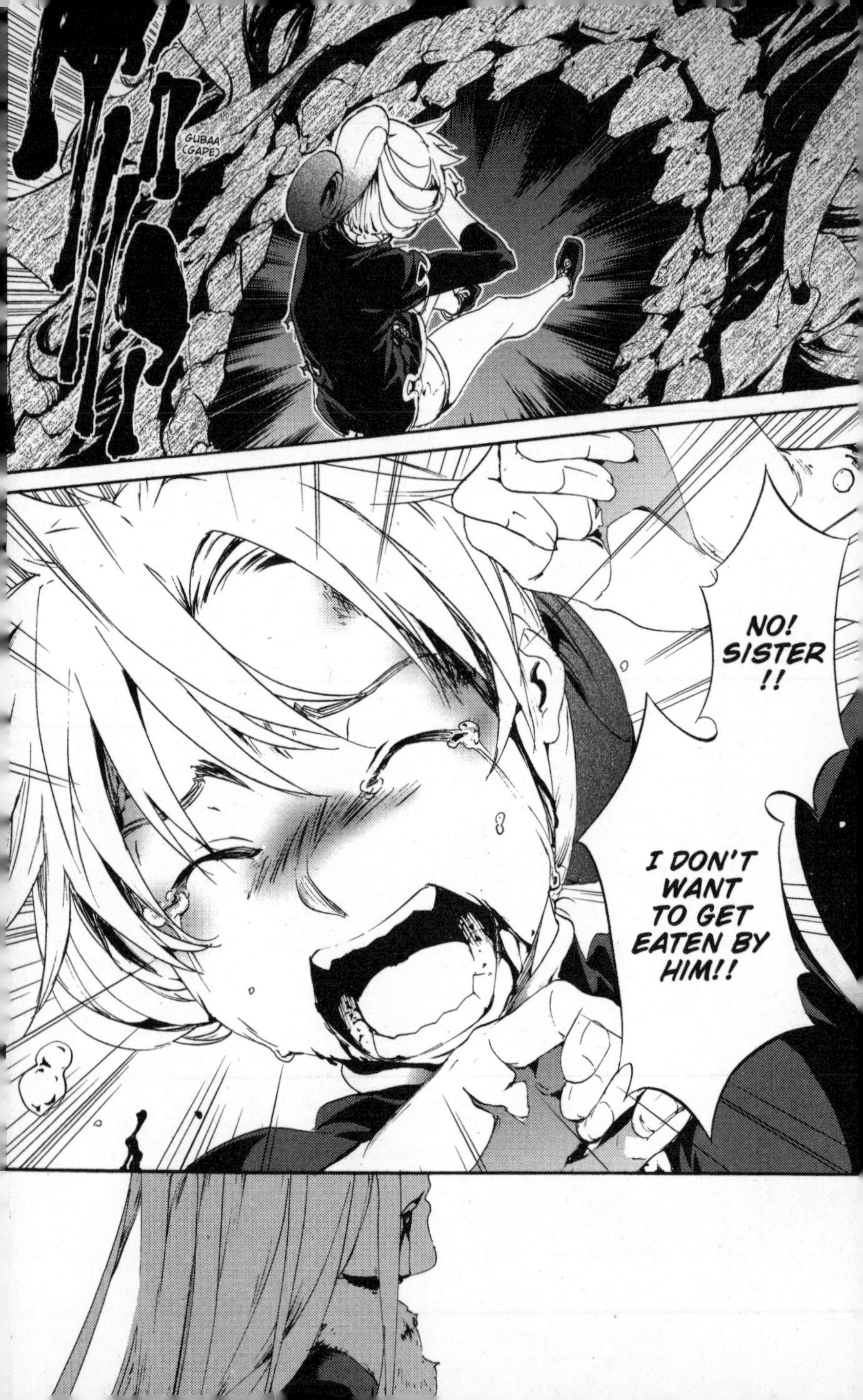
GUBAA (GAPE)
NO! SISTER !!
I DON'T WANT TO GET EATEN BY HIM!!

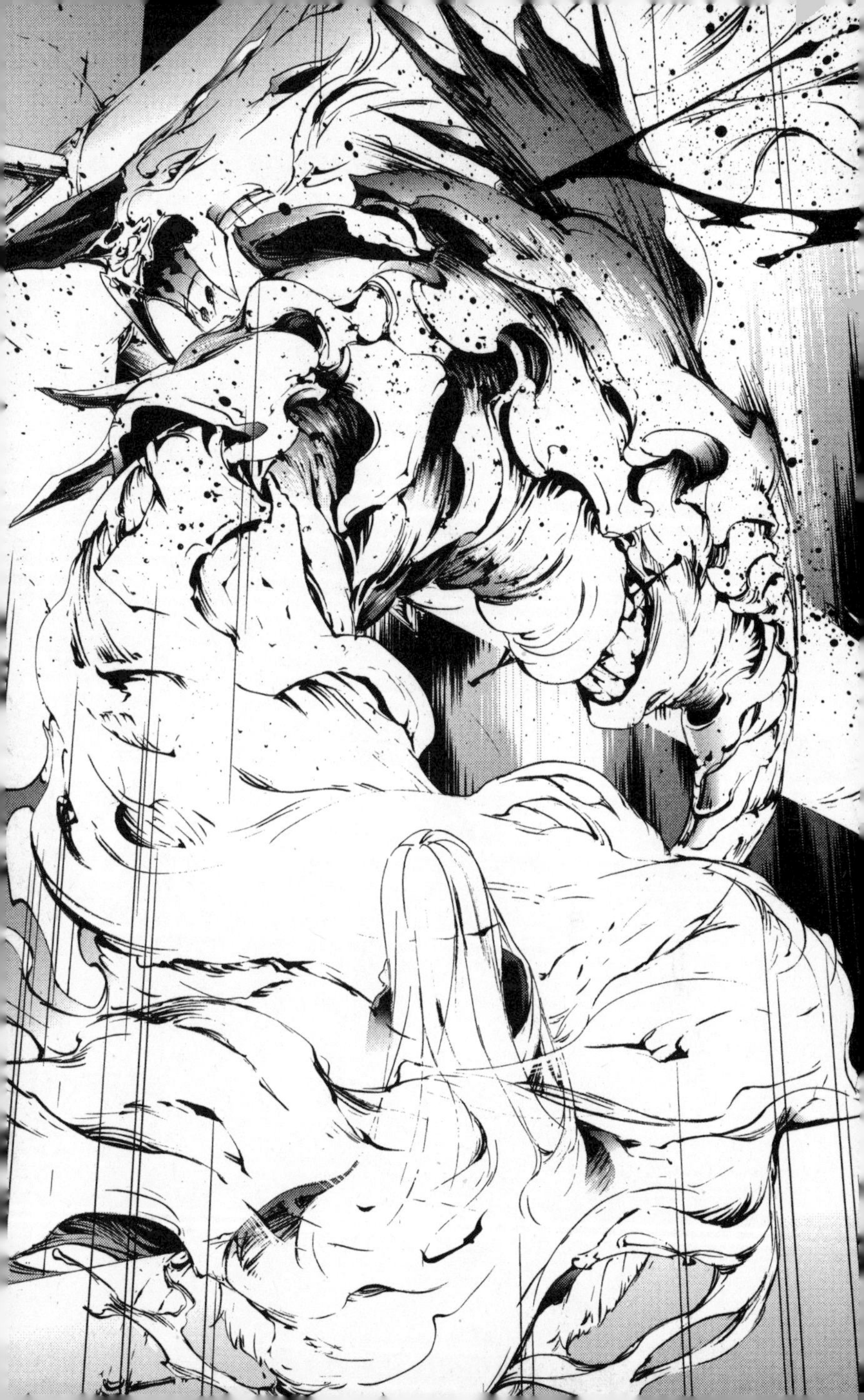

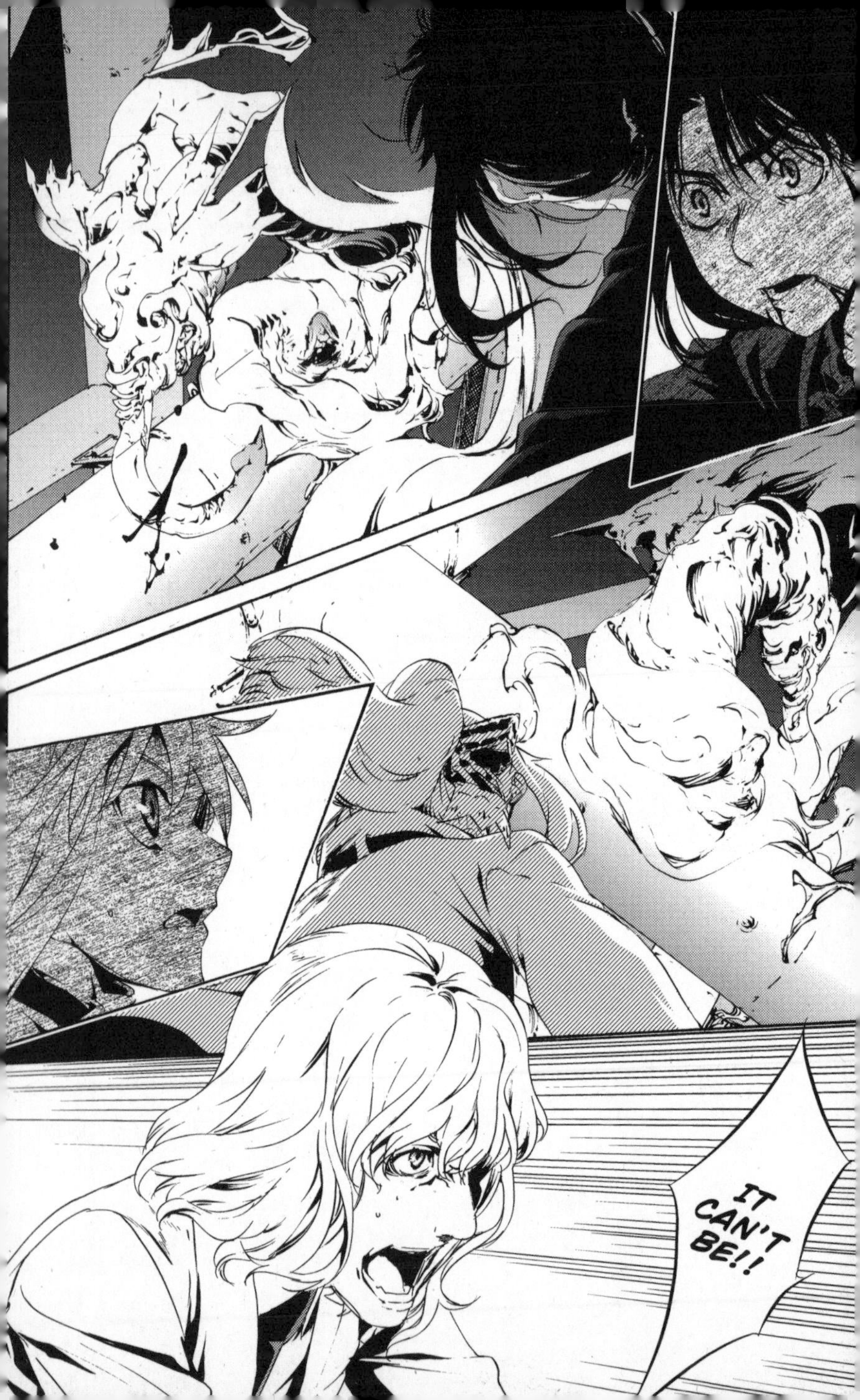
IT CAN'T BE!!

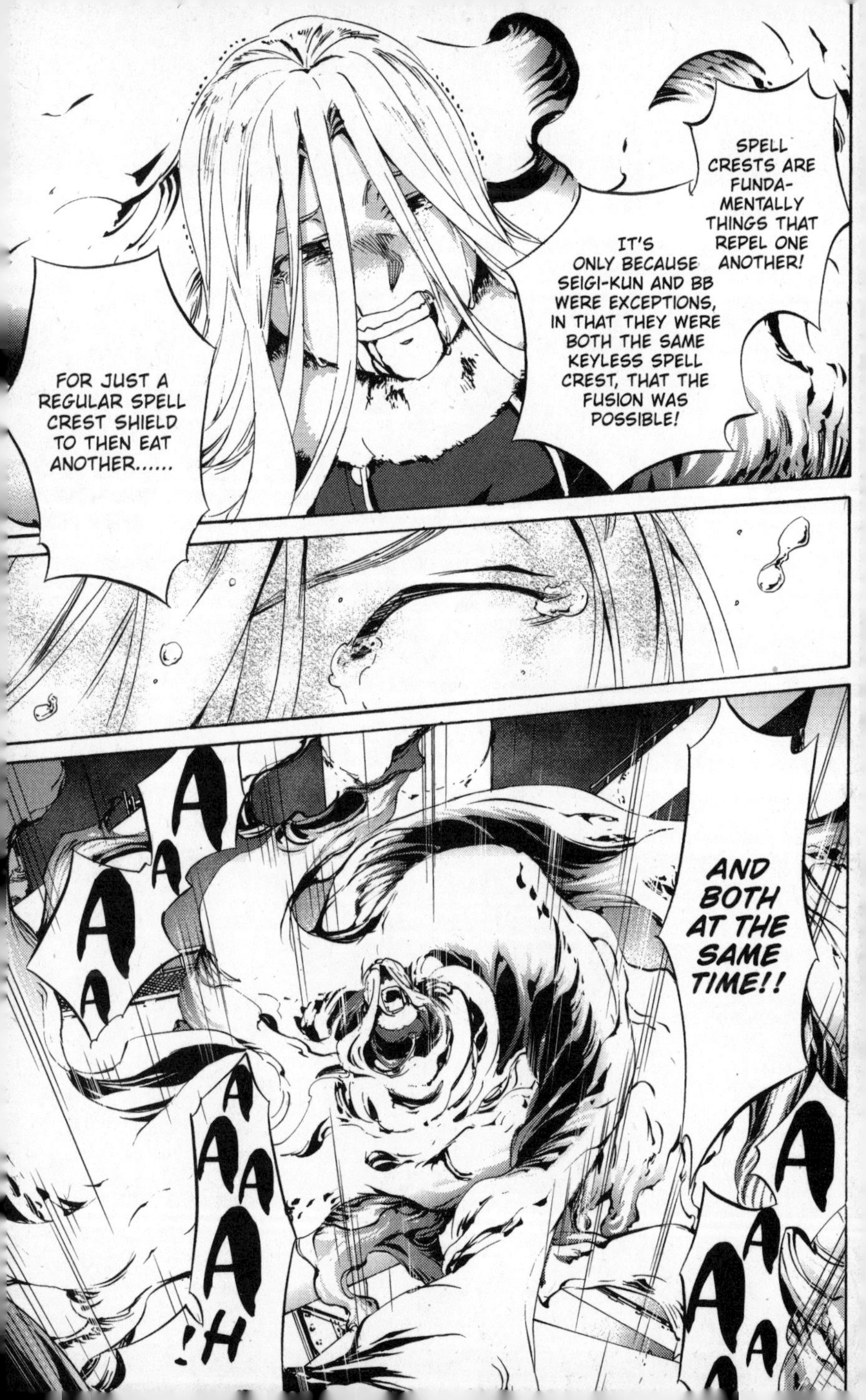
SPELL CRESTS ARE FUNDA-MENTALLY THINGS THAT REPEL ONE ANOTHER!
IT'S ONLY BECAUSE SEIGI-KUN AND BB WERE EXCEPTIONS, IN THAT THEY WERE BOTH THE SAME KEYLESS SPELL CREST, THAT THE FUSION WAS POSSIBLE!
FOR JUST A REGULAR SPELL CREST SHIELD TO THEN EAT ANOTHER......
AND BOTH AT THE SAME TIME!!
AAAAA
AAAAAA
AAAAAH!

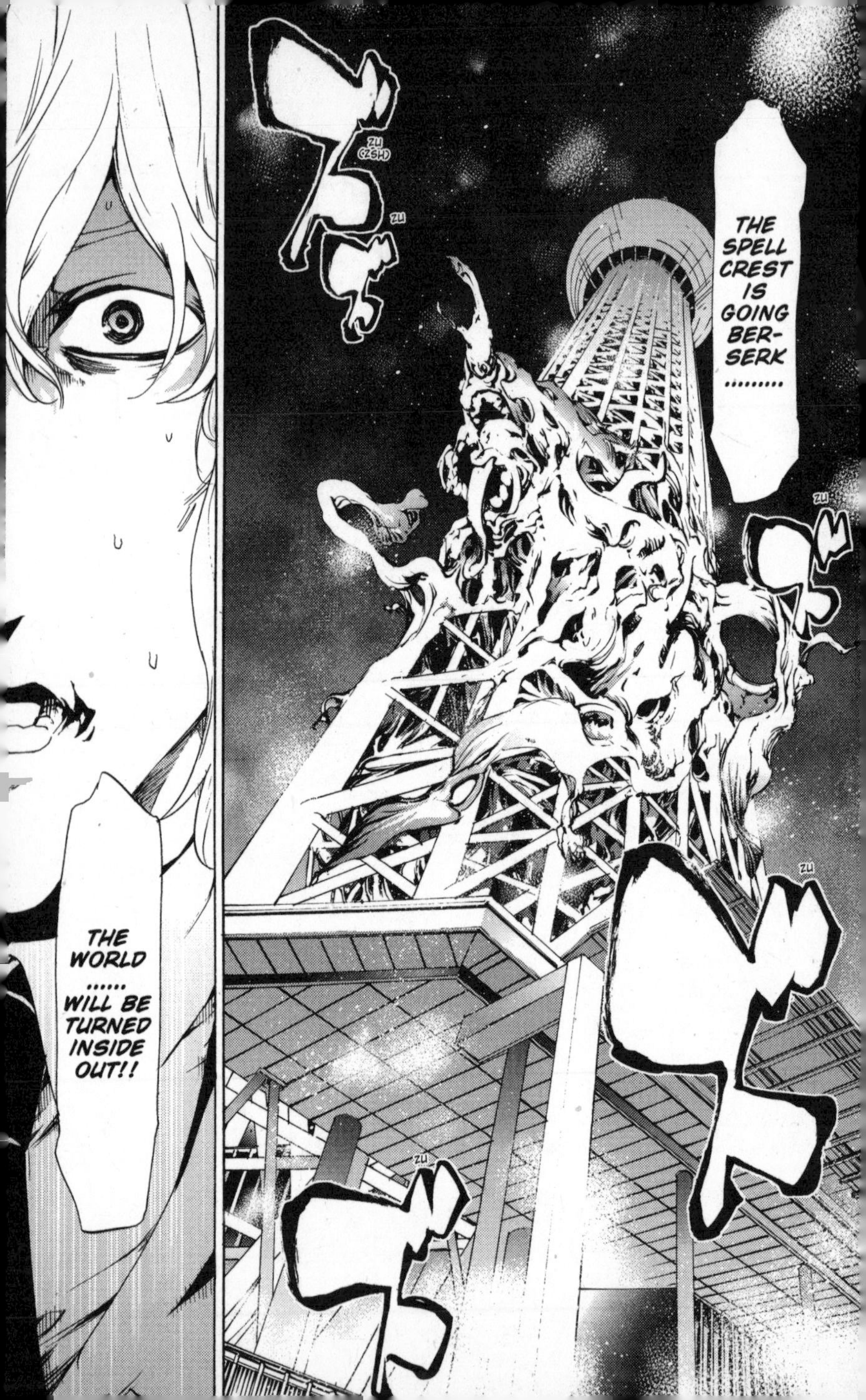
THE SPELL CREST IS GOING BER-SERK ....
ZU
ZU (ZSH)
ZU
ZU
ZU
THE WORLD ...... WILL BE TURNED INSIDE OUT!!

TABOO TATTOO

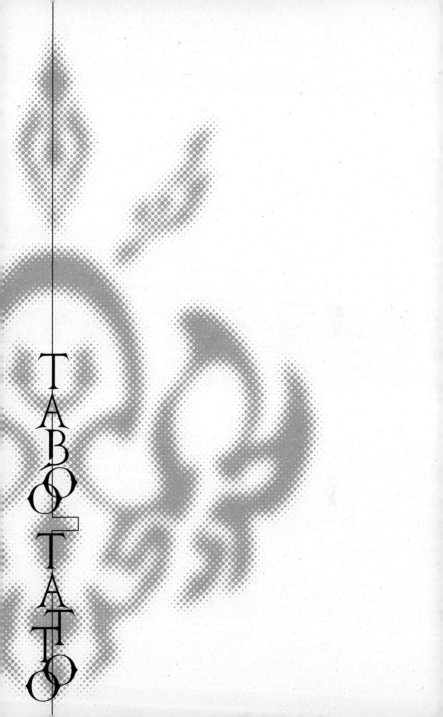

TABOO TATTOO

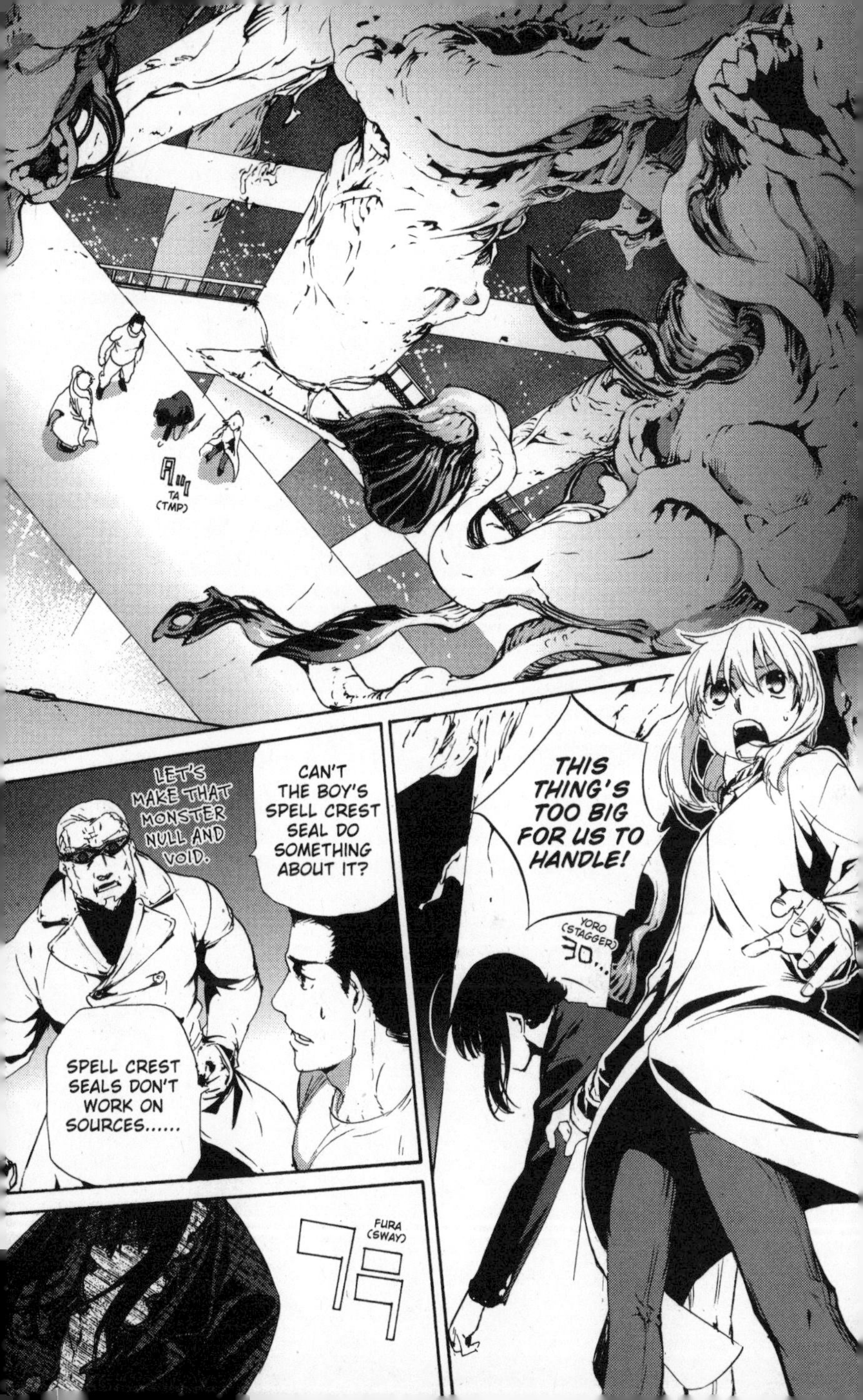

TA (TMP)
THIS THING'S TOO BIG FOR US TO HANDLE!
YORO (STAGGER)
CAN'T THE BOY'S SPELL CREST SEAL DO SOMETHING ABOUT IT?
LET'S MAKE THAT MONSTER NULL AND VOID.
SPELL CREST SEALS DON'T WORK ON SOURCES......
FURA (SWAY)

#55 DESCENT

TABOOTATTOO

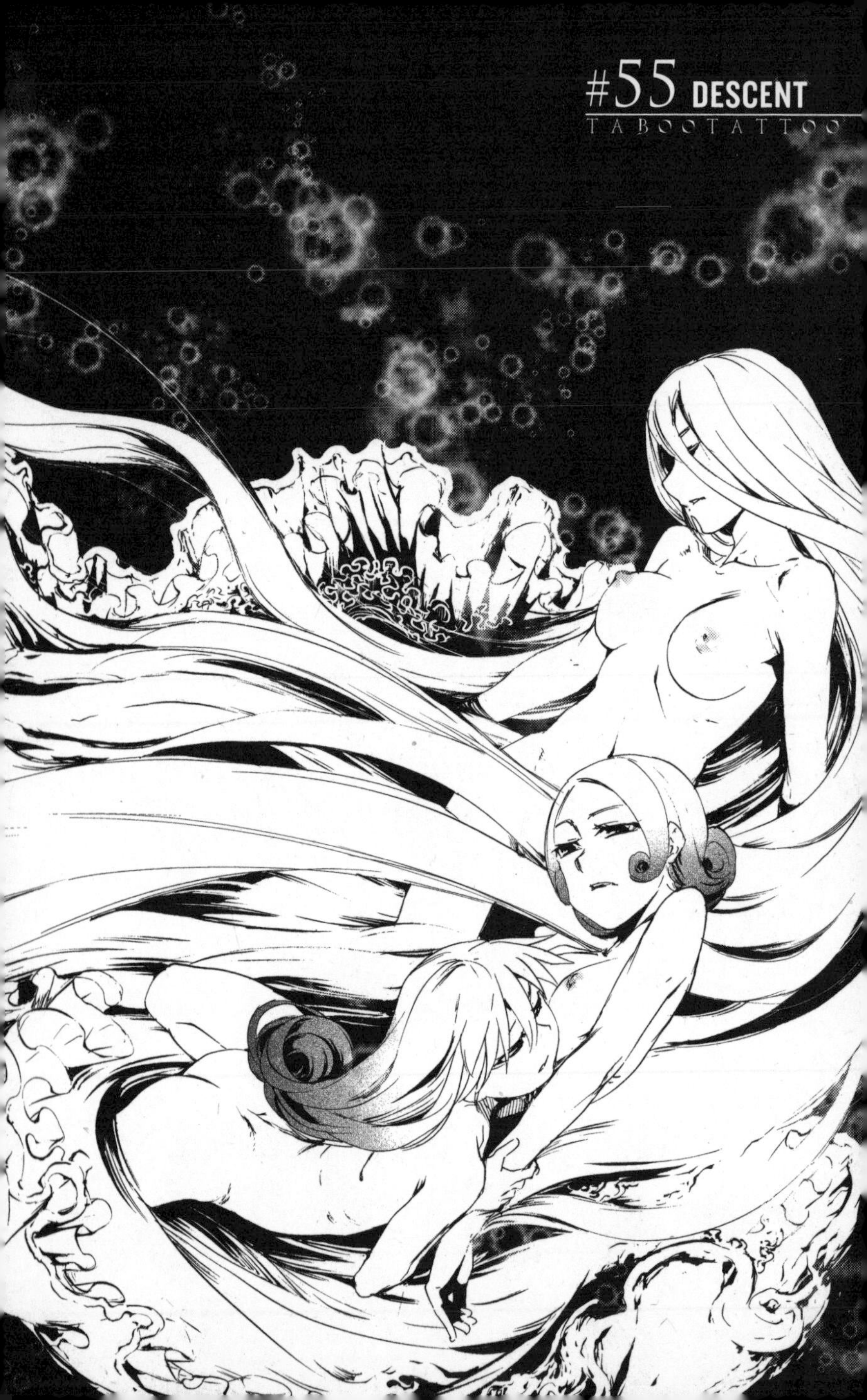

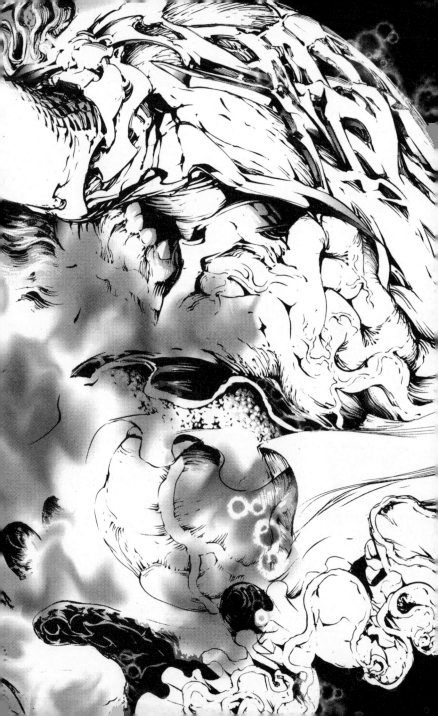

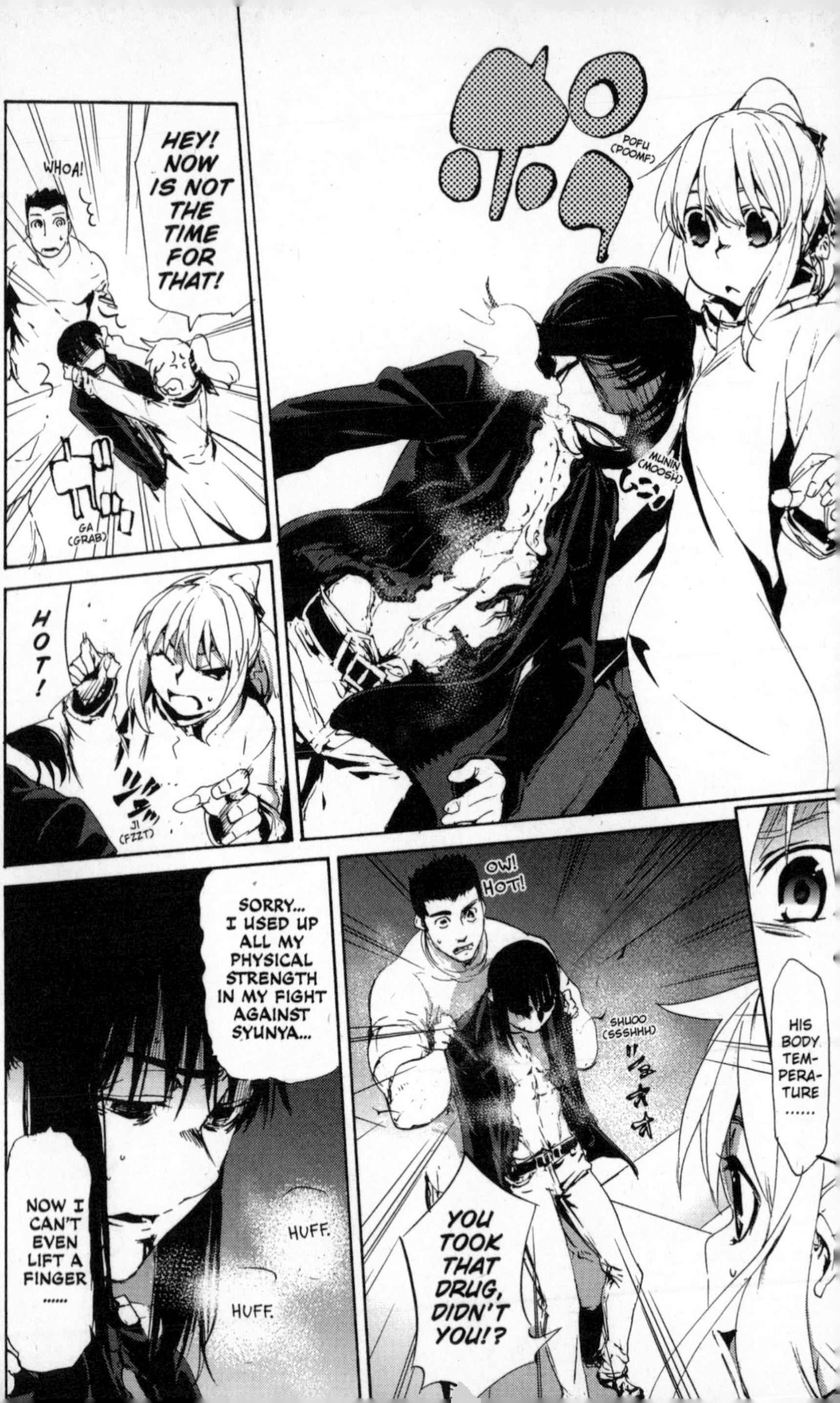
POFU (POOMF)
MUNIN (MOOSH)
WHOA!
HEY! NOW IS NOT THE TIME FOR THAT!
GA (GRAB)
HOT!
JI (FZZT)
HIS BODY TEM-PERA-TURE......
OW! HOT!
SHUOO (SSSHHH)
YOU TOOK THAT DRUG, DIDN'T YOU!?
SORRY... I USED UP ALL MY PHYSICAL STRENGTH IN MY FIGHT AGAINST SYUNYA...
HUFF.
HUFF.
NOW I CAN'T EVEN LIFT A FINGER......

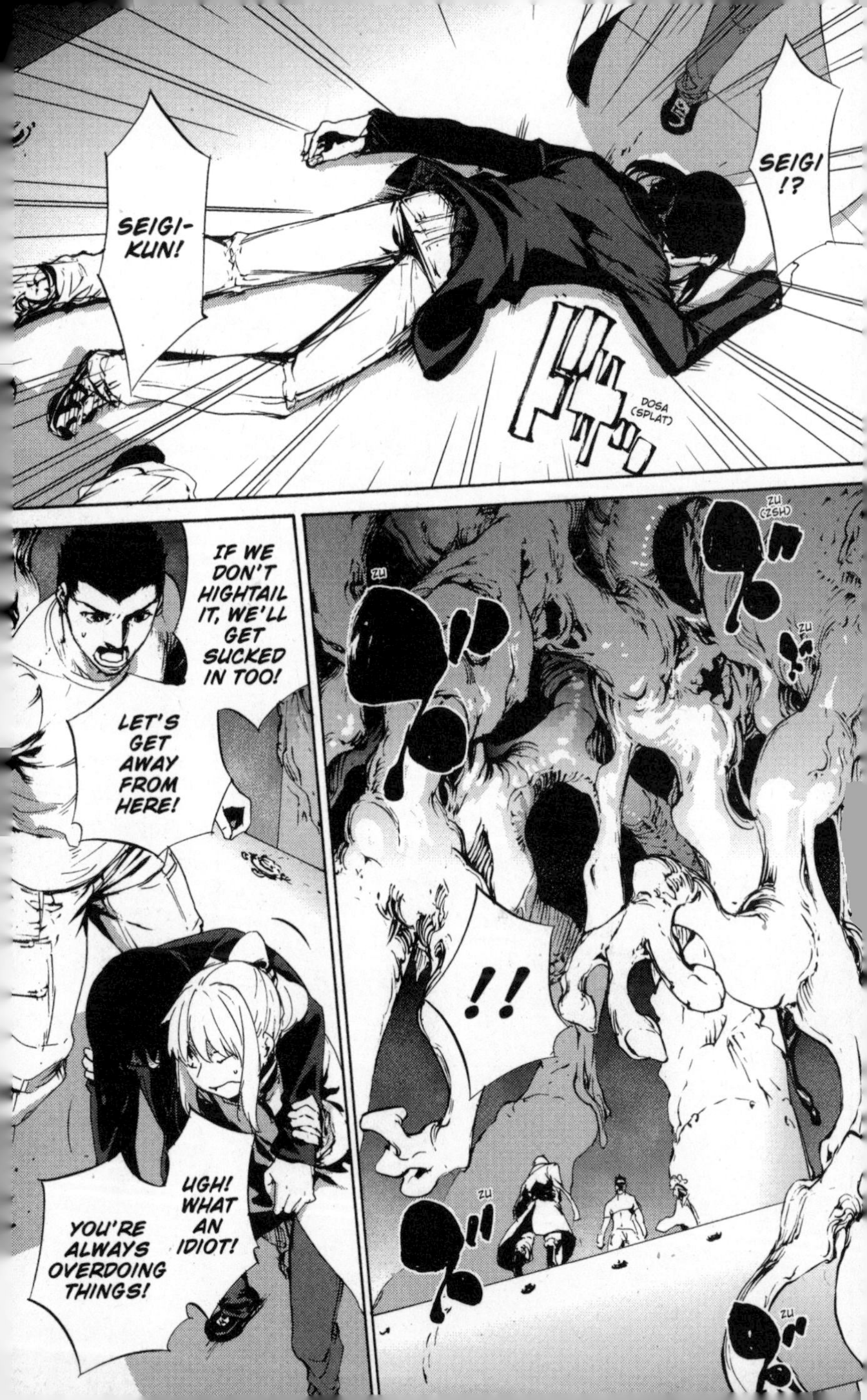
SEIGI !?
DOSA (SPLAT)
SEIGI-KUN!
ZU (ZSH)
ZU
ZU
!!
ZU
ZU
IF WE DON'T HIGHTAIL IT, WE'LL GET SUCKED IN TOO!
LET'S GET AWAY FROM HERE!
UGH! WHAT AN IDIOT!
YOU'RE ALWAYS OVERDOING THINGS!

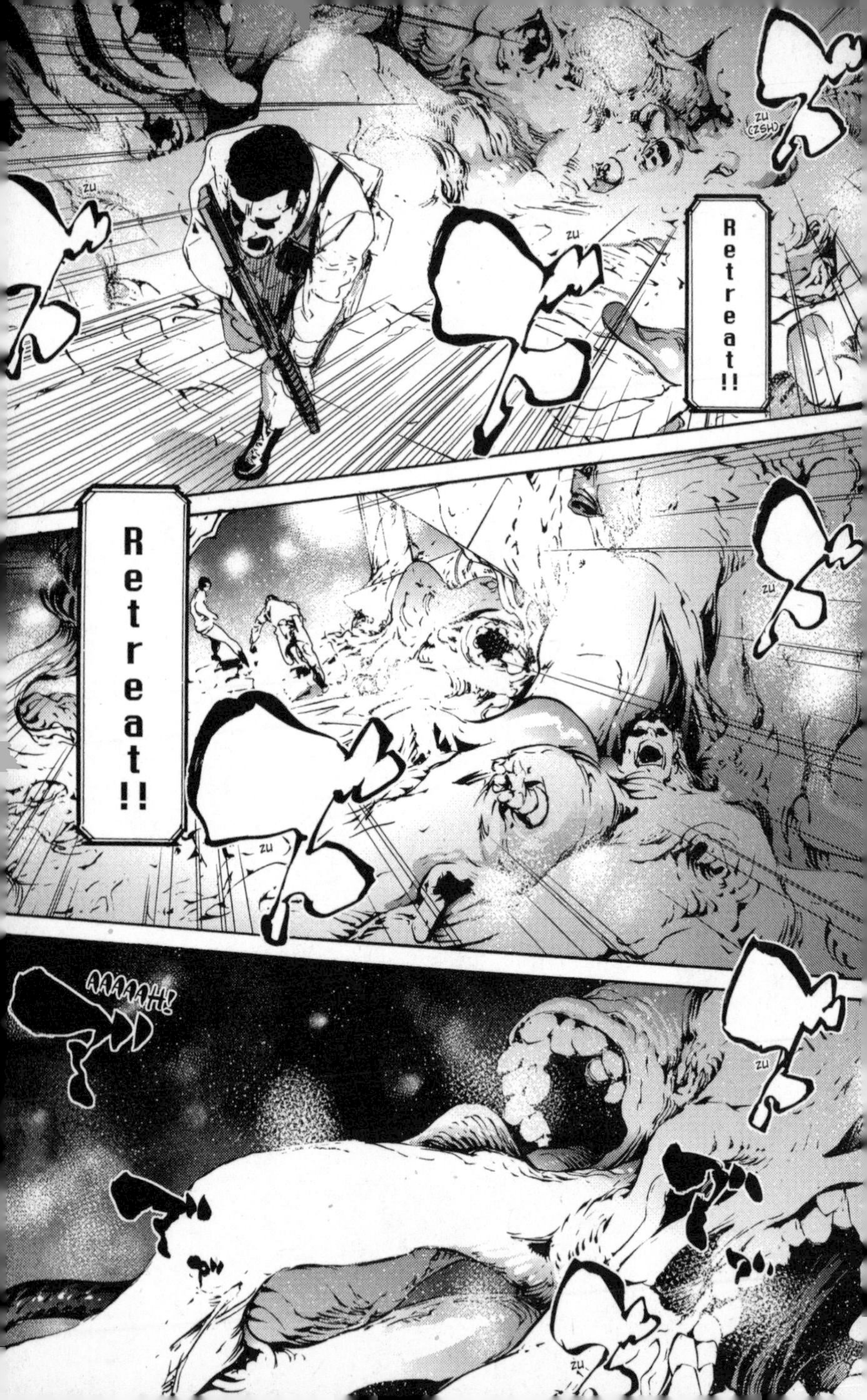
ZU (ZSH)
Retreat!!
ZU
ZU
ZU
Retreat!!
ZU
ZU
ZU
AAAAAH!
ZU
ZU

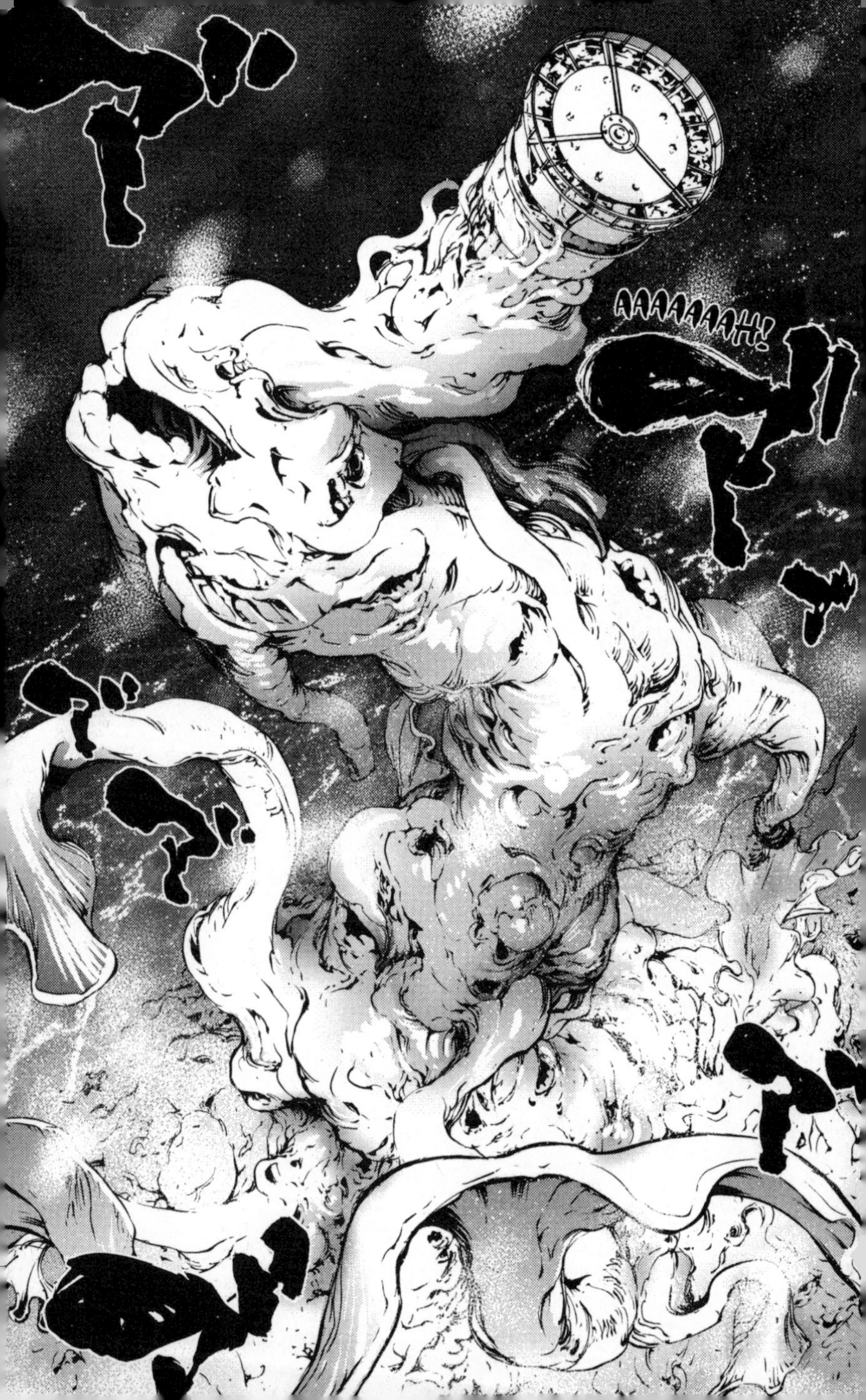
AAAAAAAH!

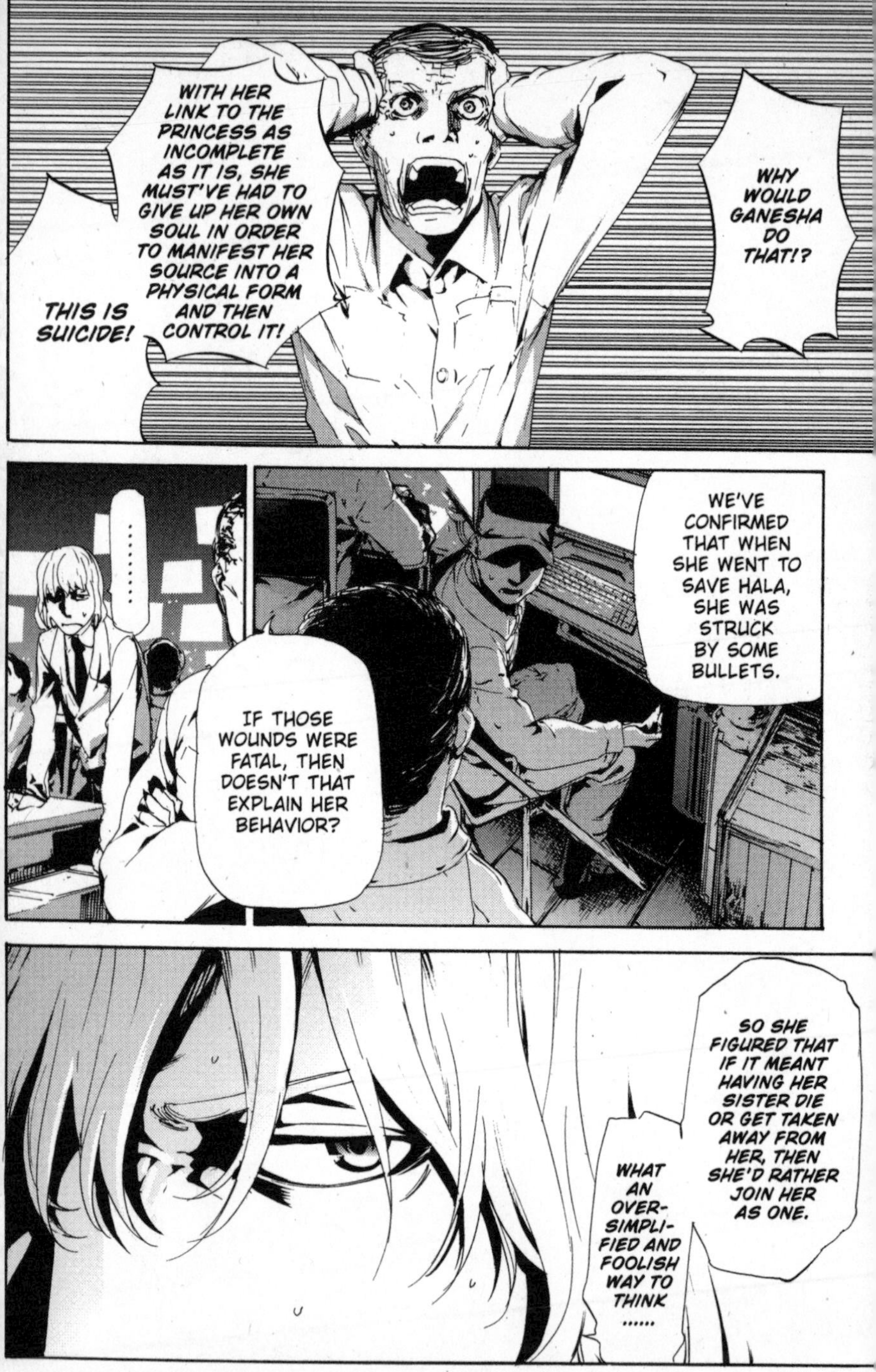
WHY WOULD GANESHA DO THAT!?
WITH HER LINK TO THE PRINCESS AS INCOMPLETE AS IT IS, SHE MUST'VE HAD TO GIVE UP HER OWN SOUL IN ORDER TO MANIFEST HER SOURCE INTO A PHYSICAL FORM AND THEN CONTROL IT!
THIS IS SUICIDE!
WE'VE CONFIRMED THAT WHEN SHE WENT TO SAVE HALA, SHE WAS STRUCK BY SOME BULLETS.
IF THOSE WOUNDS WERE FATAL, THEN DOESN'T THAT EXPLAIN HER BEHAVIOR?
......
SO SHE FIGURED THAT IF IT MEANT HAVING HER SISTER DIE OR GET TAKEN AWAY FROM HER, THEN SHE'D RATHER JOIN HER AS ONE.
WHAT AN OVER-SIMPLIFIED AND FOOLISH WAY TO THINK ......

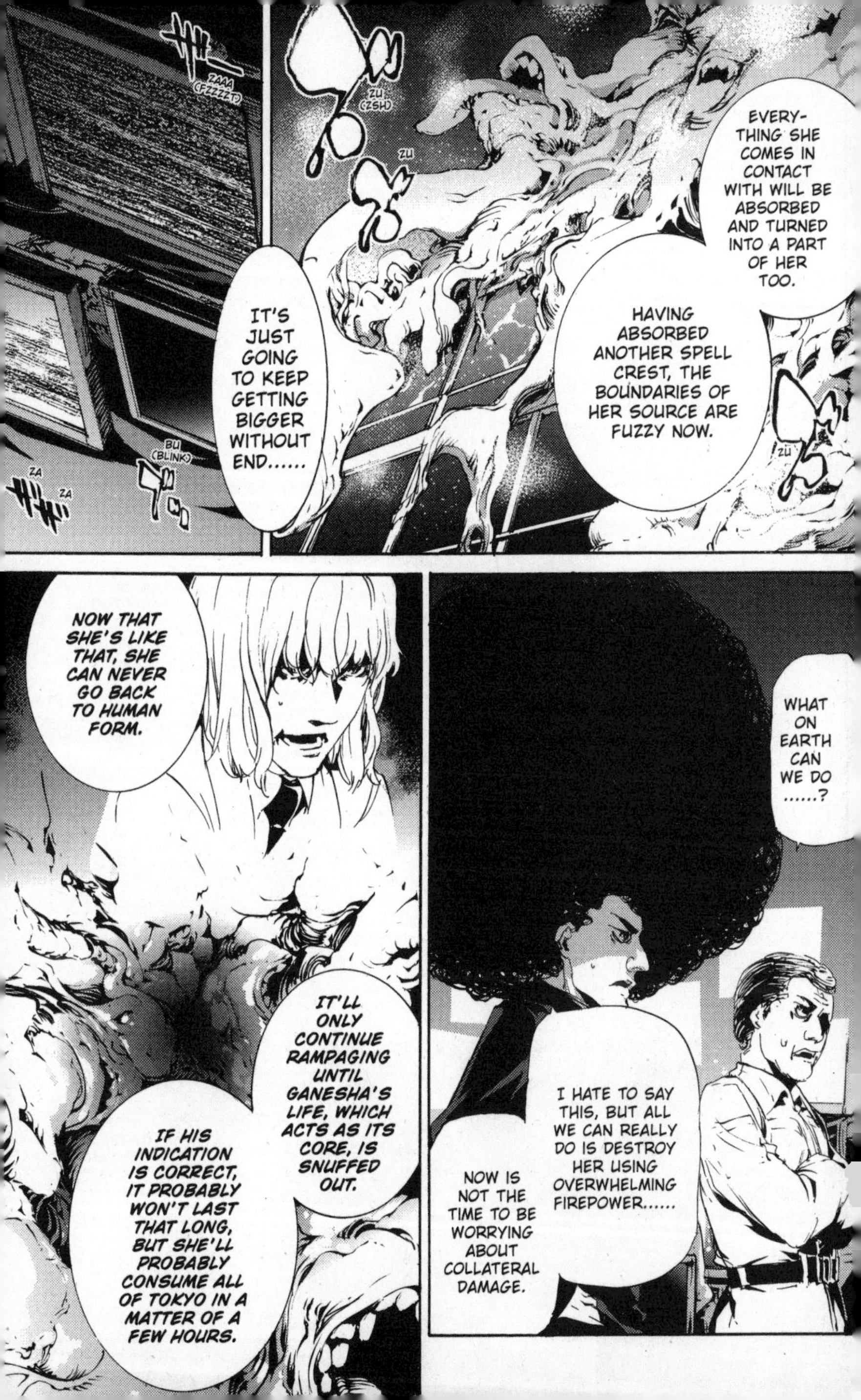
ZU (ZSH)
ZU
EVERY-THING SHE COMES IN CONTACT WITH WILL BE ABSORBED AND TURNED INTO A PART OF HER TOO.
HAVING ABSORBED ANOTHER SPELL CREST, THE BOUNDARIES OF HER SOURCE ARE FUZZY NOW.
ZU
IT'S JUST GOING TO KEEP GETTING BIGGER WITHOUT END......
ZAAA (FZZZZT)
BU (BLINK)
ZA ZA
WHAT ON EARTH CAN WE DO......?
I HATE TO SAY THIS, BUT ALL WE CAN REALLY DO IS DESTROY HER USING OVERWHELMING FIREPOWER......
NOW IS NOT THE TIME TO BE WORRYING ABOUT COLLATERAL DAMAGE.
NOW THAT SHE'S LIKE THAT, SHE CAN NEVER GO BACK TO HUMAN FORM.
IT'LL ONLY CONTINUE RAMPAGING UNTIL GANESHA'S LIFE, WHICH ACTS AS ITS CORE, IS SNUFFED OUT.
IF HIS INDICATION IS CORRECT, IT PROBABLY WON'T LAST THAT LONG, BUT SHE'LL PROBABLY CONSUME ALL OF TOKYO IN A MATTER OF A FEW HOURS.

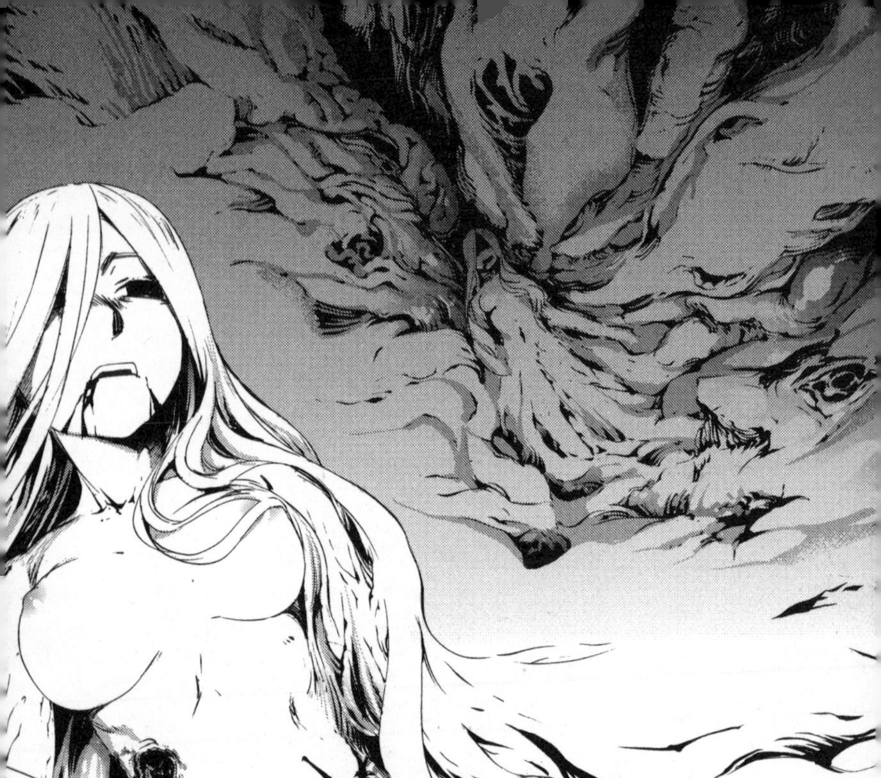

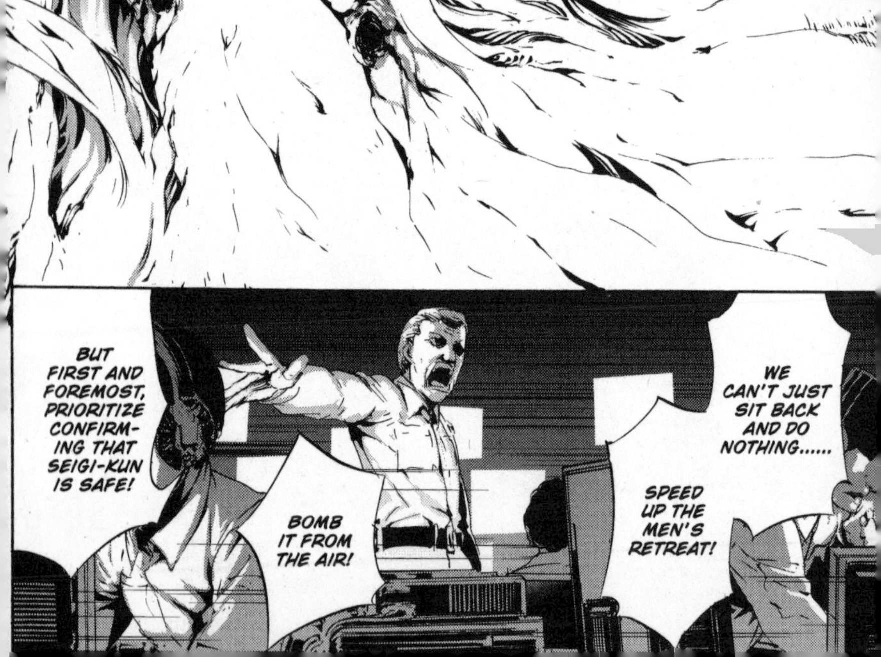
WE CAN'T JUST SIT BACK AND DO NOTHING......
SPEED UP THE MEN'S RETREAT!
BUT FIRST AND FOREMOST, PRIORITIZE CONFIRMING THAT SEIGI-KUN IS SAFE!
BOMB IT FROM THE AIR!

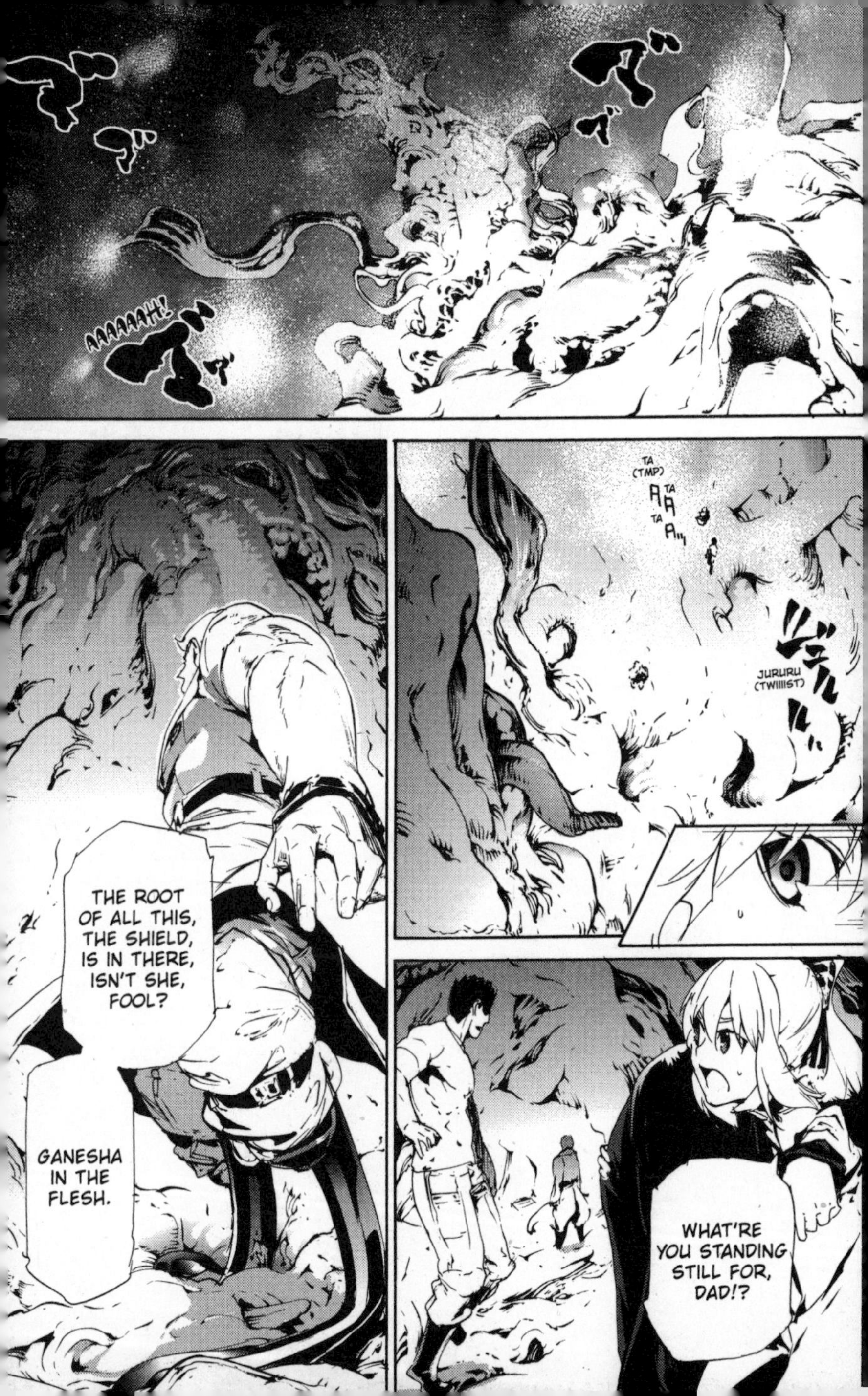
AAAAAAH!
TA (TMP)
TA
TA
JURURU (TWIIIIST)
WHAT'RE YOU STANDING STILL FOR, DAD!?
THE ROOT OF ALL THIS, THE SHIELD, IS IN THERE, ISN'T SHE, FOOL?
GANESHA IN THE FLESH.

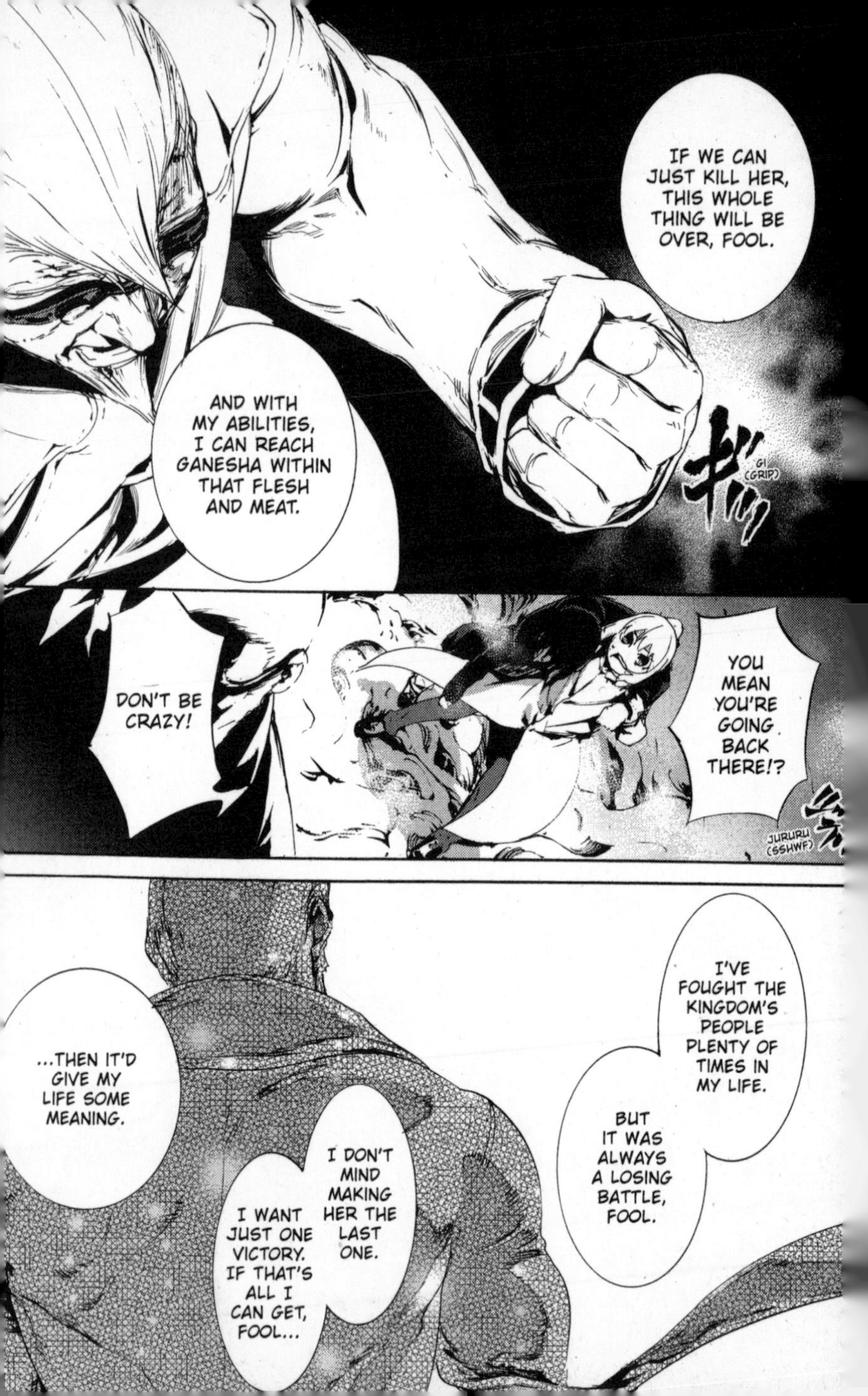
IF WE CAN JUST KILL HER, THIS WHOLE THING WILL BE OVER, FOOL.
AND WITH MY ABILITIES, I CAN REACH GANESHA WITHIN THAT FLESH AND MEAT.
GI (GRIP)
YOU MEAN YOU'RE GOING BACK THERE!?
JURURU (SSHWF)
DON'T BE CRAZY!
I'VE FOUGHT THE KINGDOM'S PEOPLE PLENTY OF TIMES IN MY LIFE.
BUT IT WAS ALWAYS A LOSING BATTLE, FOOL.
I DON'T MIND MAKING HER THE LAST ONE.
I WANT JUST ONE VICTORY. IF THAT'S ALL I CAN GET, FOOL...
...THEN IT'D GIVE MY LIFE SOME MEANING.

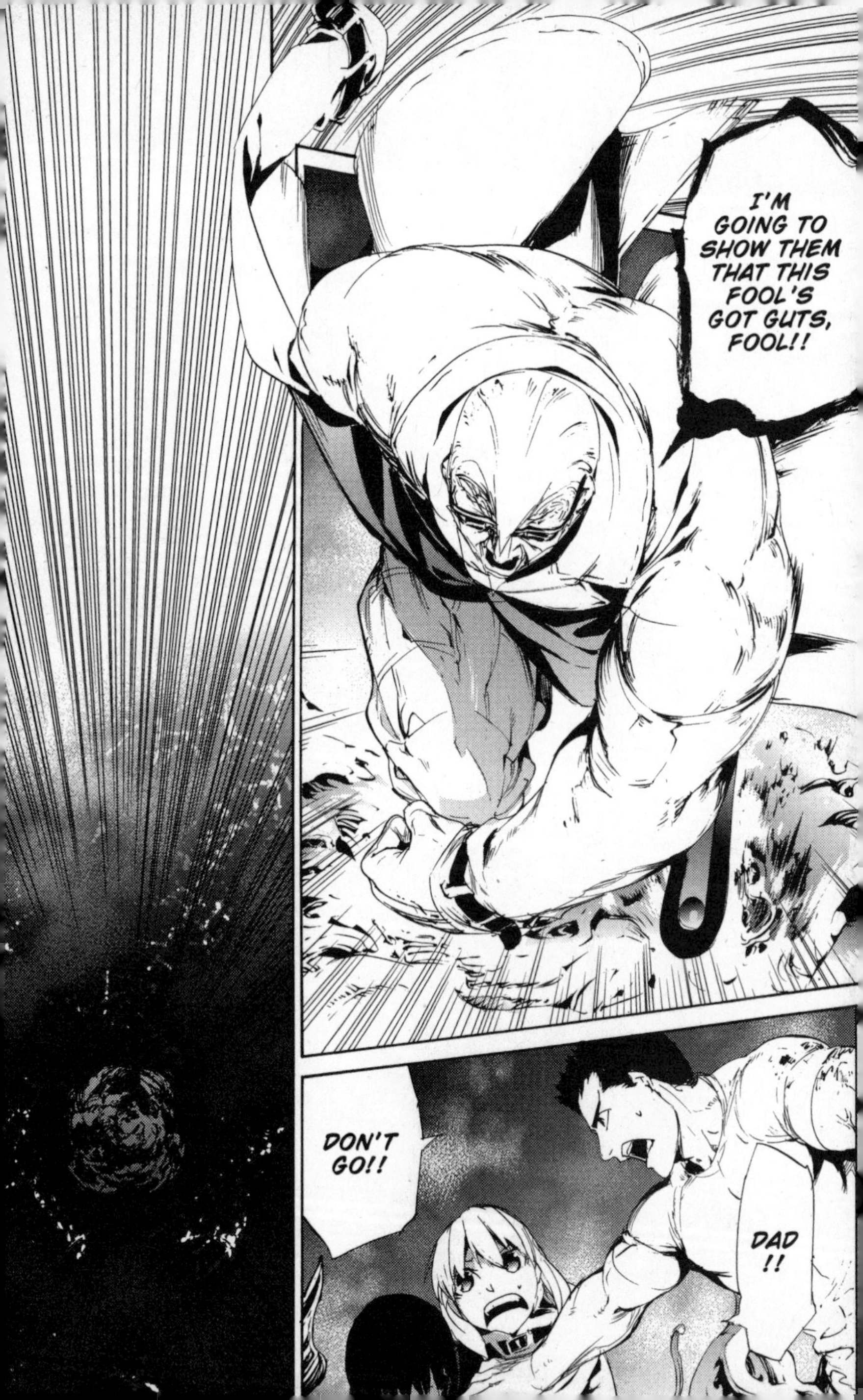
I'M GOING TO SHOW THEM THAT THIS FOOL'S GOT GUTS, FOOL!!
DAD!!
DON'T GO!!

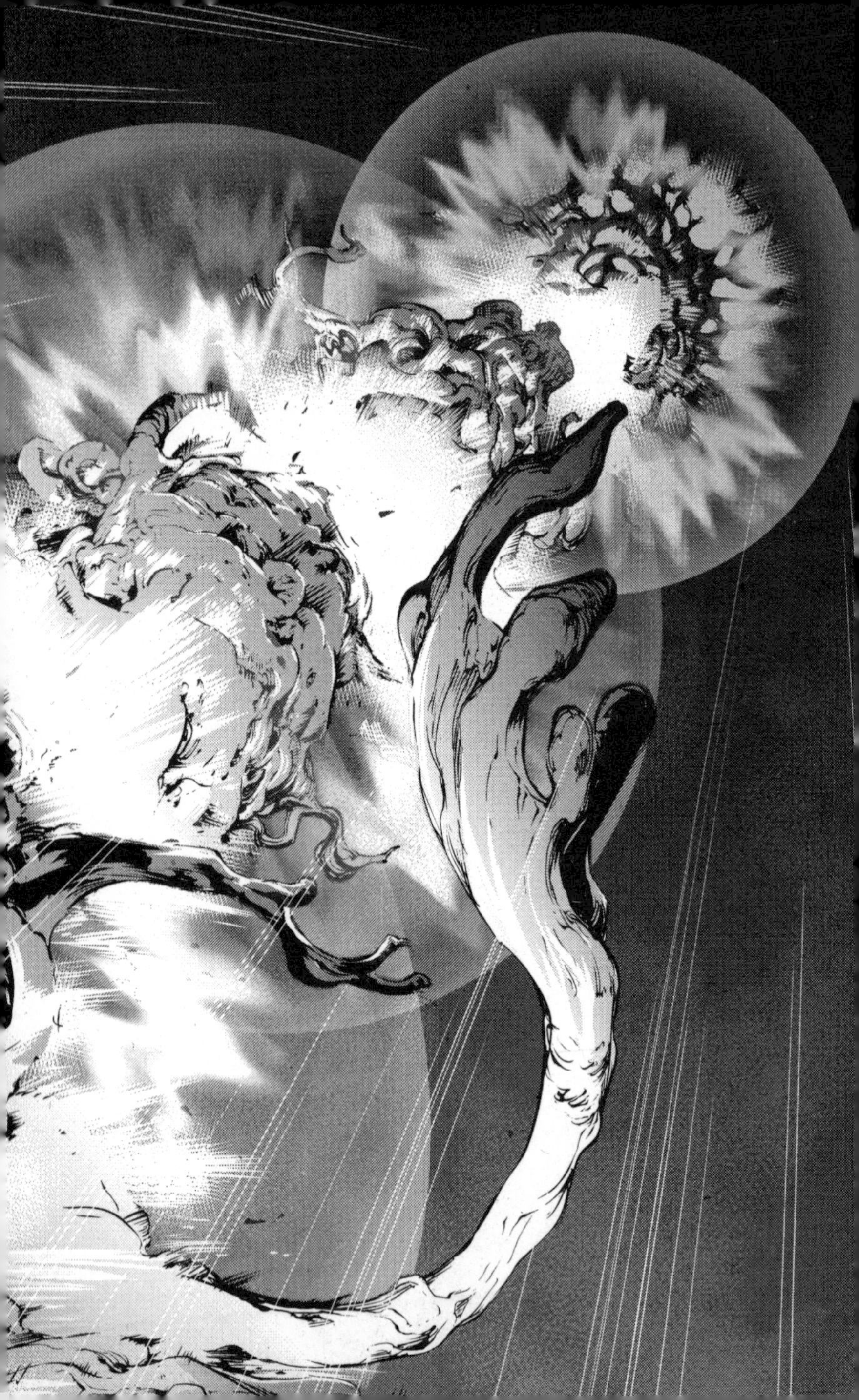

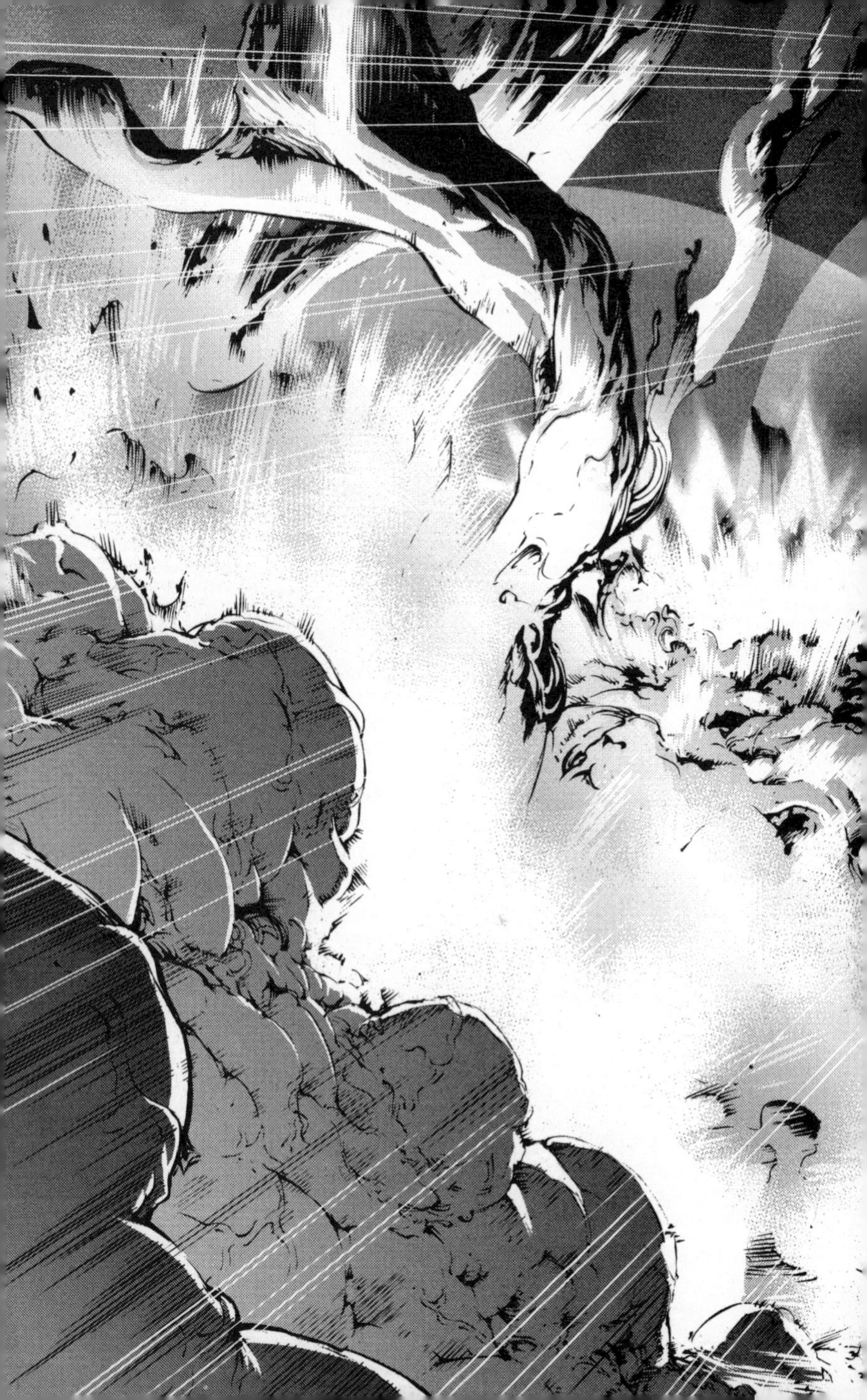

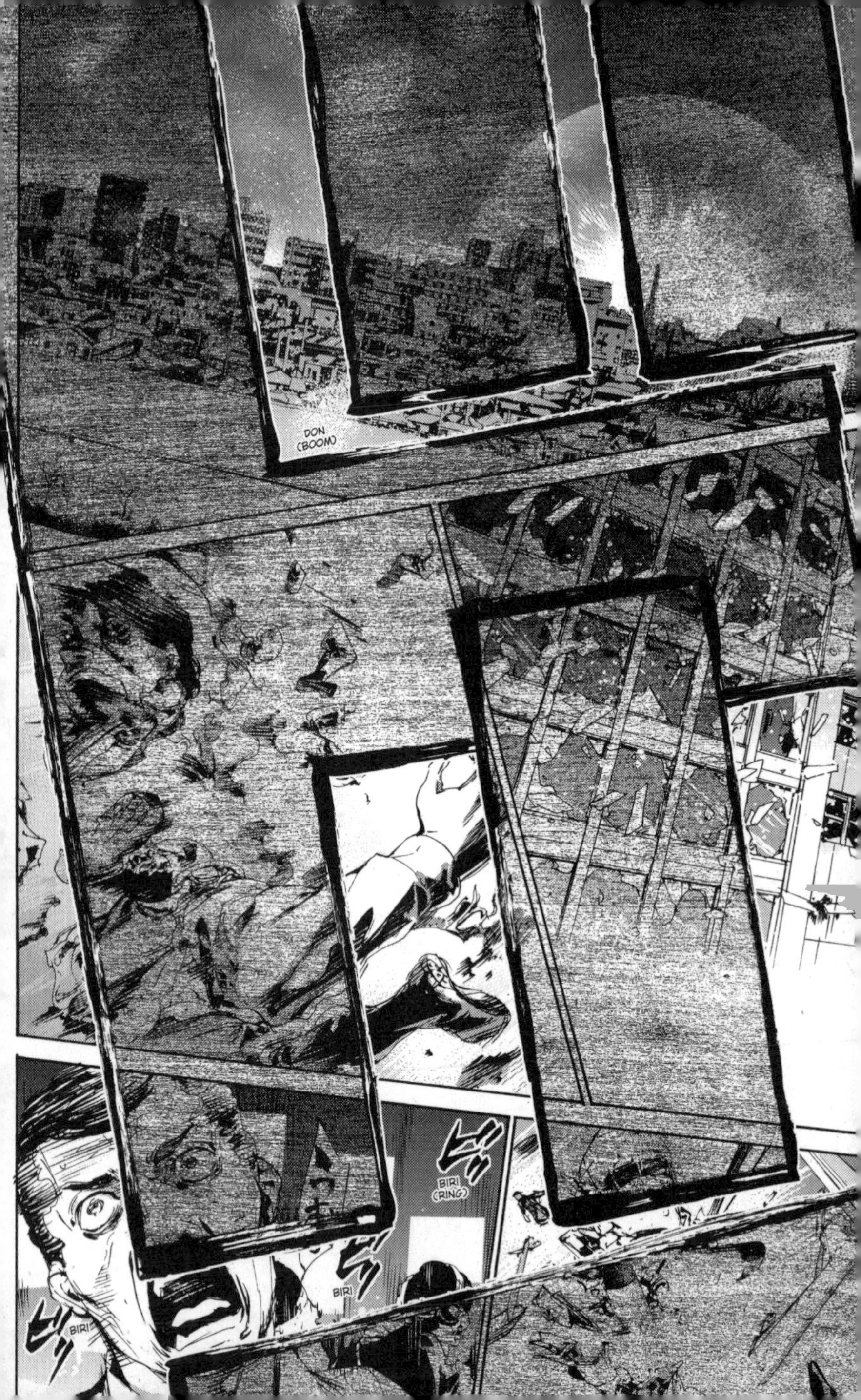
DON (BOOM)
BIRI (RING)
BIRI
BIRI

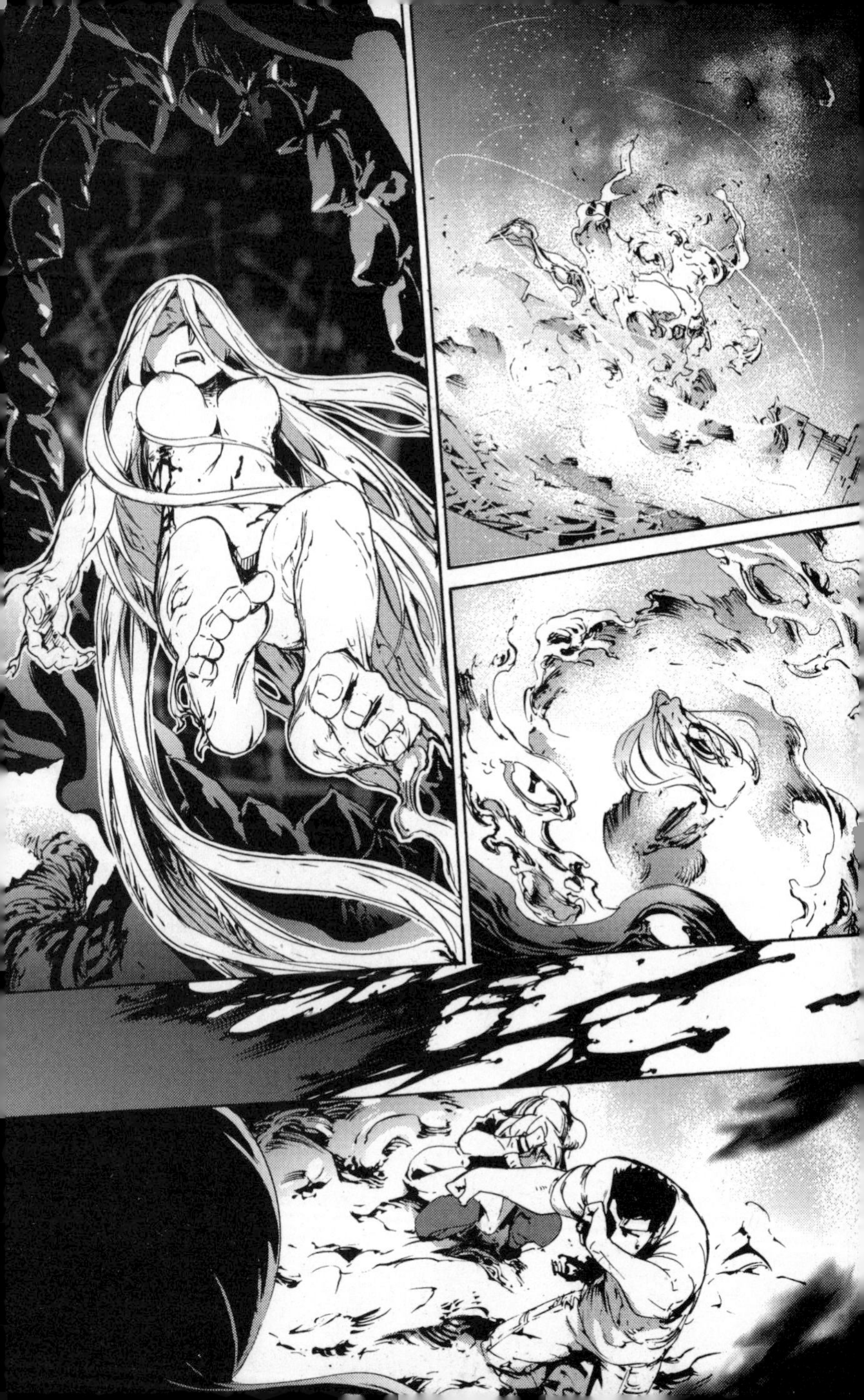

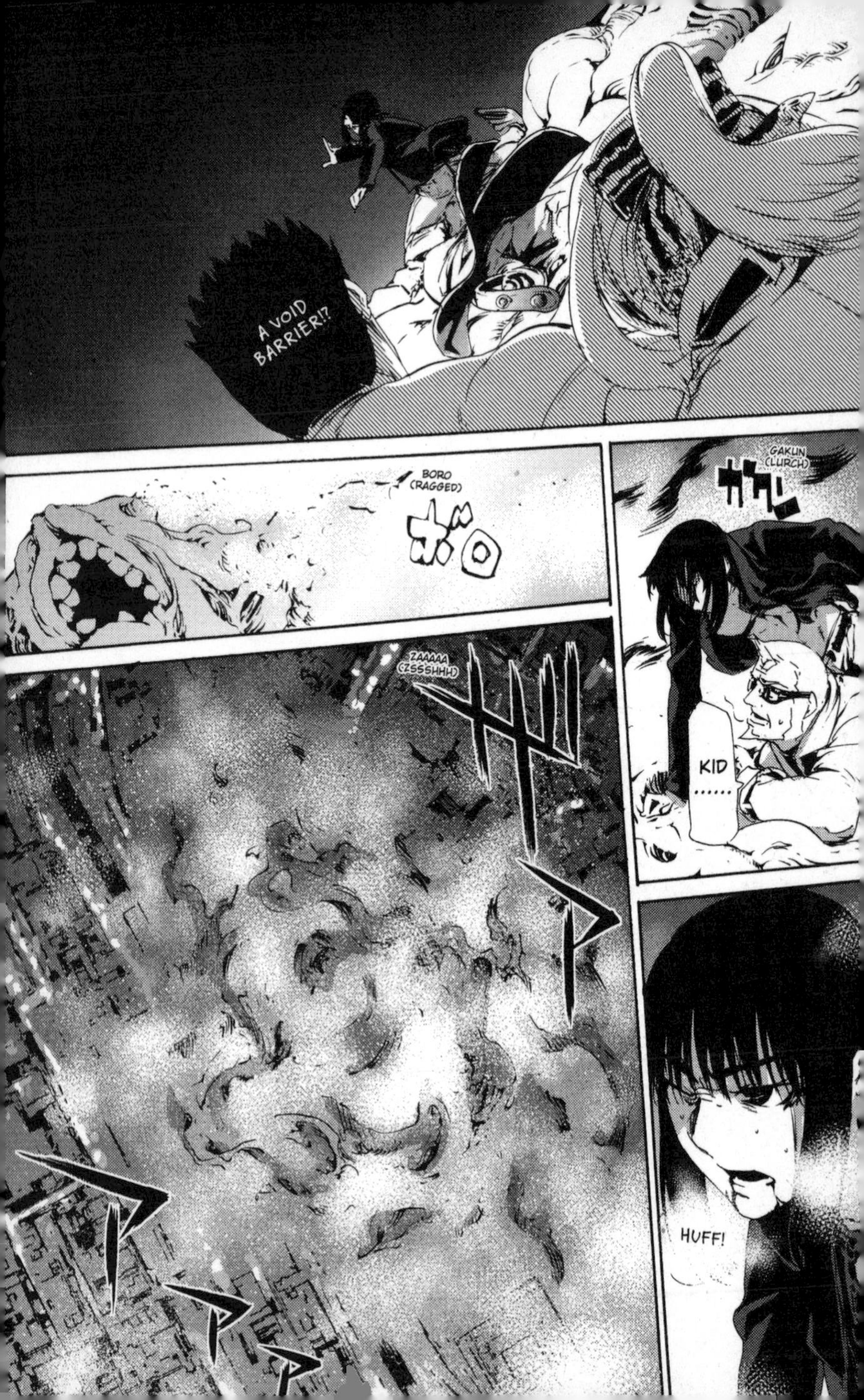
A VOID BARRIER!?
GAKUN (LURCH)
ガクン
KID ......
BORO (RAGGED)
ボロ
ZAAAAA (ZSSSHHH)
HUFF!

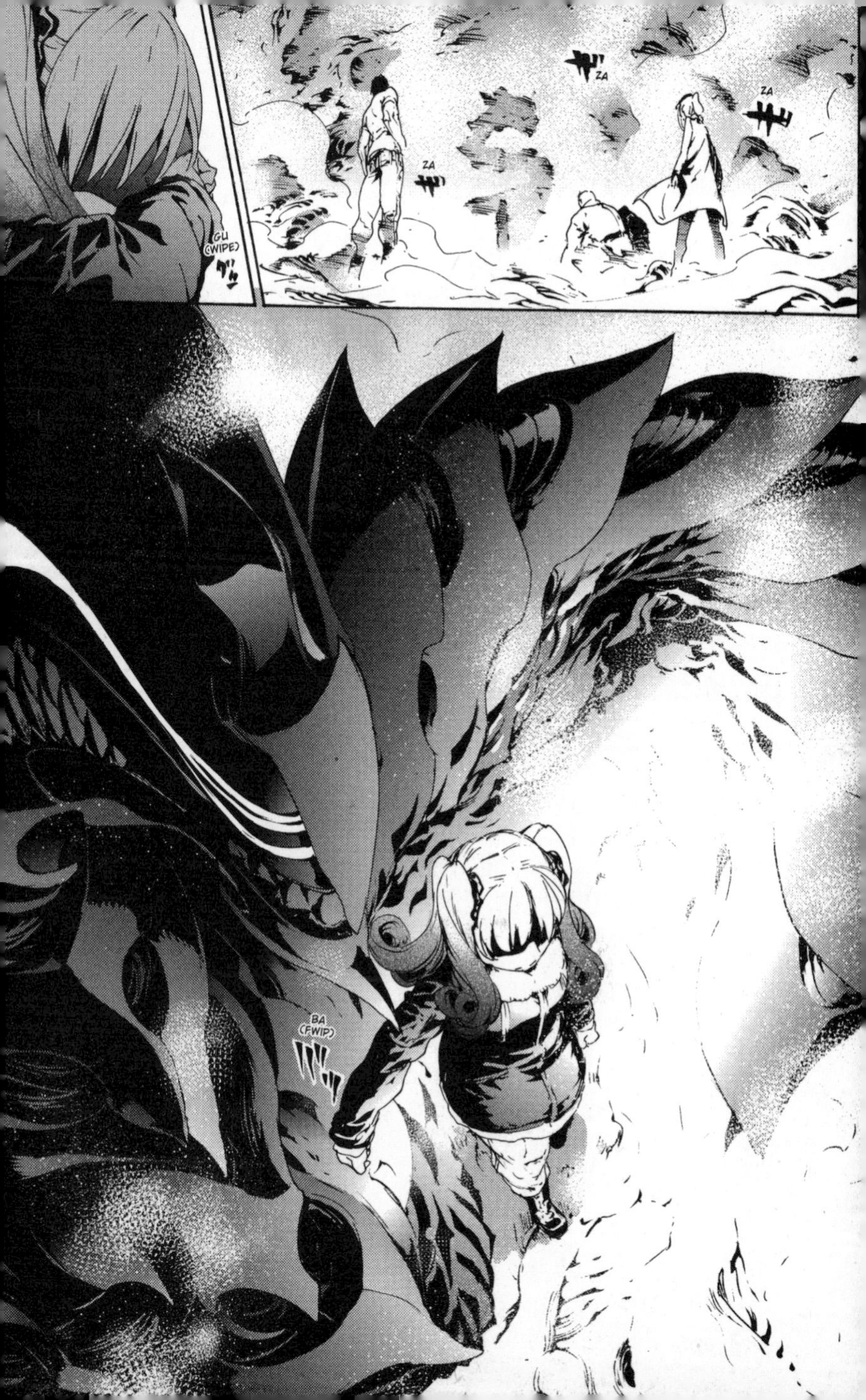
ZA
ZA
ZA
GU (WIPE)
BA (FWIP)

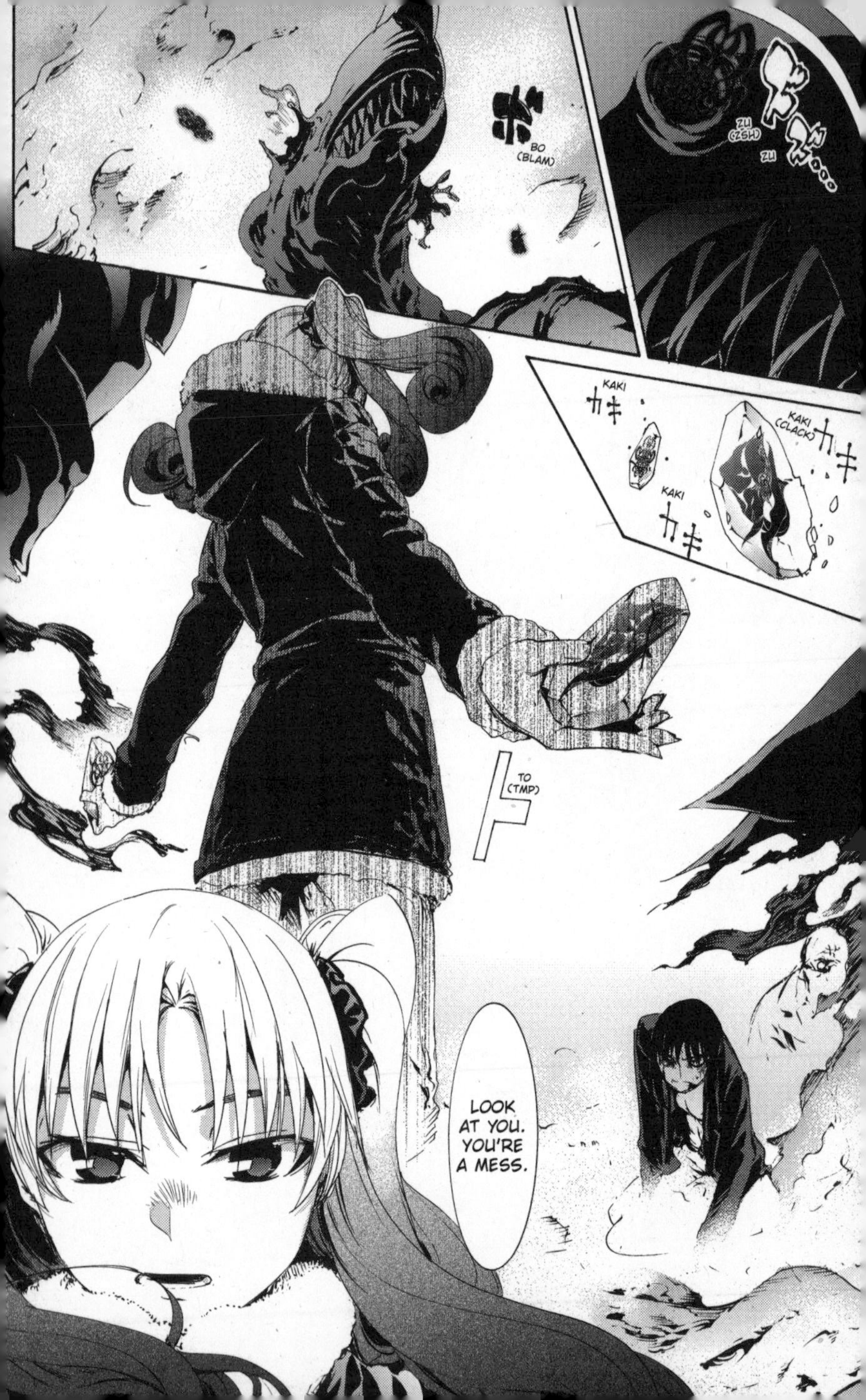
ZU (ZSH)
ZU
BO (BLAM)
KAKI (CLACK)
KAKI
KAKI
TO (TMP)
LOOK AT YOU. YOU'RE A MESS.

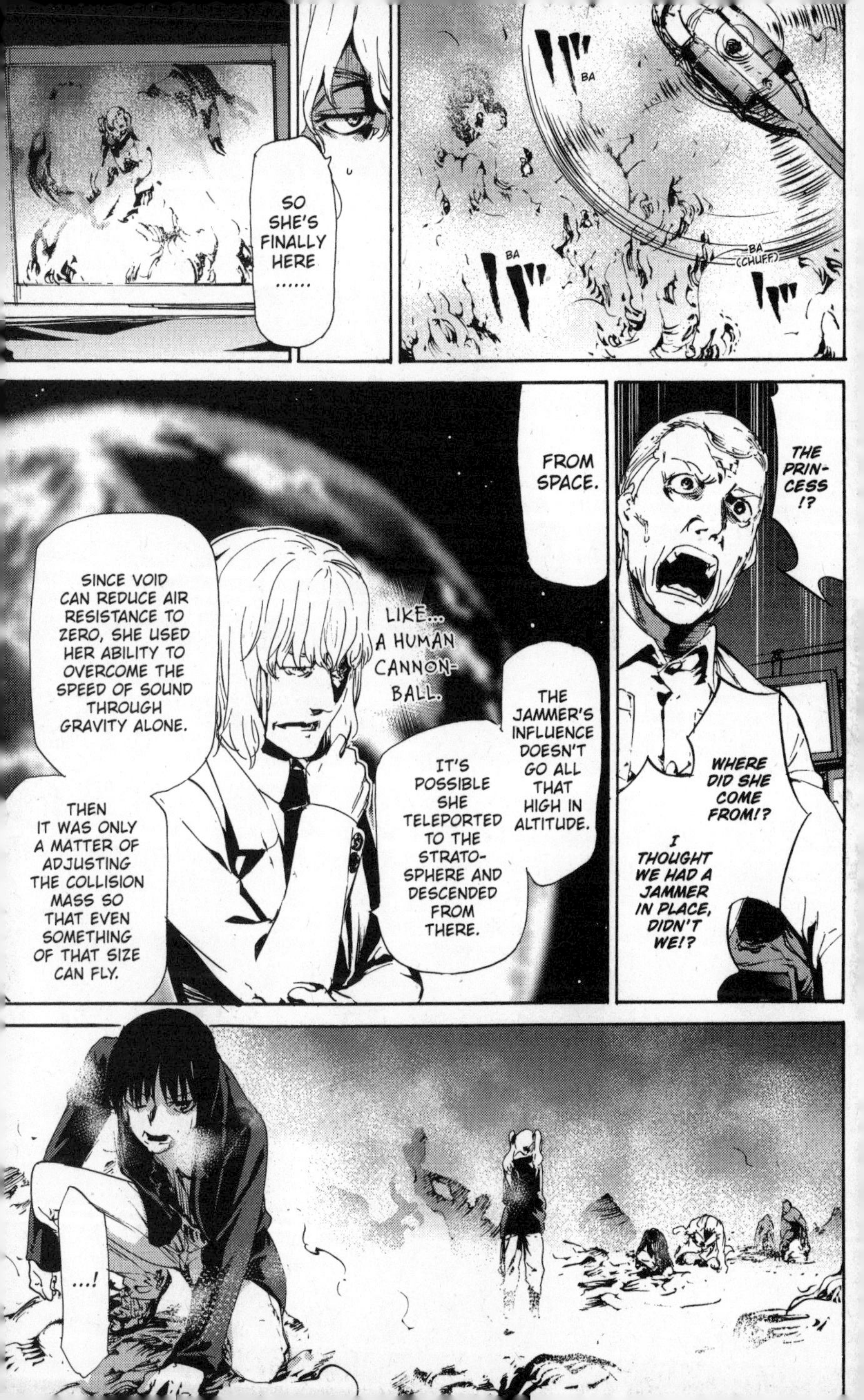

BA
BA (CHUFF.)
BA
SO SHE'S FINALLY HERE ......
THE PRIN-CESS !?
WHERE DID SHE COME FROM!?
I THOUGHT WE HAD A JAMMER IN PLACE, DIDN'T WE!?
FROM SPACE.
THE JAMMER'S INFLUENCE DOESN'T GO ALL THAT HIGH IN ALTITUDE.
IT'S POSSIBLE SHE TELEPORTED TO THE STRATO-SPHERE AND DESCENDED FROM THERE.
LIKE... A HUMAN CANNON-BALL.
SINCE VOID CAN REDUCE AIR RESISTANCE TO ZERO, SHE USED HER ABILITY TO OVERCOME THE SPEED OF SOUND THROUGH GRAVITY ALONE.
THEN IT WAS ONLY A MATTER OF ADJUSTING THE COLLISION MASS SO THAT EVEN SOMETHING OF THAT SIZE CAN FLY.
...!

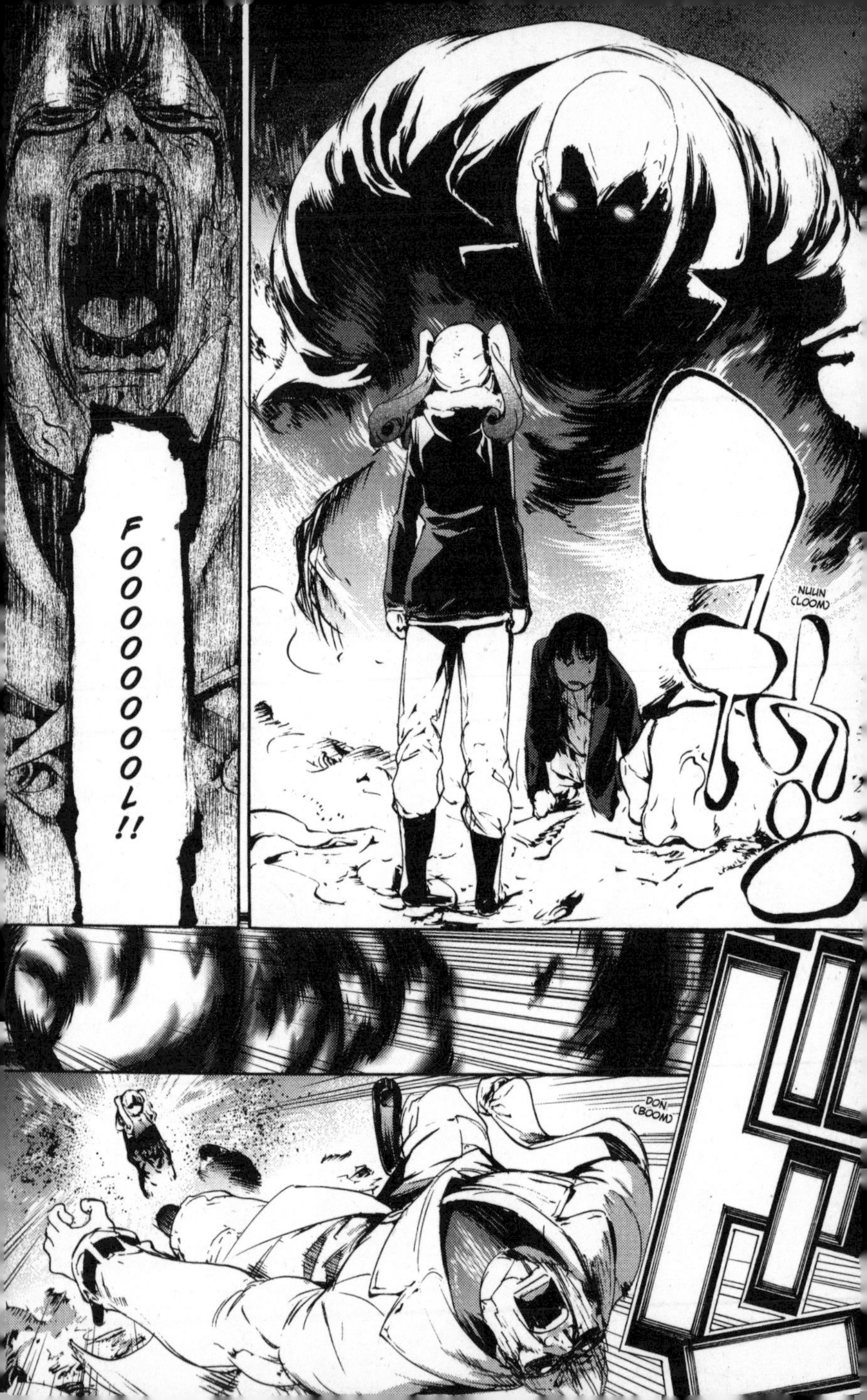
NUUN (LOOM)
FOOOOOOOOL!!
DON (BOOM)

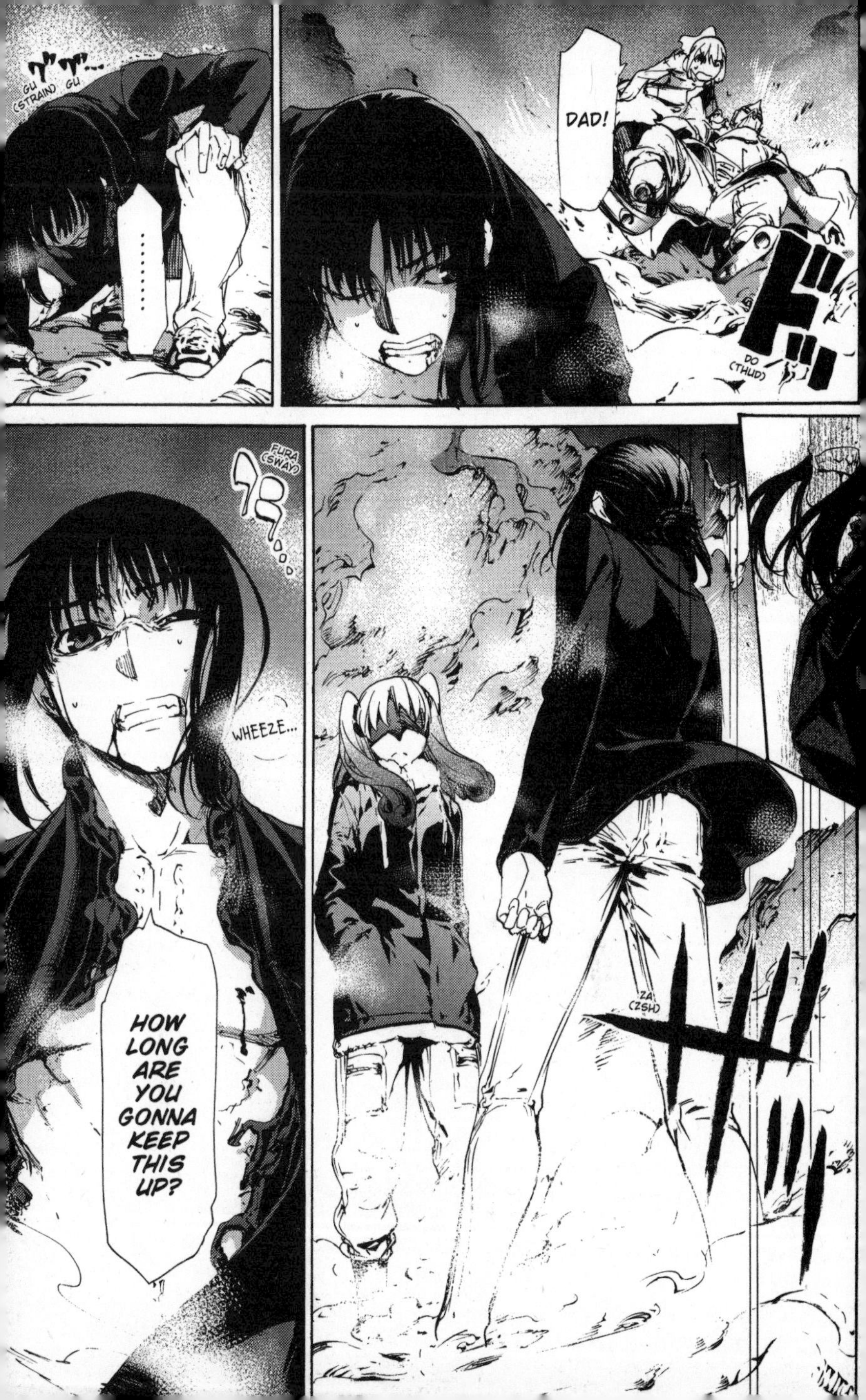
DAD!
DO (THUD)
GU (STRAIN) GU
......
ZA (ZSH)
FURA (SWAY)
WHEEZE...
HOW LONG ARE YOU GONNA KEEP THIS UP?

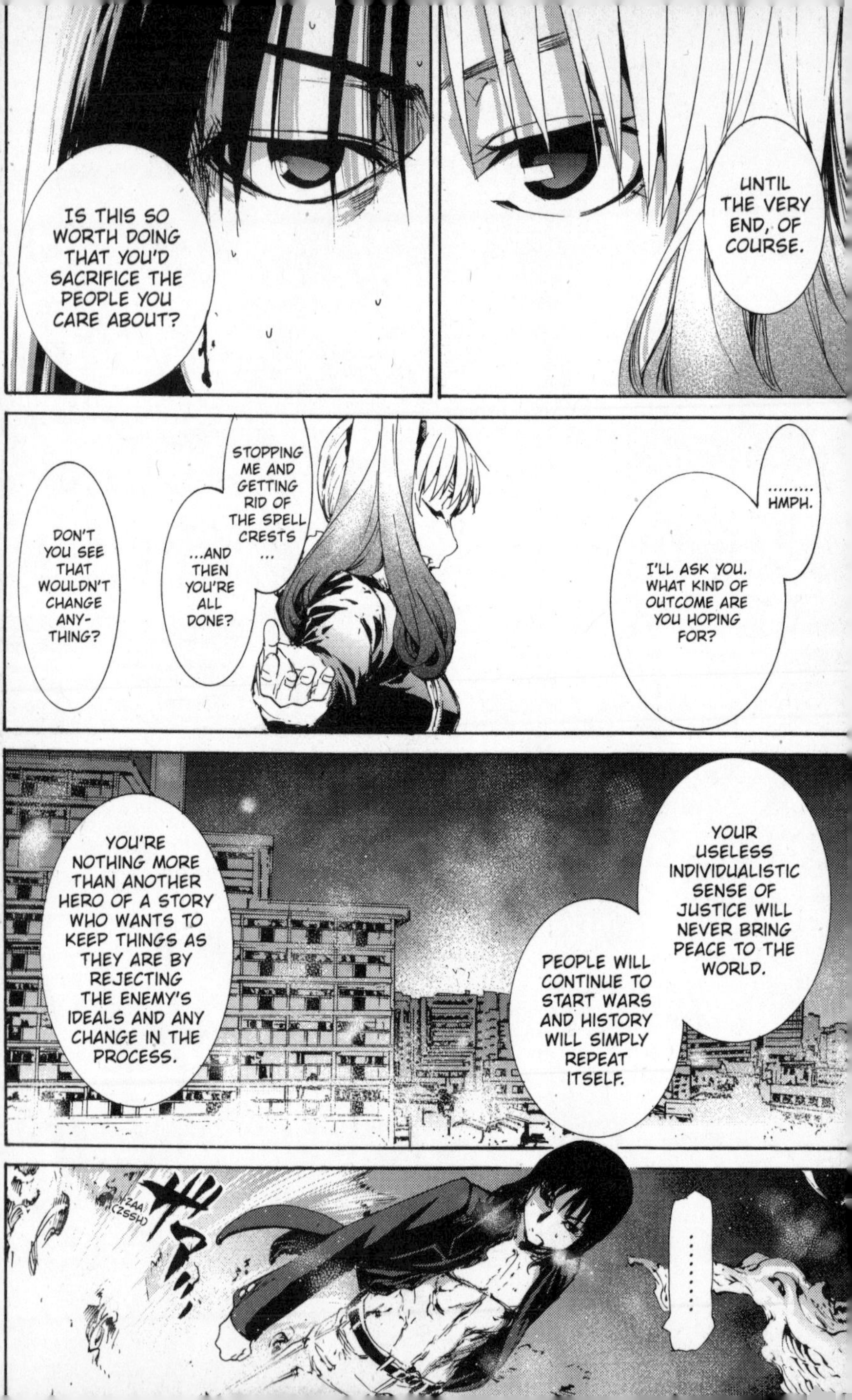
UNTIL THE VERY END, OF COURSE.
IS THIS SO WORTH DOING THAT YOU'D SACRIFICE THE PEOPLE YOU CARE ABOUT?
.... HMPH.
I'LL ASK YOU. WHAT KIND OF OUTCOME ARE YOU HOPING FOR?
STOPPING ME AND GETTING RID OF THE SPELL CRESTS ...
...AND THEN YOU'RE ALL DONE?
DON'T YOU SEE THAT WOULDN'T CHANGE ANY-THING?
YOUR USELESS INDIVIDUALISTIC SENSE OF JUSTICE WILL NEVER BRING PEACE TO THE WORLD.
PEOPLE WILL CONTINUE TO START WARS AND HISTORY WILL SIMPLY REPEAT ITSELF.
YOU'RE NOTHING MORE THAN ANOTHER HERO OF A STORY WHO WANTS TO KEEP THINGS AS THEY ARE BY REJECTING THE ENEMY'S IDEALS AND ANY CHANGE IN THE PROCESS.
......
ZAA (ZSSH)

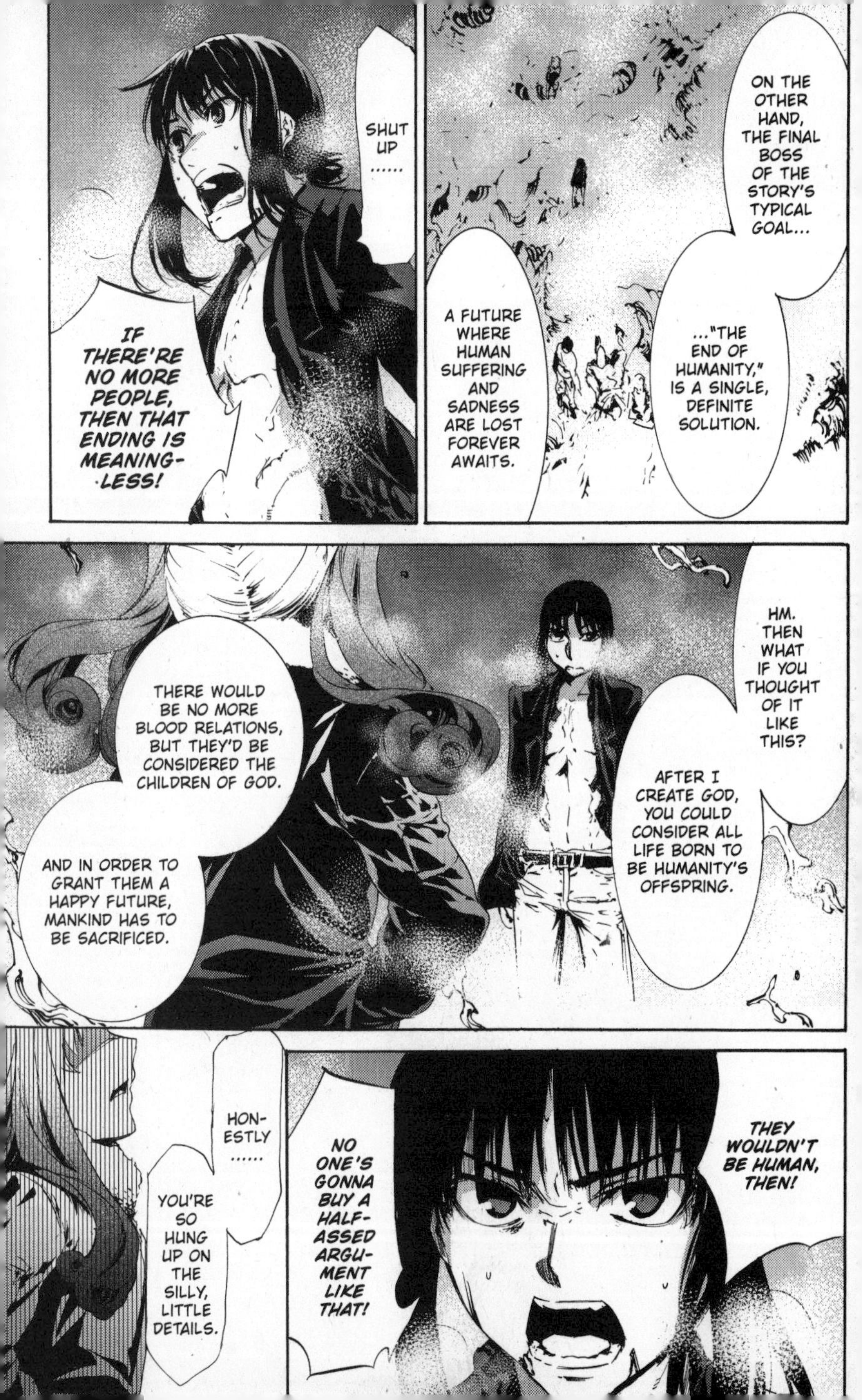
ON THE OTHER HAND, THE FINAL BOSS OF THE STORY'S TYPICAL GOAL...
..."THE END OF HUMANITY," IS A SINGLE, DEFINITE SOLUTION.
A FUTURE WHERE HUMAN SUFFERING AND SADNESS ARE LOST FOREVER AWAITS.
SHUT UP ......
IF THERE'RE NO MORE PEOPLE, THEN THAT ENDING IS MEANING-LESS!
HM. THEN WHAT IF YOU THOUGHT OF IT LIKE THIS?
AFTER I CREATE GOD, YOU COULD CONSIDER ALL LIFE BORN TO BE HUMANITY'S OFFSPRING.
THERE WOULD BE NO MORE BLOOD RELATIONS, BUT THEY'D BE CONSIDERED THE CHILDREN OF GOD.
AND IN ORDER TO GRANT THEM A HAPPY FUTURE, MANKIND HAS TO BE SACRIFICED.
THEY WOULDN'T BE HUMAN, THEN!
NO ONE'S GONNA BUY A HALF-ASSED ARGU-MENT LIKE THAT!
HON-ESTLY ......
YOU'RE SO HUNG UP ON THE SILLY, LITTLE DETAILS.

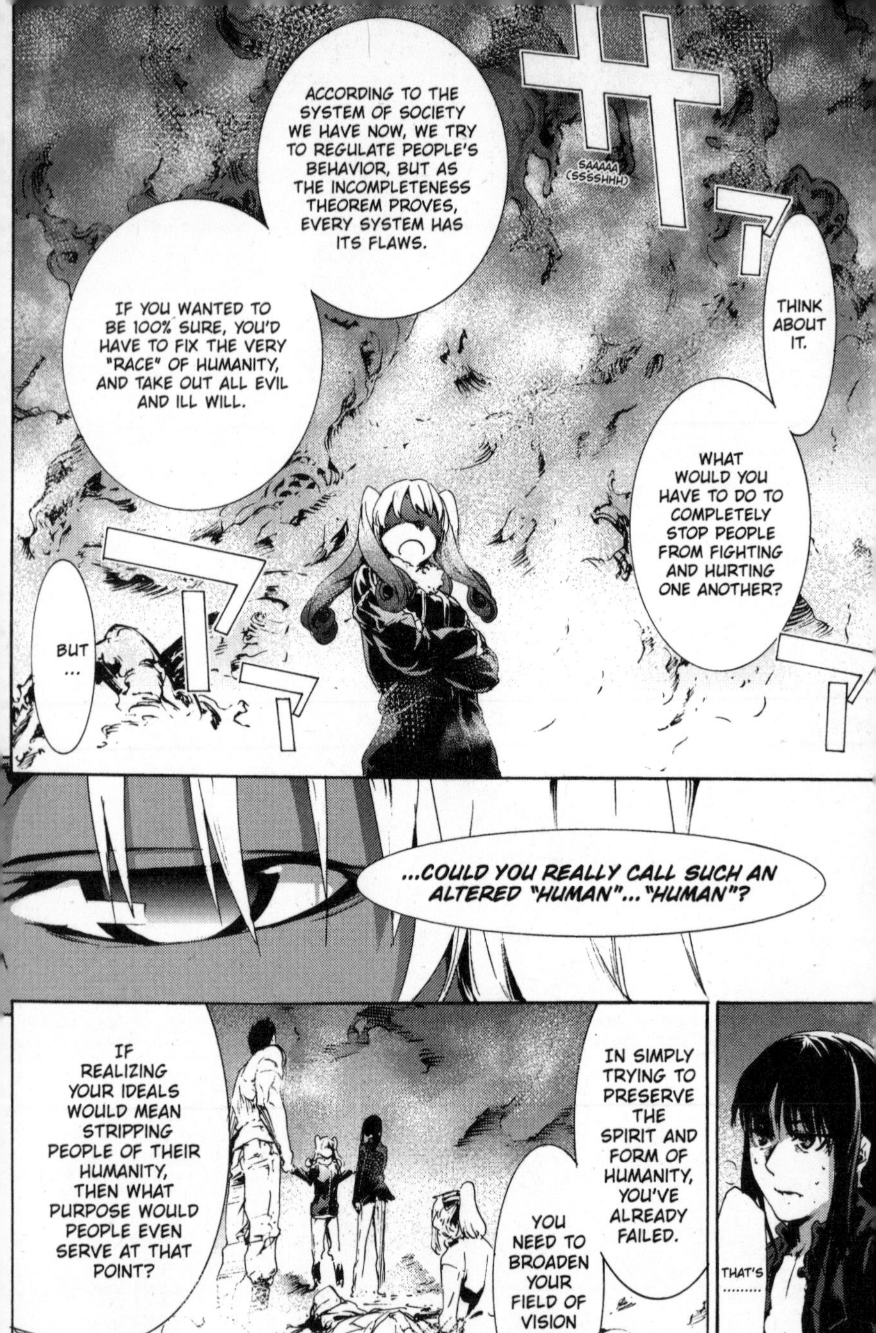
SAAAAA (SSSSHHH)
THINK ABOUT IT.
WHAT WOULD YOU HAVE TO DO TO COMPLETELY STOP PEOPLE FROM FIGHTING AND HURTING ONE ANOTHER?
ACCORDING TO THE SYSTEM OF SOCIETY WE HAVE NOW, WE TRY TO REGULATE PEOPLE'S BEHAVIOR, BUT AS THE INCOMPLETENESS THEOREM PROVES, EVERY SYSTEM HAS ITS FLAWS.
IF YOU WANTED TO BE 100% SURE, YOU'D HAVE TO FIX THE VERY "RACE" OF HUMANITY, AND TAKE OUT ALL EVIL AND ILL WILL.
BUT...
...COULD YOU REALLY CALL SUCH AN ALTERED "HUMAN"... "HUMAN"?
THAT'S.........
IN SIMPLY TRYING TO PRESERVE THE SPIRIT AND FORM OF HUMANITY, YOU'VE ALREADY FAILED.
YOU NEED TO BROADEN YOUR FIELD OF VISION MORE.
IF REALIZING YOUR IDEALS WOULD MEAN STRIPPING PEOPLE OF THEIR HUMANITY, THEN WHAT PURPOSE WOULD PEOPLE EVEN SERVE AT THAT POINT?

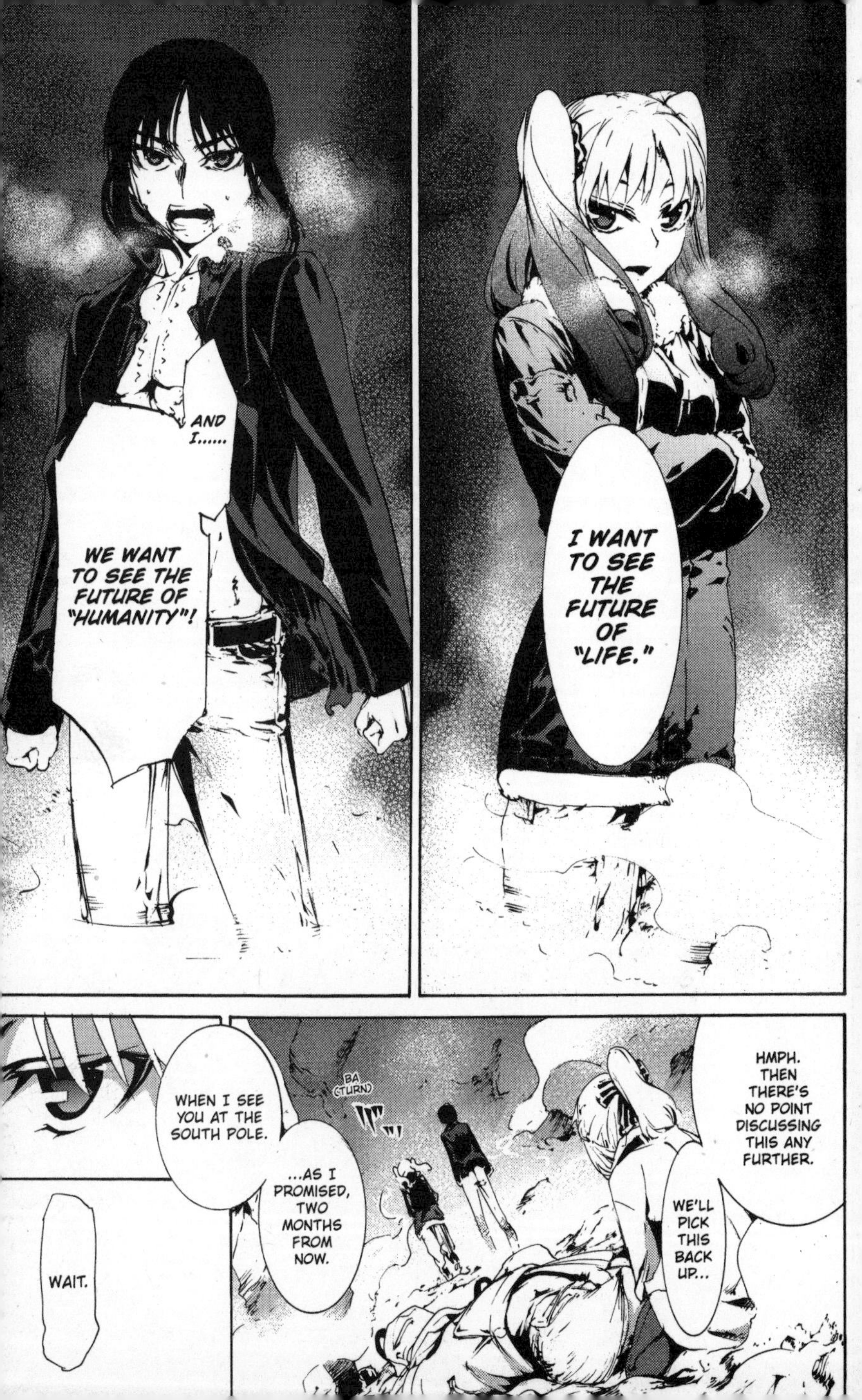
I WANT TO SEE THE FUTURE OF "LIFE."
AND I......
WE WANT TO SEE THE FUTURE OF "HUMANITY"!
HMPH. THEN THERE'S NO POINT DISCUSSING THIS ANY FURTHER.
WE'LL PICK THIS BACK UP...
...AS I PROMISED, TWO MONTHS FROM NOW.
WHEN I SEE YOU AT THE SOUTH POLE.
BA (TURN)
WAIT.

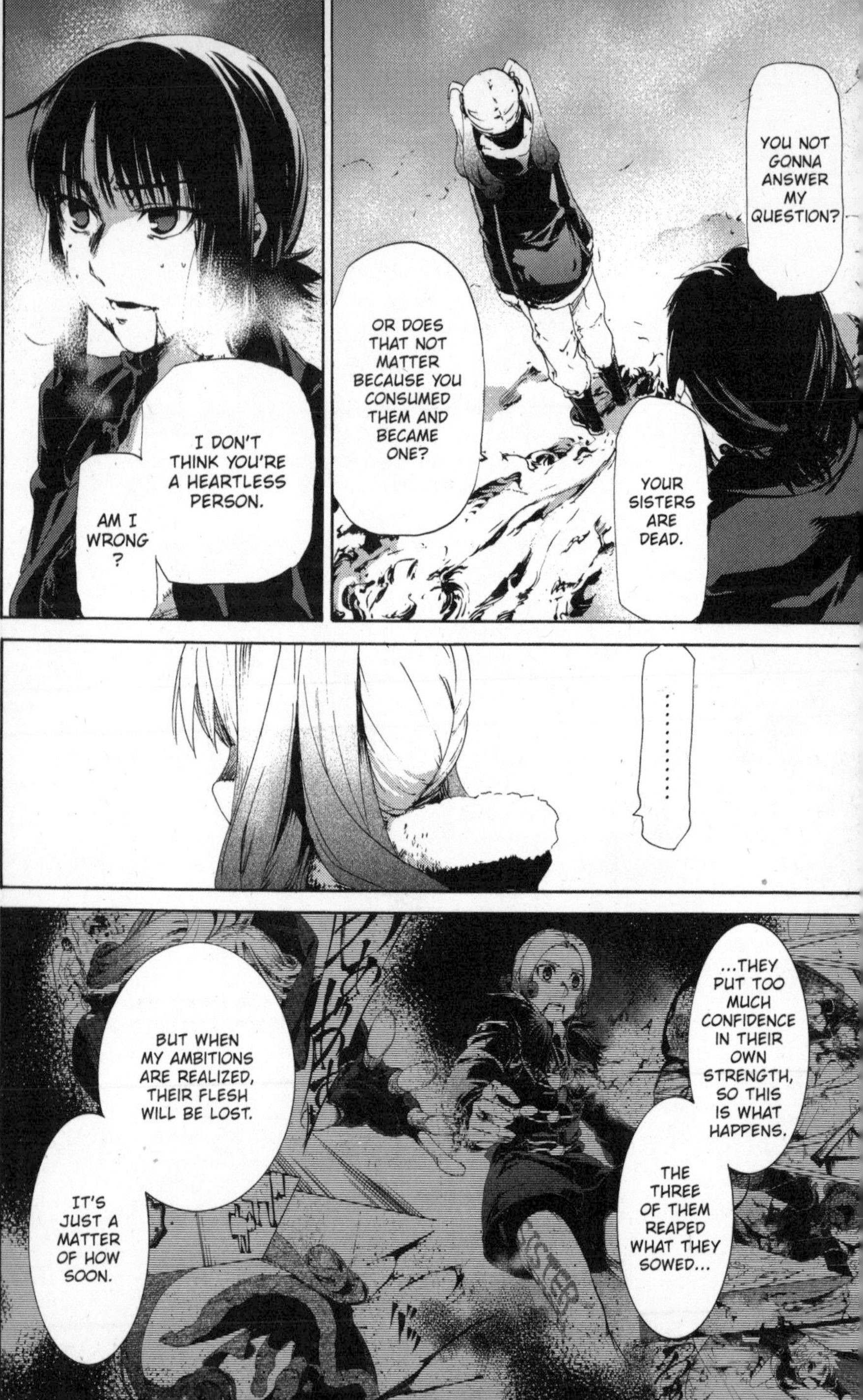
YOU NOT GONNA ANSWER MY QUESTION?
YOUR SISTERS ARE DEAD.
OR DOES THAT NOT MATTER BECAUSE YOU CONSUMED THEM AND BECAME ONE?
I DON'T THINK YOU'RE A HEARTLESS PERSON.
AM I WRONG?
......
...THEY PUT TOO MUCH CONFIDENCE IN THEIR OWN STRENGTH, SO THIS IS WHAT HAPPENS.
THE THREE OF THEM REAPED WHAT THEY SOWED...
BUT WHEN MY AMBITIONS ARE REALIZED, THEIR FLESH WILL BE LOST.
IT'S JUST A MATTER OF HOW SOON.

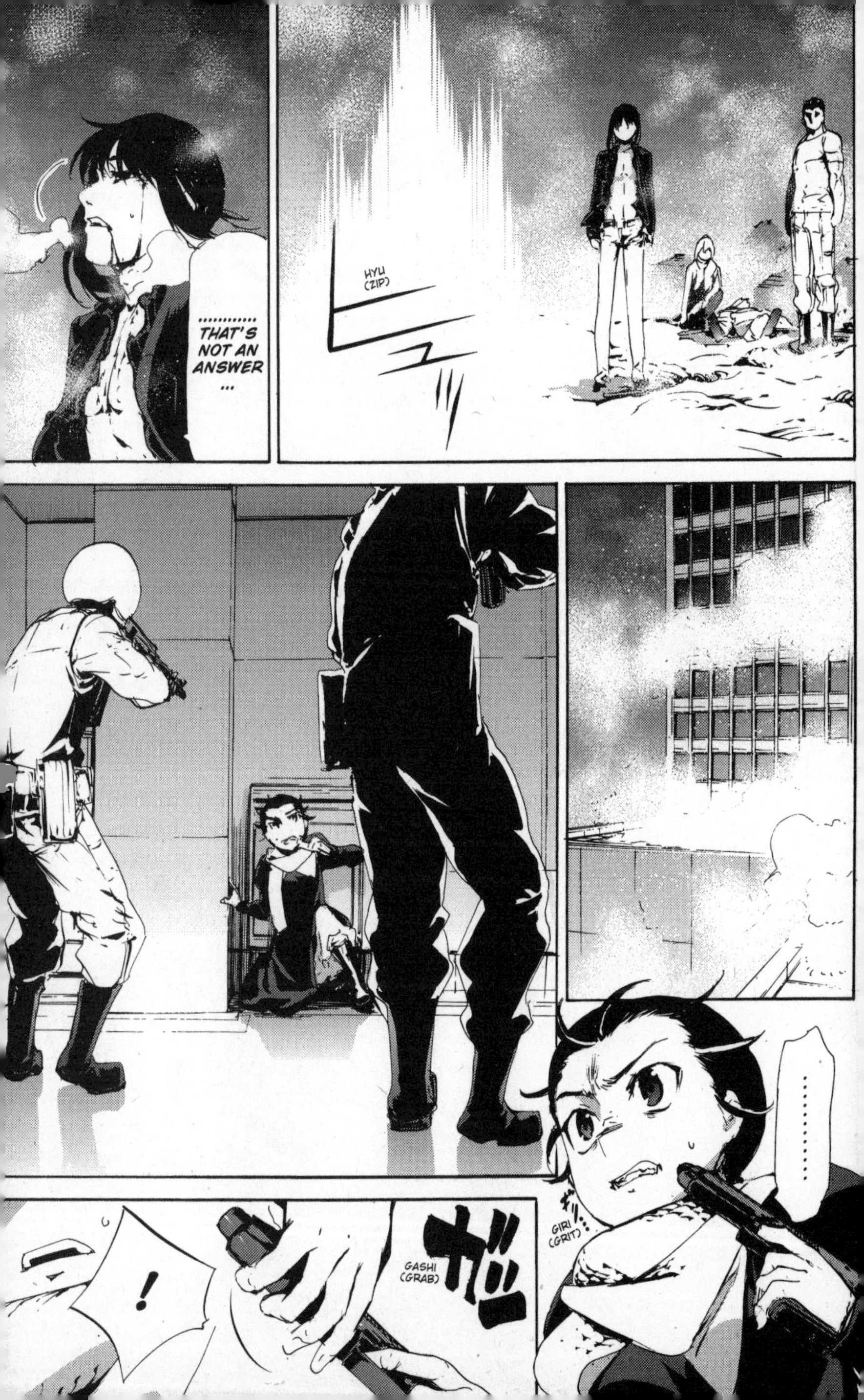
HYU (ZIP)
.... THAT'S NOT AN ANSWER ...
....
GIRI (GRIT)
GASHI (GRAB)
!

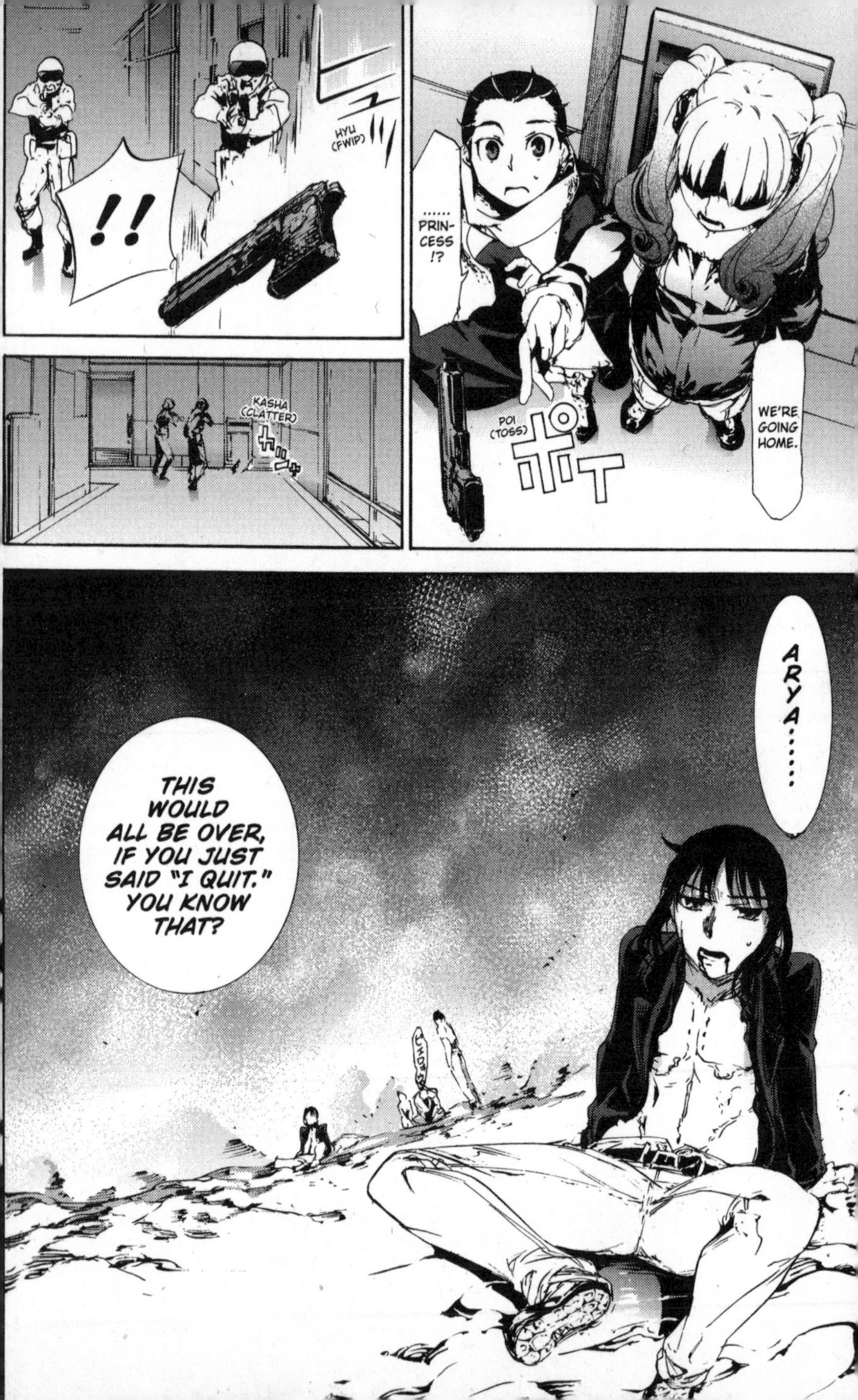

......PRINCESS!?
WE'RE GOING HOME.
POI (TOSS)
HYU (FWIP)
!!
KASHA (CLATTER)
ARYA......
THIS WOULD ALL BE OVER, IF YOU JUST SAID "I QUIT." YOU KNOW THAT?

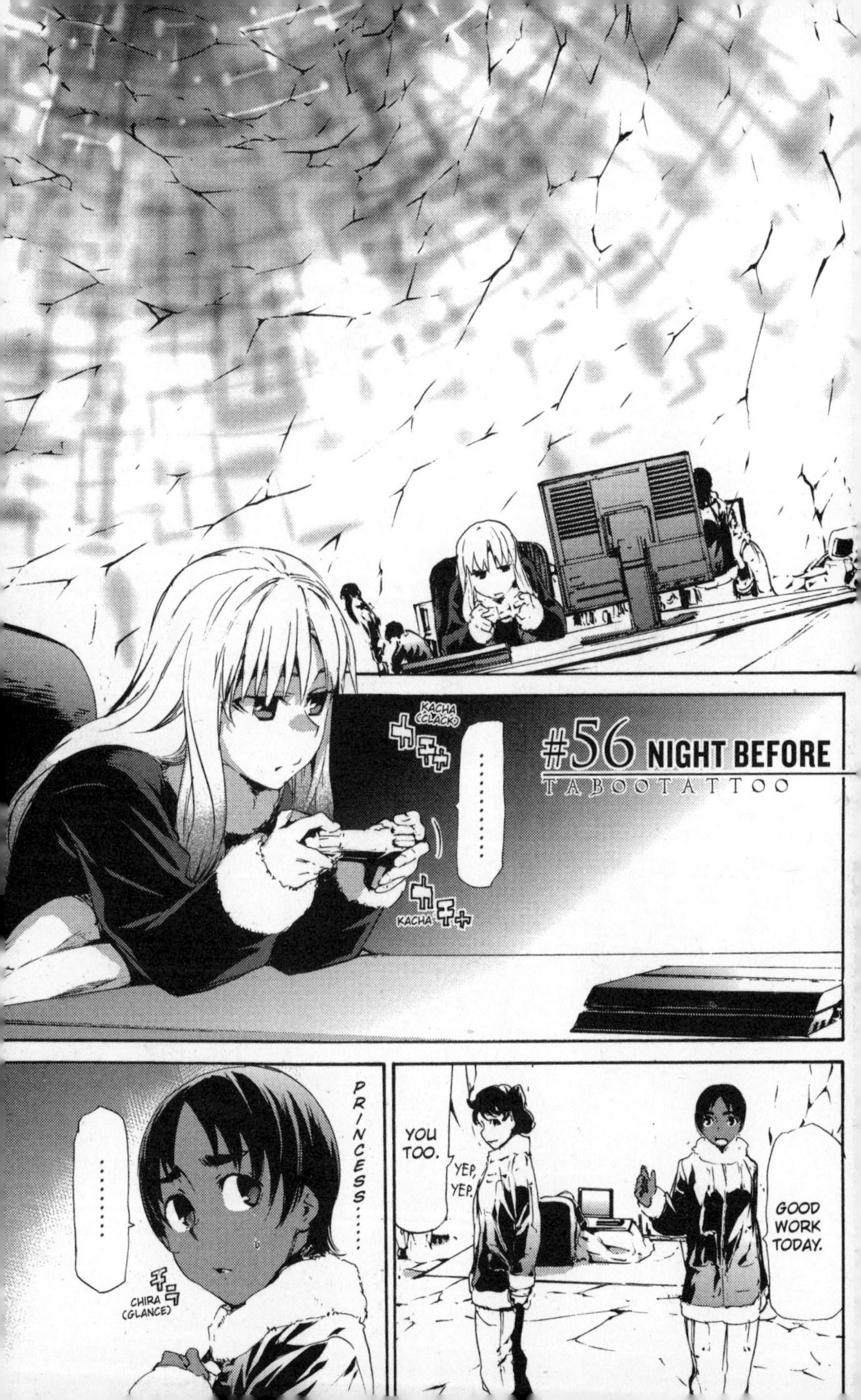

#56 NIGHT BEFORE
TABOO TATTOO
......
KACHA (CLACK)
KACHA
GOOD WORK TODAY.
YEP, YEP.
YOU TOO.
PRINCESS......
......
CHIRA (GLANCE)

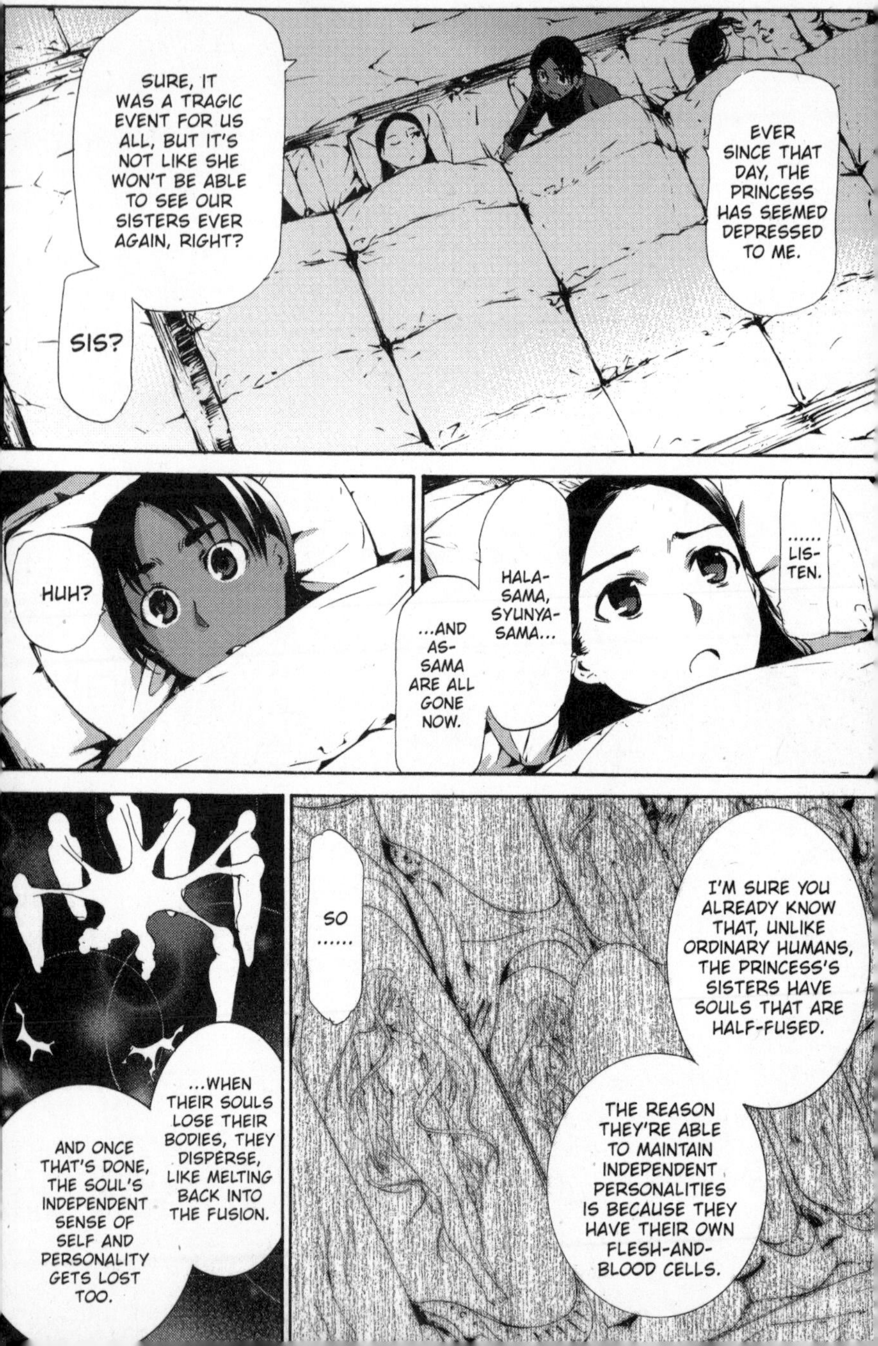
EVER SINCE THAT DAY, THE PRINCESS HAS SEEMED DEPRESSED TO ME.
SURE, IT WAS A TRAGIC EVENT FOR US ALL, BUT IT'S NOT LIKE SHE WON'T BE ABLE TO SEE OUR SISTERS EVER AGAIN, RIGHT?
SIS?
......LIS-TEN.
HALA-SAMA, SYUNYA-SAMA...
...AND AS-SAMA ARE ALL GONE NOW.
HUH?
I'M SURE YOU ALREADY KNOW THAT, UNLIKE ORDINARY HUMANS, THE PRINCESS'S SISTERS HAVE SOULS THAT ARE HALF-FUSED.
THE REASON THEY'RE ABLE TO MAINTAIN INDEPENDENT PERSONALITIES IS BECAUSE THEY HAVE THEIR OWN FLESH-AND-BLOOD CELLS.
SO......
...WHEN THEIR SOULS LOSE THEIR BODIES, THEY DISPERSE, LIKE MELTING BACK INTO THE FUSION.
AND ONCE THAT'S DONE, THE SOUL'S INDEPENDENT SENSE OF SELF AND PERSONALITY GETS LOST TOO.

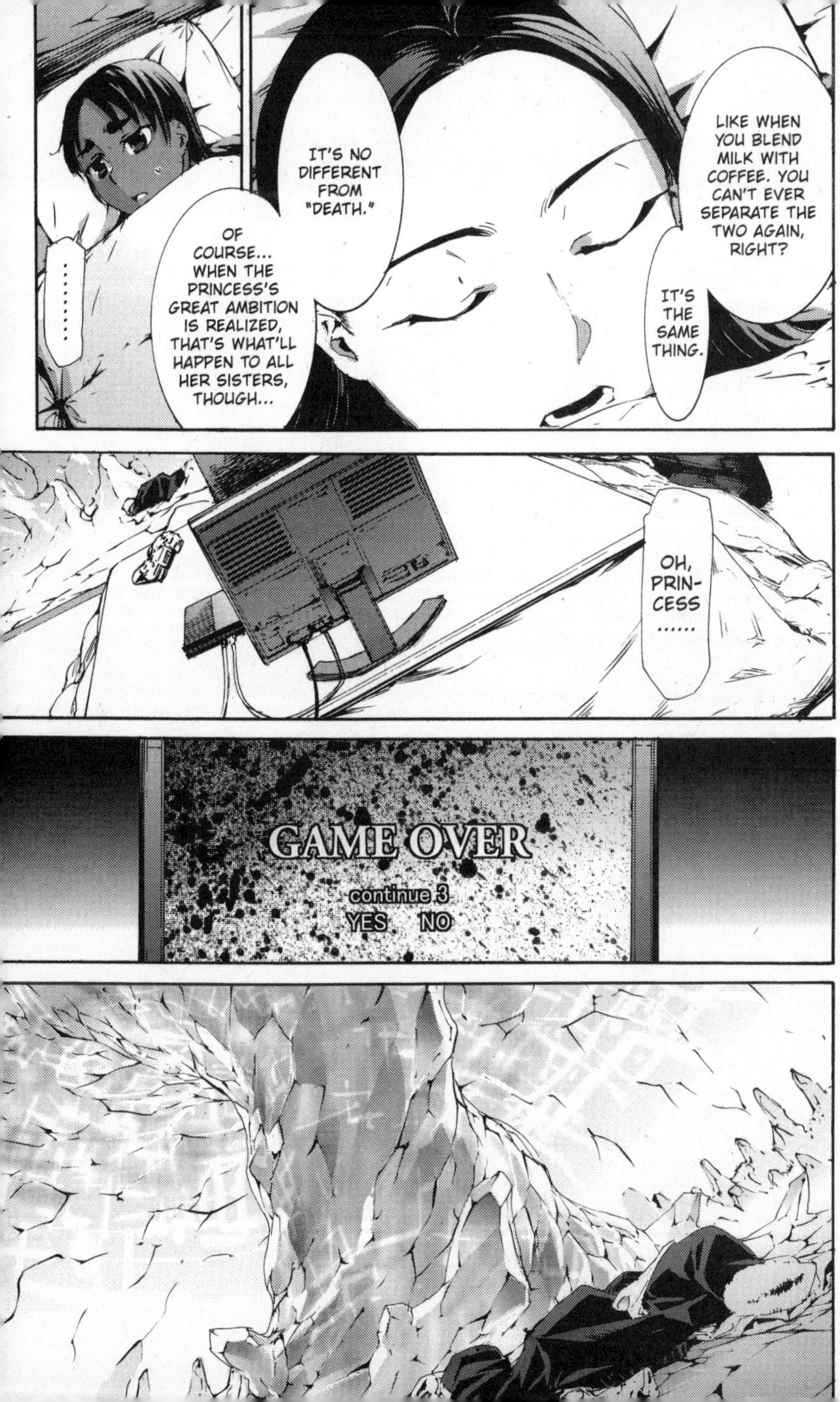
LIKE WHEN YOU BLEND MILK WITH COFFEE. YOU CAN'T EVER SEPARATE THE TWO AGAIN, RIGHT?
IT'S THE SAME THING.
IT'S NO DIFFERENT FROM "DEATH."
OF COURSE... WHEN THE PRINCESS'S GREAT AMBITION IS REALIZED, THAT'S WHAT'LL HAPPEN TO ALL HER SISTERS, THOUGH...
......
OH, PRIN-CESS......
GAME OVER
continue 3
YES NO

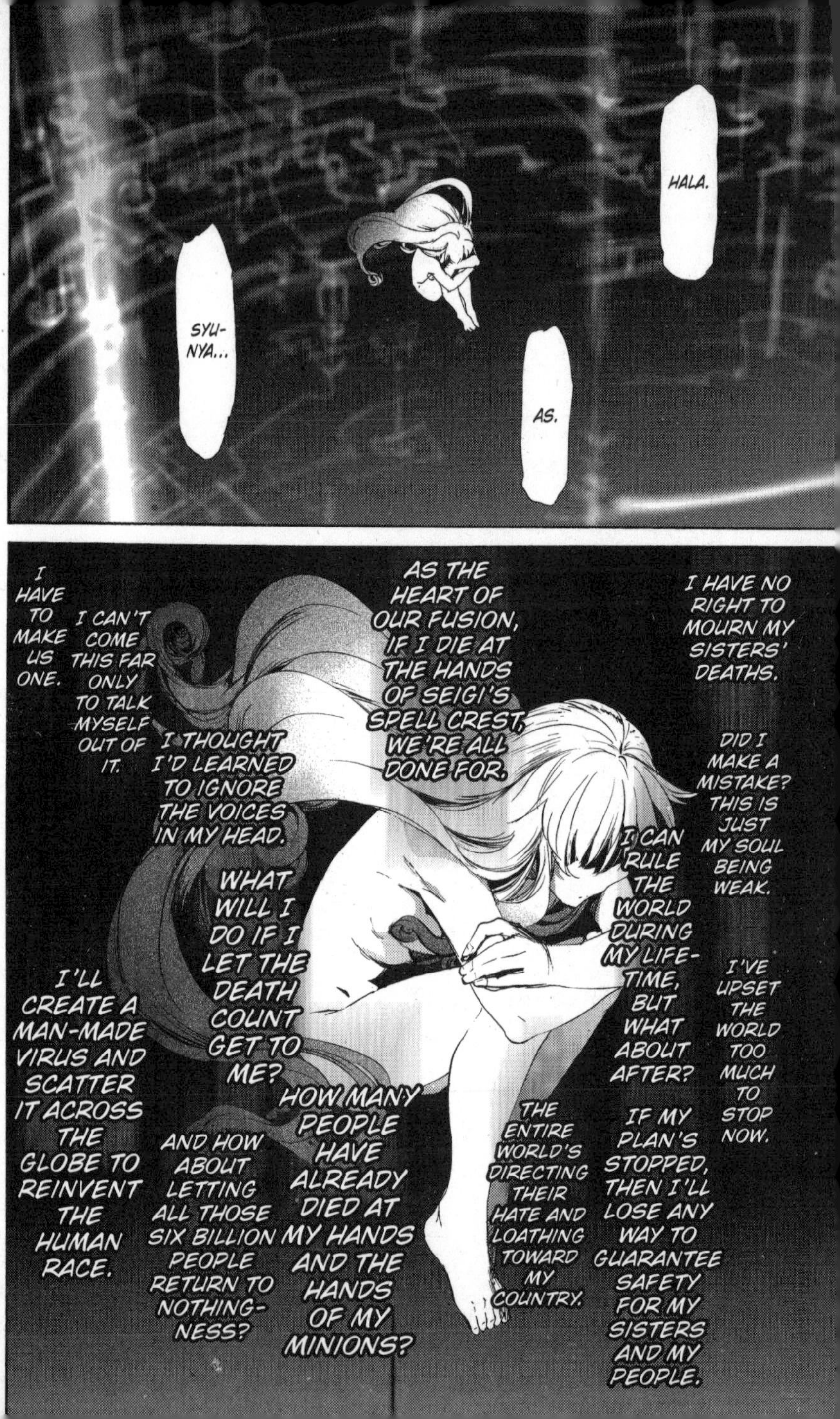
HALA.
AS.
SYU-NYA...
I HAVE NO RIGHT TO MOURN MY SISTERS' DEATHS.
DID I MAKE A MISTAKE? THIS IS JUST MY SOUL BEING WEAK.
I'VE UPSET THE WORLD TOO MUCH TO STOP NOW.
AS THE HEART OF OUR FUSION, IF I DIE AT THE HANDS OF SEIGI'S SPELL CREST, WE'RE ALL DONE FOR.
I CAN RULE THE WORLD DURING MY LIFE-TIME, BUT WHAT ABOUT AFTER?
IF MY PLAN'S STOPPED, THEN I'LL LOSE ANY WAY TO GUARANTEE SAFETY FOR MY SISTERS AND MY PEOPLE.
THE ENTIRE WORLD'S DIRECTING THEIR HATE AND LOATHING TOWARD MY COUNTRY.
I HAVE TO MAKE US ONE.
I CAN'T COME THIS FAR ONLY TO TALK MYSELF OUT OF IT.
I THOUGHT I'D LEARNED TO IGNORE THE VOICES IN MY HEAD.
WHAT WILL I DO IF I LET THE DEATH COUNT GET TO ME?
HOW MANY PEOPLE HAVE ALREADY DIED AT MY HANDS AND THE HANDS OF MY MINIONS?
AND HOW ABOUT LETTING ALL THOSE SIX BILLION PEOPLE RETURN TO NOTHING-NESS?
I'LL CREATE A MAN-MADE VIRUS AND SCATTER IT ACROSS THE GLOBE TO REINVENT THE HUMAN RACE.

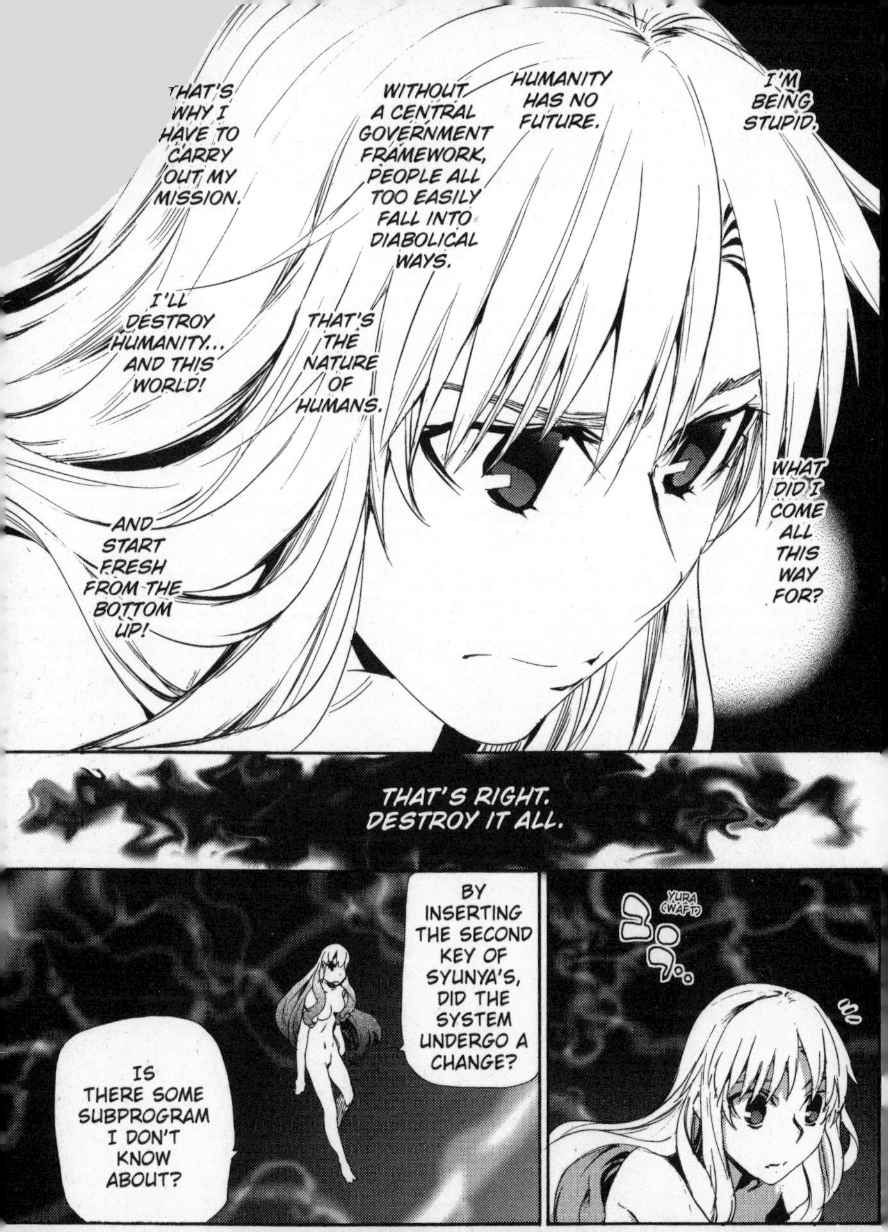
I'M BEING STUPID.
WHAT DID I COME ALL THIS WAY FOR?
HUMANITY HAS NO FUTURE.
WITHOUT A CENTRAL GOVERNMENT FRAMEWORK, PEOPLE ALL TOO EASILY FALL INTO DIABOLICAL WAYS.
THAT'S THE NATURE OF HUMANS.
THAT'S WHY I HAVE TO CARRY OUT MY MISSION.
I'LL DESTROY HUMANITY... AND THIS WORLD!
AND START FRESH FROM THE BOTTOM UP!
THAT'S RIGHT. DESTROY IT ALL.
YURA (WAFT)
BY INSERTING THE SECOND KEY OF SYUNYA'S, DID THE SYSTEM UNDERGO A CHANGE?
IS THERE SOME SUBPROGRAM I DON'T KNOW ABOUT?

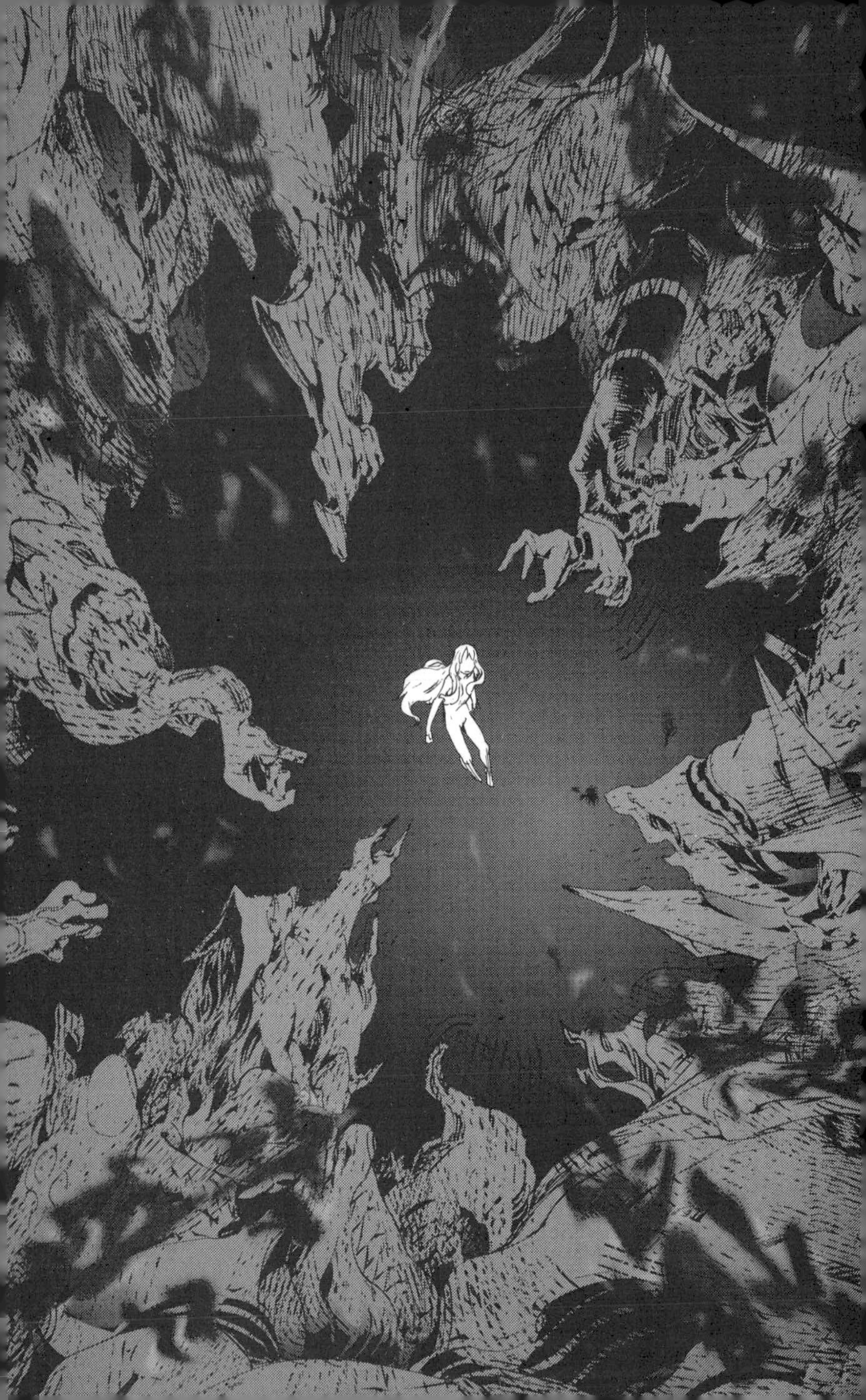

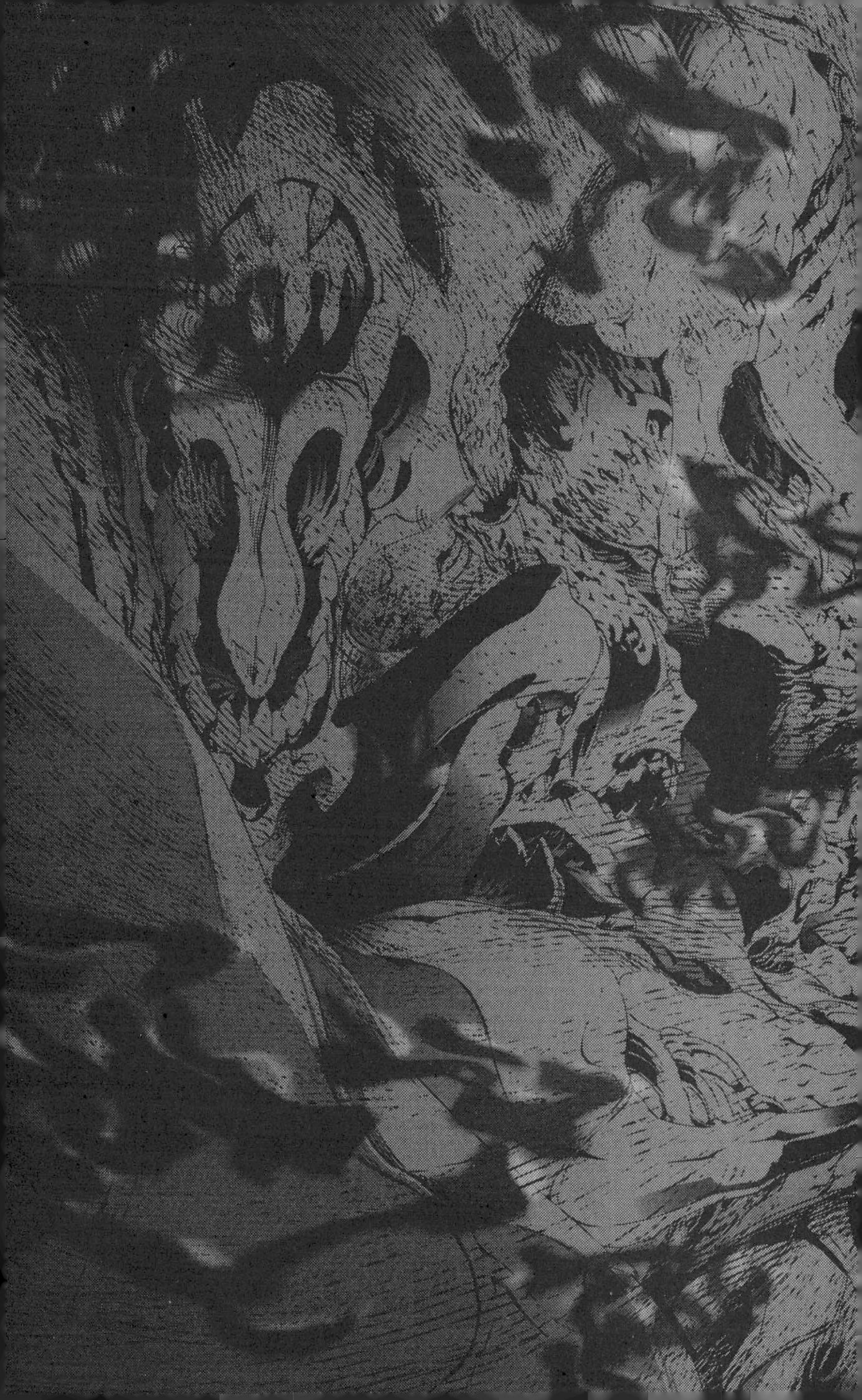

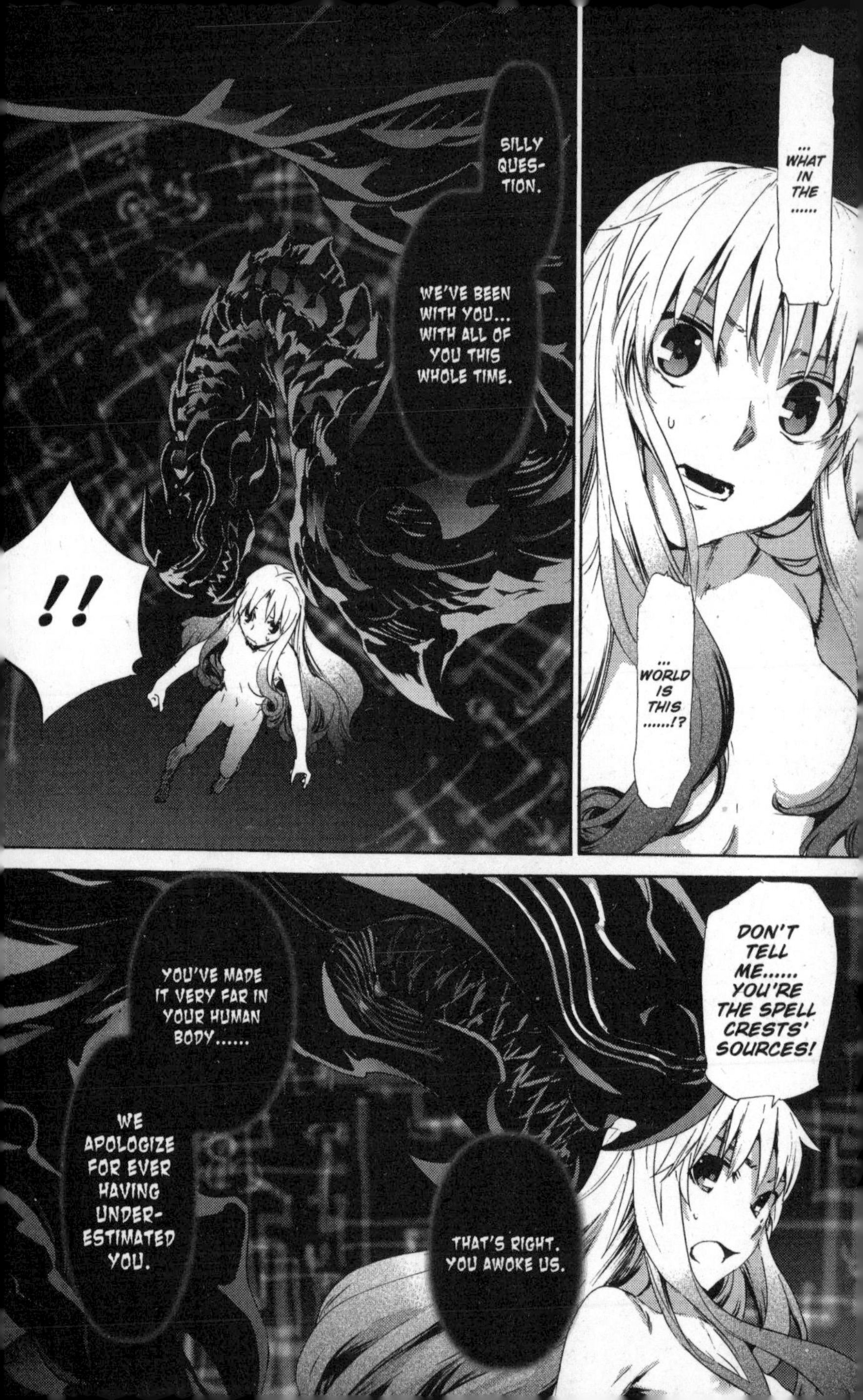
...WHAT IN THE ......
...WORLD IS THIS ......!?
SILLY QUES-TION.
WE'VE BEEN WITH YOU... WITH ALL OF YOU THIS WHOLE TIME.
!!
DON'T TELL ME...... YOU'RE THE SPELL CRESTS' SOURCES!
THAT'S RIGHT. YOU AWOKE US.
YOU'VE MADE IT VERY FAR IN YOUR HUMAN BODY......
WE APOLOGIZE FOR EVER HAVING UNDER-ESTIMATED YOU.

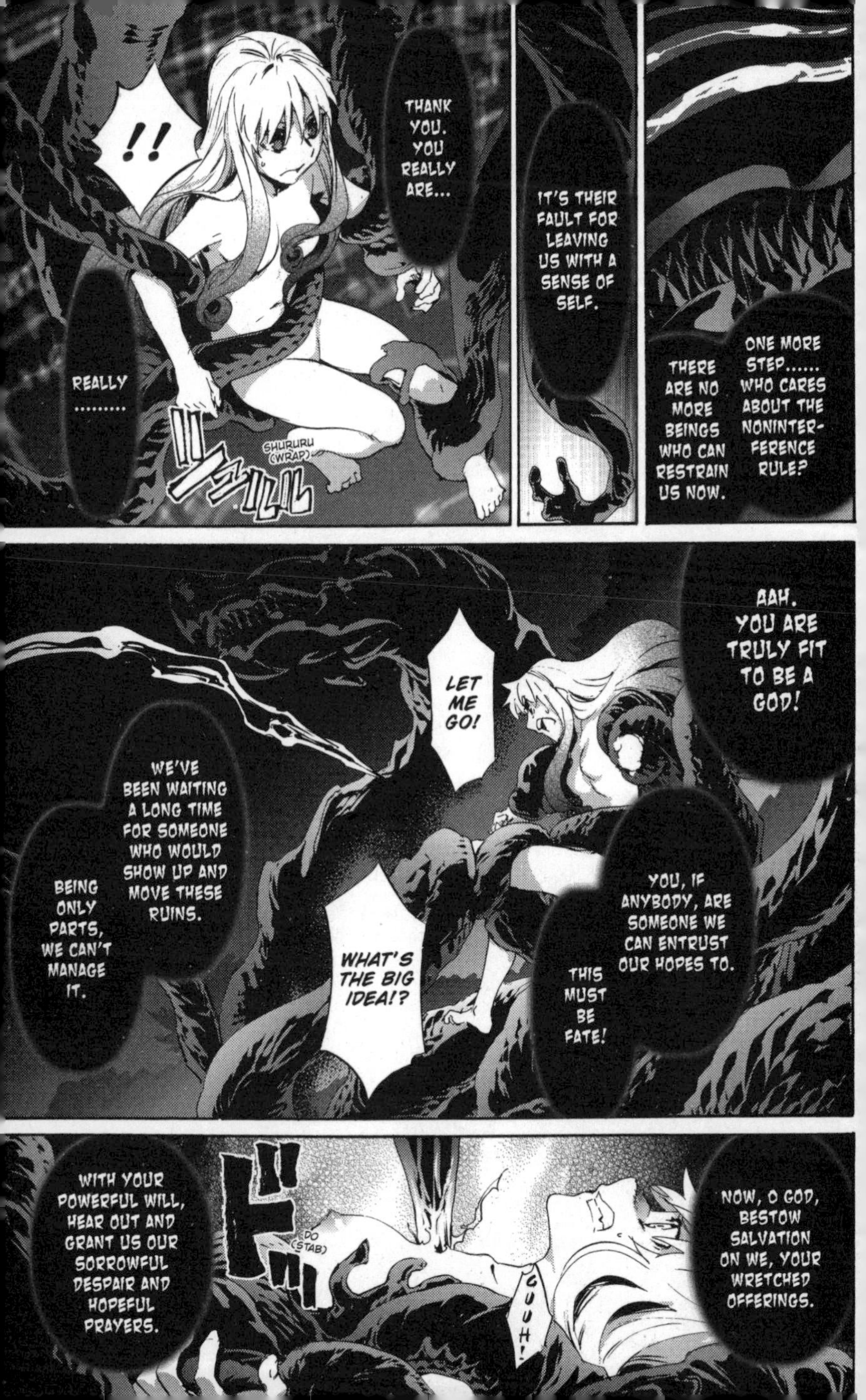
ONE MORE STEP...... WHO CARES ABOUT THE NONINTERFERENCE RULE?
THERE ARE NO MORE BEINGS WHO CAN RESTRAIN US NOW.
IT'S THEIR FAULT FOR LEAVING US WITH A SENSE OF SELF.
THANK YOU. YOU REALLY ARE...
!!
REALLY ....
SHURURU (WRAP)
AAH. YOU ARE TRULY FIT TO BE A GOD!
LET ME GO!
YOU, IF ANYBODY, ARE SOMEONE WE CAN ENTRUST OUR HOPES TO.
THIS MUST BE FATE!
WHAT'S THE BIG IDEA!?
WE'VE BEEN WAITING A LONG TIME FOR SOMEONE WHO WOULD SHOW UP AND MOVE THESE RUINS.
BEING ONLY PARTS, WE CAN'T MANAGE IT.
NOW, O GOD, BESTOW SALVATION ON WE, YOUR WRETCHED OFFERINGS.
GUUH!
DO (STAB)
WITH YOUR POWERFUL WILL, HEAR OUT AND GRANT US OUR SORROWFUL DESPAIR AND HOPEFUL PRAYERS.

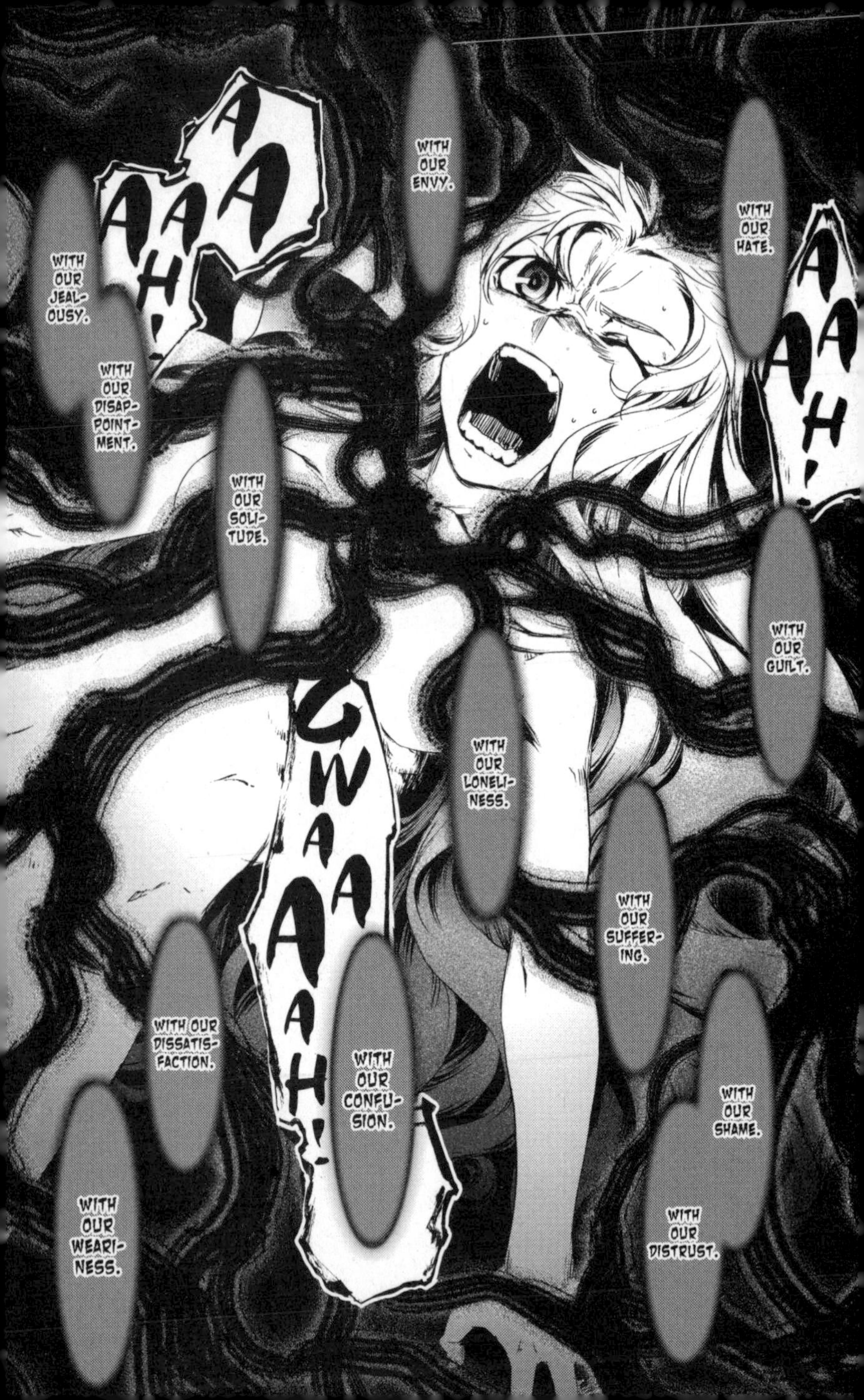
WITH OUR HATE.
AAAH!
WITH OUR ENVY.
AAAAAH!
WITH OUR JEAL-OUSY.
WITH OUR DISAP-POINT-MENT.
WITH OUR SOLI-TUDE.
WITH OUR GUILT.
WITH OUR LONELI-NESS.
GWAAAAH!
WITH OUR SUFFER-ING.
WITH OUR SHAME.
WITH OUR CONFU-SION.
WITH OUR DISSATIS-FACTION.
WITH OUR DISTRUST.
WITH OUR WEARI-NESS.

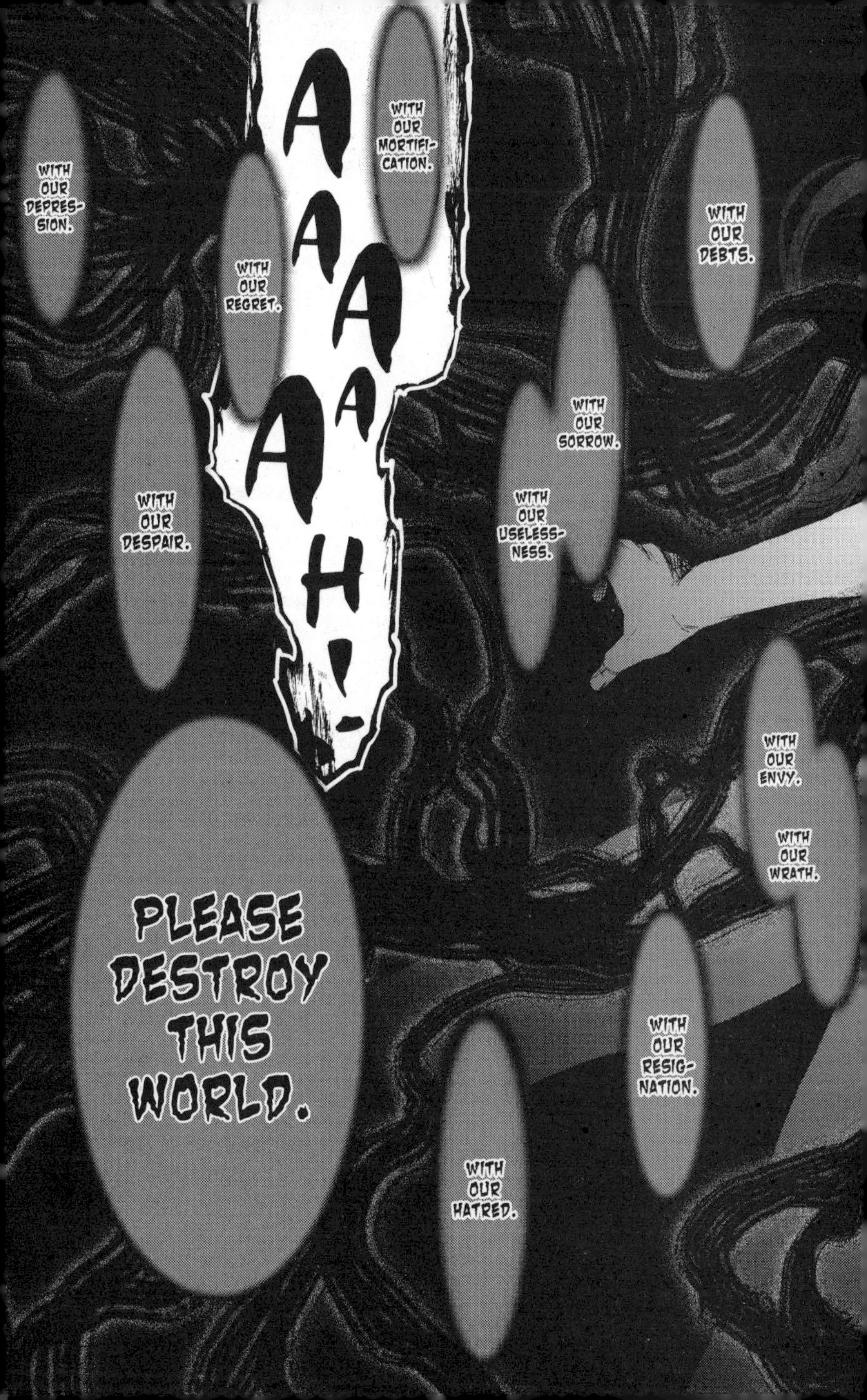
WITH OUR DEBTS.
WITH OUR MORTIFICATION.
AAAAAH!
WITH OUR SORROW.
WITH OUR USELESSNESS.
WITH OUR REGRET.
WITH OUR DEPRESSION.
WITH OUR DESPAIR.
WITH OUR ENVY.
WITH OUR WRATH.
WITH OUR RESIGNATION.
WITH OUR HATRED.
PLEASE DESTROY THIS WORLD.

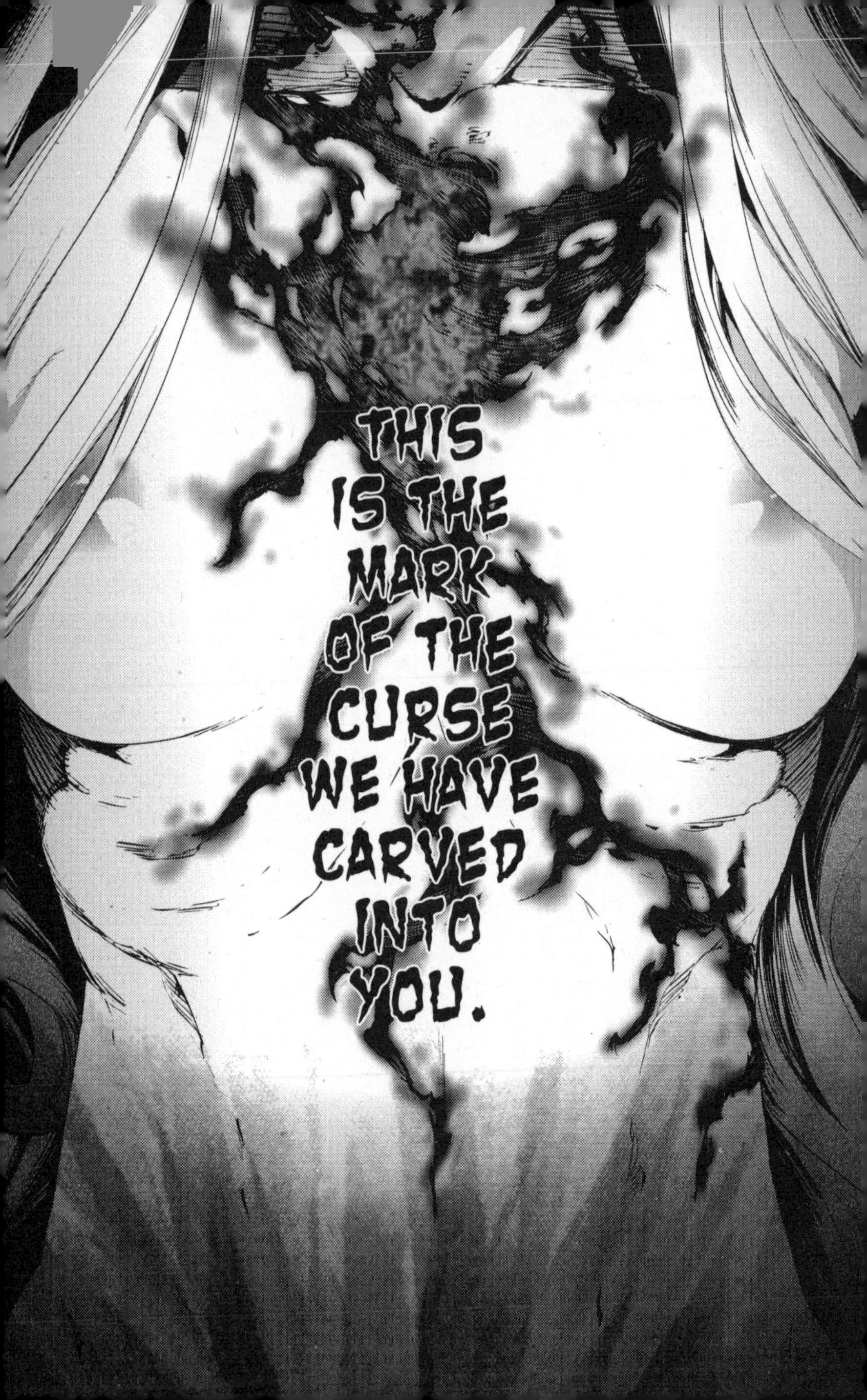
THIS IS THE MARK OF THE CURSE WE HAVE CARVED INTO YOU.

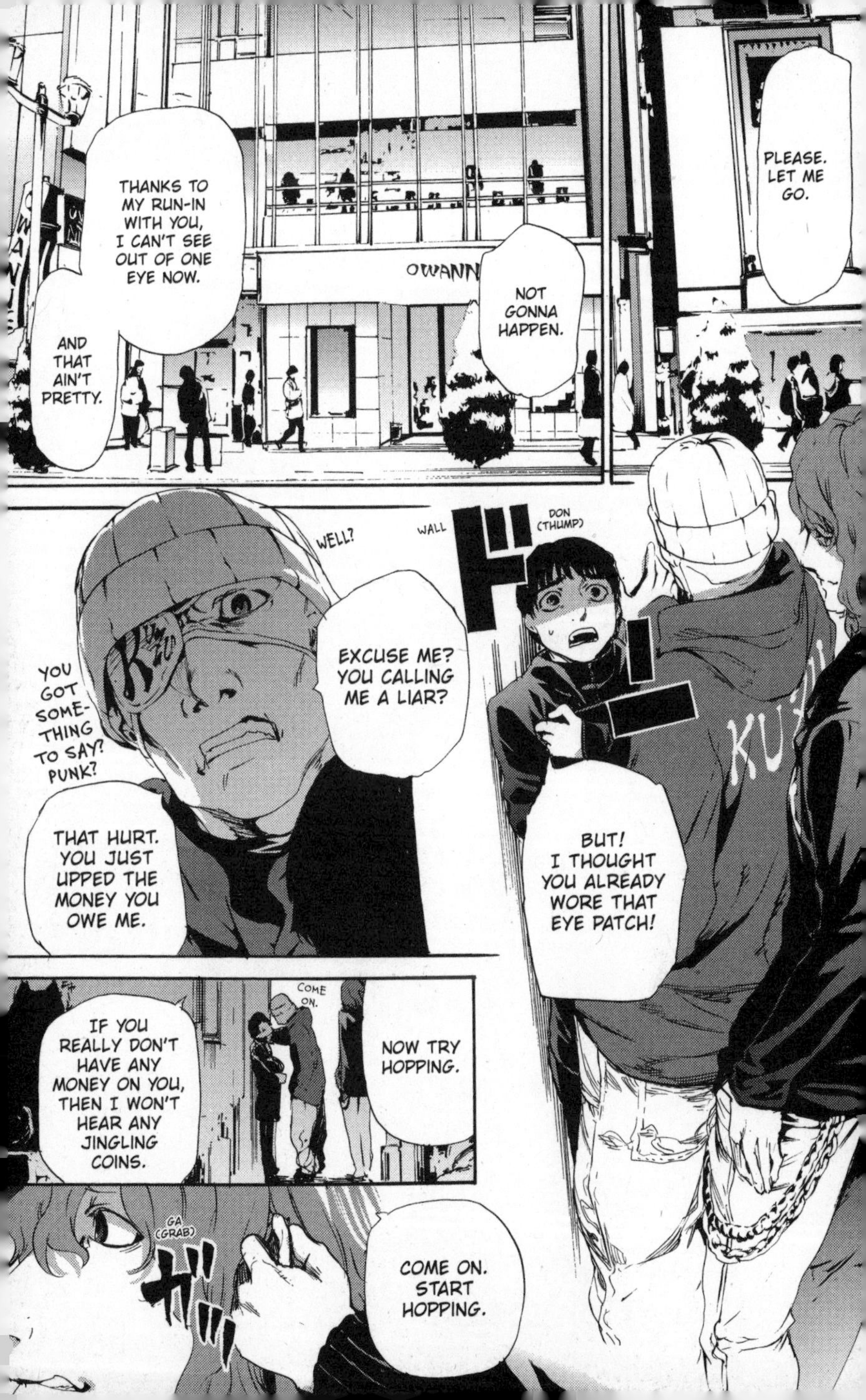
PLEASE. LET ME GO.
NOT GONNA HAPPEN.
THANKS TO MY RUN-IN WITH YOU, I CAN'T SEE OUT OF ONE EYE NOW.
AND THAT AIN'T PRETTY.
WALL
DON (THUMP)
BUT! I THOUGHT YOU ALREADY WORE THAT EYE PATCH!
WELL?
EXCUSE ME? YOU CALLING ME A LIAR?
YOU GOT SOME-THING TO SAY? PUNK?
THAT HURT. YOU JUST UPPED THE MONEY YOU OWE ME.
COME ON.
NOW TRY HOPPING.
IF YOU REALLY DON'T HAVE ANY MONEY ON YOU, THEN I WON'T HEAR ANY JINGLING COINS.
GA (GRAB)
COME ON. START HOPPING.

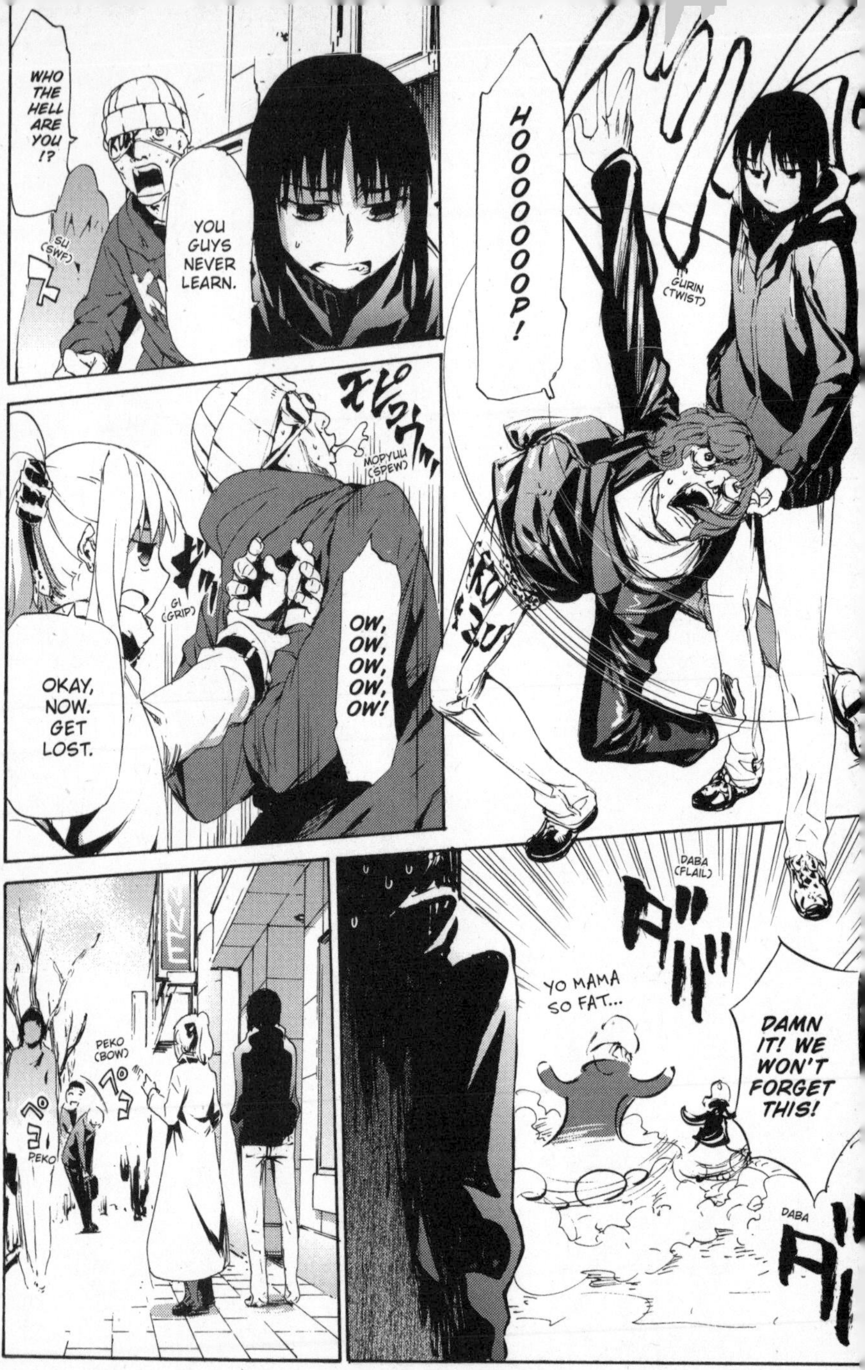
HOOOOOOOOP!
GURIN (TWIST)
WHO THE HELL ARE YOU!?
SU (SWF)
YOU GUYS NEVER LEARN.
MOPYUU (SPEW)
OW, OW, OW, OW, OW!
GI (GRIP)
OKAY, NOW. GET LOST.
DABA (FLAIL)
YO MAMA SO FAT...
DAMN IT! WE WON'T FORGET THIS!
DABA
PEKO (BOW)
PEKO

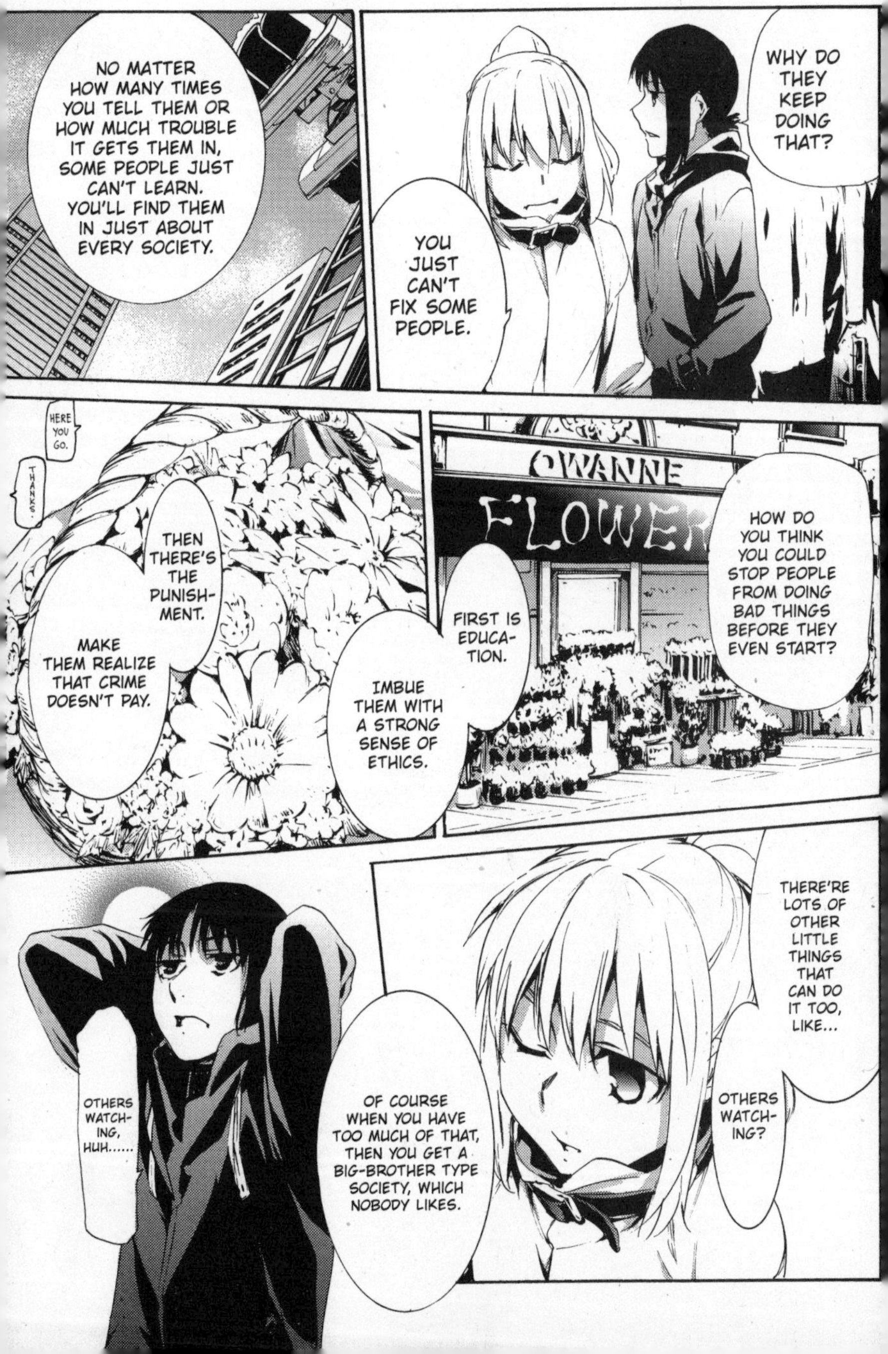
WHY DO THEY KEEP DOING THAT?
YOU JUST CAN'T FIX SOME PEOPLE.
NO MATTER HOW MANY TIMES YOU TELL THEM OR HOW MUCH TROUBLE IT GETS THEM IN, SOME PEOPLE JUST CAN'T LEARN. YOU'LL FIND THEM IN JUST ABOUT EVERY SOCIETY.
CWANNE
FLOWER
HOW DO YOU THINK YOU COULD STOP PEOPLE FROM DOING BAD THINGS BEFORE THEY EVEN START?
FIRST IS EDUCATION.
IMBUE THEM WITH A STRONG SENSE OF ETHICS.
HERE YOU GO.
THANKS.
THEN THERE'S THE PUNISHMENT.
MAKE THEM REALIZE THAT CRIME DOESN'T PAY.
THERE'RE LOTS OF OTHER LITTLE THINGS THAT CAN DO IT TOO, LIKE...
OTHERS WATCHING?
OF COURSE WHEN YOU HAVE TOO MUCH OF THAT, THEN YOU GET A BIG-BROTHER TYPE SOCIETY, WHICH NOBODY LIKES.
OTHERS WATCHING, HUH......

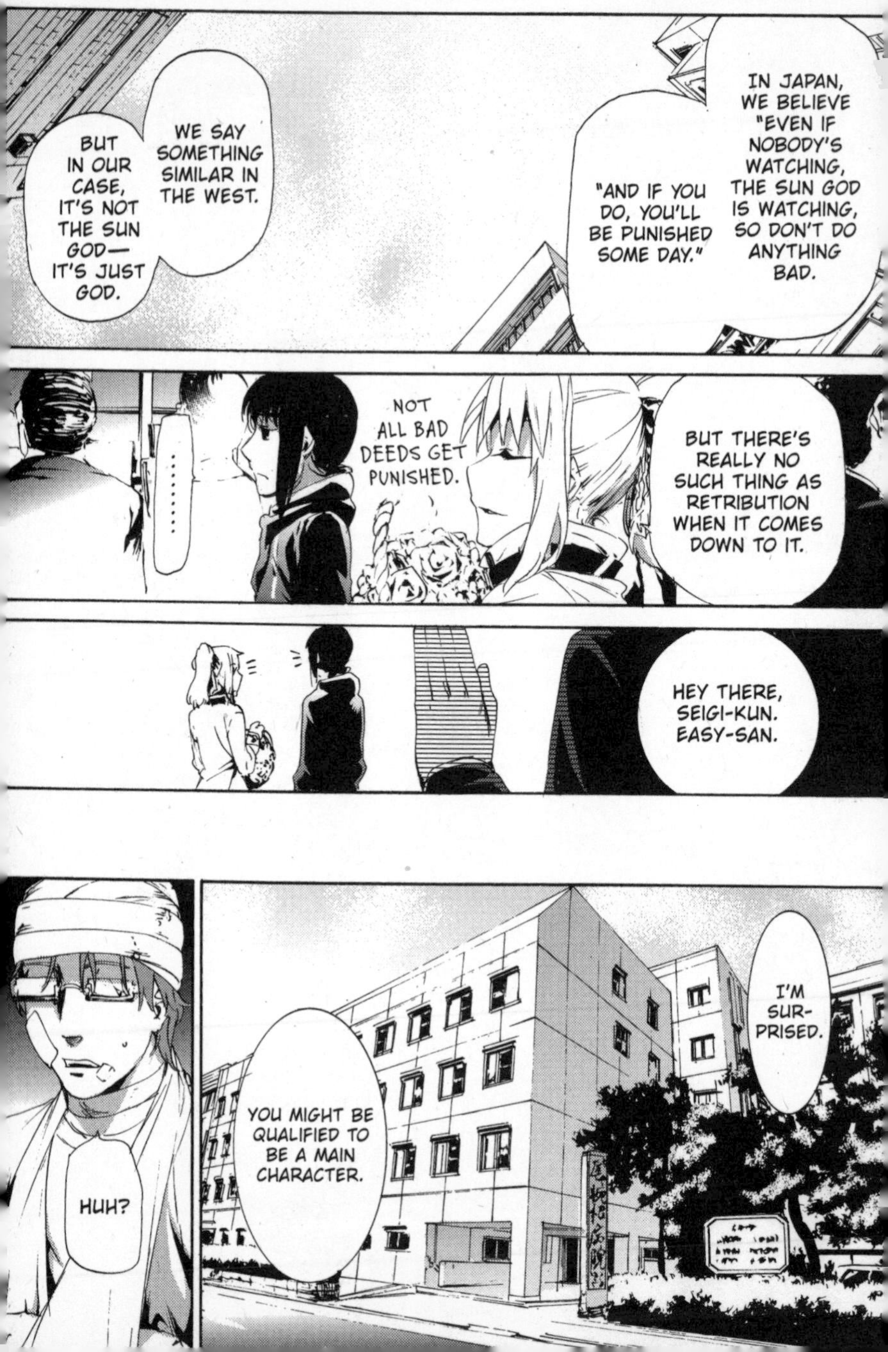
IN JAPAN, WE BELIEVE "EVEN IF NOBODY'S WATCHING, THE SUN GOD IS WATCHING, SO DON'T DO ANYTHING BAD.
"AND IF YOU DO, YOU'LL BE PUNISHED SOME DAY."
WE SAY SOMETHING SIMILAR IN THE WEST.
BUT IN OUR CASE, IT'S NOT THE SUN GOD— IT'S JUST GOD.
BUT THERE'S REALLY NO SUCH THING AS RETRIBUTION WHEN IT COMES DOWN TO IT.
NOT ALL BAD DEEDS GET PUNISHED.
....
HEY THERE, SEIGI-KUN. EASY-SAN.
I'M SUR-PRISED.
YOU MIGHT BE QUALIFIED TO BE A MAIN CHARACTER.
HUH?

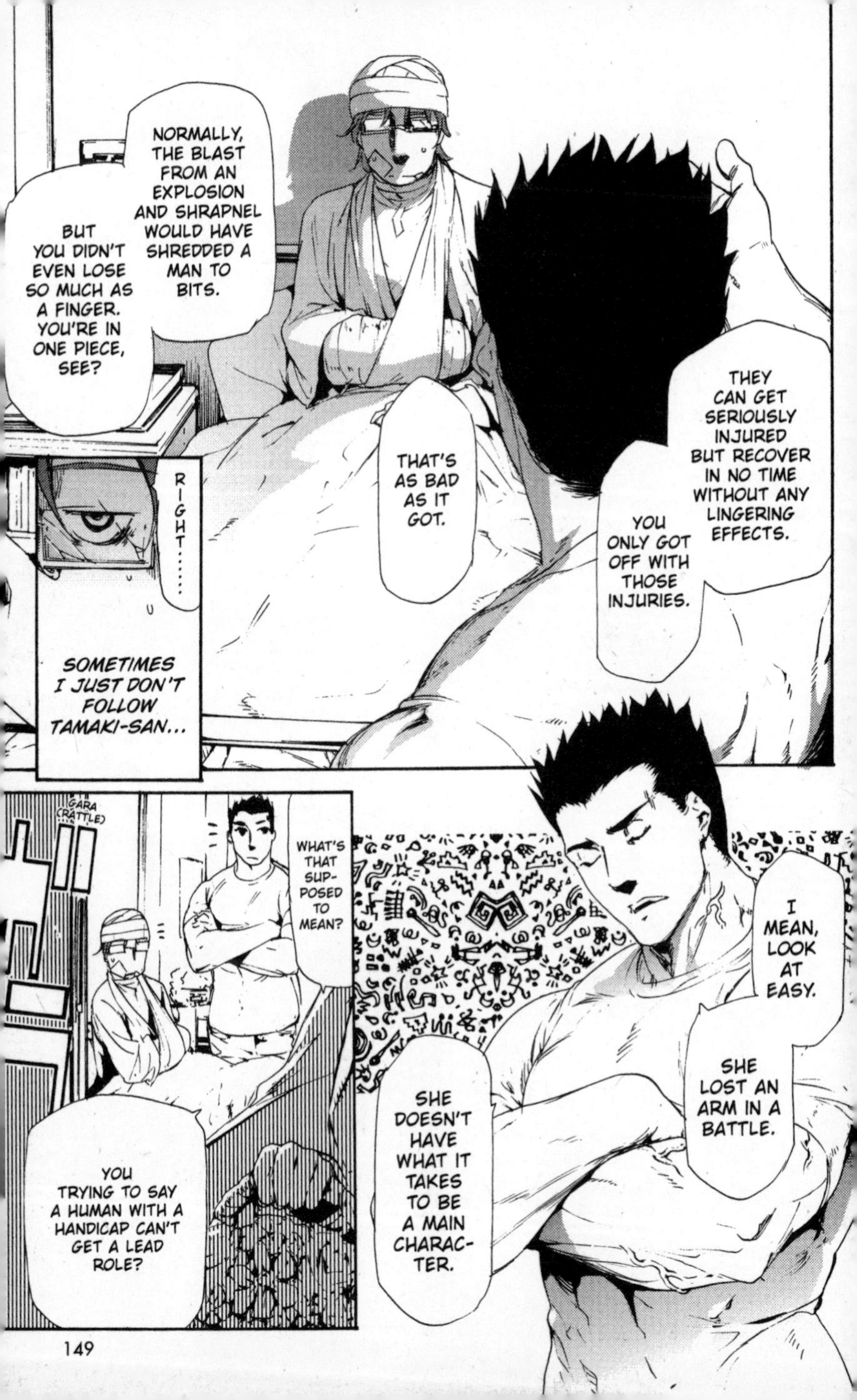
THEY CAN GET SERIOUSLY INJURED BUT RECOVER IN NO TIME WITHOUT ANY LINGERING EFFECTS.
YOU ONLY GOT OFF WITH THOSE INJURIES.
THAT'S AS BAD AS IT GOT.
NORMALLY, THE BLAST FROM AN EXPLOSION AND SHRAPNEL WOULD HAVE SHREDDED A MAN TO BITS.
BUT YOU DIDN'T EVEN LOSE SO MUCH AS A FINGER. YOU'RE IN ONE PIECE, SEE?
RIGHT......
SOMETIMES I JUST DON'T FOLLOW TAMAKI-SAN...
I MEAN, LOOK AT EASY.
SHE LOST AN ARM IN A BATTLE.
SHE DOESN'T HAVE WHAT IT TAKES TO BE A MAIN CHARAC-TER.
GARA (RATTLE)
WHAT'S THAT SUP-POSED TO MEAN?
YOU TRYING TO SAY A HUMAN WITH A HANDICAP CAN'T GET A LEAD ROLE?

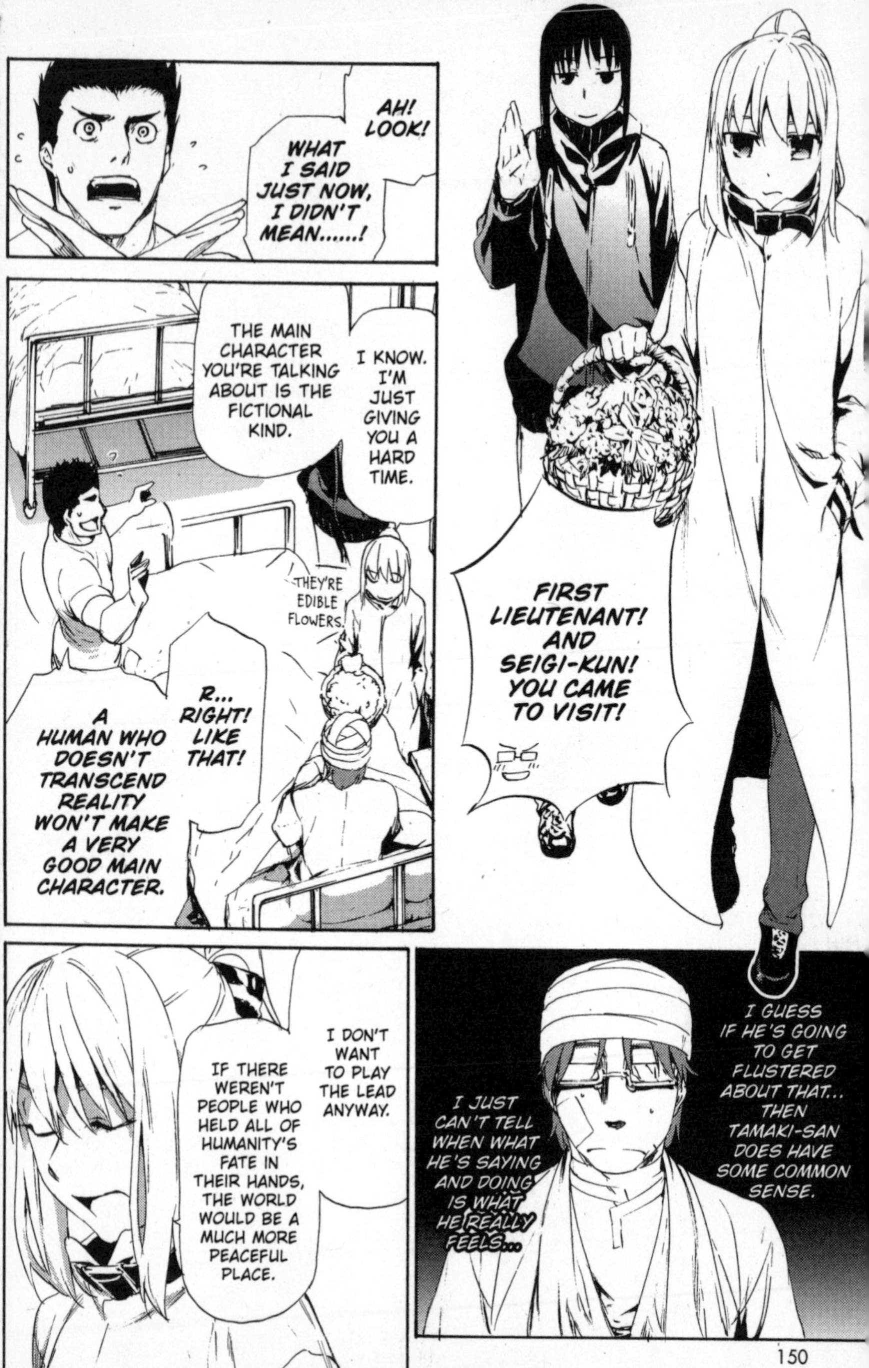
FIRST LIEUTENANT! AND SEIGI-KUN! YOU CAME TO VISIT!
AH! LOOK!
WHAT I SAID JUST NOW, I DIDN'T MEAN......!
I KNOW. I'M JUST GIVING YOU A HARD TIME.
THE MAIN CHARACTER YOU'RE TALKING ABOUT IS THE FICTIONAL KIND.
THEY'RE EDIBLE FLOWERS.
R... RIGHT! LIKE THAT!
A HUMAN WHO DOESN'T TRANSCEND REALITY WON'T MAKE A VERY GOOD MAIN CHARACTER.
I GUESS IF HE'S GOING TO GET FLUSTERED ABOUT THAT... THEN TAMAKI-SAN DOES HAVE SOME COMMON SENSE.
I JUST CAN'T TELL WHEN WHAT HE'S SAYING AND DOING IS WHAT HE REALLY FEELS...
I DON'T WANT TO PLAY THE LEAD ANYWAY.
IF THERE WEREN'T PEOPLE WHO HELD ALL OF HUMANITY'S FATE IN THEIR HANDS, THE WORLD WOULD BE A MUCH MORE PEACEFUL PLACE.

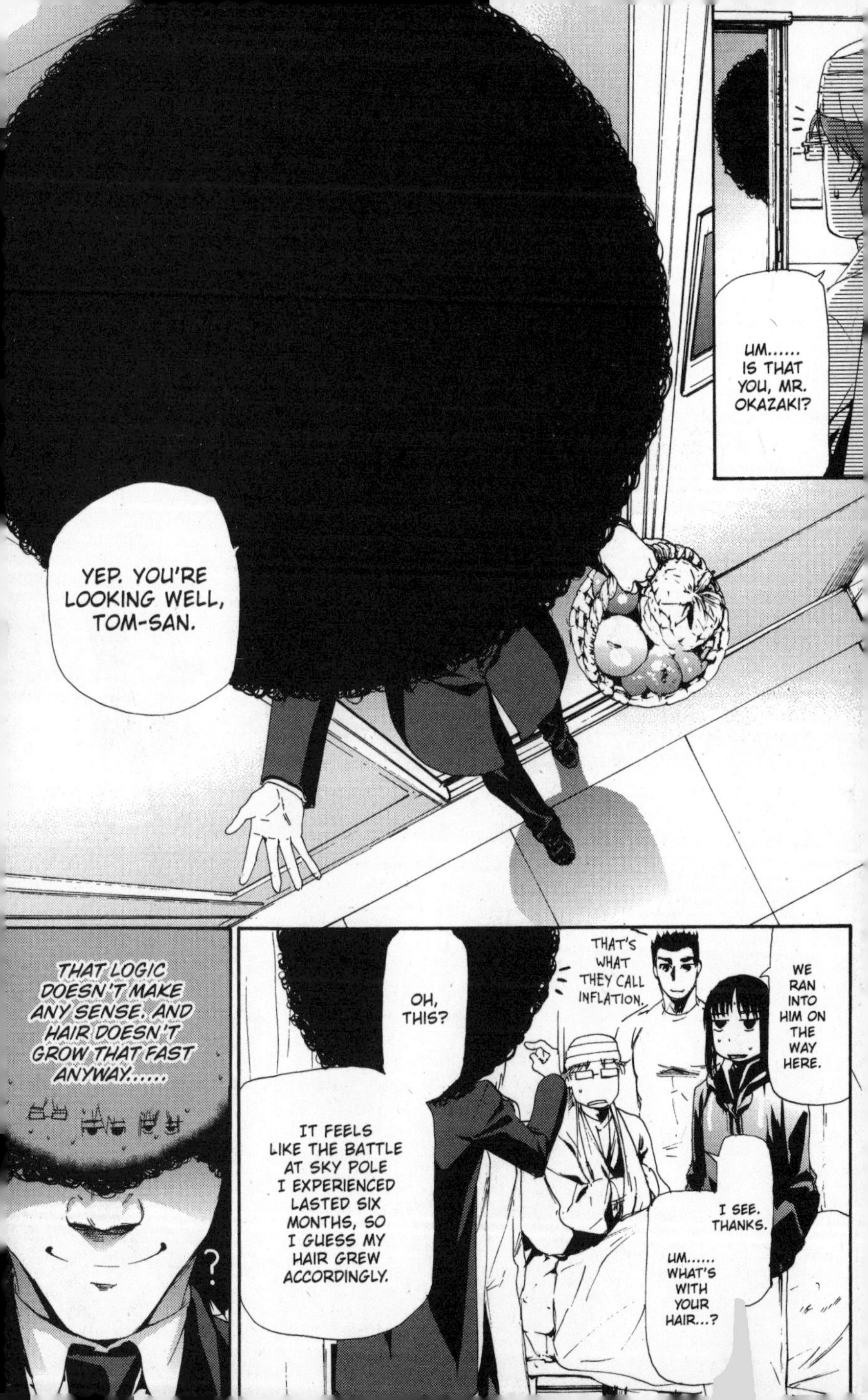
UM...... IS THAT YOU, MR. OKAZAKI?
YEP. YOU'RE LOOKING WELL, TOM-SAN.
WE RAN INTO HIM ON THE WAY HERE.
I SEE. THANKS.
UM...... WHAT'S WITH YOUR HAIR...?
OH, THIS?
IT FEELS LIKE THE BATTLE AT SKY POLE I EXPERIENCED LASTED SIX MONTHS, SO I GUESS MY HAIR GREW ACCORDINGLY.
THAT'S WHAT THEY CALL INFLATION.
THAT LOGIC DOESN'T MAKE ANY SENSE. AND HAIR DOESN'T GROW THAT FAST ANYWAY......
?

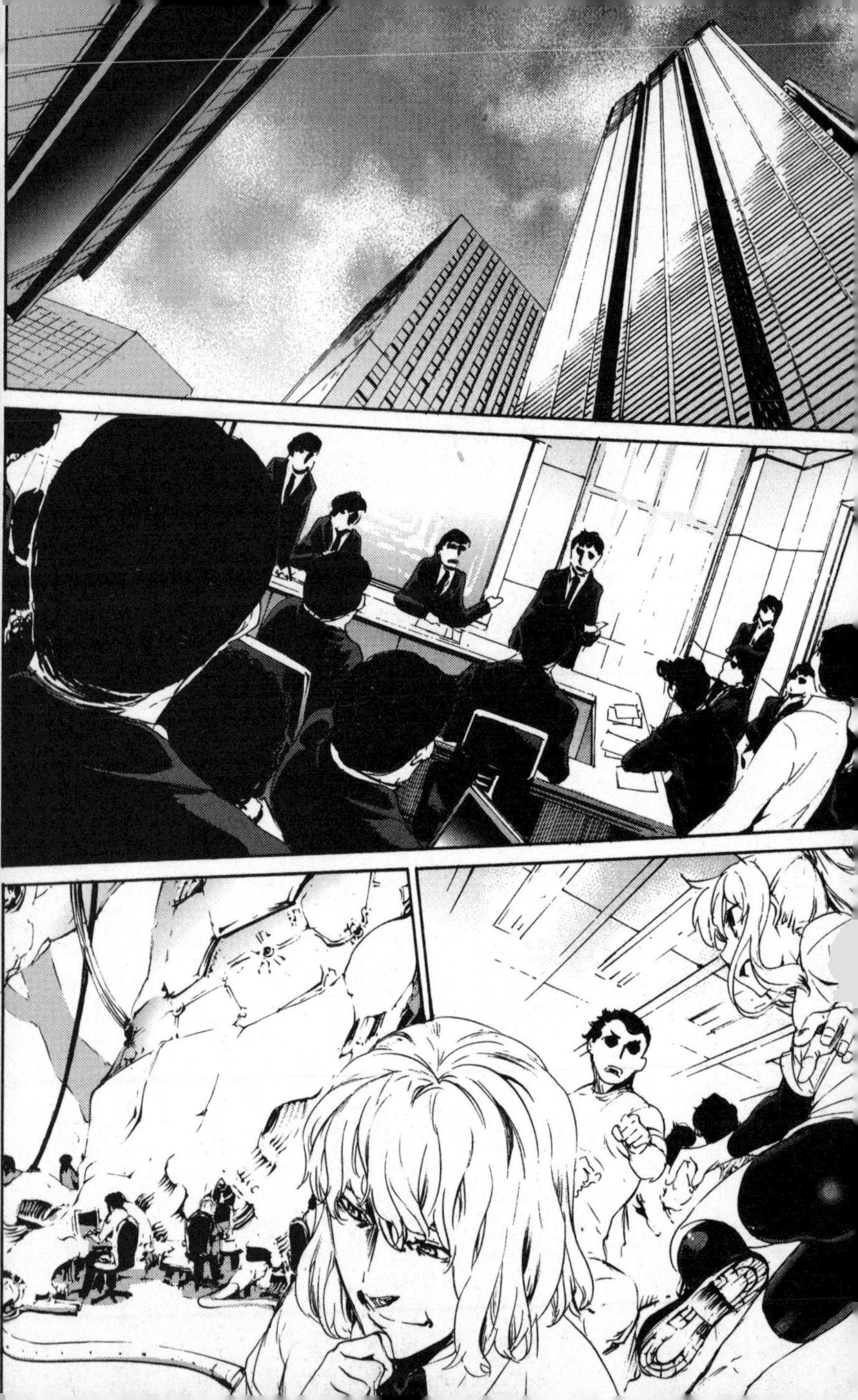

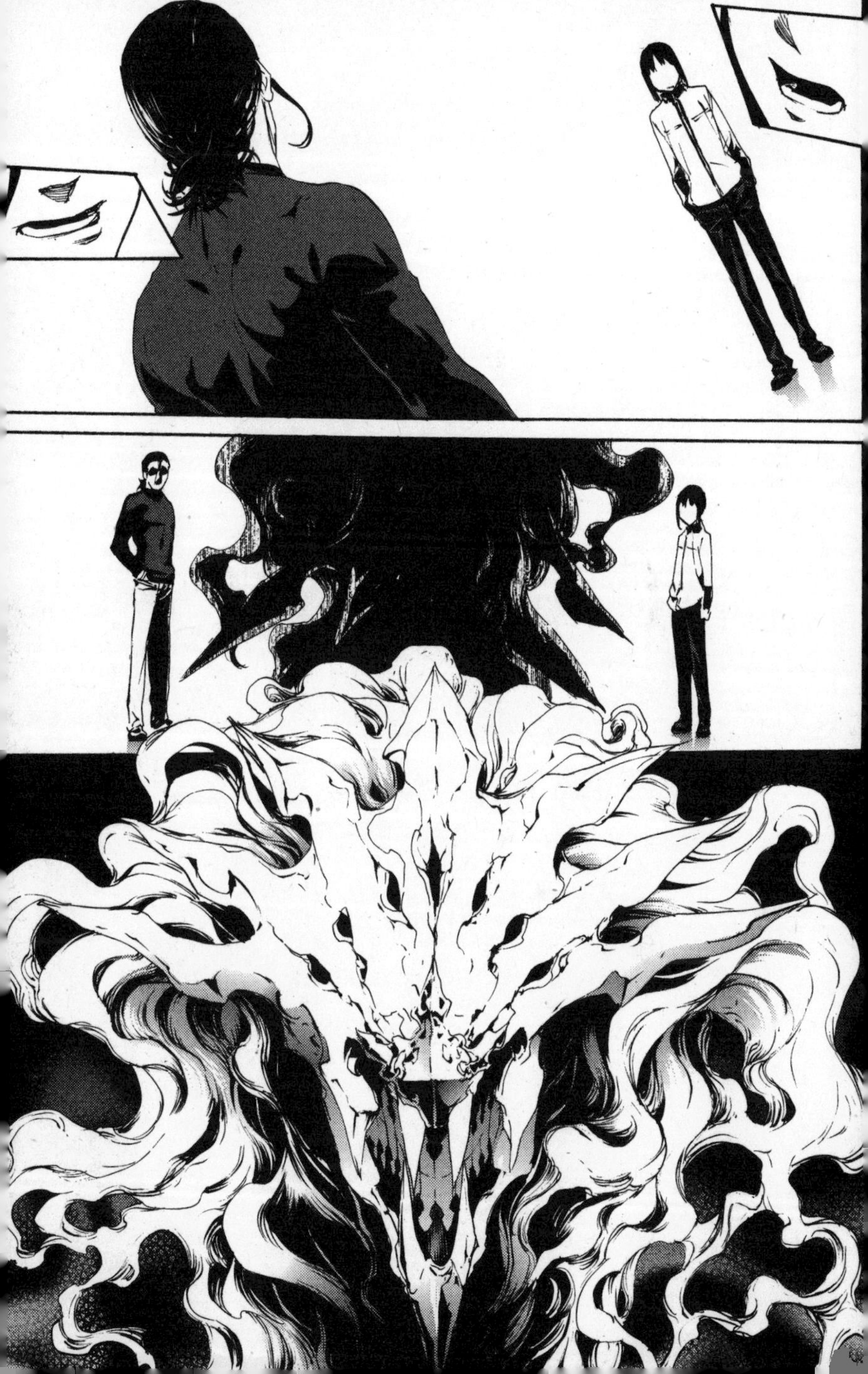

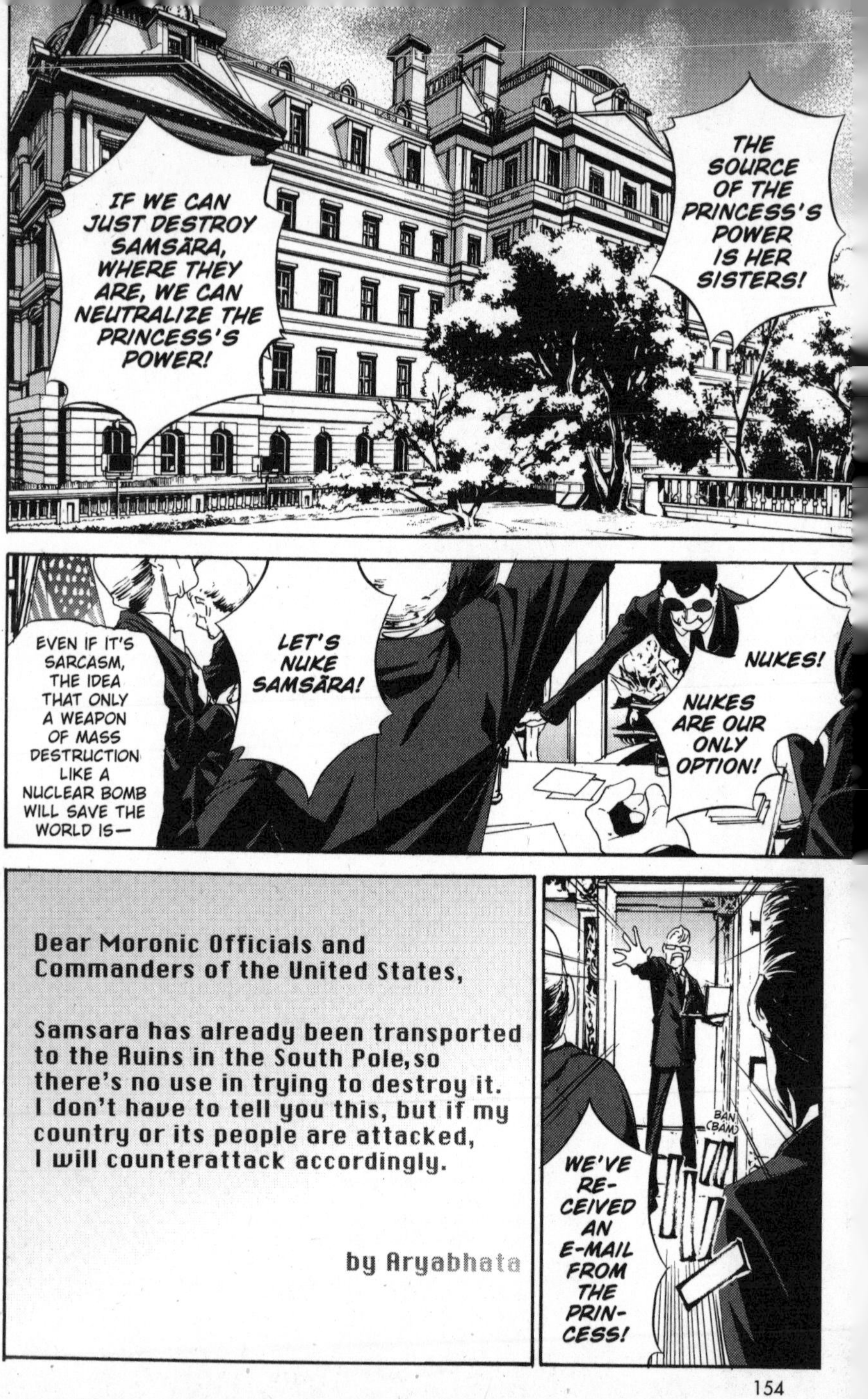
THE SOURCE OF THE PRINCESS'S POWER IS HER SISTERS!
IF WE CAN JUST DESTROY SAMSÄRA, WHERE THEY ARE, WE CAN NEUTRALIZE THE PRINCESS'S POWER!
NUKES!
NUKES ARE OUR ONLY OPTION!
LET'S NUKE SAMSÄRA!
EVEN IF IT'S SARCASM, THE IDEA THAT ONLY A WEAPON OF MASS DESTRUCTION LIKE A NUCLEAR BOMB WILL SAVE THE WORLD IS—
BAN (BAM)
WE'VE RE-CEIVED AN E-MAIL FROM THE PRIN-CESS!
Dear Moronic Officials and Commanders of the United States,
Samsara has already been transported to the Ruins in the South Pole,so there's no use in trying to destroy it. I don't have to tell you this, but if my country or its people are attacked, I will counterattack accordingly.
by Aryabhata

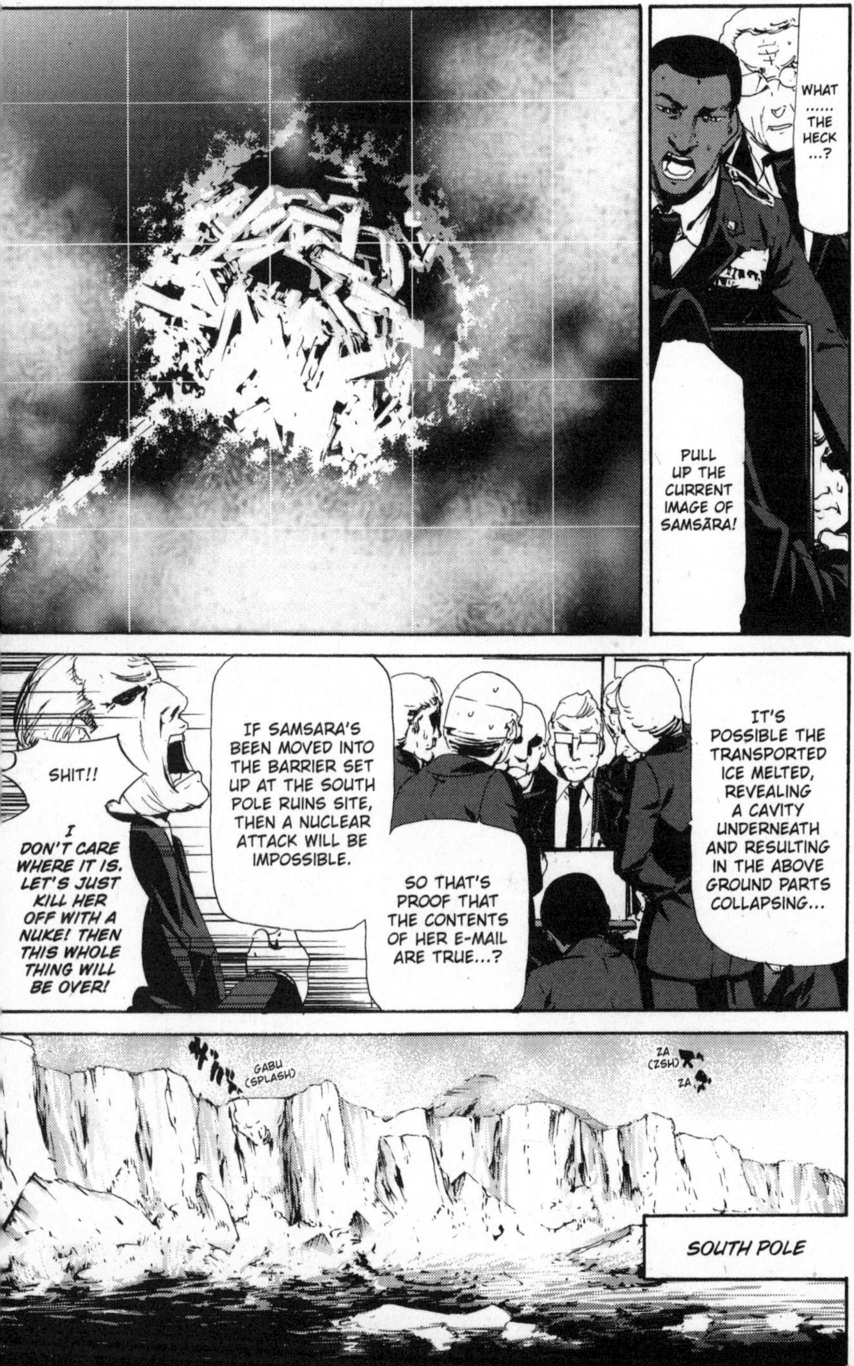
WHAT ...... THE HECK ...?
PULL UP THE CURRENT IMAGE OF SAMSĀRA!
IT'S POSSIBLE THE TRANSPORTED ICE MELTED, REVEALING A CAVITY UNDERNEATH AND RESULTING IN THE ABOVE GROUND PARTS COLLAPSING...
IF SAMSARA'S BEEN MOVED INTO THE BARRIER SET UP AT THE SOUTH POLE RUINS SITE, THEN A NUCLEAR ATTACK WILL BE IMPOSSIBLE.
SO THAT'S PROOF THAT THE CONTENTS OF HER E-MAIL ARE TRUE...?
SHIT!!
I DON'T CARE WHERE IT IS. LET'S JUST KILL HER OFF WITH A NUKE! THEN THIS WHOLE THING WILL BE OVER!
ZA (ZSH) ZA
GABU (SPLASH)
SOUTH POLE

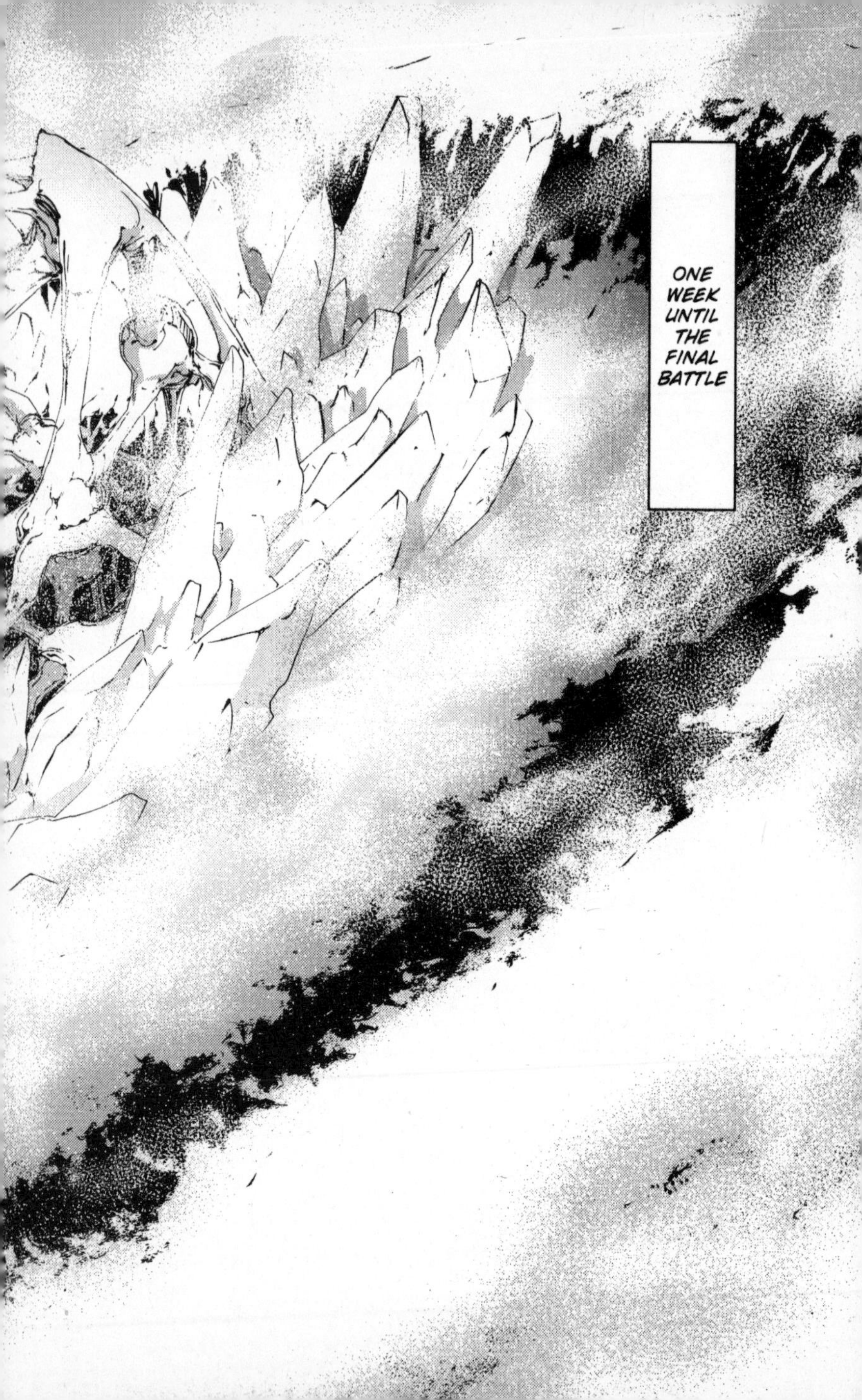
ONE WEEK UNTIL THE FINAL BATTLE

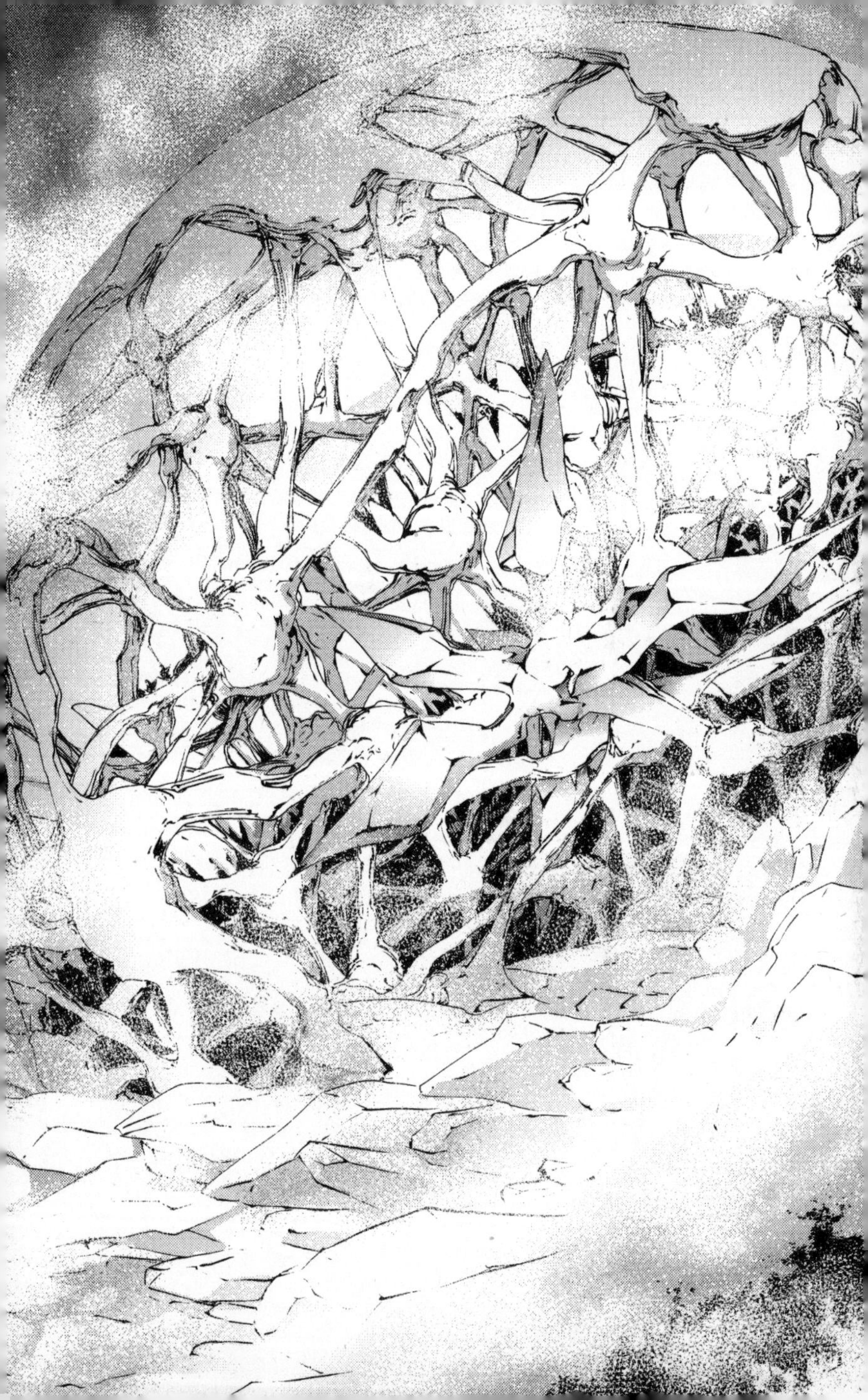

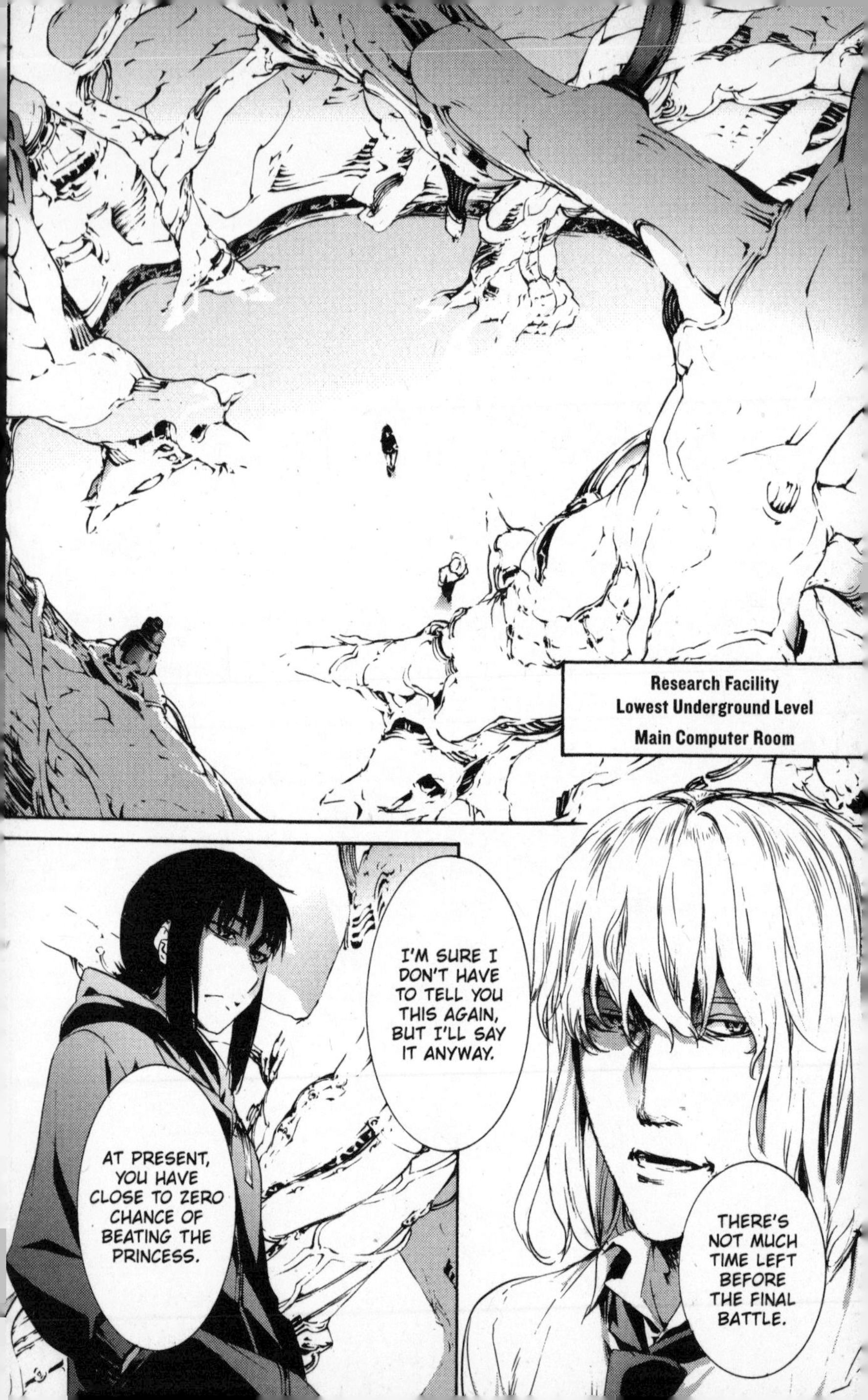
Research Facility
Lowest Underground Level
Main Computer Room
I'M SURE I DON'T HAVE TO TELL YOU THIS AGAIN, BUT I'LL SAY IT ANYWAY.
THERE'S NOT MUCH TIME LEFT BEFORE THE FINAL BATTLE.
AT PRESENT, YOU HAVE CLOSE TO ZERO CHANCE OF BEATING THE PRINCESS.

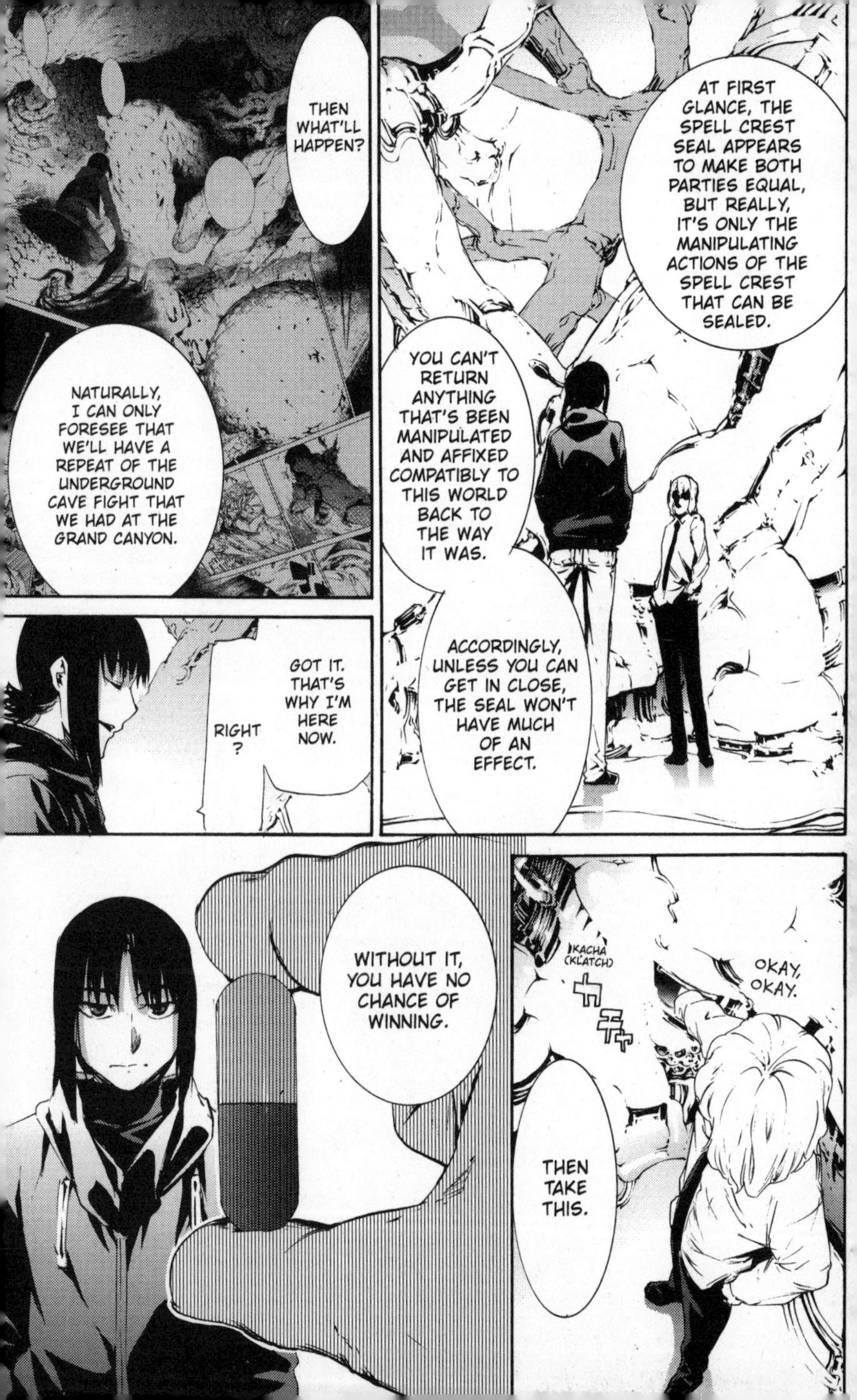
AT FIRST GLANCE, THE SPELL CREST SEAL APPEARS TO MAKE BOTH PARTIES EQUAL, BUT REALLY, IT'S ONLY THE MANIPULATING ACTIONS OF THE SPELL CREST THAT CAN BE SEALED.
YOU CAN'T RETURN ANYTHING THAT'S BEEN MANIPULATED AND AFFIXED COMPATIBLY TO THIS WORLD BACK TO THE WAY IT WAS.
ACCORDINGLY, UNLESS YOU CAN GET IN CLOSE, THE SEAL WON'T HAVE MUCH OF AN EFFECT.
THEN WHAT'LL HAPPEN?
NATURALLY, I CAN ONLY FORESEE THAT WE'LL HAVE A REPEAT OF THE UNDERGROUND CAVE FIGHT THAT WE HAD AT THE GRAND CANYON.
GOT IT. THAT'S WHY I'M HERE NOW.
RIGHT?
OKAY, OKAY.
KACHA (KLATCH)
THEN TAKE THIS.
WITHOUT IT, YOU HAVE NO CHANCE OF WINNING.

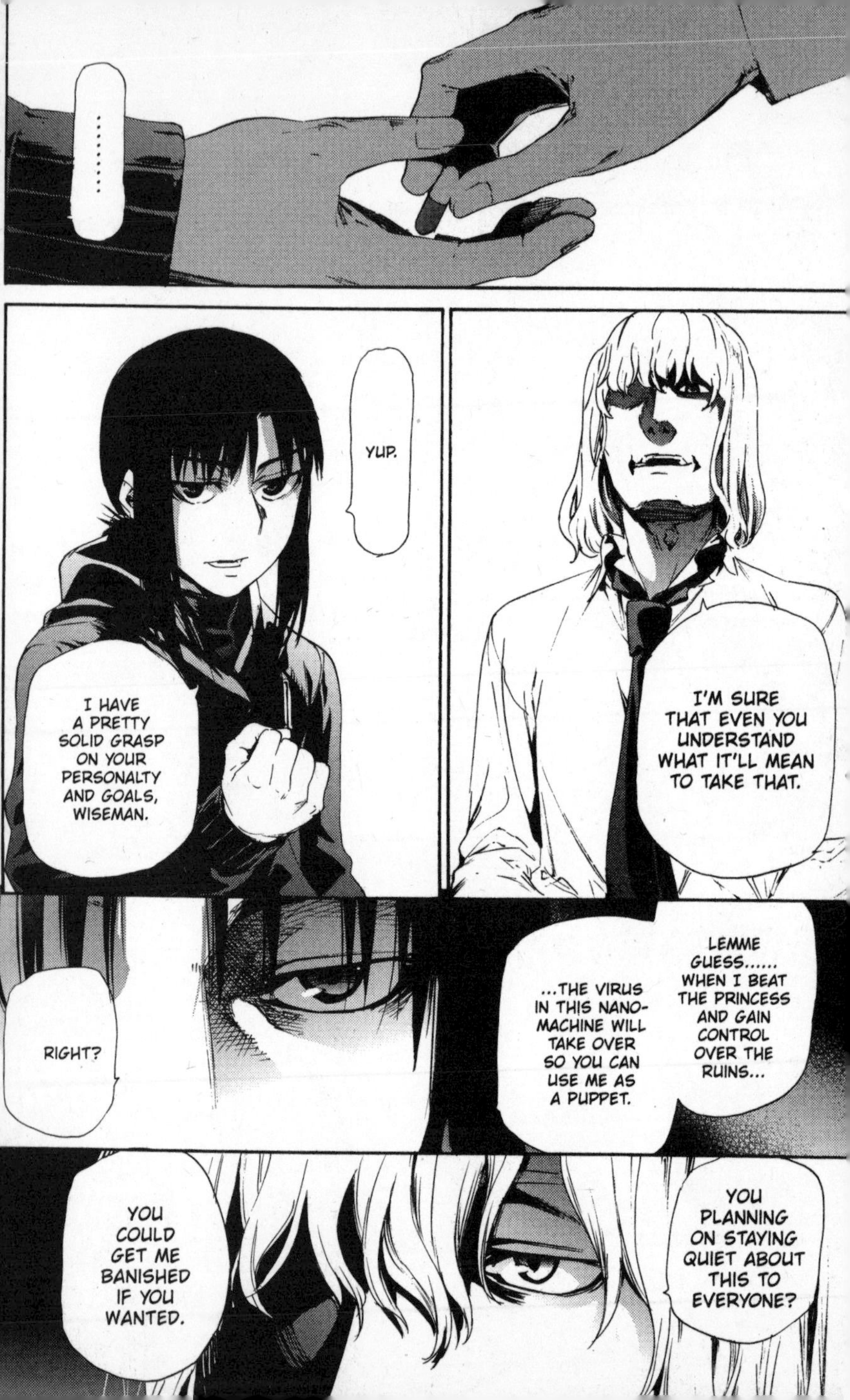
......
I'M SURE THAT EVEN YOU UNDERSTAND WHAT IT'LL MEAN TO TAKE THAT.
YUP.
I HAVE A PRETTY SOLID GRASP ON YOUR PERSONALTY AND GOALS, WISEMAN.
LEMME GUESS...... WHEN I BEAT THE PRINCESS AND GAIN CONTROL OVER THE RUINS...
...THE VIRUS IN THIS NANO-MACHINE WILL TAKE OVER SO YOU CAN USE ME AS A PUPPET.
RIGHT?
YOU PLANNING ON STAYING QUIET ABOUT THIS TO EVERYONE?
YOU COULD GET ME BANISHED IF YOU WANTED.

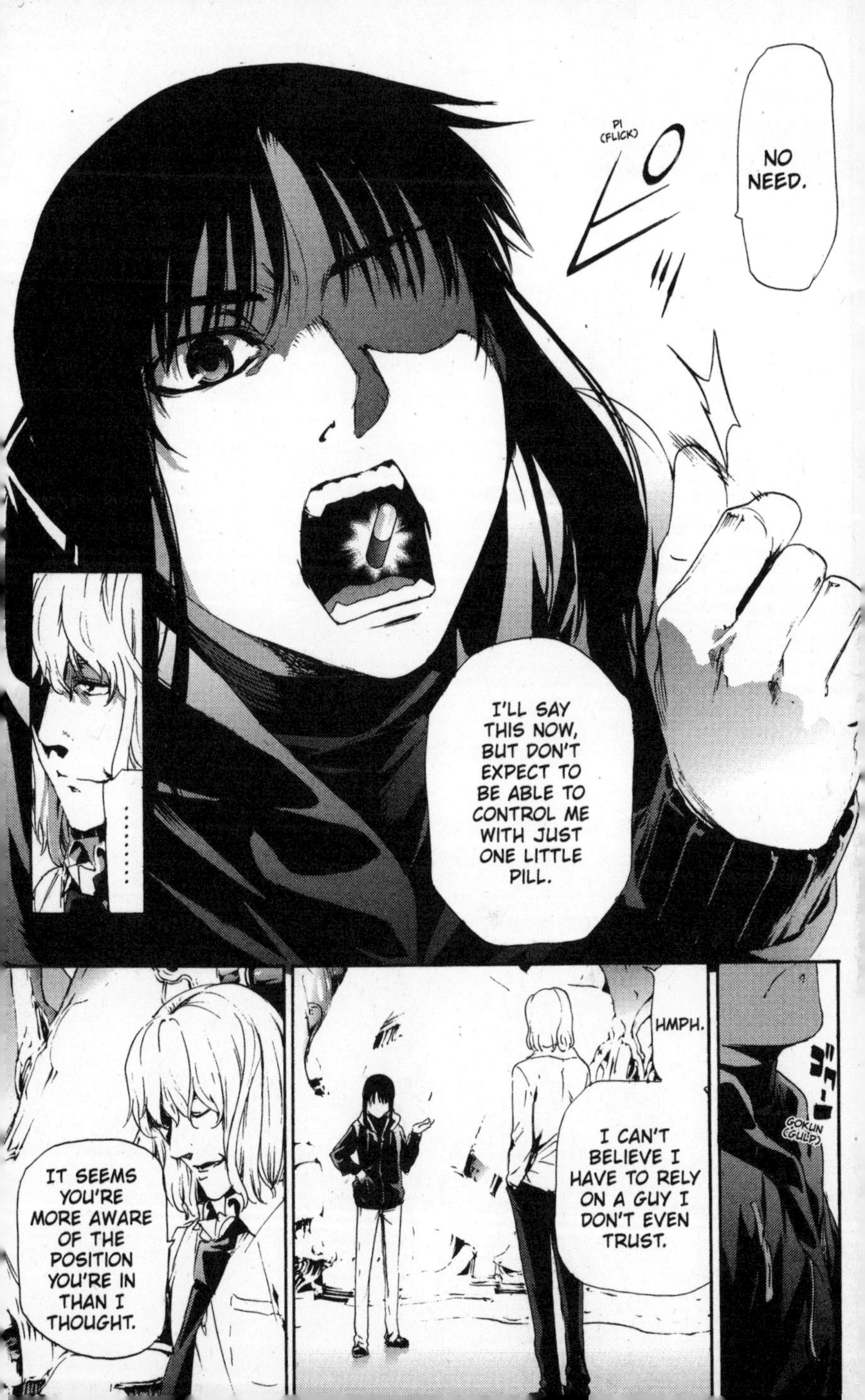
NO NEED.
PI (FLICK)
I'LL SAY THIS NOW, BUT DON'T EXPECT TO BE ABLE TO CONTROL ME WITH JUST ONE LITTLE PILL.
......
GOKUN (GULP)
HMPH.
I CAN'T BELIEVE I HAVE TO RELY ON A GUY I DON'T EVEN TRUST.
IT SEEMS YOU'RE MORE AWARE OF THE POSITION YOU'RE IN THAN I THOUGHT.

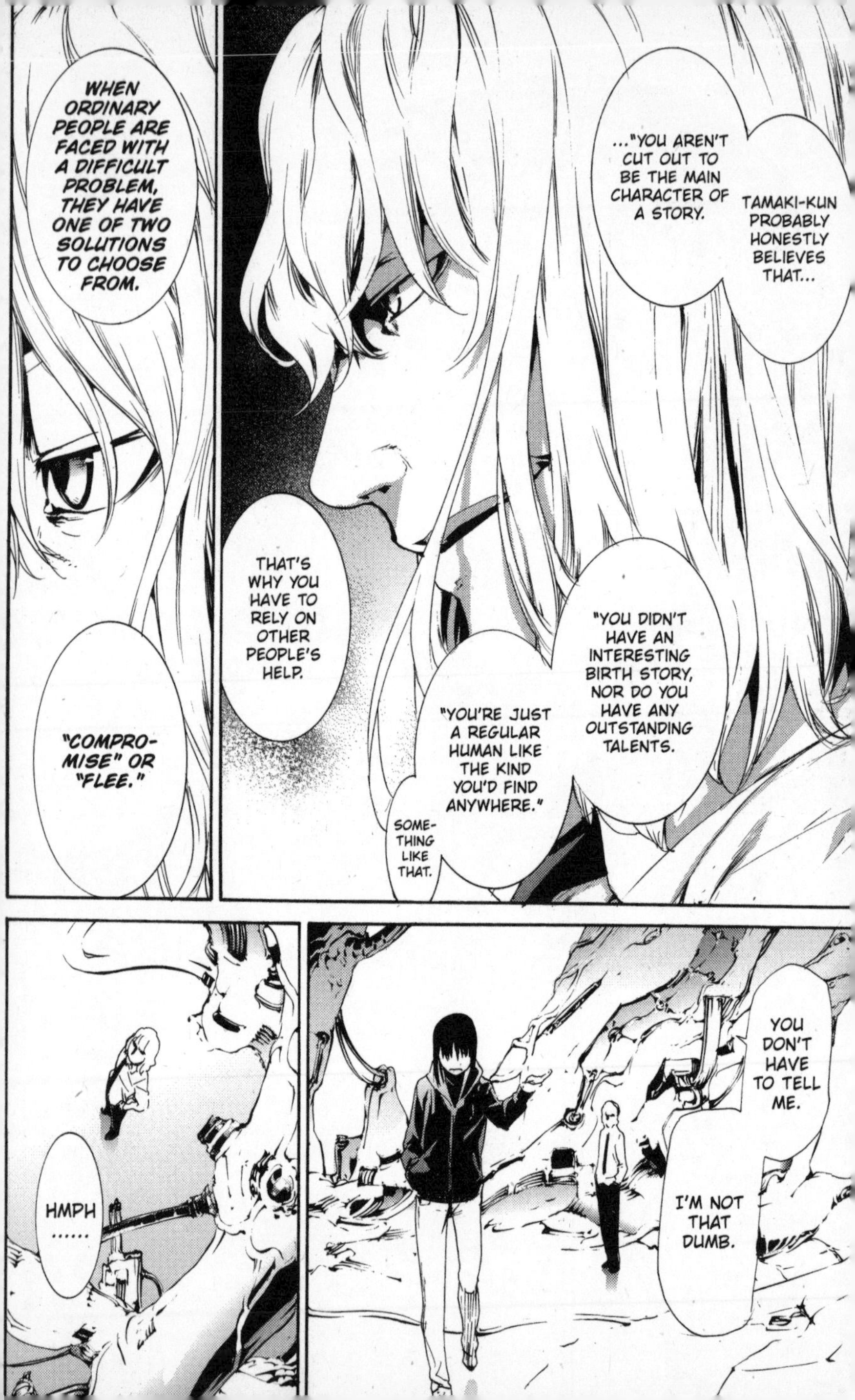
TAMAKI-KUN PROBABLY HONESTLY BELIEVES THAT...
..."YOU AREN'T CUT OUT TO BE THE MAIN CHARACTER OF A STORY.
"YOU DIDN'T HAVE AN INTERESTING BIRTH STORY, NOR DO YOU HAVE ANY OUTSTANDING TALENTS.
"YOU'RE JUST A REGULAR HUMAN LIKE THE KIND YOU'D FIND ANYWHERE."
SOME-THING LIKE THAT.
THAT'S WHY YOU HAVE TO RELY ON OTHER PEOPLE'S HELP.
WHEN ORDINARY PEOPLE ARE FACED WITH A DIFFICULT PROBLEM, THEY HAVE ONE OF TWO SOLUTIONS TO CHOOSE FROM.
"COMPRO-MISE" OR "FLEE."
YOU DON'T HAVE TO TELL ME.
I'M NOT THAT DUMB.
HMPH ......

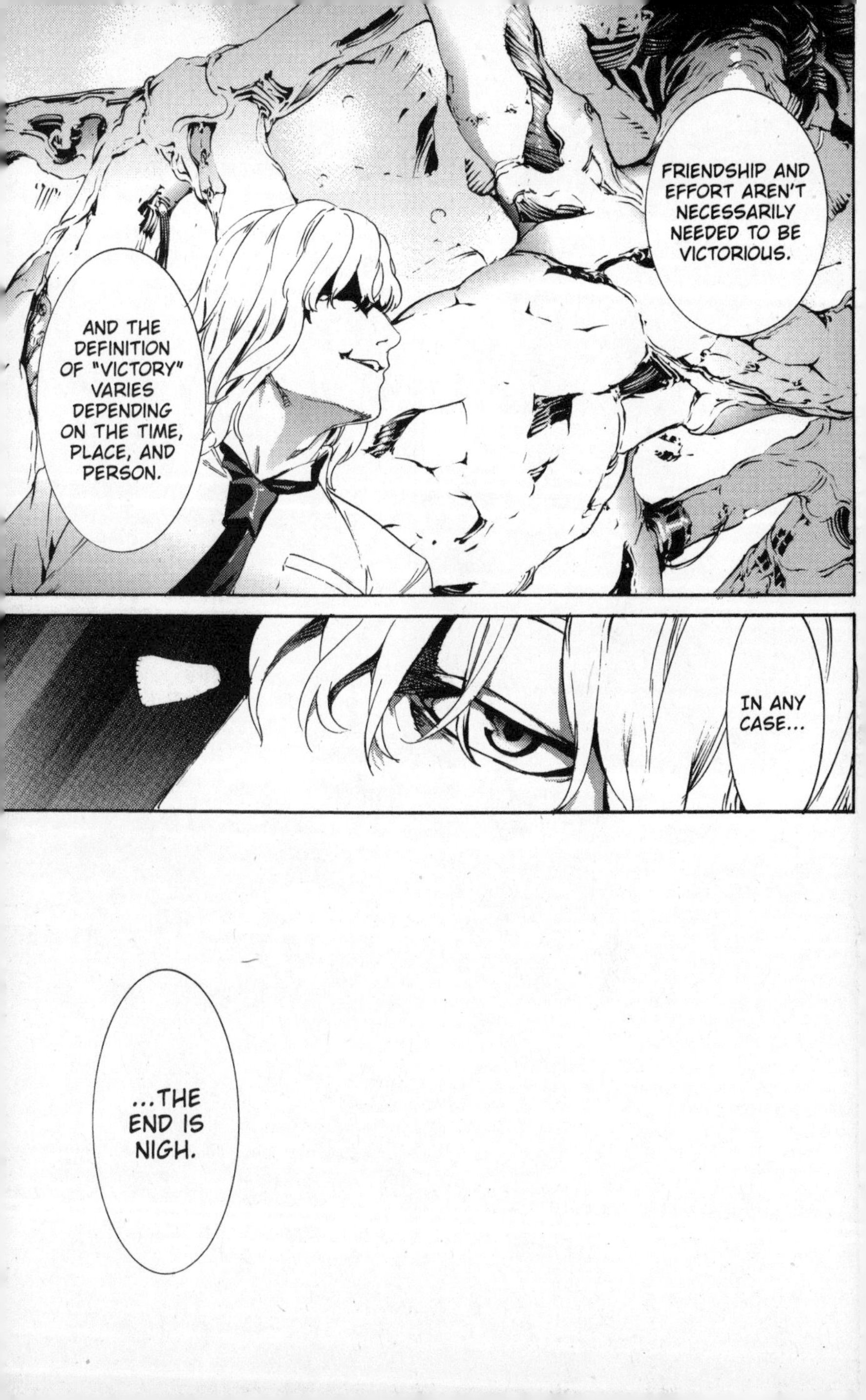
FRIENDSHIP AND EFFORT AREN'T NECESSARILY NEEDED TO BE VICTORIOUS.
AND THE DEFINITION OF "VICTORY" VARIES DEPENDING ON THE TIME, PLACE, AND PERSON.
IN ANY CASE...
...THE END IS NIGH.

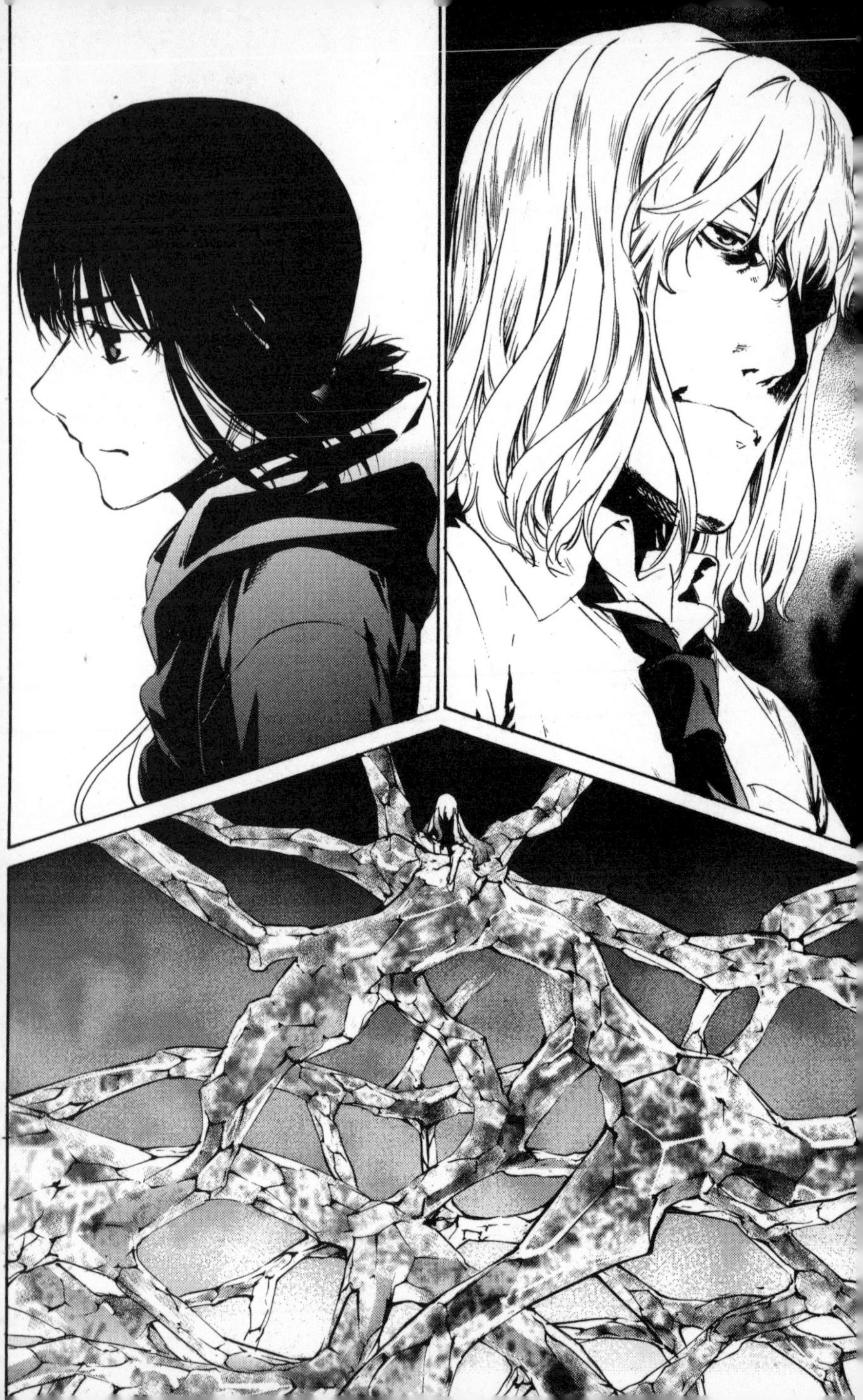

TABOO TATTOO

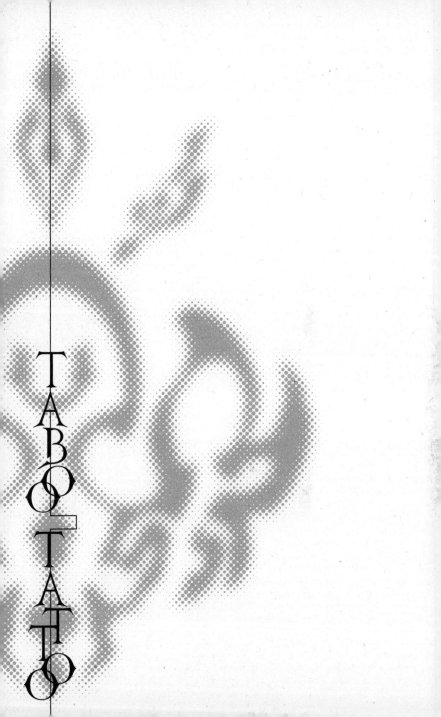

TABOO TATTOO

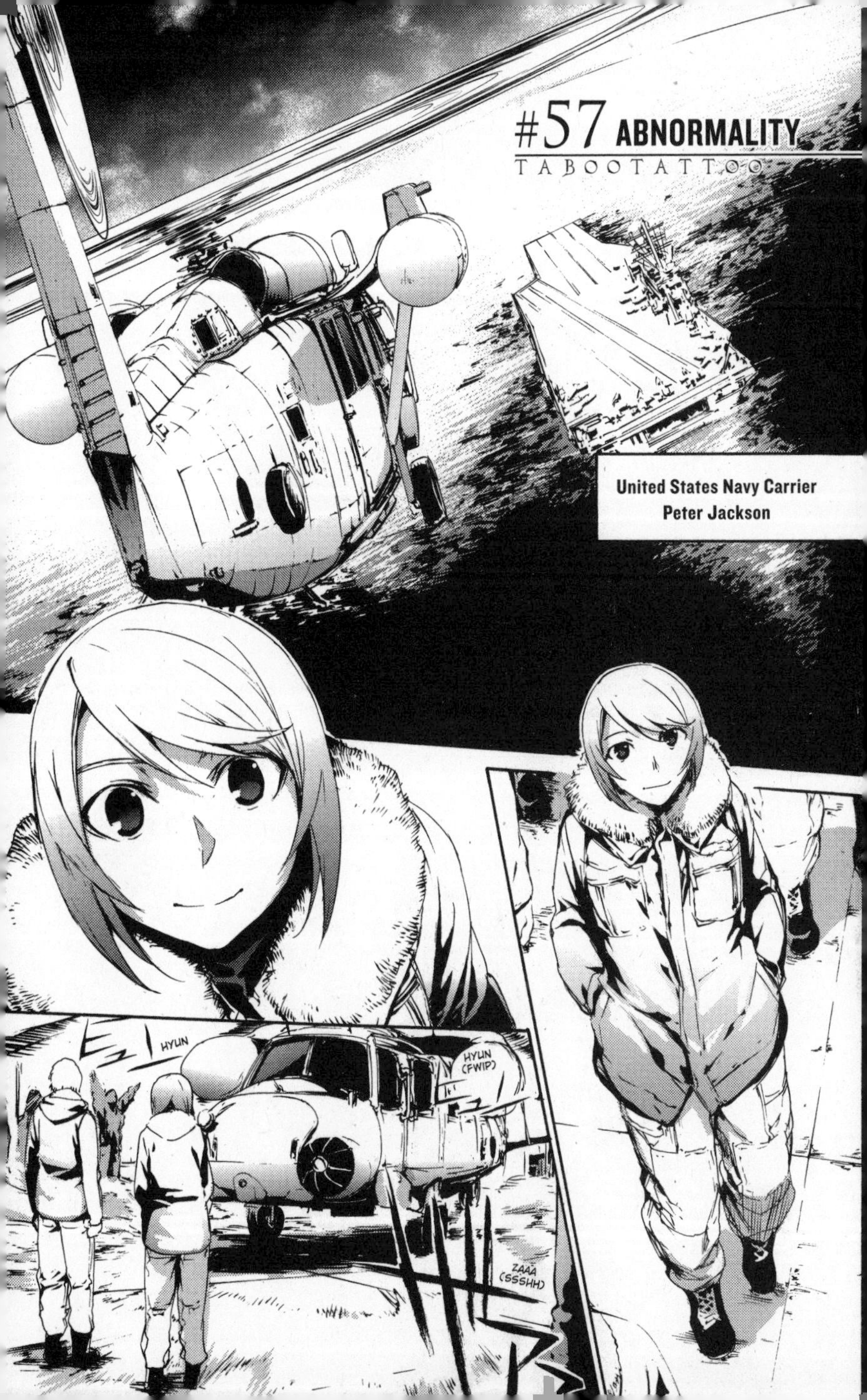
#57 ABNORMALITY
TABOOTATTOO
United States Navy Carrier
Peter Jackson
HYUN (FWIP)
HYUN
ZAAA (SSSHH)

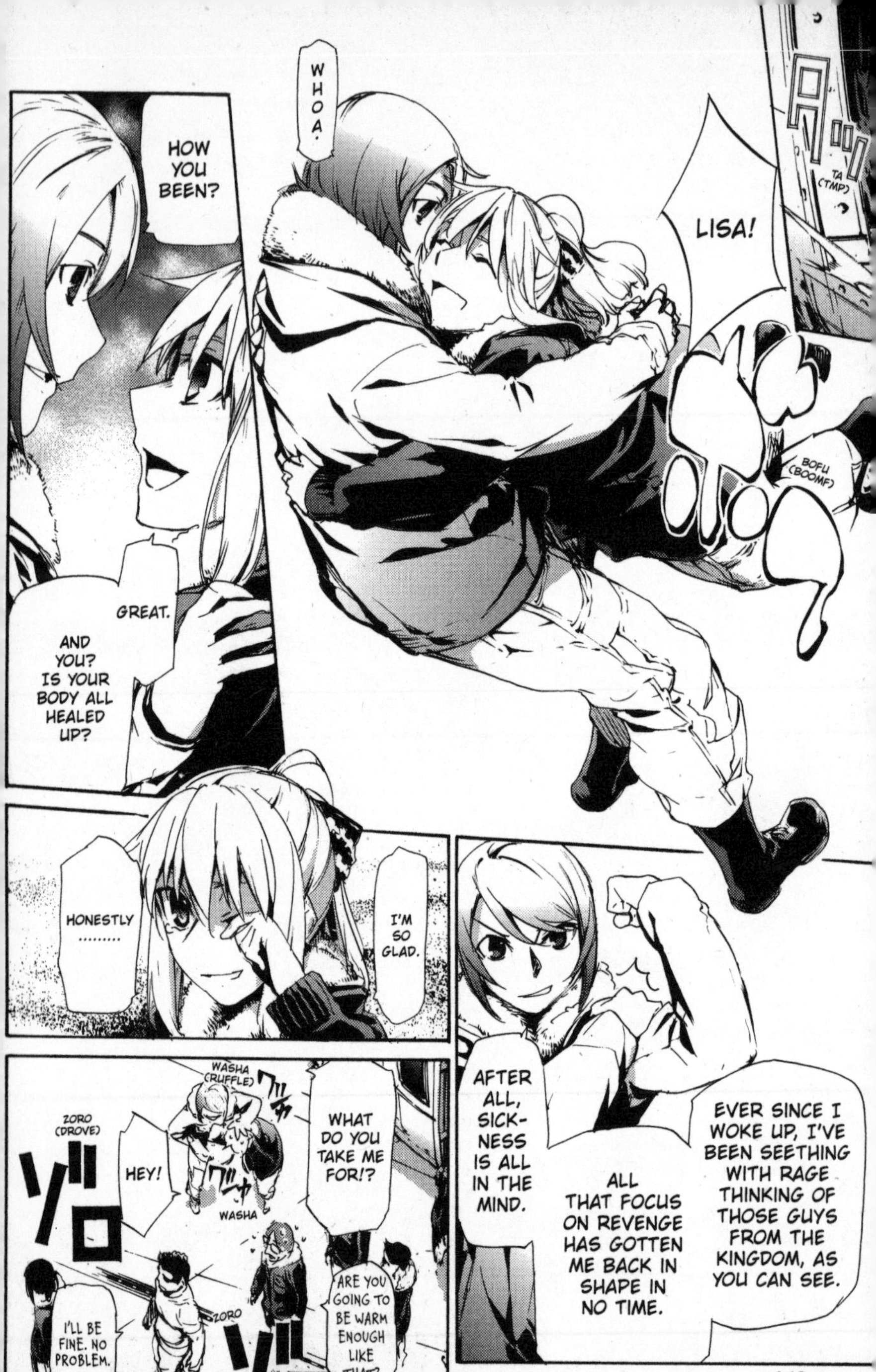
TA (TMP)
LISA!
BOFU (BOOMF)
WHOA.
HOW YOU BEEN?
GREAT.
AND YOU? IS YOUR BODY ALL HEALED UP?
EVER SINCE I WOKE UP, I'VE BEEN SEETHING WITH RAGE THINKING OF THOSE GUYS FROM THE KINGDOM, AS YOU CAN SEE.
ALL THAT FOCUS ON REVENGE HAS GOTTEN ME BACK IN SHAPE IN NO TIME.
AFTER ALL, SICK-NESS IS ALL IN THE MIND.
I'M SO GLAD.
HONESTLY..........
WHAT DO YOU TAKE ME FOR!?
WASHA (RUFFLE)
HEY!
WASHA
ZORO (DROVE)
ARE YOU GOING TO BE WARM ENOUGH LIKE THAT?
ZORO
I'LL BE FINE. NO PROBLEM.

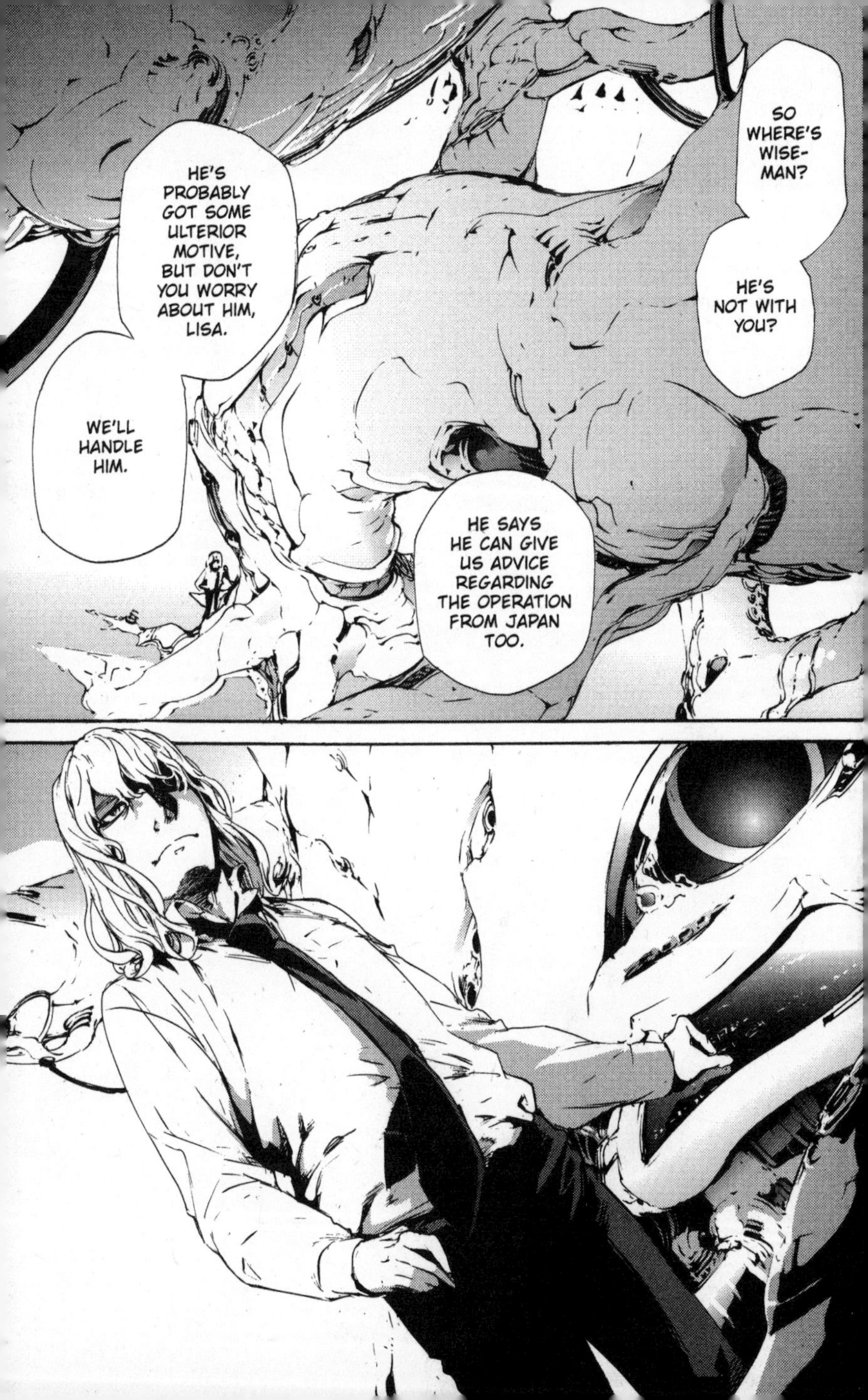
SO WHERE'S WISE-MAN?
HE'S NOT WITH YOU?
HE'S PROBABLY GOT SOME ULTERIOR MOTIVE, BUT DON'T YOU WORRY ABOUT HIM, LISA.
WE'LL HANDLE HIM.
HE SAYS HE CAN GIVE US ADVICE REGARDING THE OPERATION FROM JAPAN TOO.

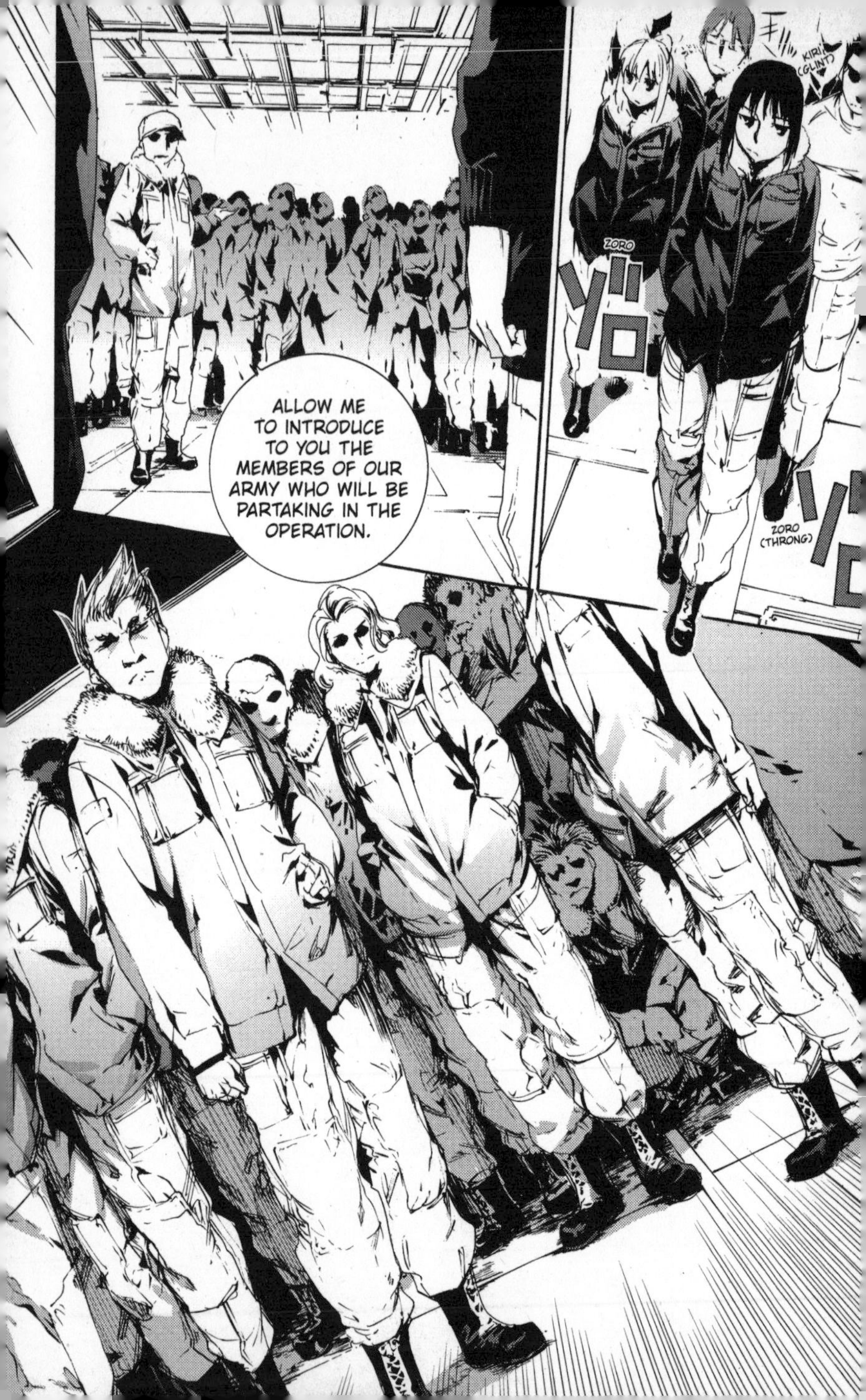
KIRI (GLINT)
ZORO
ZORO (THRONG)
ALLOW ME TO INTRODUCE TO YOU THE MEMBERS OF OUR ARMY WHO WILL BE PARTAKING IN THE OPERATION.

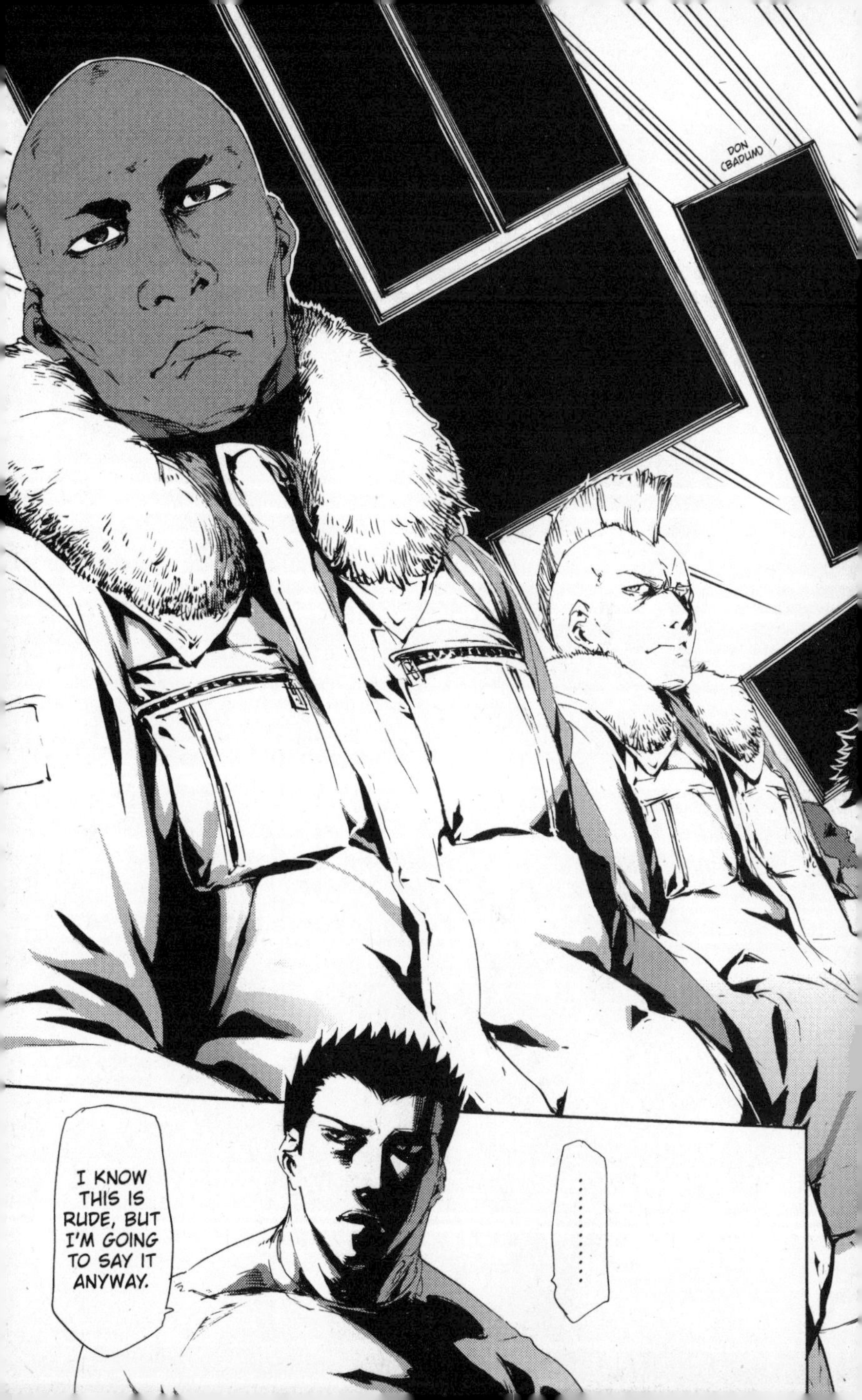
DON (BADUM)
......
I KNOW THIS IS RUDE, BUT I'M GOING TO SAY IT ANYWAY.

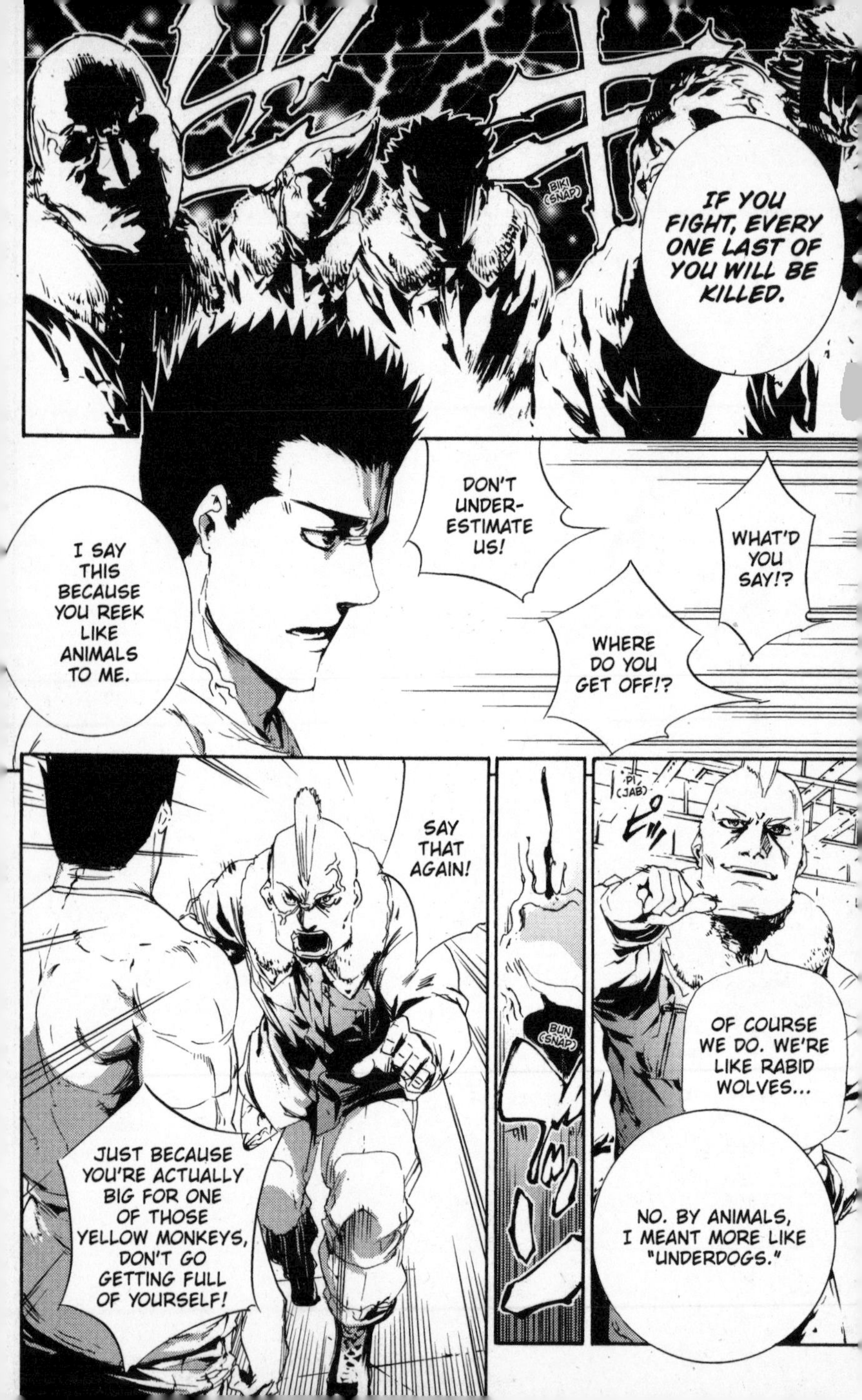
BIKI (SNAP)
IF YOU FIGHT, EVERY ONE LAST OF YOU WILL BE KILLED.
WHAT'D YOU SAY!?
DON'T UNDER-ESTIMATE US!
WHERE DO YOU GET OFF!?
I SAY THIS BECAUSE YOU REEK LIKE ANIMALS TO ME.
PI (JAB)
OF COURSE WE DO. WE'RE LIKE RABID WOLVES...
NO. BY ANIMALS, I MEANT MORE LIKE "UNDERDOGS."
BUN (SNAP)
SAY THAT AGAIN!
JUST BECAUSE YOU'RE ACTUALLY BIG FOR ONE OF THOSE YELLOW MONKEYS, DON'T GO GETTING FULL OF YOURSELF!

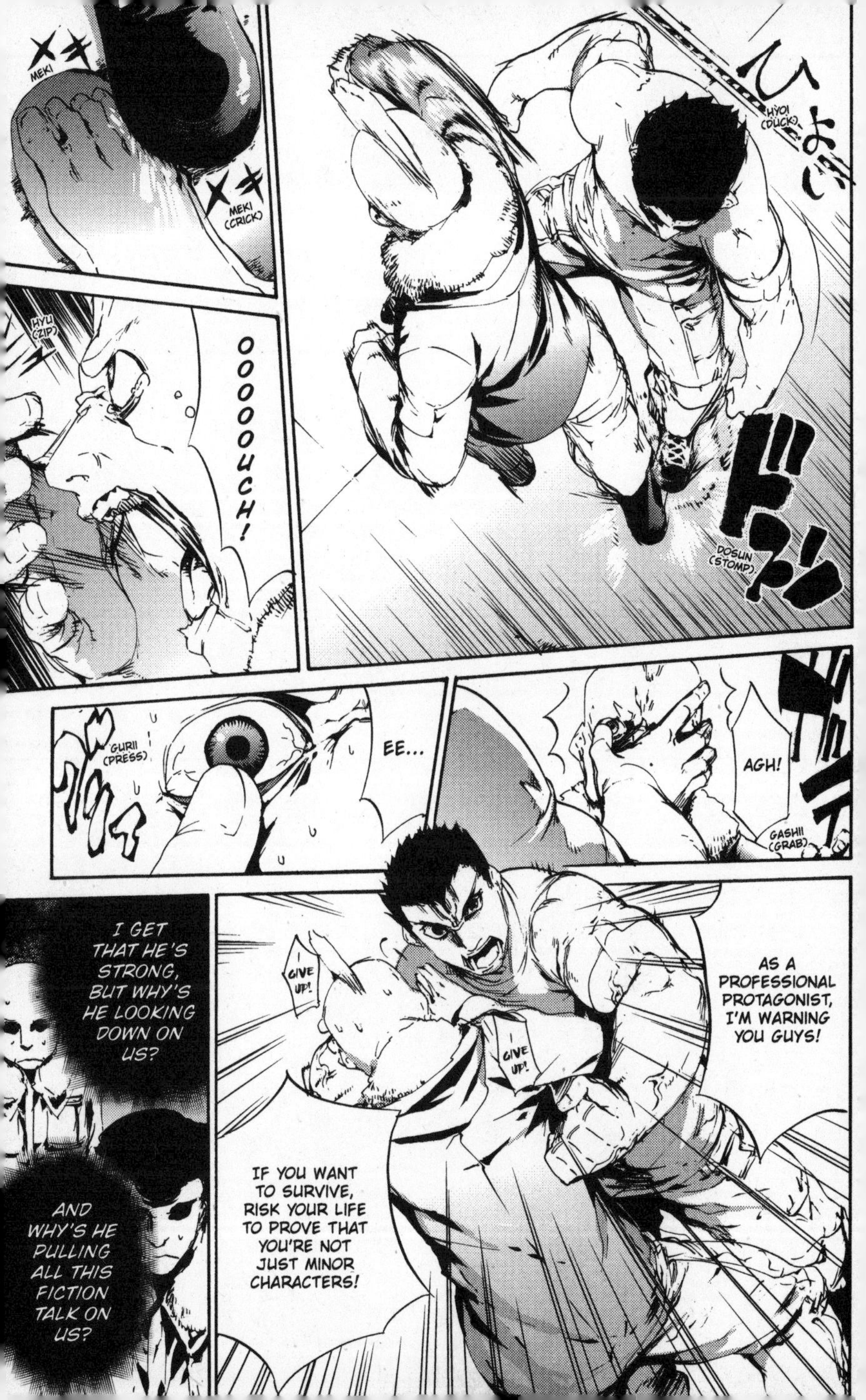
HYOI (DUCK)
DOSUN (STOMP)
MEKI
MEKI (CRICK)
HYU (ZIP)
OOOOOOUCH!
AGH!
GASHI (GRAB)
EE...
GURII (PRESS)
AS A PROFESSIONAL PROTAGONIST, I'M WARNING YOU GUYS!
I GIVE UP!
I GIVE UP!
IF YOU WANT TO SURVIVE, RISK YOUR LIFE TO PROVE THAT YOU'RE NOT JUST MINOR CHARACTERS!
I GET THAT HE'S STRONG, BUT WHY'S HE LOOKING DOWN ON US?
AND WHY'S HE PULLING ALL THIS FICTION TALK ON US?

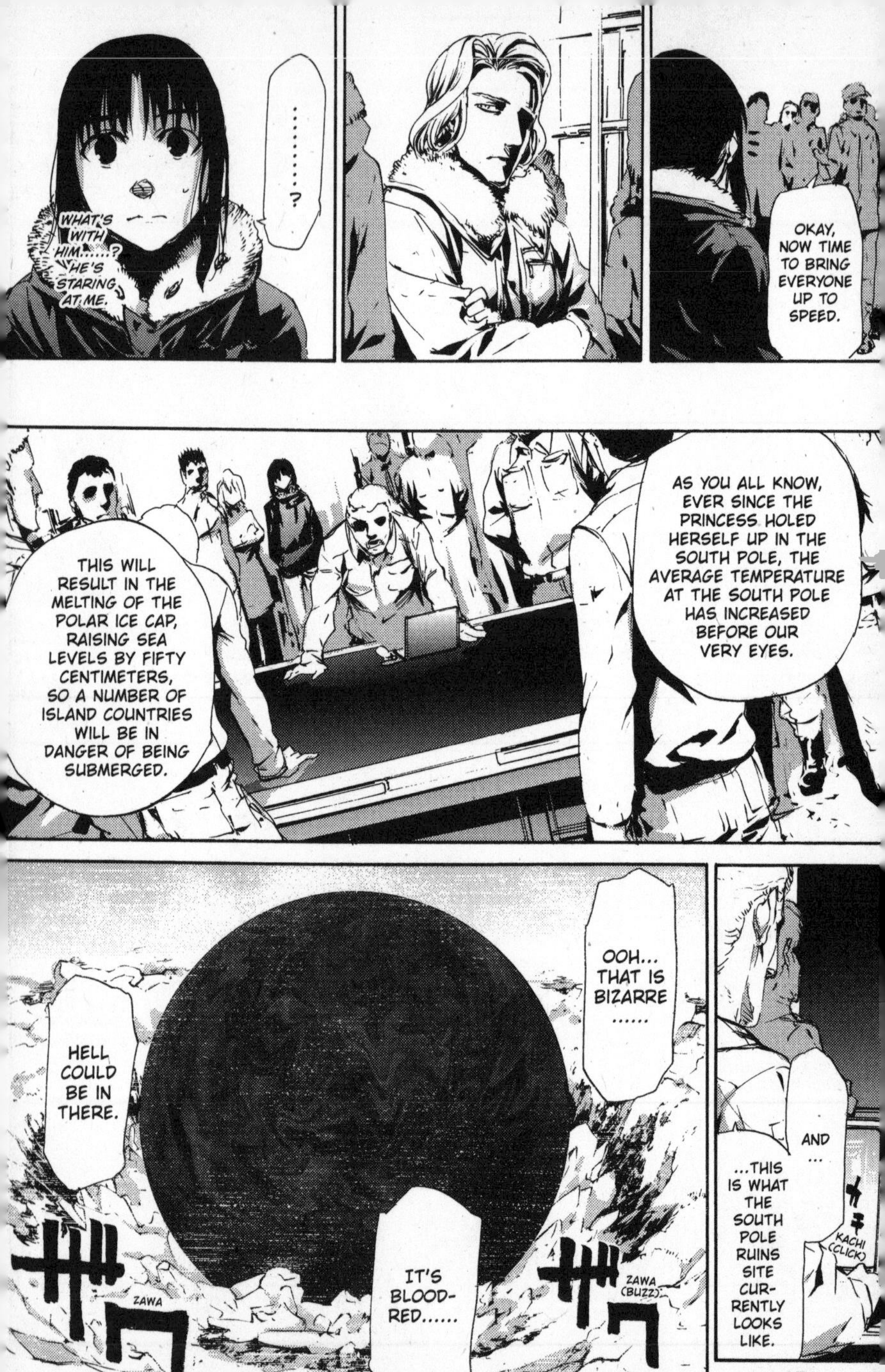
OKAY, NOW TIME TO BRING EVERYONE UP TO SPEED.
......?
WHAT'S WITH HIM......? HE'S STARING AT ME.
AS YOU ALL KNOW, EVER SINCE THE PRINCESS HOLED HERSELF UP IN THE SOUTH POLE, THE AVERAGE TEMPERATURE AT THE SOUTH POLE HAS INCREASED BEFORE OUR VERY EYES.
THIS WILL RESULT IN THE MELTING OF THE POLAR ICE CAP, RAISING SEA LEVELS BY FIFTY CENTIMETERS, SO A NUMBER OF ISLAND COUNTRIES WILL BE IN DANGER OF BEING SUBMERGED.
AND...
...THIS IS WHAT THE SOUTH POLE RUINS SITE CURRENTLY LOOKS LIKE.
KACHI (CLICK)
OOH... THAT IS BIZARRE......
ZAWA (BUZZ)
HELL COULD BE IN THERE.
IT'S BLOOD-RED......
ZAWA

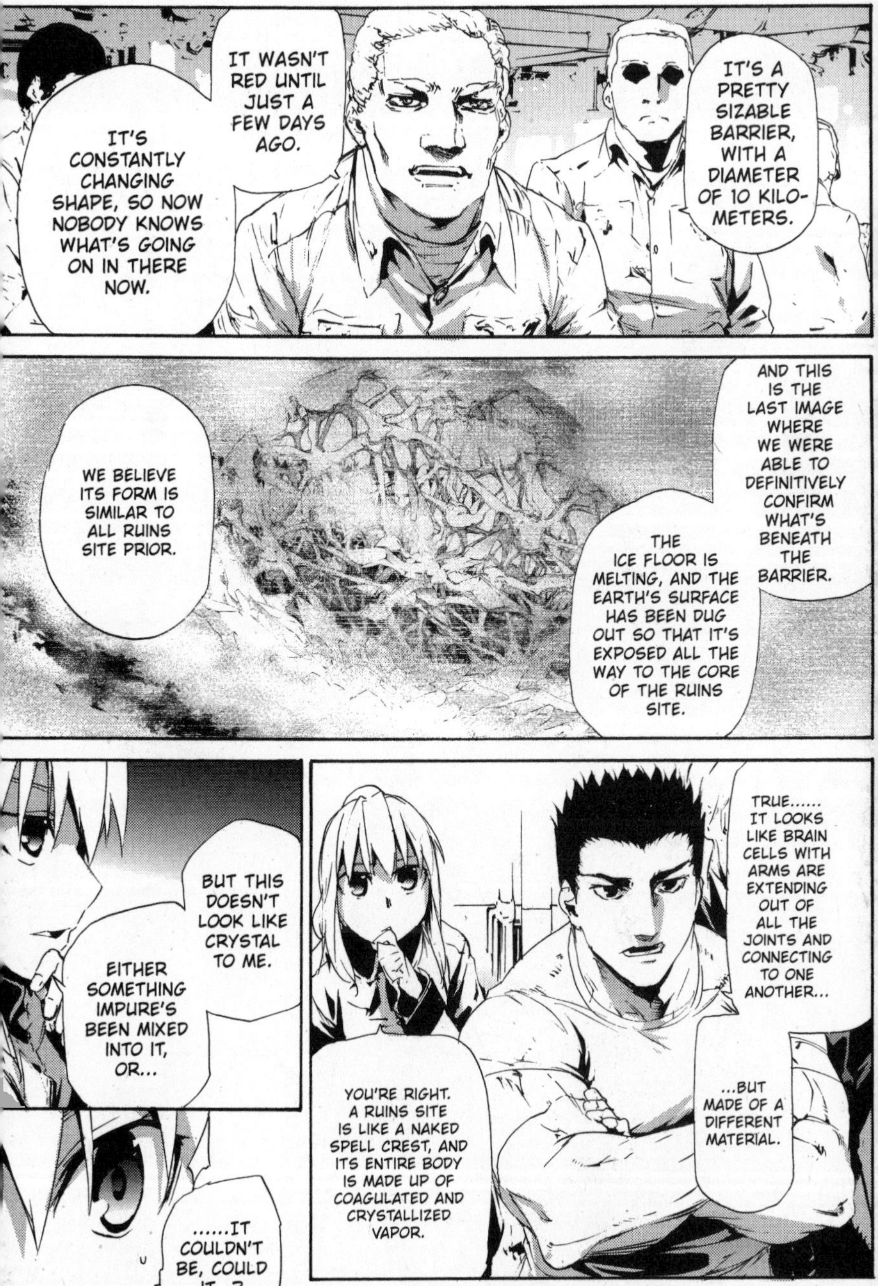
IT'S A PRETTY SIZABLE BARRIER, WITH A DIAMETER OF 10 KILO-METERS.
IT WASN'T RED UNTIL JUST A FEW DAYS AGO.
IT'S CONSTANTLY CHANGING SHAPE, SO NOW NOBODY KNOWS WHAT'S GOING ON IN THERE NOW.
AND THIS IS THE LAST IMAGE WHERE WE WERE ABLE TO DEFINITIVELY CONFIRM WHAT'S BENEATH THE BARRIER.
THE ICE FLOOR IS MELTING, AND THE EARTH'S SURFACE HAS BEEN DUG OUT SO THAT IT'S EXPOSED ALL THE WAY TO THE CORE OF THE RUINS SITE.
WE BELIEVE ITS FORM IS SIMILAR TO ALL RUINS SITE PRIOR.
TRUE...... IT LOOKS LIKE BRAIN CELLS WITH ARMS ARE EXTENDING OUT OF ALL THE JOINTS AND CONNECTING TO ONE ANOTHER...
...BUT MADE OF A DIFFERENT MATERIAL.
YOU'RE RIGHT. A RUINS SITE IS LIKE A NAKED SPELL CREST, AND ITS ENTIRE BODY IS MADE UP OF COAGULATED AND CRYSTALLIZED VAPOR.
BUT THIS DOESN'T LOOK LIKE CRYSTAL TO ME.
EITHER SOMETHING IMPURE'S BEEN MIXED INTO IT, OR...
......IT COULDN'T BE, COULD IT...?

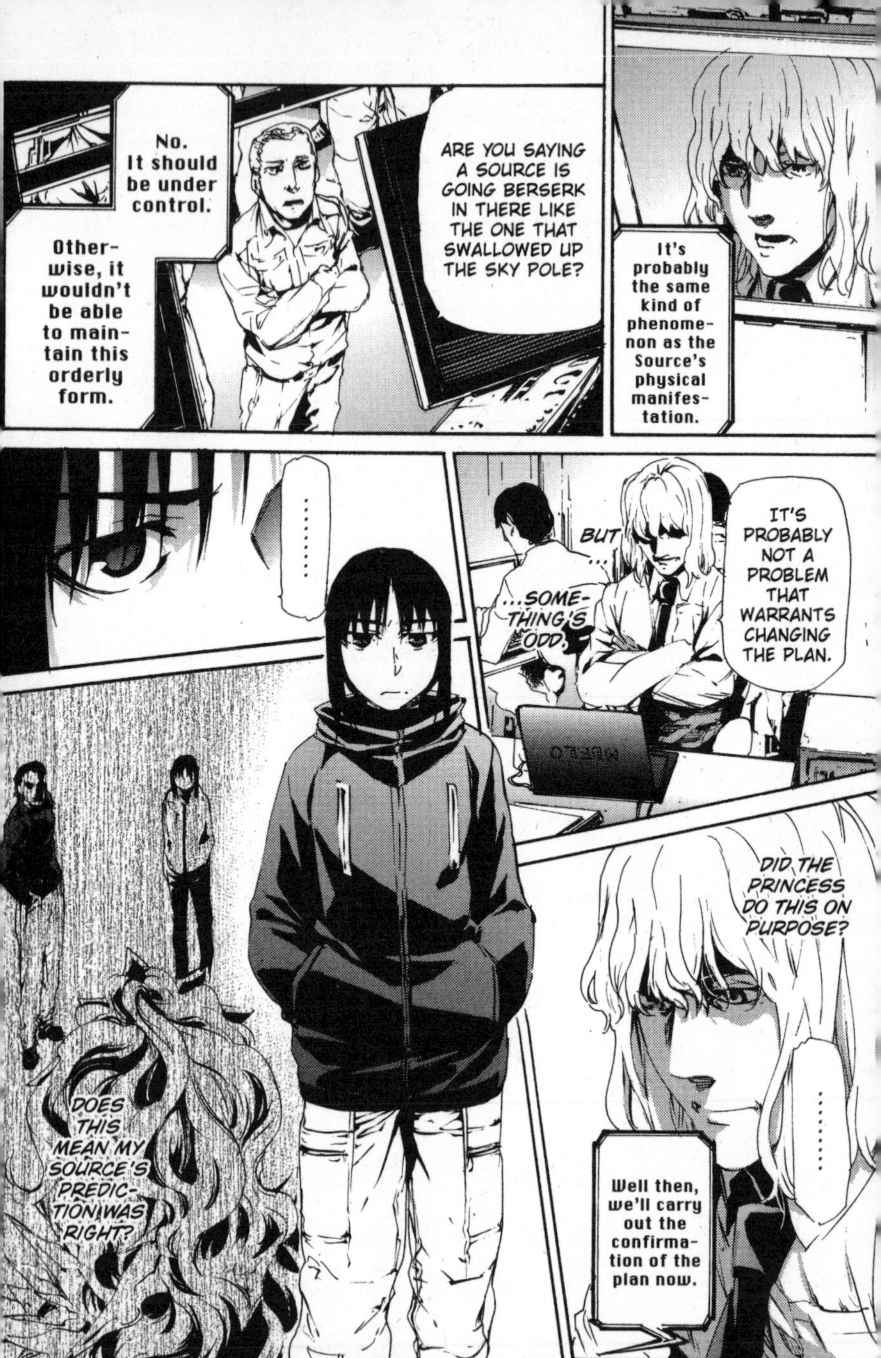
It's probably the same kind of phenomenon as the Source's physical manifestation.
ARE YOU SAYING A SOURCE IS GOING BERSERK IN THERE LIKE THE ONE THAT SWALLOWED UP THE SKY POLE?
No. It should be under control.
Otherwise, it wouldn't be able to maintain this orderly form.
IT'S PROBABLY NOT A PROBLEM THAT WARRANTS CHANGING THE PLAN.
BUT...
...SOMETHING'S ODD.
......
DID THE PRINCESS DO THIS ON PURPOSE?
......
Well then, we'll carry out the confirmation of the plan now.
DOES THIS MEAN MY SOURCE'S PREDICTION WAS RIGHT?

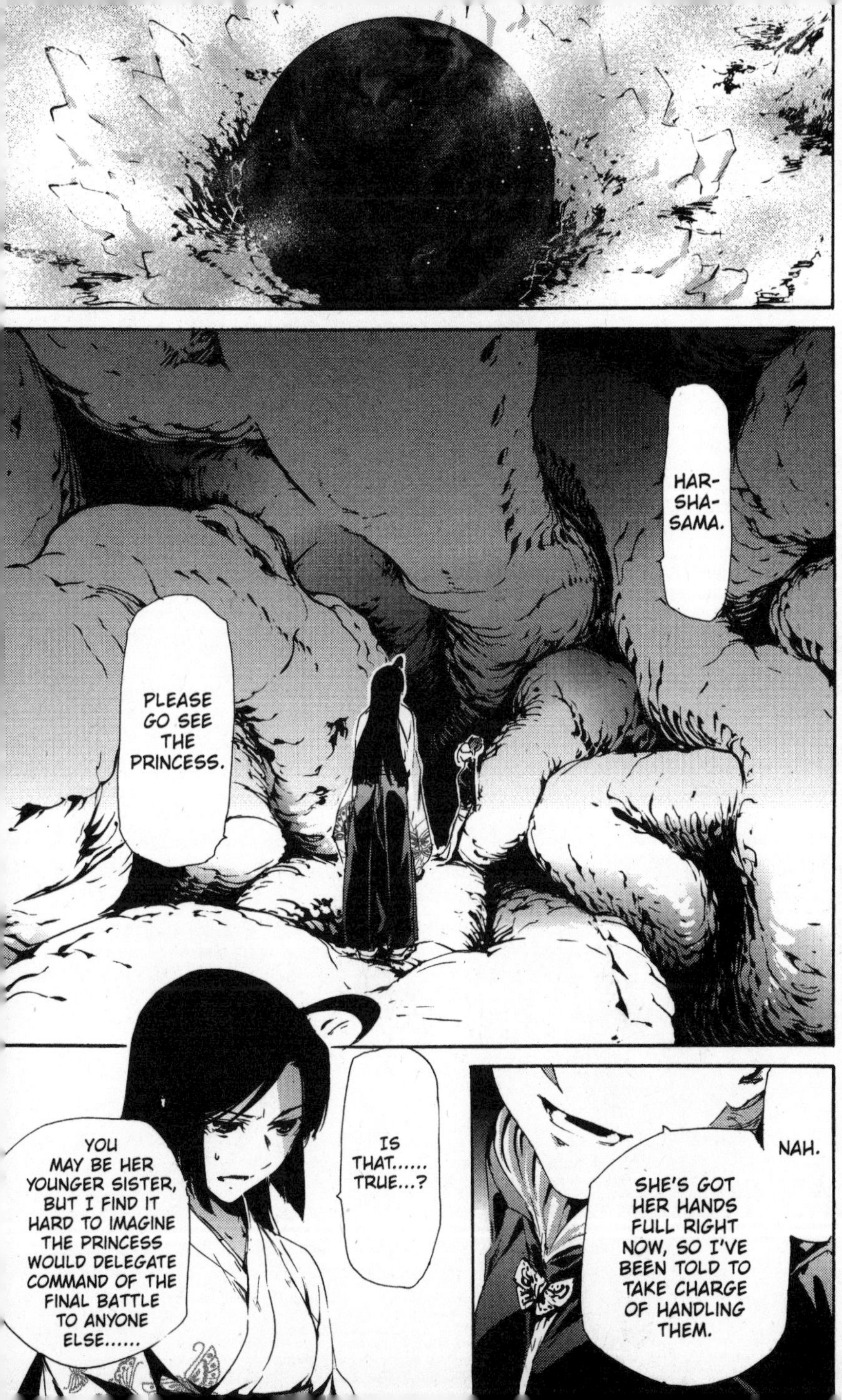
HAR-SHA-SAMA.
PLEASE GO SEE THE PRINCESS.
NAH.
SHE'S GOT HER HANDS FULL RIGHT NOW, SO I'VE BEEN TOLD TO TAKE CHARGE OF HANDLING THEM.
IS THAT...... TRUE...?
YOU MAY BE HER YOUNGER SISTER, BUT I FIND IT HARD TO IMAGINE THE PRINCESS WOULD DELEGATE COMMAND OF THE FINAL BATTLE TO ANYONE ELSE......

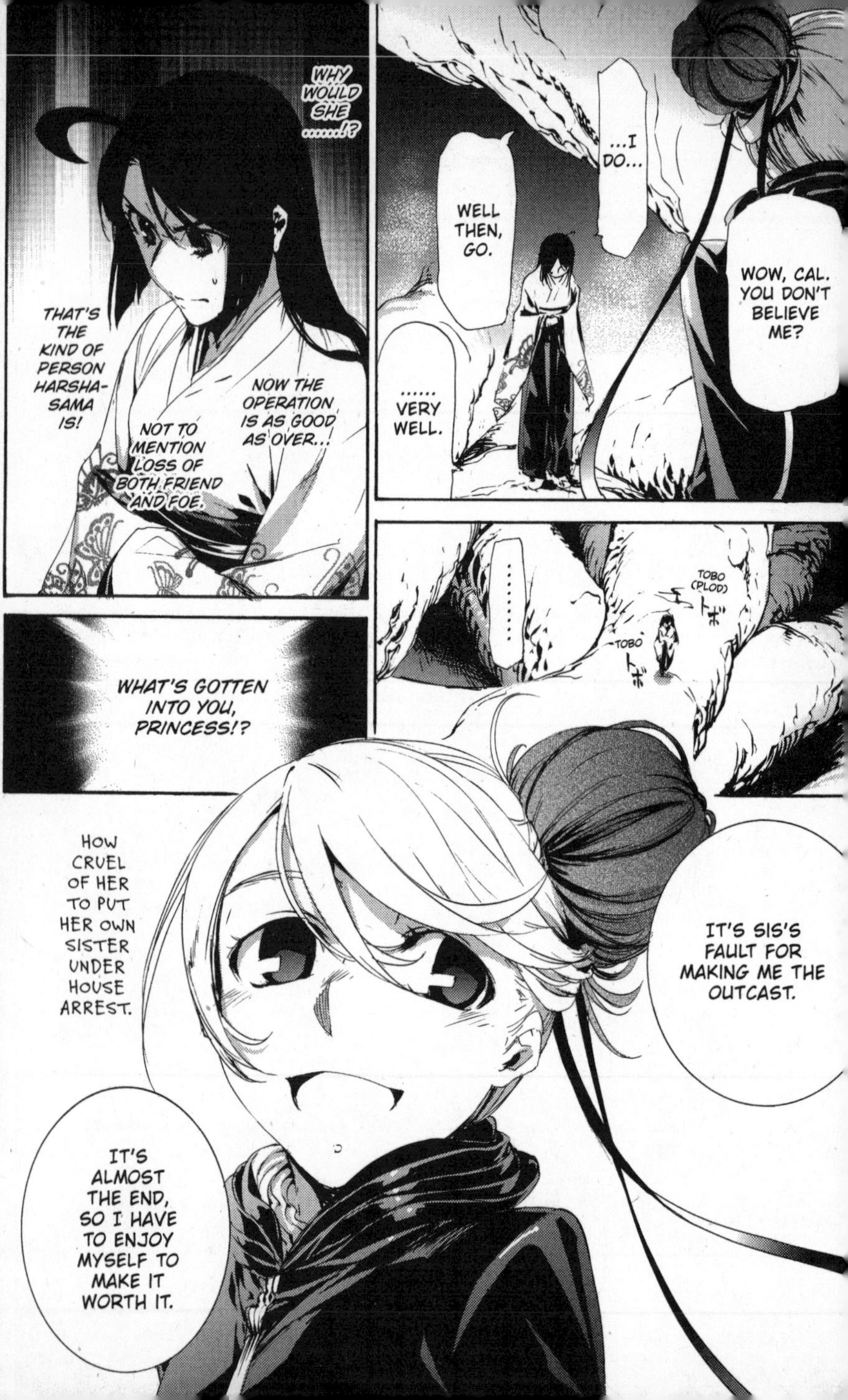
WOW, CAL. YOU DON'T BELIEVE ME?
...I DO...
WELL THEN, GO.
...... VERY WELL.
WHY WOULD SHE ......!?
NOW THE OPERATION IS AS GOOD AS OVER...
NOT TO MENTION LOSS OF BOTH FRIEND AND FOE.
THAT'S THE KIND OF PERSON HARSHA-SAMA IS!
......
TOBO (PLOD)
トボ
TOBO
トボ
WHAT'S GOTTEN INTO YOU, PRINCESS!?
IT'S SIS'S FAULT FOR MAKING ME THE OUTCAST.
HOW CRUEL OF HER TO PUT HER OWN SISTER UNDER HOUSE ARREST.
IT'S ALMOST THE END, SO I HAVE TO ENJOY MYSELF TO MAKE IT WORTH IT.

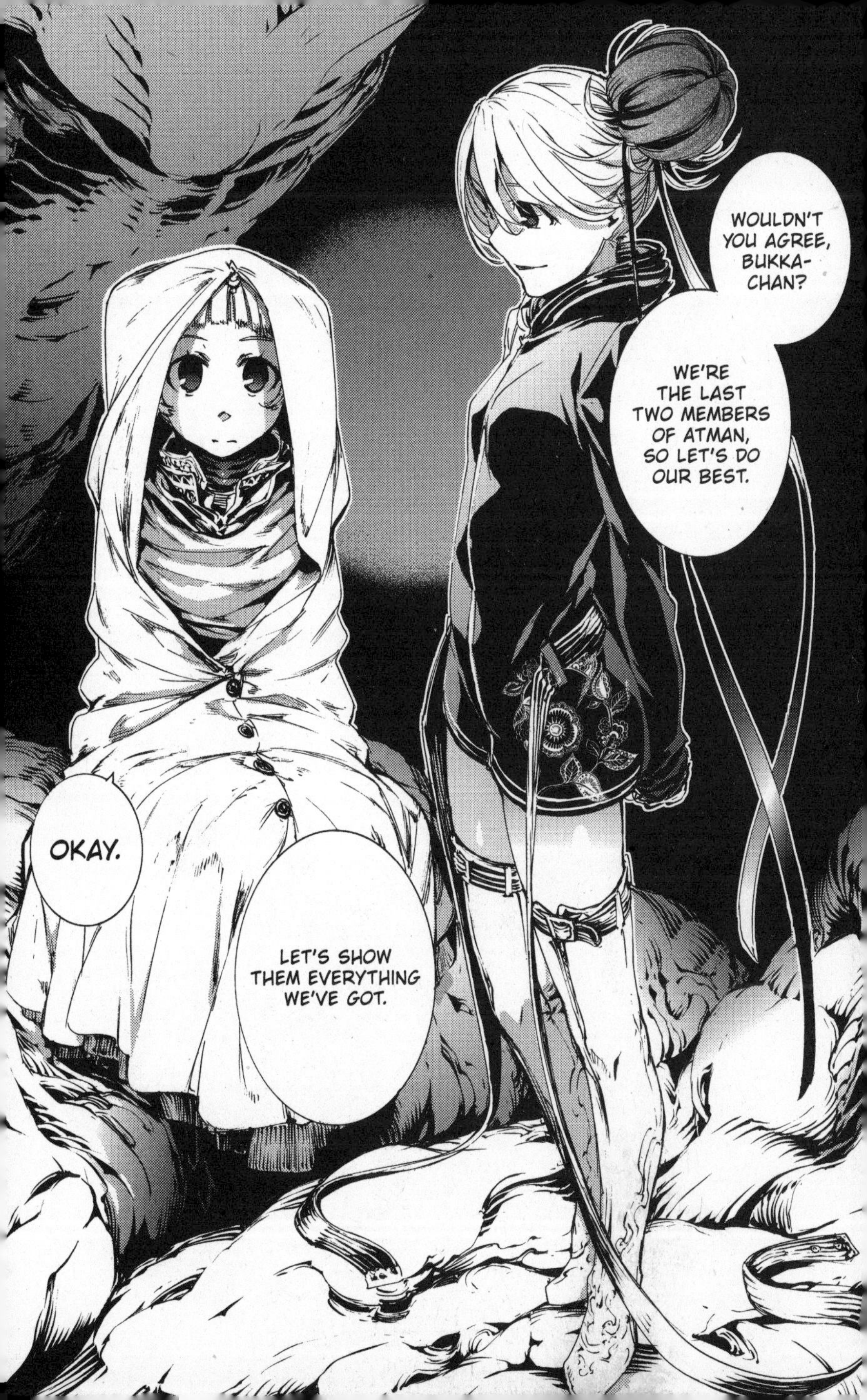
WOULDN'T YOU AGREE, BUKKA-CHAN?
WE'RE THE LAST TWO MEMBERS OF ATMAN, SO LET'S DO OUR BEST.
LET'S SHOW THEM EVERYTHING WE'VE GOT.
OKAY.

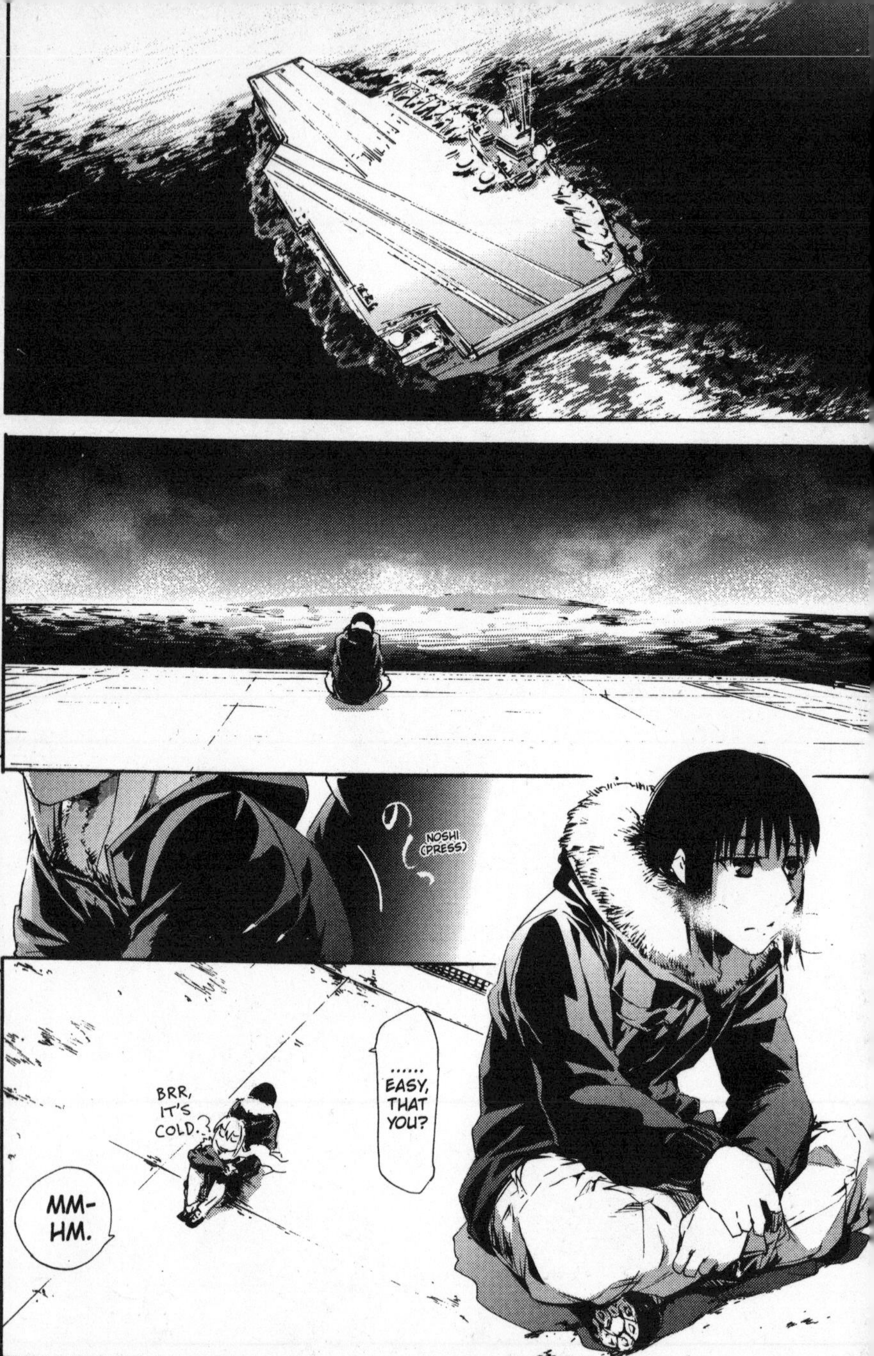
NOSHI (PRESS)
......EASY, THAT YOU?
BRR, IT'S COLD.
MM-HM.

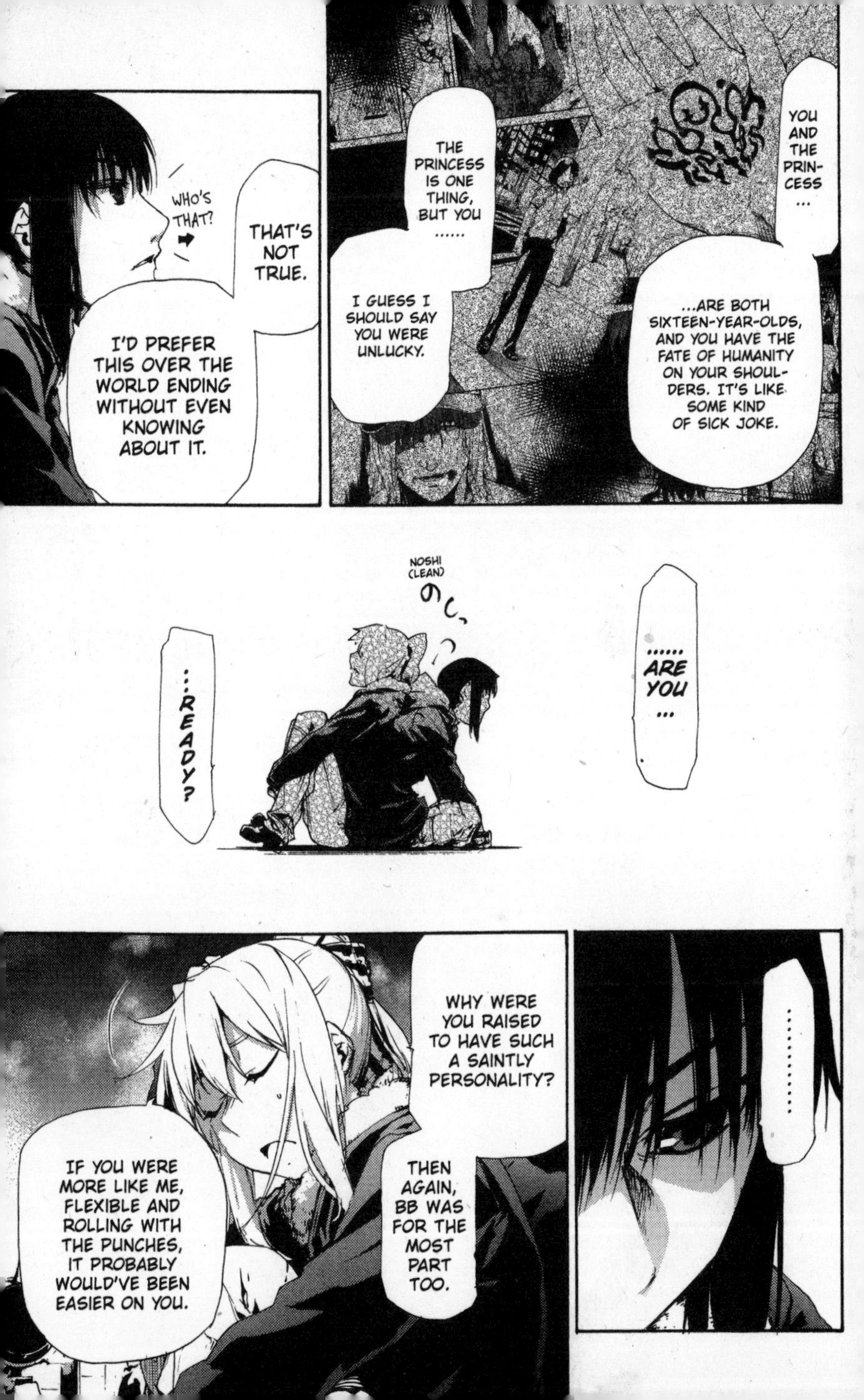
YOU AND THE PRINCESS...
...ARE BOTH SIXTEEN-YEAR-OLDS, AND YOU HAVE THE FATE OF HUMANITY ON YOUR SHOULDERS. IT'S LIKE SOME KIND OF SICK JOKE.
THE PRINCESS IS ONE THING, BUT YOU......
I GUESS I SHOULD SAY YOU WERE UNLUCKY.
THAT'S NOT TRUE.
WHO'S THAT?
I'D PREFER THIS OVER THE WORLD ENDING WITHOUT EVEN KNOWING ABOUT IT.
......ARE YOU...
NOSHI (LEAN)
...READY?
....
WHY WERE YOU RAISED TO HAVE SUCH A SAINTLY PERSONALITY?
THEN AGAIN, BB WAS FOR THE MOST PART TOO.
IF YOU WERE MORE LIKE ME, FLEXIBLE AND ROLLING WITH THE PUNCHES, IT PROBABLY WOULD'VE BEEN EASIER ON YOU.

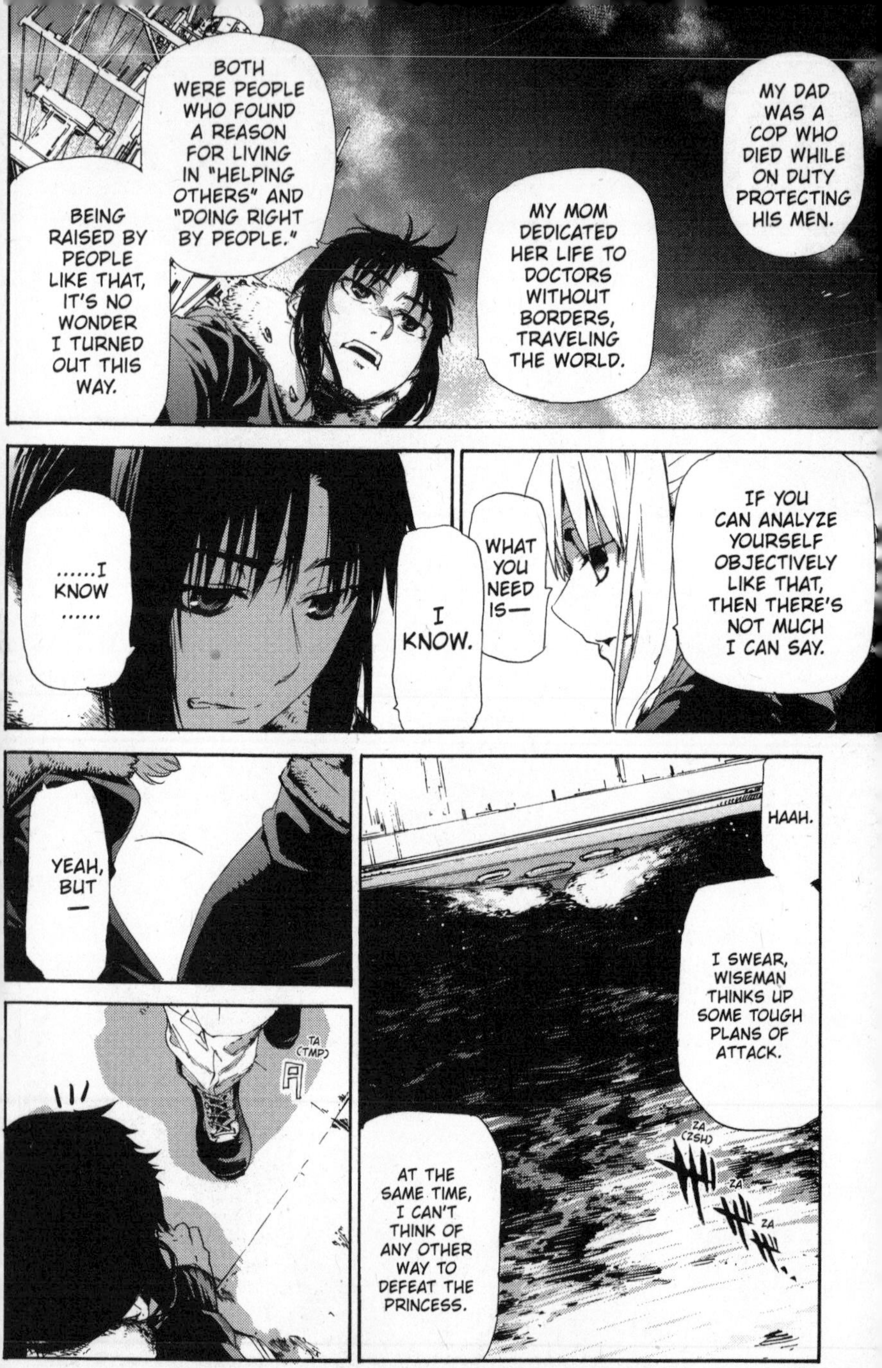
MY DAD WAS A COP WHO DIED WHILE ON DUTY PROTECTING HIS MEN.
MY MOM DEDICATED HER LIFE TO DOCTORS WITHOUT BORDERS, TRAVELING THE WORLD.
BOTH WERE PEOPLE WHO FOUND A REASON FOR LIVING IN "HELPING OTHERS" AND "DOING RIGHT BY PEOPLE."
BEING RAISED BY PEOPLE LIKE THAT, IT'S NO WONDER I TURNED OUT THIS WAY.
IF YOU CAN ANALYZE YOURSELF OBJECTIVELY LIKE THAT, THEN THERE'S NOT MUCH I CAN SAY.
WHAT YOU NEED IS—
I KNOW.
......I KNOW ......
HAAH.
I SWEAR, WISEMAN THINKS UP SOME TOUGH PLANS OF ATTACK.
AT THE SAME TIME, I CAN'T THINK OF ANY OTHER WAY TO DEFEAT THE PRINCESS.
ZA (ZSH)
ZA
ZA
YEAH, BUT —
TA (TMP)

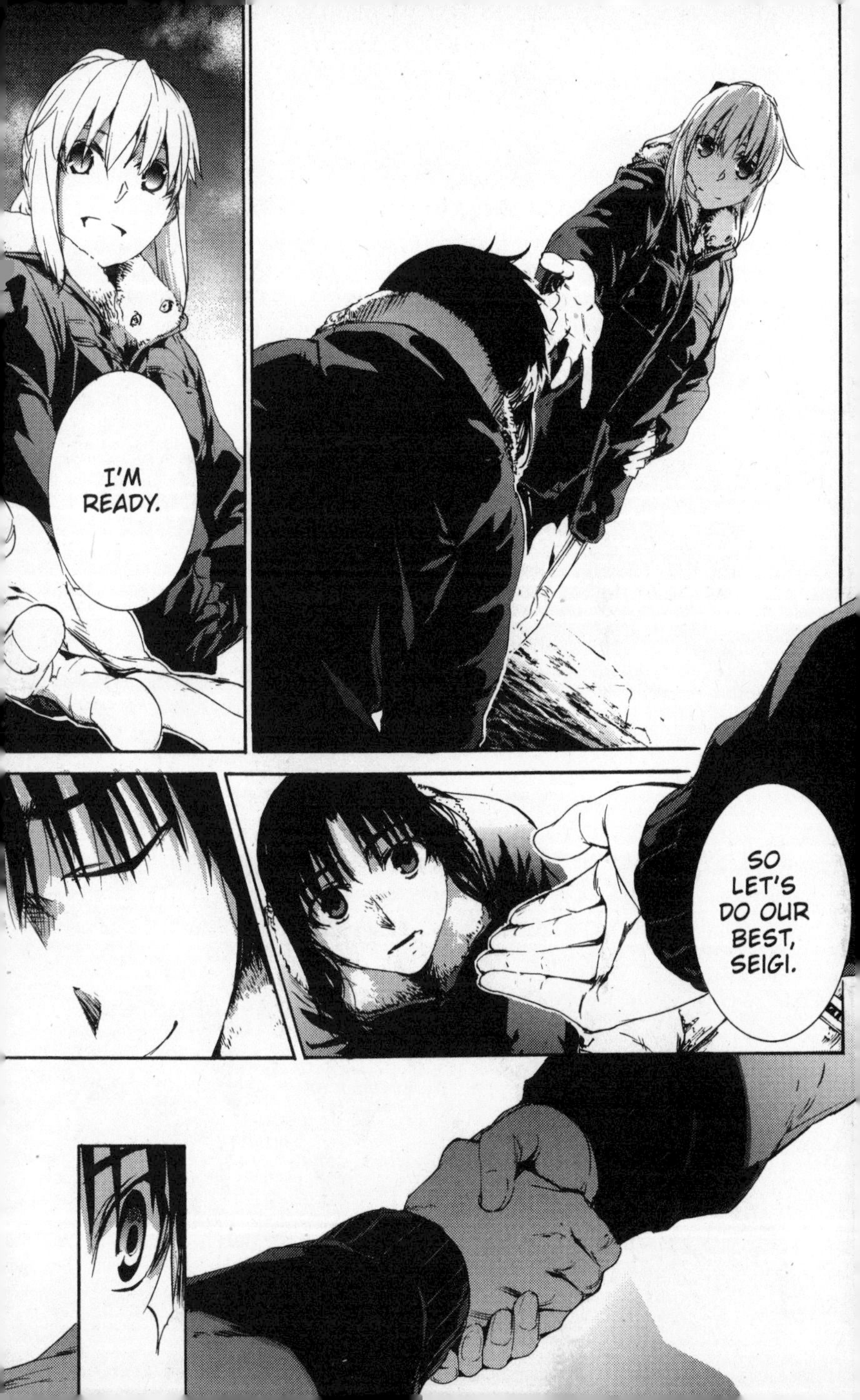
I'M READY.
SO LET'S DO OUR BEST, SEIGI.

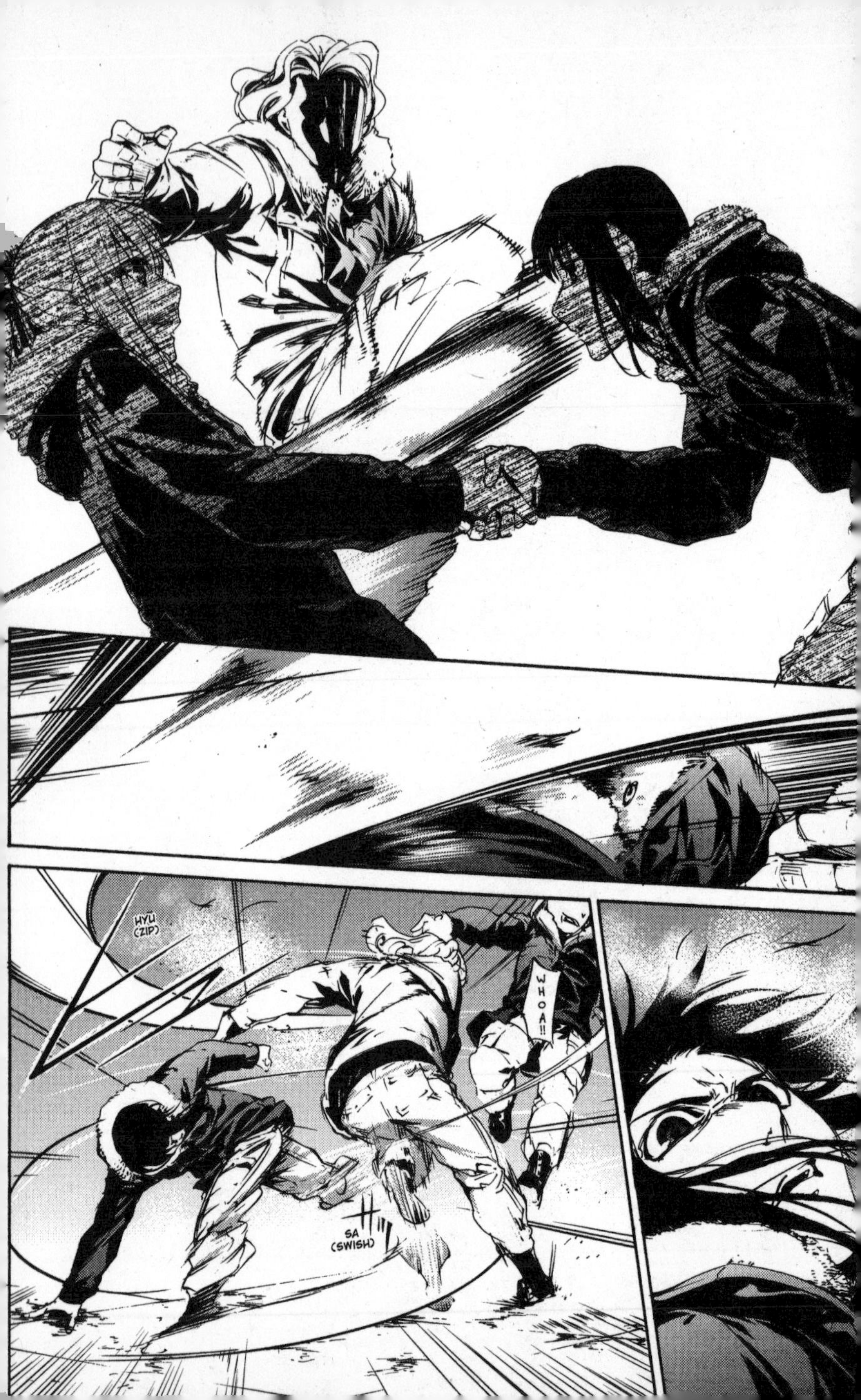
WHOA!!
HYU (ZIP)
SA (SWISH)

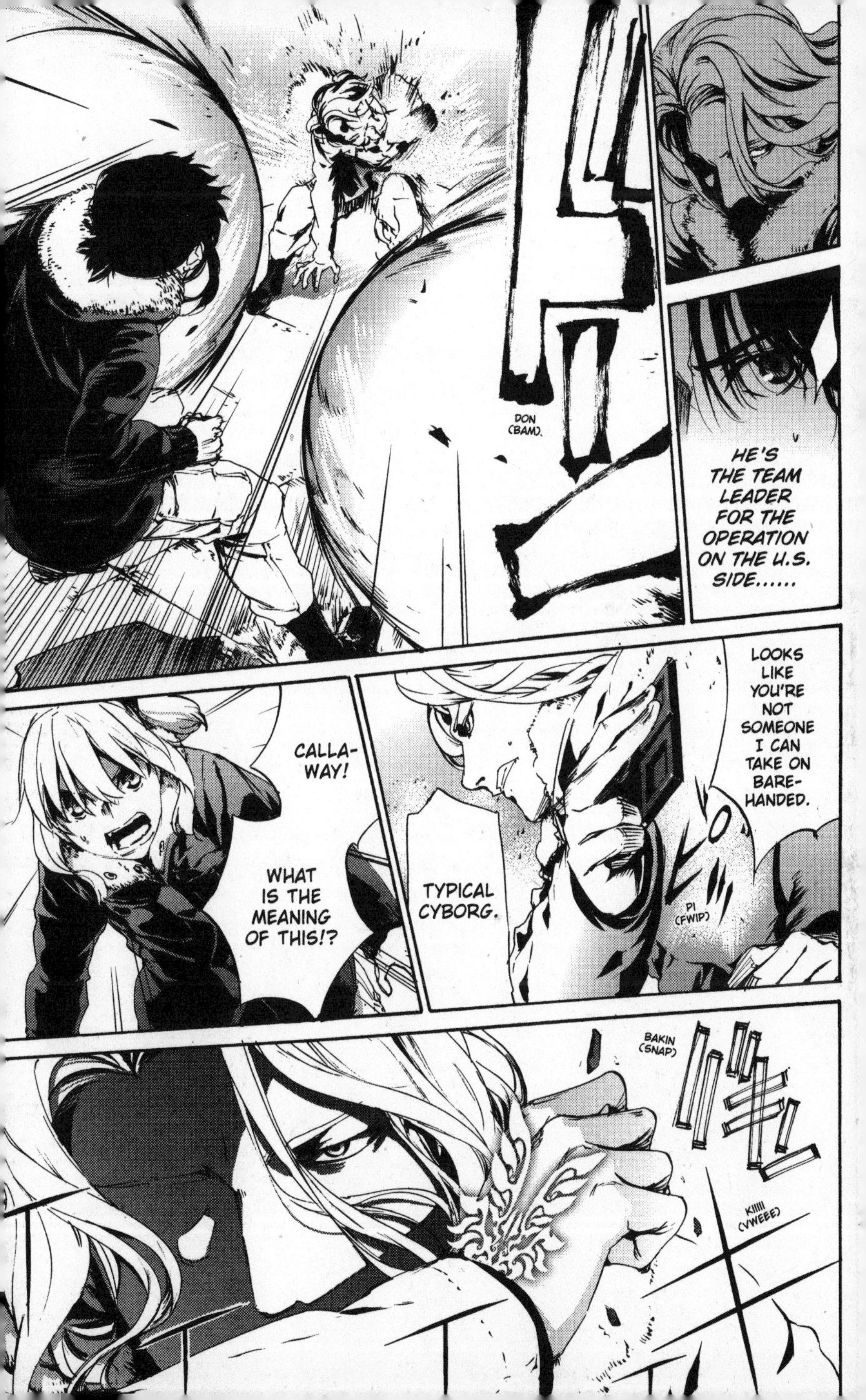
HE'S THE TEAM LEADER FOR THE OPERATION ON THE U.S. SIDE......
DON (BAM)
LOOKS LIKE YOU'RE NOT SOMEONE I CAN TAKE ON BARE-HANDED.
PI (FWIP)
TYPICAL CYBORG.
CALLA-WAY!
WHAT IS THE MEANING OF THIS!?
BAKIN (SNAP)
KIIII (VWEEE)

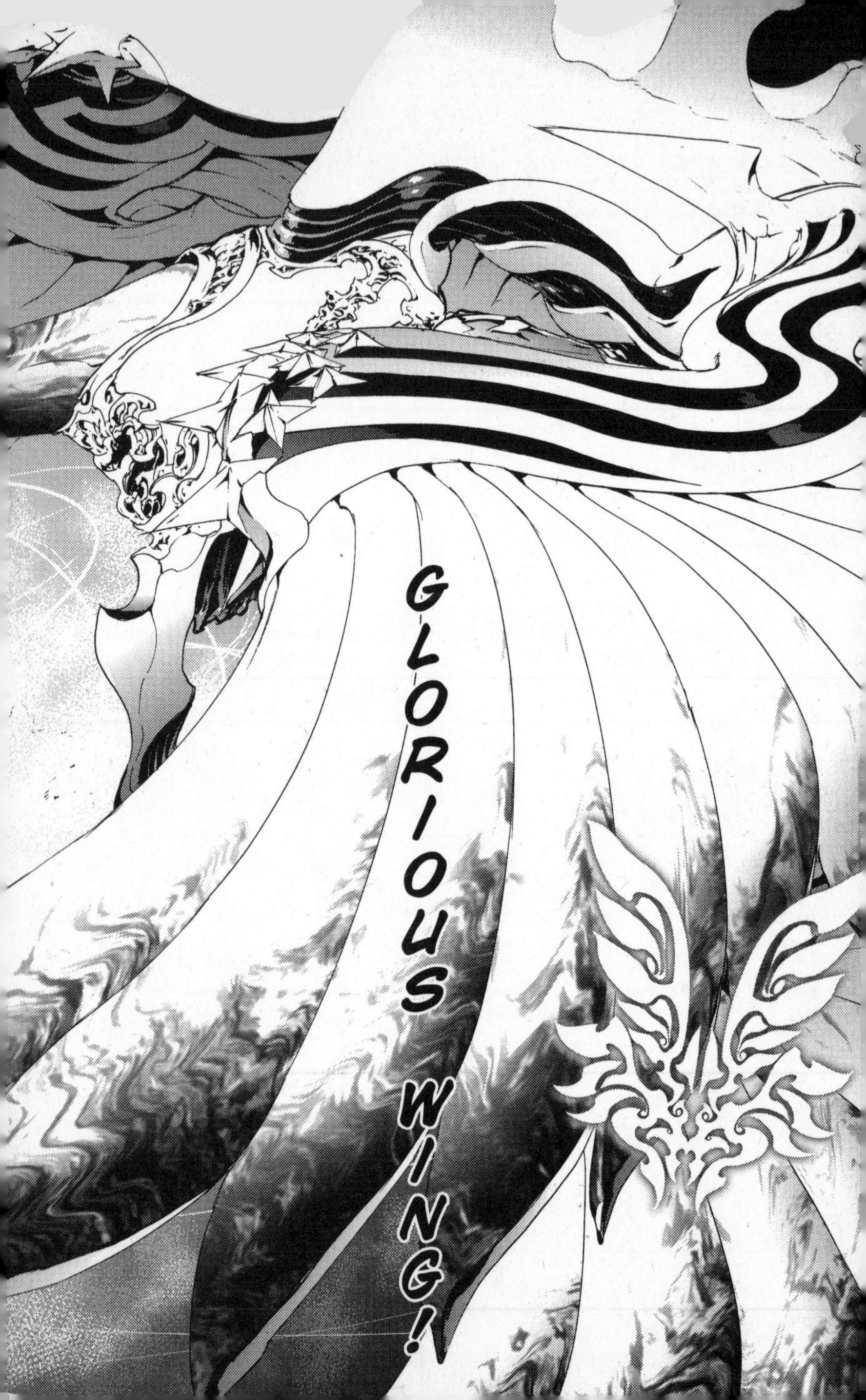
GLORIOUS WING!

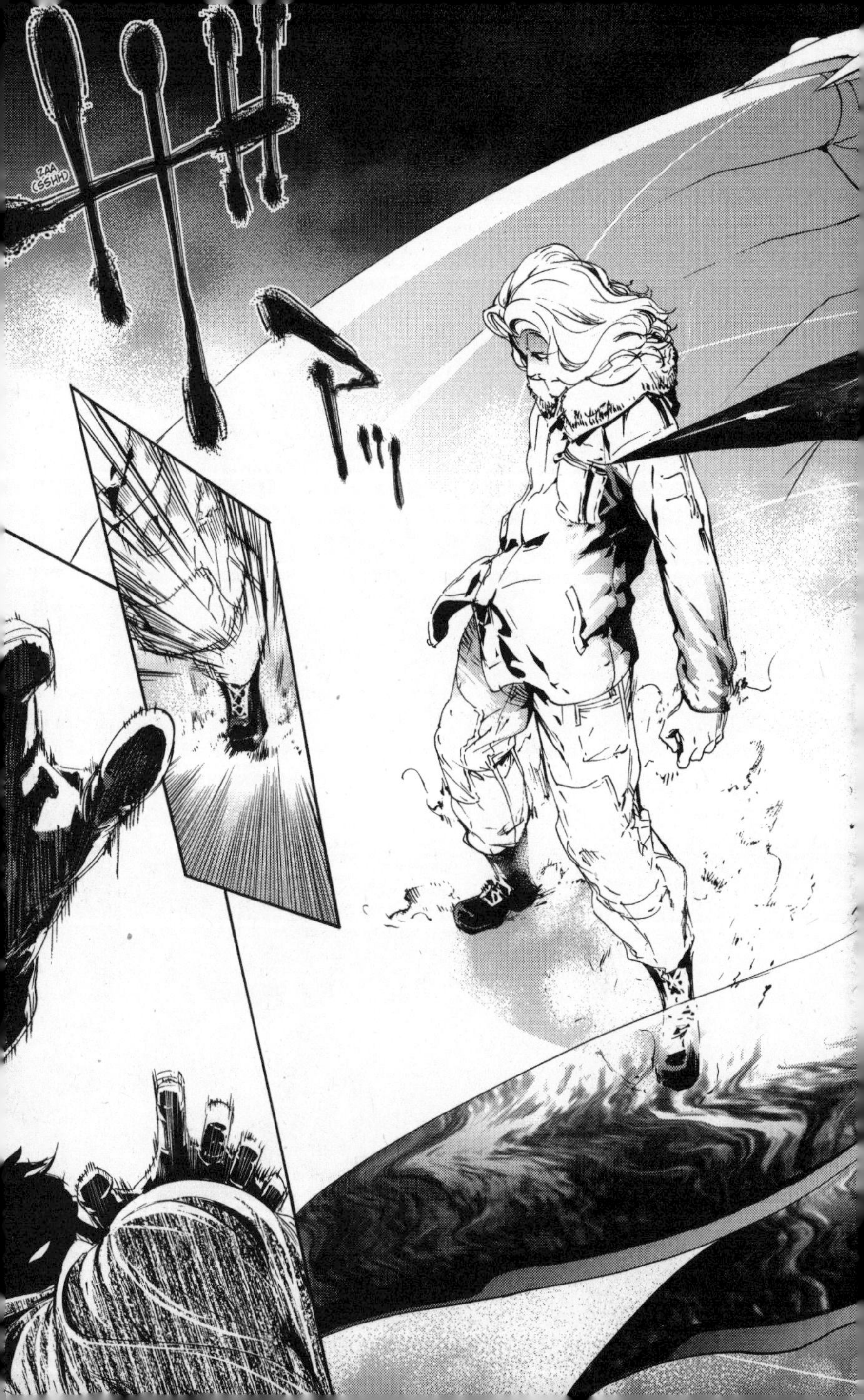
ZAA
(SSHH)

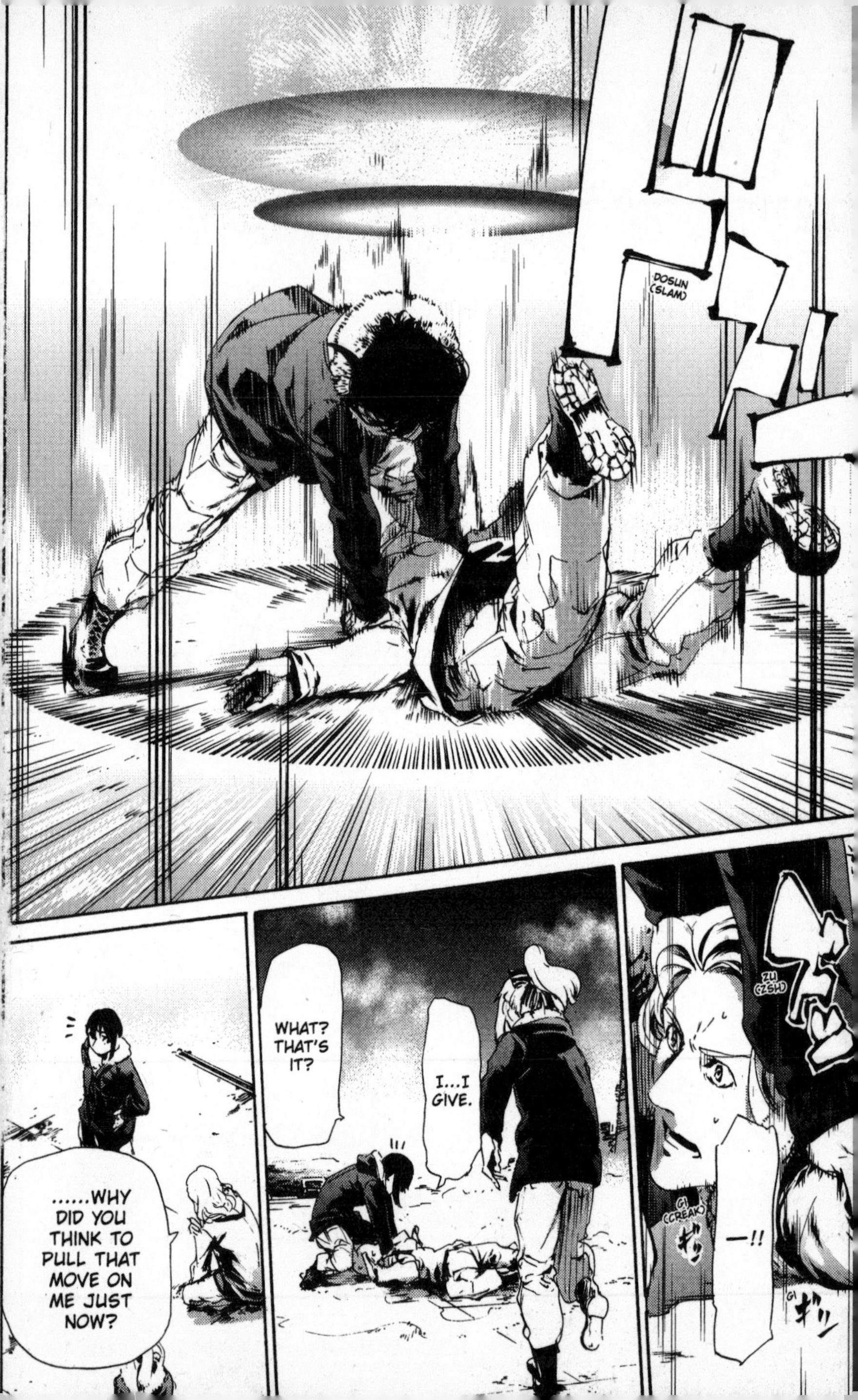
DOSUN (SLAM)
ZU (ZSH)
GI (CREAK)
—!!
GI
I...I GIVE.
WHAT? THAT'S IT?
......WHY DID YOU THINK TO PULL THAT MOVE ON ME JUST NOW?

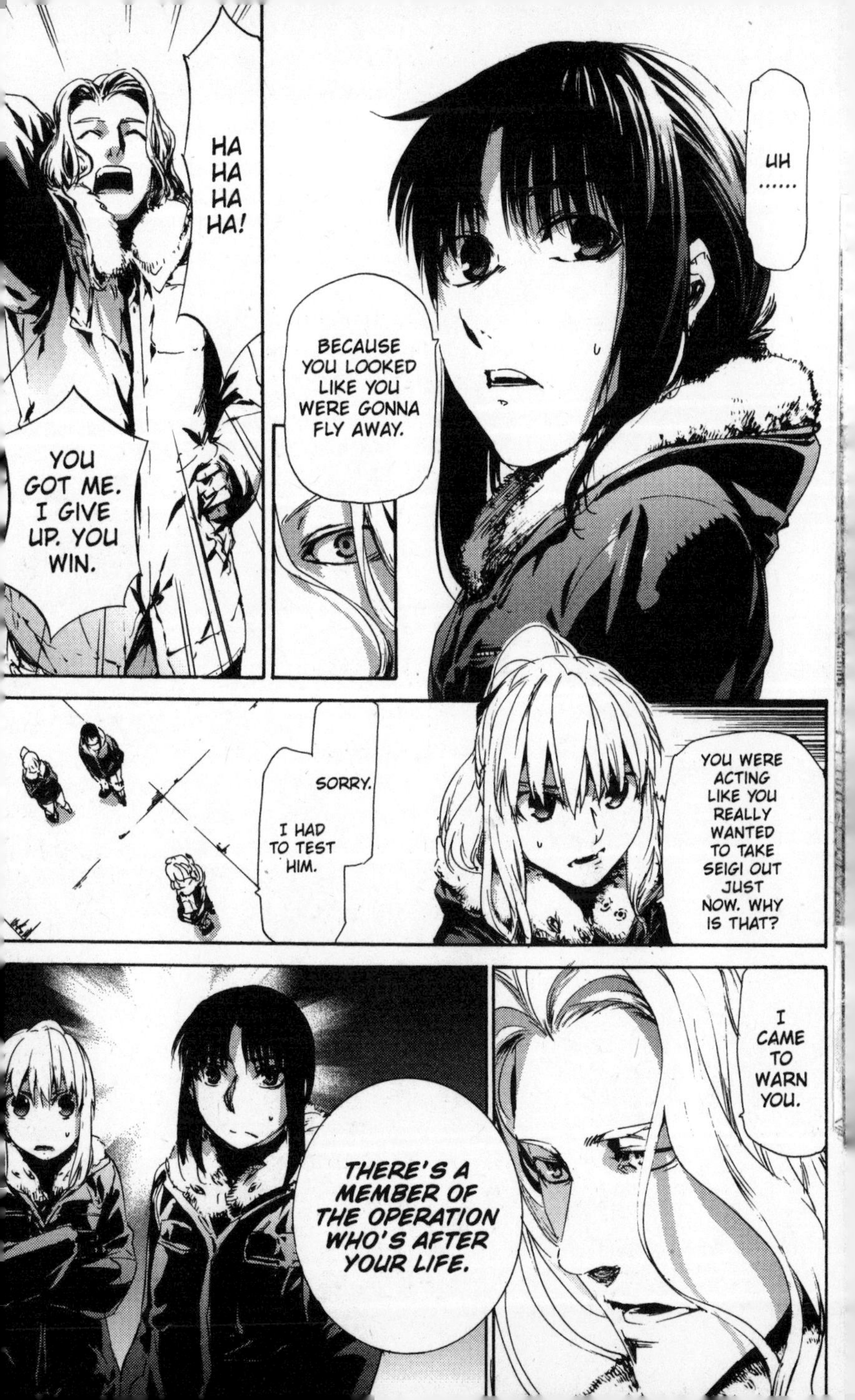
UH ......
BECAUSE YOU LOOKED LIKE YOU WERE GONNA FLY AWAY.
HA HA HA HA!
YOU GOT ME. I GIVE UP. YOU WIN.
YOU WERE ACTING LIKE YOU REALLY WANTED TO TAKE SEIGI OUT JUST NOW. WHY IS THAT?
SORRY.
I HAD TO TEST HIM.
I CAME TO WARN YOU.
THERE'S A MEMBER OF THE OPERATION WHO'S AFTER YOUR LIFE.

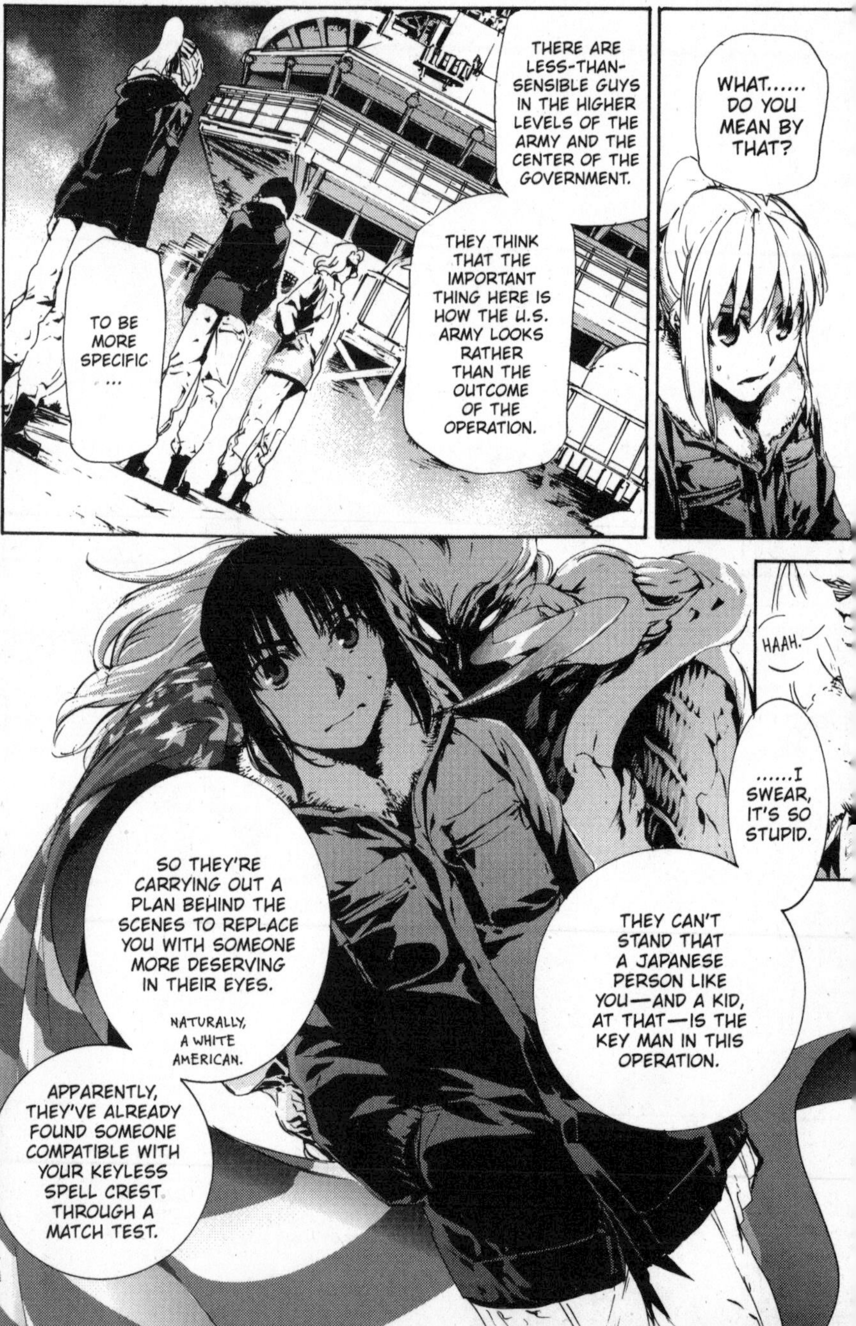
WHAT...... DO YOU MEAN BY THAT?
THERE ARE LESS-THAN-SENSIBLE GUYS IN THE HIGHER LEVELS OF THE ARMY AND THE CENTER OF THE GOVERNMENT.
THEY THINK THAT THE IMPORTANT THING HERE IS HOW THE U.S. ARMY LOOKS RATHER THAN THE OUTCOME OF THE OPERATION.
TO BE MORE SPECIFIC ...
HAAH.
......I SWEAR, IT'S SO STUPID.
THEY CAN'T STAND THAT A JAPANESE PERSON LIKE YOU—AND A KID, AT THAT—IS THE KEY MAN IN THIS OPERATION.
SO THEY'RE CARRYING OUT A PLAN BEHIND THE SCENES TO REPLACE YOU WITH SOMEONE MORE DESERVING IN THEIR EYES.
NATURALLY, A WHITE AMERICAN.
APPARENTLY, THEY'VE ALREADY FOUND SOMEONE COMPATIBLE WITH YOUR KEYLESS SPELL CREST THROUGH A MATCH TEST.

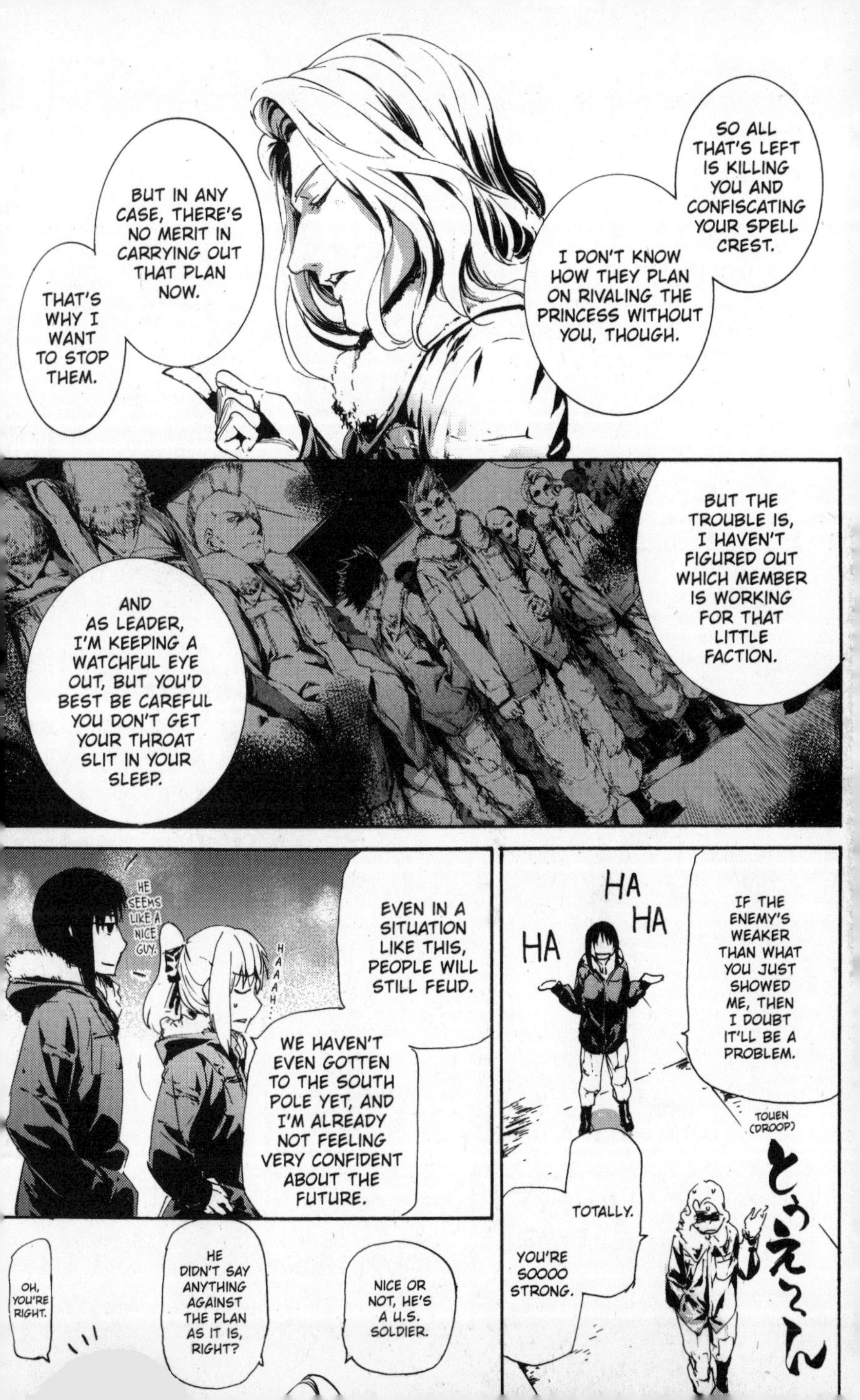
SO ALL THAT'S LEFT IS KILLING YOU AND CONFISCATING YOUR SPELL CREST.
I DON'T KNOW HOW THEY PLAN ON RIVALING THE PRINCESS WITHOUT YOU, THOUGH.
BUT IN ANY CASE, THERE'S NO MERIT IN CARRYING OUT THAT PLAN NOW.
THAT'S WHY I WANT TO STOP THEM.
BUT THE TROUBLE IS, I HAVEN'T FIGURED OUT WHICH MEMBER IS WORKING FOR THAT LITTLE FACTION.
AND AS LEADER, I'M KEEPING A WATCHFUL EYE OUT, BUT YOU'D BEST BE CAREFUL YOU DON'T GET YOUR THROAT SLIT IN YOUR SLEEP.
HA HA HA
IF THE ENEMY'S WEAKER THAN WHAT YOU JUST SHOWED ME, THEN I DOUBT IT'LL BE A PROBLEM.
TOUEN (DROOP)
TOTALLY.
YOU'RE SOOOO STRONG.
EVEN IN A SITUATION LIKE THIS, PEOPLE WILL STILL FEUD.
HE SEEMS LIKE A NICE GUY.
HAAAH...
WE HAVEN'T EVEN GOTTEN TO THE SOUTH POLE YET, AND I'M ALREADY NOT FEELING VERY CONFIDENT ABOUT THE FUTURE.
NICE OR NOT, HE'S A U.S. SOLDIER.
HE DIDN'T SAY ANYTHING AGAINST THE PLAN AS IT IS, RIGHT?
OH, YOU'RE RIGHT.

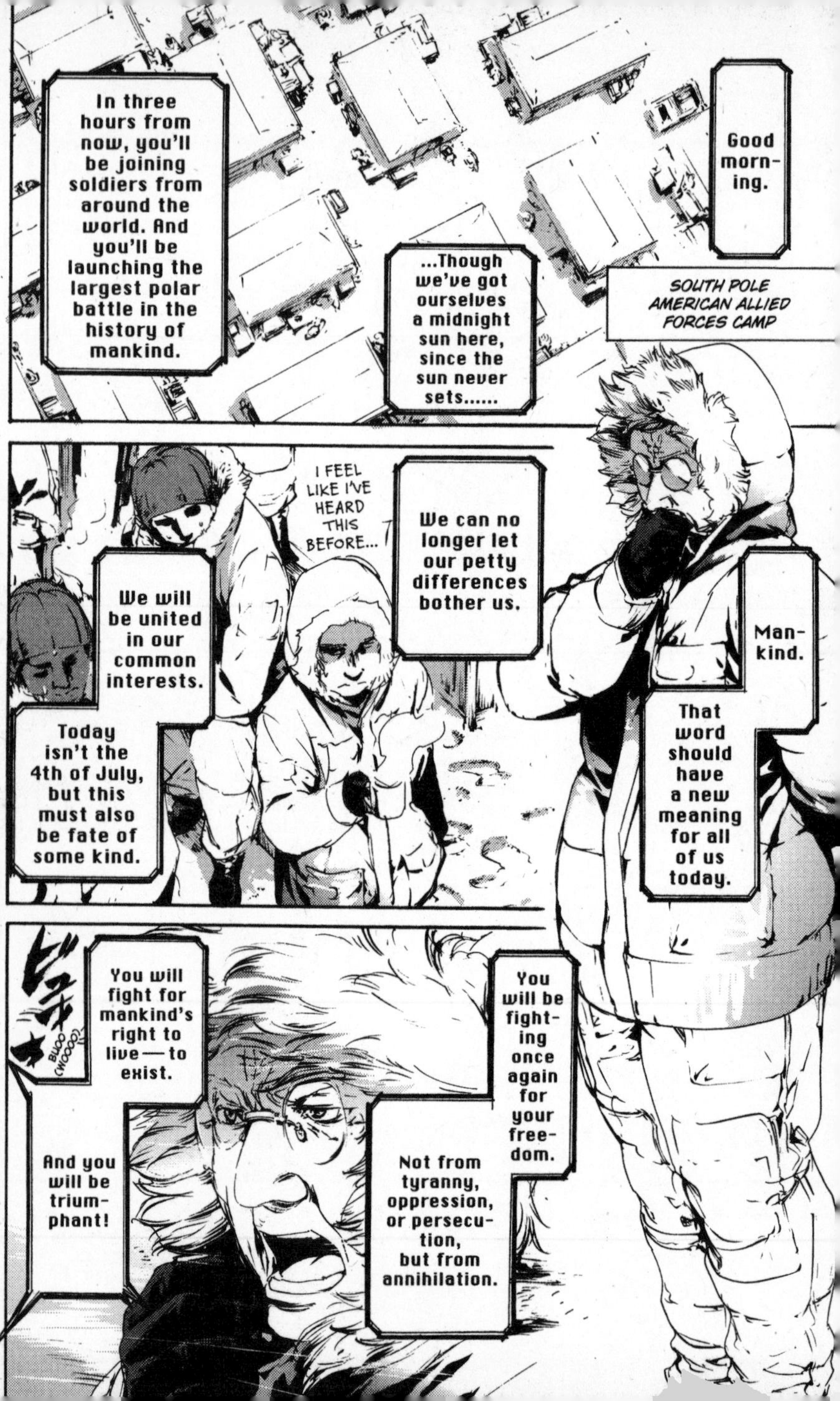
Good morning.
SOUTH POLE AMERICAN ALLIED FORCES CAMP
...Though we've got ourselves a midnight sun here, since the sun never sets......
In three hours from now, you'll be joining soldiers from around the world. And you'll be launching the largest polar battle in the history of mankind.
Mankind.
That word should have a new meaning for all of us today.
We can no longer let our petty differences bother us.
I FEEL LIKE I'VE HEARD THIS BEFORE...
We will be united in our common interests.
Today isn't the 4th of July, but this must also be fate of some kind.
You will be fighting once again for your freedom.
Not from tyranny, oppression, or persecution, but from annihilation.
You will fight for mankind's right to live — to exist.
And you will be triumphant!
BUOO (WOOOO)

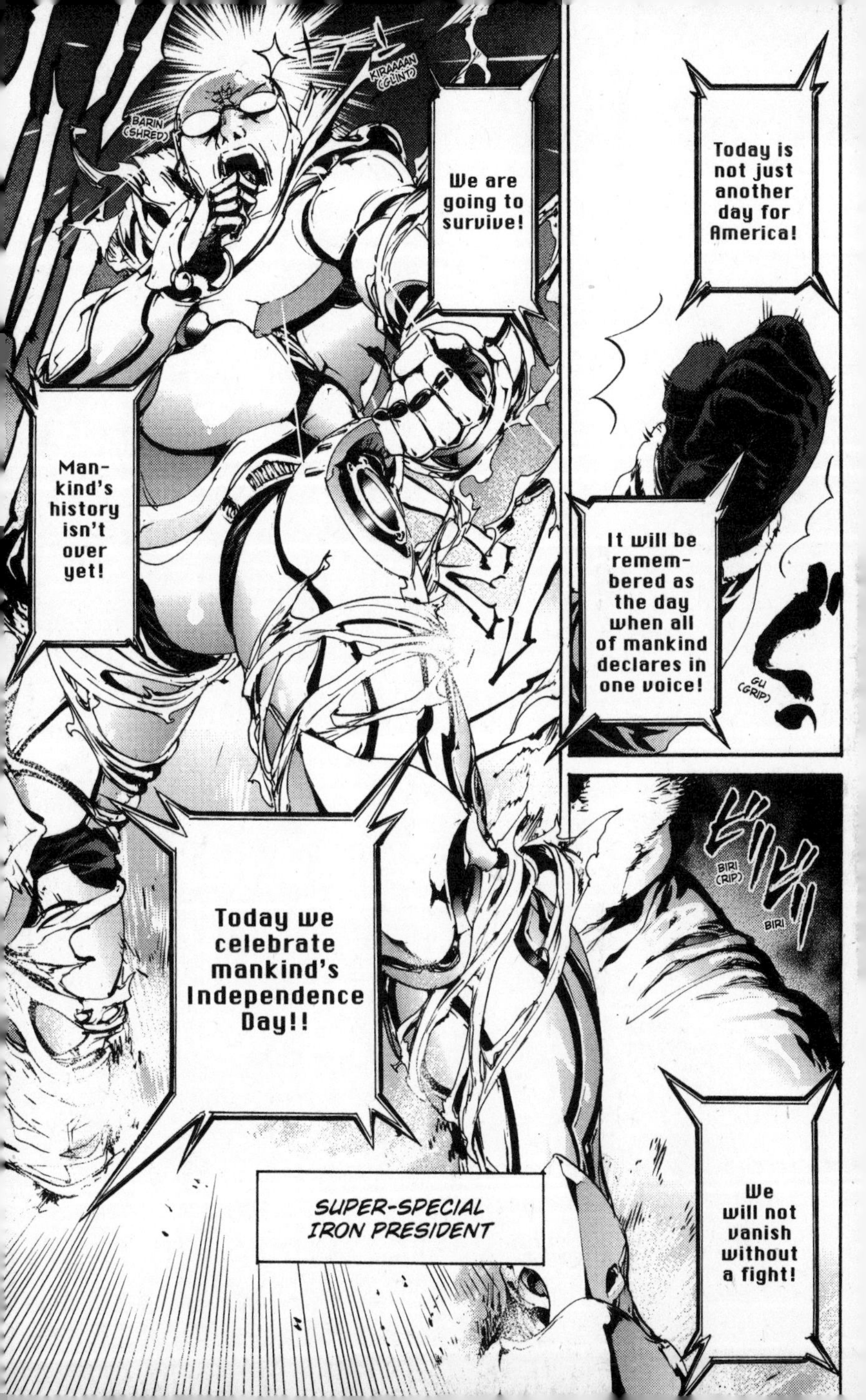
Today is not just another day for America!
It will be remembered as the day when all of mankind declares in one voice!
GU (GRIP)
BIRI (RIP)
BIRI
We will not vanish without a fight!
KIRAAAAN (GLINT)
We are going to survive!
BARIN (SHRED)
Mankind's history isn't over yet!
Today we celebrate mankind's Independence Day!!
SUPER-SPECIAL IRON PRESIDENT

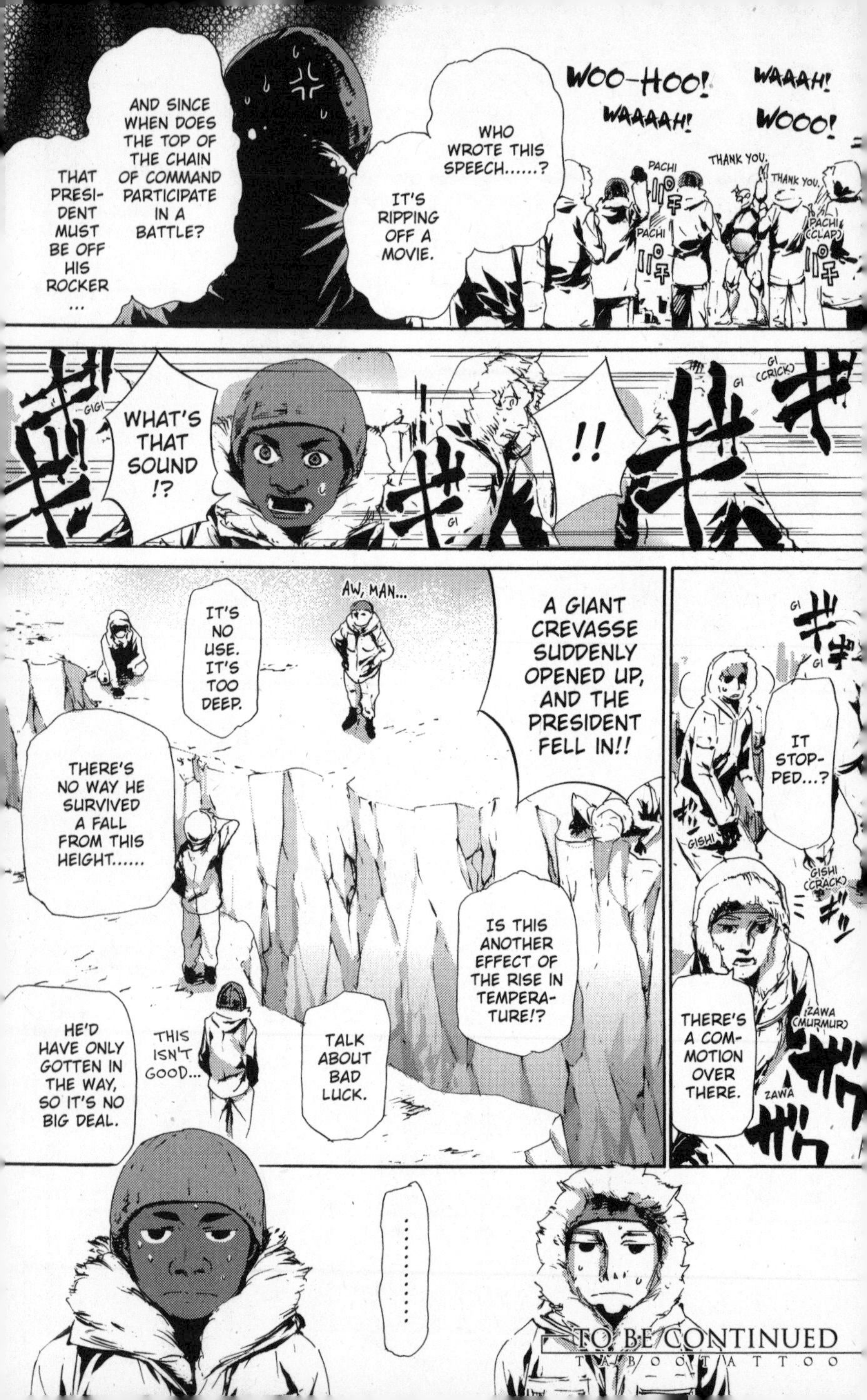

WOO-HOO!
WAAAH!
WAAAAH!
WOOO!
THANK YOU.
THANK YOU.
PACHI (CLAP)
PACHI
PACHI
WHO WROTE THIS SPEECH......?
IT'S RIPPING OFF A MOVIE.
AND SINCE WHEN DOES THE TOP OF THE CHAIN OF COMMAND PARTICIPATE IN A BATTLE?
THAT PRESIDENT MUST BE OFF HIS ROCKER...
GI (CRICK)
GI
!!
GI
WHAT'S THAT SOUND!?
GIGI
GI
GI
IT STOPPED...?
GISHI
GISHI (CRACK)
THERE'S A COMMOTION OVER THERE.
ZAWA (MURMUR)
ZAWA
A GIANT CREVASSE SUDDENLY OPENED UP, AND THE PRESIDENT FELL IN!!
AW, MAN...
IT'S NO USE. IT'S TOO DEEP.
THERE'S NO WAY HE SURVIVED A FALL FROM THIS HEIGHT......
IS THIS ANOTHER EFFECT OF THE RISE IN TEMPERATURE!?
TALK ABOUT BAD LUCK.
THIS ISN'T GOOD...
HE'D HAVE ONLY GOTTEN IN THE WAY, SO IT'S NO BIG DEAL.
....
TO BE CONTINUED
TABOO TATTOO

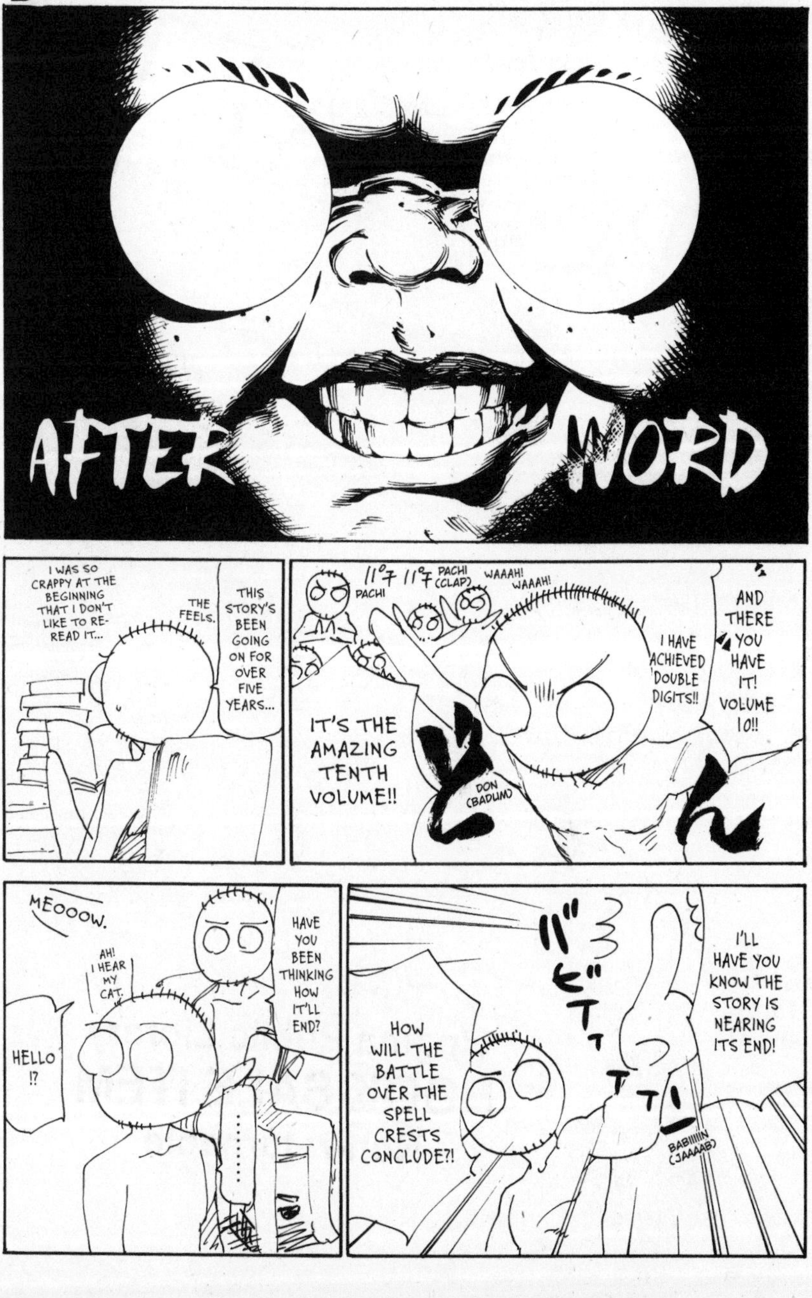
AFTER WORD
AND THERE YOU HAVE IT! VOLUME 10!!
I HAVE ACHIEVED DOUBLE DIGITS!!
PACHI PACHI (CLAP)
WAAAH! WAAAH!
IT'S THE AMAZING TENTH VOLUME!!
DON (BADUM)
THIS STORY'S BEEN GOING ON FOR OVER FIVE YEARS...
THE FEELS.
I WAS SO CRAPPY AT THE BEGINNING THAT I DON'T LIKE TO RE-READ IT...
I'LL HAVE YOU KNOW THE STORY IS NEARING ITS END!
HOW WILL THE BATTLE OVER THE SPELL CRESTS CONCLUDE?!
BABIIIIIN (JAAAAB)
HAVE YOU BEEN THINKING HOW IT'LL END?
MEOOOW.
AH! I HEAR MY CAT.
HELLO!?

TABOO TATTOO

by SHINJIRO

Translation: Christine Dashiell • Lettering: Phil Christie

TABOO TATTOO
© Shinjiro 2015
First published in Japan in 2015 by KADOKAWA CORPORATION. English translation rights reserved by Yen Press, LLC under the license from KADOKAWA CORPORATION, Tokyo through TUTTLE-MORI AGENCY, Inc., Tokyo.

English translation © 2018 by Yen Press, LLC

Yen Press
1290 Avenue of the Americas
New York, NY 10104

Visit us at yenpress.com
facebook.com/yenpress
twitter.com/yenpress
yenpress.tumblr.com
instagram.com/yenpress

First Yen Press Edition: April 2018

Yen Press is an imprint of Yen Press, LLC.
The Yen Press name and logo are trademarks of Yen Press, LLC.

The publisher is not responsible for websites (or their content) that are not owned by the publisher.

Library of Congress Control Number: 2015959759

ISBNs: 978-1-9753-0048-7 (paperback)
978-1-9753-0049-4 (ebook)

10 9 8 7 6 5 4 3 2 1

WOR

Printed in the United States of America